Computer Aided Design
Software and Analytical Tools

Computer Aided Design
Software and Analytical Tools

Second Edition

C.S. Krishnamoorthy[†]

S. Rajeev

A. Rajaraman

Alpha Science International Ltd.

Harrow, U.K.

C.S. Krishnamoorthy[†]
S. Rajeev
A. Rajaraman

Department of Civil Engineering
Indian Institute of Technology, Madras
Chennai, India

Alpha Science International Ltd
Hygeia Building, 66 College Road
Harrow, Middlesex HA1 1BE, U.K.

ISBN 1-84265-126-9

Printed in India

To
Our Parents

Preface to the Second Edition

All chapters in the first edition have been retained as they are and modifications in terms of updating and inclusion of object oriented and C++ approaches have been made mainly to reflect the ten years difference in knowledge from the first edition brought out in 1991.

The first Author Prof. C.S. Krishnamoorthy, classmate and close friend of mine for the last three decades, died in a tragic accident in 2000 and when Shri Mehra of Narosa Publishing House approached me to revise and update the book, I gladly took up the task with the approval of the second author Shri Rajeev. I wanted to retain the outlook of the earlier edition and at the same time add object oriented approach and C++ to enhance the contents. I also wanted to add softcomputing techniques but keeping in view the size of the book, I thought it better to bring out a seaparate companion volume *Computer Graphics for Engineers*. This is in progress.

Grateful thanks are placed on record to Mrs C.S. Krishnamoorthy and S. Rajeev for according approval and Civil Engineering Department of IITM, in particular Profs. Kalyanaraman and Meher Prasad for all the help they provided.

This Edition is dedicated to the memory of Prof C.S. Krishnamoorthy.

A. Rajaraman

Preface to the First Edition

Computer Aided Design is a process where the designer works with the computer to develop an engineering system. CAD is fast developing as a discipline of specialisation in all branches of engineering. The advances in computer science and technology have resulted in the emergence of very powerful hardware and software tools that offer scope for use in analysis, design and construction/manufacturing phases of engineering systems. Knowledge of hardware and software tools is required for developing CAD systems that would lead to effective use of computers in the entire design process. It is observed that many topics of software engineering form specialised areas in computer science and are treated independently in different books and other publications, and they are not available in a synthesized form for use by CAD programmers. The main aim of this book is to bring the developments in software tools to the domain of students and application programmers involved in Computer Aided Design of engineering systems.

One of the essential features of the book is that it brings to the student the recent advances made in the application of Artificial Intelligence (AI) techniques leading to the development of Knowledge-Based Expert Systems (KBES) that are finding increasing application in civil, mechanical and other engineering disciplines. CAD systems are dynamic and advances in hardware do produce an impact on the application environment. Viewing in this context the authors have carefully chosen and presented the tools that form the basis of software technology for CAD.

To understand the process of Computer Aided Design, the various steps involved in an engineering design and the role of computers in the whole process are described in chapter 1. The computer forms the heart of the CAD system and it is essential to know some of the fundamental features of computer hardware. A brief introduction to computer hardware is presented in this chapter. As part of the system software, the operating systems do play a vital role and some of the commonly used Operating Systems like UNIX and DOS are discussed. To the developer, programming languages provide the basis for interaction with the machine. Various low and high level languages that are available and the basis for choice of a particular language for CAD are described in this chapter.

Though FORTRAN language has been widely used in the development of analysis and other algorithm based packages, it is increasingly felt that serious system developers of CAD systems require knowledge of other languages. It has been brought out in chapter 1 that C language is being favoured in many situations like the development of user interfaces, graphics functions etc. The C programming language is described in chapter 2. A number of examples are included in this chapter to illustrate the language features discussed herein.

In engineering design problems the data items are many and one has to carry out a number of operations on the data items at different stages of processing. The organisation of data and development of algorithms to manipulate data are important steps in any software development project for CAD. Chapter 3 presents the concepts of Programming and Data Structures. The abstract data types such as Lists, Stacks, Queues and Trees that lead to efficient organisation of information are described. Implementation details of various abstract data types with reference to programming techniques for CAD are discussed in this chapter. Number of examples from engineering domain are solved to illustrate the concepts of algorithm development and design of data structures. More than the detailed engineering aspects of the problems, the issues related to information management for efficient problem solving is discussed in greater detail.

Computer Graphics forms the core of CAD programs and is used at every stage of design process. In chapter 4 a comprehensive treatment is given on the basic principles of computer graphics, manipulation of images and geometric modelling. The GKS (Graphical Kernal System) is being accepted as an international standard for computer graphics and an introduction is given to graphics programming through GKS. In addition the principles of computer aided drafting and use of AutoCAD are described in this chapter along with a brief overview of the developments that are going on in the field of computer graphics with special reference to CAD/CAM/CAE.

Programs for Computer Aided Design applications require handling of large amount of data generated during the problem solving process. In addition it is found that large amount of data in related activities need to be stored and retrieved for integrating various phases of design and manufacturing/construction leading to computer aided engineering of large systems. This requires a study of *data base* and its management referred to as Data Base Management System (DBMS). Though DBMS is widely known in commercial applications its use in engineering software is of recent origin. Chapter 5 deals with DBMS and its significance to CAD software development. The three data models, hierarchical, network and relational models used in DBMS are briefly presented in chapter 5. The relational model is finding increasing application and a brief introduction to Relational Data Base Management System is given in this chapter.

There is excitement in engineering community in the use of Artificial Intelligence techniques for engineering design. A number of problems encountered in design are ill-structured and a considerable amount of expertise in the concerned discipline is required to solve them. Conventional programming tools do not address these problems. The recent advances in AI technology make it possible now to develop programs that reach the performance of human expert in the same specialised domain and these systems are called Knowledge Based Expert Systems (KBES). It is observed that KBES will form part of all the CAD systems of the future. The architecture of the KBES and its components are described in chapter 6. The important schemes of knowledge representation and inferece mechanisms are discussed with suitable examples. The recent developments in knowledge based approaches to engineering problem solving and the potential for application to design are highlighted in this chapter.

With the advent of computers, there have been tremendous advances made in the realm of analysis and design of engineering systems. In the field of analysis Finite Element Method forms a powerful numerical method for stress analysis of structural systems and machine components of complex geometry and complicated boundary conditions. Optimization techniques provide useful tools in the area of design. Since these two analytical tools would be useful for a CAD system, an introduction to these topics are presented in chapter 7.

The basic philosophy of the finite element technique is presented in chapter 7. A full treatment of the subject is beyond the scope of the book and the role of this technique in CAD environment is emphasized here along with a brief description of some of the software packages available. To the user of the finite element analysis package pre and post processing dealing with finite element modelling and presentation of final results respectively are important and they are described in this chapter. With the development of mathematical programming techniques it is now possible to formulate and solve the engineering design problems with the objective of minimizing the cost or weight and satisfying all the design requirements expressed as constraints. An introduction to optimization techniques and potential for application are brought out in the second part of chapter 7. In order to give the students an experience in optimization techniques, the authors have chosen to describe a simple but efficient technique of using interior penalty/barrier function to modify the constrained problem into an unconstrained function. The steps for programming using pattern search technique based on Hooke and Jeeves algorithm for sequential unconstrained minimization are presented in this chapter.

The material presented in this book is based on the short-courses conducted on the subject for the benefit of practising engineers and the post-graduate course on CAD in Civil Engineering developed by the authors over the last five years at the Indian Institute of Technology, Madras. A number of CAD projects have been carried out by the authors with the support of the CAD/CAM Programme of Indian Institute of Technology, Madras funded by the Minstry of Human Resources Development, Government of India. The most significant project is the development of PENCAD (Programming Environment for Computer Aided Design). PENCAD provides on personal computers a programming environment to a CAD program developer with a set of libraries that can be used by an application programmer through C language. The three main components of PENCAD are (i) IITM-GKS, a CAD oriented graphics support system, (ii) ENDBMS, an engineering database management system based on relational model and (iii) KBSS, a knowledge-based system development shell.

The authors would like to express their deep appreciation to Mr. Shaikh Karimulla Raja, Project Associate, CAD/CAM Programme for his significant contribution to the development of PENCAD and his enthusiastic support to CAD projects. A number of research scholars and graduate students have helped the authors in the preparation of this book and the authors would like to extend their grateful thanks to Messers Anil Mukundan, Benny Raphael, Rajesh G. Shenoi, C. Srinivasa Rao and Miss. A.P. Thenmozhi. The authors are grateful to Dr. R. Krishnakumar of Department of Mechanical Engineering and Mr. S. Jayaprakash of

Department of Computer Science for their comments and discussions. Thanks are also due to Mr. R. Muthusamy of Civil Engineering Departmental Computer Facility, and Mrs. S. Sankari, project staff of CAD/CAM programme for their help in the preparation of this book. The authors would like to appreciate the support extended to them by their families during the writing of this book.

C.S. Krishnamoorthy
S. Rajeev

Contents

4. Programming Techniques   102

5. Computer Graphics   172

CHAPTER 1

Introduction

1.1 COMPUTER AIDED DESIGN–AN OVERVIEW

Engineering design is a creative activity, where the creative skills of the designer are used with the help of the engineering knowledge he/she has acquired to produce the design of an engineering system. The completed design should meet all the engineering requirements in addition to optimum performance. The advances in computer science and technology have resulted in the emergence of very powerful hardware and scftware tools that offer scope for use in the entire design process resulting in improvement in the quality of the design. The emergence of *Computer Aided Design* as a field of specialisation will help the engineer to acquire the knowledge and skills needed in the use of these tools in an efficient and effective way in the design process. This chapter presents first an overview of Computer Aided Design, followed by the distinct roles played by the designer as well as the computer in the process of design and finally describes the hardware and software tools.

1.1.1 Engineering Design

As we have seen earlier, Computer Aided Design is a process, where the designer and the computer work together to produce an engineering design. The creative ideas of the designer is transformed into a design, with the help of analytical and software tools on a hardware platform. To understand the process of Computer Aided Design, let us analyse the process of engineering design in greater detail.

Engineering systems were developed, designed and used for centuries. Existence of many buildings, bridges, automobiles, aero-planes, ships, highways, machine components etc. are excellent testimonials for the engineering design activity. The process of engineering design can be thought of as a sequence of tasks as given below:

1. *Conceptualisation of the design model to meet the functional requirements.*   

2. *Preliminary design, to select suitable configuration and proportioning the components of the artifact to be designed.*

3. *Analysis of the design model to understand the behaviour under realistic working conditions.*

4. *Evaluation of the performance of the system with the help of results of analysis.*

5. *If the performance can be improved, then modify the design mode, to improve the performance.*

6. *Repeat the steps 4 and 5, until an improved design with optimum performance is obtained.*

7. *Carry out any detailing if required, depending on the engineering aspects of the system being designed.*

8. *Produce detailed drawings for construction or manufacturing.*

The above eight steps form the sequence of activities leading to an optimum design of engineering systems. Now let us analyse each of these steps and explore each activity in greater depth.

In the first stage, i.e., conceptualization of the design model, the designer comes out with a preliminary model of the artifact to be designed. The creative skills of the designer along with his engineering knowledge play a very important role at this stage to arrive at a reasonably good design mode. Since there can be many solutions to a design problem, the performance level of one solution will be different from the other. The factors that affect the performance of the design solution are many. The conceptual design model developed by a more experienced designer will always be better compared to the one developed by a novice. The expertise of the designer improves the designer's creative skills, which finally result in a better design solution.

The sizing and proportioning of the components of the conceptual model are done at the second stage. The engineering system to be designed is hierarchically decomposed into subsystems and subsystems into components. There may be many levels of subsystems depending on the type and behaviour of the artifact to be designed. A design synthesis is generally carried out at this stage, where different feasible alternatives are tried for each one of the components to arrive at a feasible configuration of the mode, with components proportioned.

Now the preliminary model is analysed to obtain its behaviour under real working conditions. At this stage, the designer uses an appropriate analytical model to obtain a realistic response of the system. Generally this stage demands large amount of numerical computations and storage space for data, depending on the type of the system and analytical model.

The results of analysis stage are evaluated to check for any violations of provisions provided in the standard codes of practice and other behavioural constraints. If there are any violations, the system is modified and analysed again. This cycle of analysis and evaluation of responses is repeated until a system with optimum performance is obtained.

Now detailed design of various subsystems and components are carried out. Some examples of detailed design are: design of connections between components and subsystems, design and detailing of reinforcement in concrete structures etc. The preliminary design as well as detailed design completes the actual design process. But to pass on this design information to the manufacturing unit or construction site, it has to be represented in the form of drawings. The preparation of drawings form a very important step in design process, which ultimately is the concluding step in a design sequence.

1.1.2 Designer vs Computer

A review of the engineering design process described so far enumerates the different sequential steps involved in a conventional design process. A computer can contribute at various stages of the design, which will result in improvement of quality of the design produced and also of the design process itself. Before investigating into the details of the role that a computer can play in design, let us compare the capabilities of a designer and a computer from the engineering design point of view.

- A designer has creative skills and uses the engineering knowledge, imagination and judgement to generate ideas. But a computer can only carry out systematic reasoning using programs stored in it.

- A designer can input large amount of information at an instance of time. Eyes, ears and other organs are used to pass the information to the brain parallelly. Only a sequential input is possible in the case of a computer through input devices like keyboard, mouse, graphic tablet etc.

- Information is organised and stored by a designer with little effort. Whereas large amount of programming work has to be done to properly organise and store information in a computer.

- The amount of information, that a designer can store at a time is very less than that compared to a computer. Also the information is lost from a human brain in due course of time. But a computer can store a large amount of information for a long time.

- Production of errors is more frequent in the case of a designer compared to that of a computer. While a designer can respond to erroneous information, a computer cannot. A designer always tries to relate numbers to physical entities and tries to infer its validity, whereas a computer treats all the numbers in equal manner.

- The designer has good intuitive analysis capability, whereas the computer has good numerical analysis capability. Computer can do a large amount of number crunching work with reasonable accuracy, in a very short span of time. A designer is very slow in numerical computations. Designer tends to use short cuts, which may affect the quality of design.

The above comparison shows that the designer who is a human being has some capabilities, which the computer does not have. But a few superior capabilities of the computer, which the designer does not possess, will be of great help in the design process. In Computer Aided Design, the designer and the computer divide the total work and perform in activities in which each one is best suited. That means the designer and the computer work together, interacting with each other, towards the goal of producing better and efficient designs.

1.2 COMPUTER AS A DESIGN MEDIUM

Designers have been using paper and pencil as medium to carry out designs for centuries. Right from the conceptualization to the final drafting stage, the ideas are expressed on paper; and also the exchange of information from one stage to the other. As paper is a passive medium, it just retains what is scribbled on it. The paper cannot respond to something that has been written on it. Thus the conventional design process becomes a passive activity, where the designer does the complete job, with paper and pencil acting as passive design medium.

Computer Aided Design uses the computer primarily as a design medium. Once it is programmed to act as a medium for design, it can be made to respond to whatever has been put into it by the designer. Thus basically computer becomes an active medium to carry out engineering design. This itself is a major step towards improving the quality of designs. Use of many other capabilities of computers gives many additional advantages for computer- aided design over the conventional one.

To use computer as a design medium, the designer should have good amount of knowledge on hardware and software tools, so that the computer system can be effectively used. Selection of these tools very much depends on the type and size of engineering systems to be designed using them. As both the designer and the computer have their own roles to play in computer aided design, let us examine their involvement in the design process from the very first stage of conceptualization to the final drafting.

The conceptualization stage is where the designer generates ideas on the design to meet the functional requirements of the artifact to be designed. The engineering knowledge and creative skill of the designer play a very important role at this stage. Instead of putting the ideas on the paper, it can be put into a computer using appropriate input devices. A suitable computer program can be written to accept the ideas from the designer, transform them into a computer model and then properly represent it in the computer. This computer model can be used as a basic design to start with. It has been pointed out that the expertise of the designer can make significant difference in the conceptual model developed. So what a novice designer will do, if he/she is asked to carry out a design? A novice cannot generally have access to the expert knowledge, which only the experienced designer has. Since the computer can store large amount of information, expert knowledge of experienced designers could be acquired and stored in the computer. Recent advances in Artificial Intelligence make it possible now, to write programs for systematic reasoning so that designers get guidance from these stored knowledge. Hence at the conceptualization stage, the computer is not only used as a medium to store ideas, but also it is made to respond to these ideas, which will help the designer. In addition, reasoning programs base on expert knowledge stored in the computer guides the designers in improving their ideas.

In the preliminary design stage, where the selection of configuration and proportioning of components are carried out, the designer again makes use of ideas from previous designs, his experience and guidance from standard codes of practices and handbooks. As in the previous task, knowledge based programs stored in the computer can guide the designer. Also large amount of information on standard practices and from handbooks can be stored in databases, so that they are available to the designer for ready reference at any time. Also arriving at a feasible design configuration requires, testing the model with many alternate configurations. Such repeated tasks can easily be programmed in a computer. Finally by evaluating the performances of each alternative, the designer takes the decision to select an appropriate configuration of the model.

The analysis stage primarily involves transforming the preliminary design model into an analytical model to compute the responses. The analytical model depends on the type of engineering system and its requirements. Before the real analysis starts, the designer would like to confirm the correctness of the transformation from the preliminary design to the analytical model. At this stage the computer should convey information on the description of the analytical model to the designer, and he/she should be able to interact with the computer to properly modify the model if necessary. This step is very important since carrying out analysis on a wrong model can be avoided. Once the analysis is completed, the response of the system to real working conditions has to be evaluated. For this purpose, suitable methods for information exchange with the design have to be devised. Based on the performance evaluation, the designer can decide whether the model has to be improved or not.

The next stage of detailed design deals with detailing of the design if necessary. Knowledge based programs along with databases could help the designers to complete the detailed design. Finally the graphics capability of the computer provides the designer necessary assistance in preparing working drawings.

It is evident from the above description that the designer is still on the driver's seat of the design process. He/she is assisted by the computer, which processes the design information, based on the instructions received. At every stage of the design sequence, the decisions are taken by the designer and not by the computer. The designer and computer interact and exchange information from time to time to do the tasks assigned to them for achieving the goal of better design.

1.2.1 Software Tools

As computer aided design is an interactive process, the exchange of information
between the designer and the computer has to be made as simple and effective as possible. It is always better to have a natural way of communication between the participants of the design task. Designers of engineering systems always put down the ideas in the form of sketches. The natural way of using computers as a medium to put down the ideas is to use computer graphics techniques, which provide capabilities to model the design ideas. A graphics tablet based input and a surface or solid modeling software would provide the designer immense capabilities for modeling design ideas. Graphics based information exchange, convey more information in less time and also the pictorial representation helps the designer to make use of his intuitive thinking capability to take better and correct decisions. This leads to the conclusion that **Interactive Computer Graphics** is one of the most important software tools for computer- aided design.

In the conceptual and preliminary design stages as well as detailed design stage, it is required to store expertise of experienced designers in the computer, so that they can be used to guide the designer in taking better design decisions. Application of artificial intelligence techniques provides software tools like **Knowledge Based Expert Systems,** which deals with representation and management of knowledge bases. They also provide techniques for writing reasoning programs where an algorithmic formulation of the design problem becomes either very difficult or practically impossible.

Depending on the type and size of design problems, the amount of data that has to be handled during the design process varies considerably. In many cases, huge amount of data has to be managed for effective exchange of information between various design tasks. In addition, the designer or the programmer should not get lost in the data management process, as a result of which the concentration on the real design problem may get affected. The huge data storage capabilities of computers has to be properly exploited with an efficient data management system, which will relieve the designer or the programmer from writing lower level programs that handle and manipulate data. **Data Base Management System** is a software tool, which provides the programmers and designers with facilities for effective use of computer memory, proper organization of data without losing its physical significance and also effective manipulation of data stored in databases.

But finally there should be a medium of communication between the computer and the application program developer, which can be achieved only through a programming language. Generally application program developers prefer to use high level programming languages along with specialized packages for different tasks. **Alternate Programming Languages** are available for a programmer to select from depending on his/her choice. A brief description on evaluation of programming languages is given at the end of this chapter.

1.2.2 Analytical Tools

The analysis stage of the design process deals with the engineering analysis of the physical model. Transformation of the physical model into the analytical model and then using numerical techniques to compute the responses are the major tasks of this stage. The role of computer graphics in analysis stage has already been mentioned. The other two software tools, viz., data base management systems and knowledge-based expert systems greatly help in proper analytical modelling and effective handling of data during analysis. The type of analysis to be carried out depends on the engineering behaviour of the model. Hence the designer should have adequate knowledge of analytical and numerical tools to be used depending on the nature of the engineering system. The **Finite Element Method** provides a powerful numerical tool and is widely used in various disciplines of engineering design.

It has been pointed out that the performance level of design is a very important criterion in evaluating a design. Search for better and better designs means improvement in performance level at every stage. Design problems can be mathematically formulated, so that mathematical programming techniques can be used to arrive at designs with optimum performance. **Optimization Techniques** based on mathematical programming provide the designers robust analytical tools, which help them in their quest for best design.

1.2.3   Development of CAD Software

So far we have seen a few software and analytical tools and their roles in engineering design process. The study of Computer Aided Design thus becomes the study of these software and analytical tools, which will help the designer in carrying out designs with the help of computers in a much more effective, efficient and elegant manner. A thorough knowledge of these tools not only improves the productivity of the design activity, but also provides the designer with powerful techniques for exploring and experimenting innovative design ideas.

A very good programming knowledge is essential for the implementation of programs, which use the analytical and software tools. Even though many programming languages are in use to write programs, one should select a language, which is capable of addressing different programming domains. It was felt that C programming language with its extension to C++ to handle object oriented programming –OOP- approaches perfectly fits into the Computer Aided Design scene. Three chapters are provided in this book, which deal with programming using C and C++ language. Out of the three chapters, the first one provides a detailed description of the language with many programming examples. The second one concentrates more on data structures and programming techniques, which provide efficient data organisation methods for easy and efficient programming. The third chapter provides a brief overview on OOP and the use of C++. It is very much essential that the designers should have adequate knowledge on hardware tools and system software used in CAD. The remaining portion of this chapter is devoted to brief description of the essential components of computer hardware and system software.

1.3   HARDWARE COMPONENTS OF A COMPUTER

Present day computers are more of information processing machines rather than just calculators. All information is handled in computers in the form of symbols. Only two symbols are used to represent any information in computers. They are BInary digiTS; i.e, BITS. This representation using bits is for our convenience only. These two digits represent only two items of information, if considered alone. Hence to represent many items they are taken in groups. A group of 8 bits is called a byte. A group of bits of any length, which is handled together by the computer is called a word. The word length is usually multiple of eight bits. Thus the computers based on microprocessors Intel-8085 and Z-80 have a word length of 8 bits, those based on Intel's 8086, 8088 and 80286 have a word length of 16 bits and those based on Intel's 80386 and Motorola's 68020 and 68030 have a word length of 32 bits. The word lengths of mini and mainframe computers vary generally from 32 to 64 bits.

A group of n bits can be written in 2n different combinations and hence can represent or code 2n different items. The American Standard Code for Information Interchange (ASCII), which is a 7-bit code with an optional parity bit is used generally as the standard code for representing alphanumeric characters, punctuation marks and a few other control symbols. Picture information also can be converted into binary form using scan conversion techniques, which is described in detail in the chapter on computer graphics. To effectively use the resources offered by the computer system, like any other computer users, design engineers also should have a reasonably good knowledge on the hardware organisation and functions of system software. A brief description of the hardware organisation of a computer system is given in the following section.

1.3.1 Computer System Organisation

The basic organisation of computer hardware consists of the following physical devices. In general, all present-day computers have four components. They are:

1. Central Processing Unit
2. Secondary storage Devices
3. Input/Output Devices and
4. Communication devices

All these components are physically connected through proper interfaces so that they can communicate with each other to send and accept data. Fig. 1.1 shows the schematic diagram of physical devices in a computer system. The capabilities and features of each one of these components vary from one system to other. The overall performance of a computer system is very much influenced by the organisation and nature of these components and also how they are connected to each other.

The Central Processing Unit, popularly called CPU, controls all the activities of a computer. It has three components, viz., controller, memory and Arithmetic Logic Unit (ALU). The controller loads the program and data into the memory, examines the program instructions and interacts with arithmetic logic unit to carry out arithmetic and logical operations. Alongwith the interaction between the components of a CPU, it interacts with the secondary storage as well as input/output devices.

The capabilities of the three components of the CPU influence the performance of a computer system to a great extent. For instance, take the amount of main memory available.

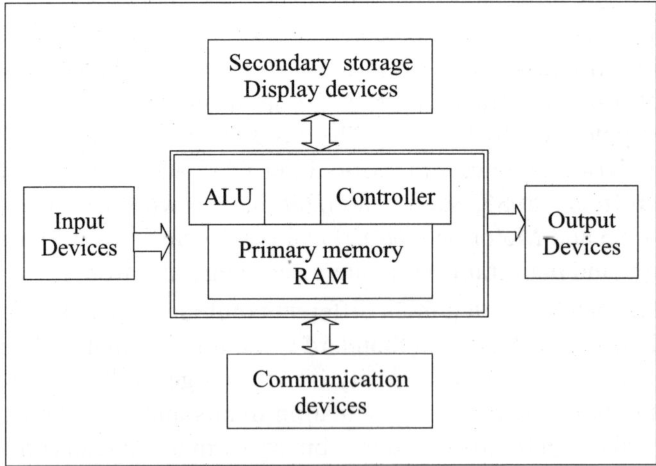

Fig. 1.1 Current day Computer System

The size of program that can be loaded into or the amount of data that can be stored for fast access depends on the available size of main memory. The main memory is organised as a collection of many small storage cells that are directly addressable by CPU. The main memory is also called Random Access Memory (RAM), because of its capability of addressing the individual storage cells directly. Direct access means, the time required to access any individual storage cell is the same. Generally the size of programs written for CAD activities are very large, since they are interactive, graphics oriented and has to handle a number of large vectors and arrays. Hence, large memory is one of the very important requirements for a computer system to be used for engineering design work.

The primary function of the Arithmetic Logic Unit (ALU) is to carry out the arithmetic computations and logical comparisons. In general, most ALUs do only integer computations. Floating point computations are either simulated using software or are done by adding another hardware device called floating point processor. The floating point processor accelerates the numerical computing speed of the computer system. Most of the engineering design problems handle floating point numbers and corresponding programs do a large amount of number crunching work. A floating point processor not only accelerates the speed of computations, but also minimizes the found-off errors and keeps the accuracy. Hence, a floating point processor is a must in a hardware used for CAD work.

The controller is the brain of the computer system. Controller primarily examines the instructions and directs the operations of the computer. It also monitors the overall operations of the CPU. The controller continuously performs an instruction-execution cycle. These steps of instruction and execution are synchronized by an electronic clock that emits millions of regularly spaced pulses each second. Instructions are interpreted and executed at proper intervals and are timed by a specific number of these pulses. Thus the speed at which an instruction is executed is directly related to the computer's build-in clock-speed, which is measured generally in megahertz (MHz). For example, modern microcomputers have clock-speed in the range of 4.77 MHz to about 35 MHz. Larger machines have faster clock-speeds.

The type of secondary storage required for a particular computer system depends on the way the data are to be organised and processed. Punched cards, magnetic tapes, magnetic disks etc. are used to store data that are sequentially organised and processed. Magnetic disks have direct access capability. In magnetic storage media, data is stored on the surface in a number of invisible concentric circles called tracks. Tiny magnetic spots representing data are recorded on and read from their tracks by one or more read/write head(s). The data density on the disk media is determined by the bits per inch of track and the number of tracks that can be placed on each disk surface. Two types of magnetic disks are commonly used. They are flexible disks and hard disks. Flexible disks are also called floppy disks and hard disks are sometimes called Winchester disks. Winchester disk systems have very high data density. The advantages of magnetic disk storage are that information can be processed sequentially or directly. The storage capacity of one flexible disk varies anywhere from 360 kilo bytes to 1.2 mega bytes, whereas that of Winchester disks vary from 10 mega bytes to 400 mega bytes. Large computer installations may have Winchester disks with much higher capacity. Other devices used for direct access secondary storage include RAM disks, magnetic bubble chips and optical disks.

Input/Output devices primarily act for interpretation and communication between humans and computers. Input devices have features for accepting data from the users of the computer. Some devices accept data in the form of alpha-numeric characters. As and when the characters are typed they are transferred to the primary storage. Keyboard is one such device. Some devices transform relative movement of a stylus or that of a ball to corresponding data and pass it on to the computer. But some devices first require data to be recorded on an input storage medium such as magnetisable material. All these devices interpret and communicate information from the individual to the computer.

Like input devices, output devices are instruments for interpretation and communication of information from a computer to the individuals. It converts the computer representation of data into a form, which humans can understand. These devices receive the output results from CPU, converts them into a form that can be used by people. Monitor screens, printers, plotters etc. are a few popular output devices. Various input-output devices used for CAD work are described in detail in chapter 4.

A new dimension to computer usage has come in the form of Internet which provides global access to data and information. Modems and Ethernet cards are devices which are essential for communication computing and additional features like audio and video players and TV connectors help in raising the level of the usage of computers to incredible heights.

For the CPU to communicate with other subsystems like main memory, I/O subsystems etc., a set of parallel communication lines each capable of transmitting a single bit of information at one time are provided. This set of communication lines is called a bus. Usually the buses are divided into three groups, viz., those carrying data, those carrying address and those carrying control signals. The number of parallel communication lines in a set is one of the factors, which determines the speed of communication through the bus. The external input and output devices like mouse, digitizer, plotter, printer etc. are connected to the CPU through external communication interfaces. Generally two different types of interfaces are commonly used. They are: (i) parallel interface and (ii) serial interface. The mode of data communication through these interfaces is different. Devices, which have only parallel interface should be connected to the CPU only with the parallel interface on the CPU side; similarly for the serial interface also. In parallel interface, all the 8 bits in a byte are sent in parallel, whereas, in a serial interface, bits are sent sequentially at a predetermined speed. Generally the speeds are in the order of 1200 bits to 9600 bits per second.

Depending on the size, architecture, cost and system performance, computer systems are classified into micro, mini, mainframe and supercomputers. Since these categories overlap, the most powerful system in one category may exceed the capabilities and cost of the least powerful system in another. As hardware and software technology are changing fast, within a matter of months after a new computer model comes to the market, it is faced with two potential successors. One that costs the same but has a much higher performance; the other has the same performance at a reduced cost. Thus a recently introduced small computer systems outperform large models of few years back. The present day microcomputer does the work of an earlier mini computer at a much lower cost. Computers of past years require skilled operators to operate them. In contrast to that the present day micros do not require such skilled personnel to operate them. The users of the computer themselves can do all the operations. This was made possible with the advancement of software technology, which resulted in development of user friendly operating systems and programming environments which made these micro computers *personal*. Most personal computers are self- contained units and designed to be used by one person at a time. Connected to the CPU of typical personal computers are limited number of peripheral devices to perform input, secondary storage and output functions.

Workstations are becoming more popular for carrying out computer aided design works, due to many special features provided in them, which make them the most suitable machines for CAD work. They are different from conventional multi-user systems and personal computers. Of course the users themselves have to acquire the skill of operating them, which makes the workstations also personal to some extent. Personal computers allow only one process to be run at any time. Conventional multi-user systems allow one to connect large number of terminals so that large number of processes can be run simultaneously, but only one from one terminal. In contrast to these a workstation permits a single user to run a number of processes simultaneously from the same terminal. In addition to a good amount of numerical computing capability, a workstation consists of a set of graphics components arranged with attention to ergonomic aspects. Essentially a 32 bit CPU with a floating point accelerator, large amount of primary as well as secondary storage, a large high resolution colour graphics screen, a specialised keyboard with a mouse attached to it, and optionally a digitizer makes a workstation ideal to be used for CAD work. On the software side, a number of software tools enhance the capabilities of the workstation. The essential software tools that are necessary on a workstation consist of a display manager with multiple window management capability, a set of application program development tools, language compilers, debuggers, graphics support software systems and a set of driver as well as server modules for connection various peripheral devices to the workstations. The workstation should also have capability for networking with other systems. This makes it possible to share software resources available on other systems.

1.4 SYSTEM SOFTWARE

So far we have briefly discussed the basic hardware components of a computer system. A properly integrated hardware, when powered on will not work as a computer system, unless some basic programs are loaded into the memory. The most basic programs, generally called microcodes are stored in Read Only Memory (ROM) chips, which automatically gets loaded into the memory while the system is switched on and makes the machine ready to accept the next level of system program called operating system. The operating system is an integrated set of specialised programs that is used to manage the resources and overall operations of a computer. It permits the computer to supervise its own operations. The operating system is stored on secondary storage devices. The operating system programs can be broadly classified into two categories, viz., essential programs also called supervisor program and a set of utilities. The essential programs should always be loaded into the memory for the computer to work. The utilities are invoked as and when it is required. Immediately after the micro-codes get loaded, they look for the essential programs of the operating system. These programs are then loaded into the main memory. This process of loading the operating system is called bootstrapping the computer. These essential programs consist of modules for managing the hardware resources and a command language interpreter. The command language interpreter provides a set of commands by which the user of the computer can interact with it. Whatever command that is keyed-in by the user, is first interpreted by the command language interpreter and later the corresponding module is invoked to carry out actions required by the command. Thus the operating system permits the computer to supervise its own operations by automatically calling in the application programs and managing the data needed to produce the output desired by the users. The operating system tends to isolate the hardware from the user.

The supervisor program of the operating system (OS), which is always primary (main) memory resident, controls and coordinates all other parts of the OS. Other programs in the operating system, i.e., the utilities are kept in online system-resident secondary storage device so that the supervisor can retrieve them as and when needed. In most of the modern large computer systems, multiple jobs are scheduled to balance the I/O processing requirements. Multiprogramming is the name given to the interleaved or concurrent execution of two or more different independent programs by the same computer. But in multi-processing systems, two or more CPUs are linked together. Instructions from two or more programs are processed at the same instance of time in multiprocessing but not in multiprogramming. Computers with virtual storage capability keeps active program segments called pages in primary storage and assigns other program parts to an on-line secondary storage device. The OS handles the swapping of program pages between primary and on-line secondary storage.

A few popular operating systems are DOS (Disk Operating Systems) on family of personal computers, VAX / VMS on VAX family of computers right from microvax to mainframe VAX systems and UNIX on workstations, mini and many 32 bit micros. DOS is a single user operating system, whereas UNIX and VMS are multi-user type. Both VMS and UNIX provide virtual memory capabilities, which do not put any restriction on the size of the program with respect to the primary storage available in the machine. UNIX operating system developed at AT & T laboratories, USA has been installed on a variety of computer systems and is becoming a *defacto* standard operating system in computing industry.

In addition to the facilities provided by the operating systems, additional capabilities are required for development of application programs. They are language compilers, linkers, general purpose as well as special purpose libraries, debuggers, programming environments etc. The language compilers are also programs which converts the programs written in high level languages to machine language, so that they can be loaded into the memory and directly executed. Solving problems using computers involve a series of tasks. They are shown in the form of a flowchart in figure 1.2. It may be noted that they are the minimum number of tasks required. Depending on the type of problem one may require additional capabilities. The minimum system software support required in addition to operating system for solving problems using computers are: text editors, language compilers, linkers and debuggers. The text editor allows one to enter or make corrections in the program entered. The language compiler checks the program for any possible errors in syntax and semantics of the language use. The linker resolves external references of functions and symbols, links with standard or

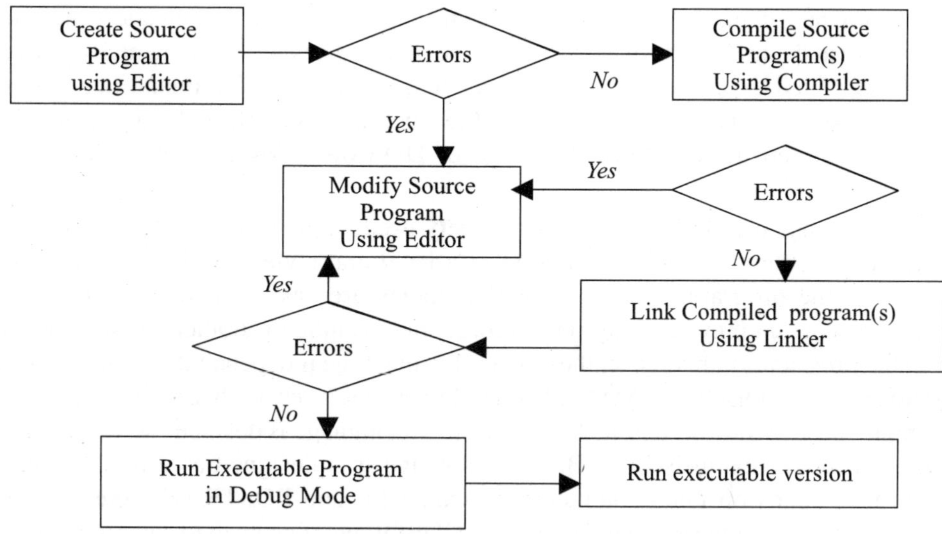

Fig. 1.2 Different stages of Program Development

specified libraries and creates an executable version of the program, which can directly be loaded and run. It is often required to test the program with different input data. During the testing stage, one has to examine the values of different variables at different stages, without making the program to modify every time. Debugger provides facilities to execute a program step by step controlled by the user, watch values of variables, evaluate expressions for verification and modify values of variables for the rest of the run. A good debugger considerably brings down the total time for program development. Editors, compilers, linkers and debuggers are separate programs. The present trend is to integrate these programs into a development environment, which provide the programmers a total environment for fast and easy development of programs. Most of the present day interactive computers support such programming environments for many languages.

1.4.1 Programming Languages

A programming language is a medium of communication between computer and the programmer. They consist of different symbols, characters and usage rules that permit people to communicate with computers. Many different programming languages are in use, depending on the type of applications for which the programs are written. They are generally classified by their level and by their principal applications. The four major categories of programming languages are the following:

- command languages
- high level languages
- assembly languages
- machine languages

The command languages are English like in their expressive power and functionality. Hence, they are at the highest level compared to the others. They are fundamentally dominated by statements which express *what to do* rather than *how to do*. Command languages like Digital Command Language (DCL) of VAX/VMS operating system, shell language of UNIX operating system and the command language of DOS operating system come under this category.

High level languages are the ones most widely used languages for programming. These languages allow algorithms to be expressed in a level and style of writing which is easily understood by the programmers. As these languages are easily implemented on several machines; the program may be easily ported from one machine to another without substantial change in the program. In this sense, they are called machine independent languages. BASIC, FORTRAN, Pascal, COBOL, C, ADA, LISP, Prolog etc. are a few high level languages, which are commonly used in various application areas. Each language is designed with some king of application in mind. For insistance, BASIC language was designed as a tool for teaching computing techniques on microcomputers. Pascal, APL and FORTRAN were specifically meant for scientific and engineering computing. COBOL was designed to cater to the needs of data processing applications. Language designed for artificial intelligence application are LISP and Prolog. C and ADA languages are primarily meant for systems programming applications. A few general purpose languages were also designed to do programming for various application areas. PL/I is one such language, which is fairly good in programming different application domains.

The assembly languages and machine languages are machine dependent. The assembly language is simply a symbolic representation form of its associated machine language, allowing less tedious programming than the latter. A good knowledge of underlying machine architecture is necessary for effective programming in either of these languages. The following three equivalent program segments as shown by Thucker [10] illustrate the basic distinction between high-level, assembly and machine language.

High-level Language	Assembly Language	Machine Language
Z=W+X*Y	L 3, X	41 3 OC1A4
	M 2,Y	3A 2 OC1A8
	A 3,W	1A 3 OC1A0
	ST 3,Z	50 3 OC1A4

Programming in high-level and assembly language, therefore requires some sort of interface with the machine language at the time the program is to be run. Three most common such interfaces are: Assembler, Compiler and Interpreter. The assemblers and compilers translate the programs into respective machine language prior to execution. The interpreter on the other hand, directly executes the instruction in the high-level language without a prior processing step. But every program line is then and there converted to corresponding machine code segment and executed. Compilation is a more efficient step than interpretation. This is because statements within *loops* must be interpreted each time they are executed by the interpreter; whereas in the case of a compiler, even the statements within a loop are translated into machine language code only once. Some languages are mainly only interpretive type, for example, languages like BASIC, Prolog, LISP etc. Most of the other languages are compiled languages. In some cases, a compiler will be alternatively available for an interpreted language such as BASIC and LISP. Interpretation is preferable to compilation in experimental programming environment, where each run involve some changes in the program text. The efficiency advantage that is traditionally enjoyed by compiled languages over interpreted ones may soon be eliminated due to the evolution of machines whose operating languages themselves are high-level languages. An example of this is the new LISP-machines, which have been recently introduced.

The application areas for which programs are generally written can be classified into five categories: scientific, data processing, artificial intelligence, text processing and systems programming. Scientific applications predominantly manipulate numbers and arrays of numbers using mathematical principles as a basis for the algorithms. Amount of input data in such problems is relatively small. The mathematical complexity of engineering problems is a significant characteristic of these problems, which usually require more of computer's central processor than the input/output devices. Most of the computing time is consumed by arithmetic computations. Data processing applications primarily deal with creation, extraction and summarisation of data records and its maintenance. The volume of data involved in these applications is very large, whereas, the arithmetic computations carried out are very low. Data processing programs spend most of its time in doing input/output operations compared to central processing. The scarce resource in a data processing task is the secondary storage. Manipulation of natural language text is what the text processing programs do. The evolution of modern word-processing technology relies primarily on text processing algorithms to perform formatting and other functions that the typist uses during report and document preparation. Simulation of intelligent behaviour of human beings is done in artificial intelligence applications. In these programs symbols are manipulated than numbers. These include game playing algorithms, computer vision, robotics and knowledge based expert systems. Systems programming applications involve programs that interface the computer hardware with the program or operator. These include compilers, interpreters, assemblers, input-output management routines, operating systems, program management facilities and managing the various resources that comprise the computer system. Two major characteristics of the system programs are: (I) the capability to effectively deal with unpredictable events like errors and (ii) the capability to coordinate various tasks.

It may be noted that a program for Computer Aided Engineering may contain many modules with different characteristics. Some may be of intensive number crunching type while some other modules may have to handle large amount of data. Also some modules have to simulate intelligent design procedures whereas, some others have to coordinate various activities where a good amount of systems programming input is required. Hence, Computer Aided Design programs cannot be viewed as one of the application among the above mentioned five different fields. They require inputs from almost all the different programming paradigms. This requirement of CAD programs puts a greater emphasis on proper selection of programming language for CAD programming. Some issues pertaining to the evaluation of programming languages based on several criteria are discussed below.

A programming language should have the ability to clearly express the meaning intended by the programmer. An expressive language has constructs consistent with those that are commonly used in the field. For instance, a mathematician or an engineer expects to find algebraic expression in a programming language to be consistent with those used in conventional algebra. The ability to have symbols to denote operations has a direct influence on the language's expressivity. FORTRAN, C and Pascal have good expressivity from the scientific and engineering programming point of view.

The language's syntax and semantics should be free from ambiguity and should be consistent. The structured programming features of Pascal and C make them execllent as far as well defined-ness is concerned. The portability of programs improves if the syntax and semantics of the language in which it is written are well defined.

More *number of data types and better data structuring* capability is an essential feature of any language to be accepted for CAD programming. In addition to the primary data types like integer, real and character, there should be facility to group similar as well as dissimilar data types. FORTRAN is only reasonably good in this aspect, whereas C and Pascal are excellent.

Modern software engineering concepts demand *program development in a modular fashion.* The software is completely designed first and tasks are divided into subtasks. Modules for each subtask are developed separately and tested before integrating them to form the complete software. To follow such software engineering methodologies the programming language should support two features, viz., sub-programming and programmer defined data typing. Sub-programming allows one to independently define procedures and functions and communicate via parameters or global variables with the invoking program. Pascal and C languages are strong in this regard with C being exceptionally good.

A language's input/output handing capability has to be thoroughly examined before a selection is made. These include, support for sequential and direct access file systems, database access and information retrieval functions. Files reside on secondary storage devices and the language should support different programming strategies for their management. FORTRAN, Pascal and C have reasonably good features as far as input/output handling is concerned.

One of the major requirements of any CAD program is that the program developed on one machine should be transportable onto other machines. That means thc language in which the program is developed should be machine-independent. American National Standard Institute (ANSI) and International Standards Organisation (ISO) have set specifications for many programming languages. Those languages which follow these standards are generally portable. The ANSI FORTRAN (1977) or ANSI COBOL (1974) or ANSI C are supported on many machines, because they are standardised. Even though BASIC is a well-defined language and available on number of hardware platforms, it is the least portable one. It is implemented in almost every machine imaginable, each implementation reflects different dialect. Thus when trying to port a BASIC program from one machine to another, the programmer must be aware of both the dialects and must modify the program. A truly portable language should not have such dialects. C is an excellent language for portability aspect compared to either Pascal or FORTRAN.

From the above discussion on the evaluation criteria of languages, it can be clearly seen that C programming language is superior in almost all aspects shadowing other languages, which are commonly used for engineering computing. Moreover C's strength extends into systems programming area, for which it was principally designed. C language contains most unified approach to procedures and functions among all the programming languages, virtually eliminating the artificial dichotomy that has existed between them for decades.

We have seen in the previous section that, programming for Computer Aided Design involve different programming paradigms, which demand different features and capabilities. Hence a language suitable for CAD programming should be general enough to handle a wide range of programming applications. Each language is designed with a specific purpose, even then they seem suitable for other application paradigms also. C programming language, even though designed for systems programming, it is found to be the most general language today. It is found to be efficient both in systems programming as well as in engineering applications programming. The various language evaluation criteria discussed above compare the languages used for procedural programming applications, where numerical computing based on algorithms forms the major part of programs.

In addition to procedural programming, other three programming paradigms which are being commonly used, are functional programming, logic programming and object oriented programming. In conventional procedural programs data as well as algorithms are distinct and separate, whereas, in functional programming, they co-exist with functions and data exchange their identify depending on the context. The recursive nature of the functional programming languages make them suitable in special applications like symbolic processing and list processing for artificial intelligence applications. LISP is a functional programming language. Logic Programming languages also manipulate symbols but represent them as clauses. The built-in inferencing mechanisms like backtracking drive the symbolic processing by such languages. Prolog is one such logic programming language. Object oriented programming is becoming more and more popular among CAD programmers. Object oriented programming is one step forward from the conventional structured programming with abstract data types, where objects or classes are defined to classify values with common operations and common properties. Object oriented programming approach places more emphasis on program design in detail first by defining classes or objects and then use these objects for information processing. C++ and Smalltalk are two popular languages used for object oriented programming.

1.5 PROGRAMMING LANGUAGE FOR CAD

Selection of a particular language for a specific application area, depends very much on the efficiency of the language for the application under consideration. Programming for Computer Aided Design involves implementation of complex algorithms, design of good data structures, interaction with data bases and providing interactive graphics facilities. The programming language to be selected for CAD must have the following capabilities to meet the above requirements.

1. *Explicit support abstraction and modular design at an efficient level of implementation.*
2. *The language must provide a functional style and a higher level of data abstraction.*
3. *Provision of a language mechanism which unifies the representation and the operation of the programmer defined data types.*
4. *The language must provide a programming environment including all the facilities and tools which a software designer or programmer requires in the design, development, testing, implementation and maintenance of a system of programs.*

The C programming language has the capabilities to meet most of the above requirements. It embodies a modular programming style. The executable construct in the language is an instance of an expression, which consists of a series of applications of functions to arguments. The first effective formal link between a programming language and the programming environment was achieved by C and its host operating system UNIX. Comprising a highly portable library and a set of tools, UNIX has become a standard operating environment for CAD software design and development. All these points to C as an effective and efficient programming language for Computer Aided Design. The C operators, data types, and function library are unusually rich C is very portable, making its applications potentially widespread. Since C is the host language for UNIX, and the current use of UNIX in engineering programming undoubtedly enhance the use of C in Cad programming. The current day invasion of PCs and 32-bit workstations in practically every field of life and efficient C programming environments in these machines have made the language very popular in almost all the areas of applications including programming for artificial intelligence.

The historical development of C parallels with that of UNIX itself. An original version of UNIX operating system was written on a PDP-7 computer in 1969 at Bell Laboratories, USA in assembler language. During the same period, an experimental language B was being developed there, which was an improvement on the earlier systems programming language BCPL. In 1972, the language C was designed, as an extension of B, the primary difference was that C had an extensive collection of standard types. In 1973, UNIX was substantially extended and was rewritten in C. Because of this liberation from assembly language, UNIX and hence C became quite portable. Moreover C language, UNIX and its function library have since had a very stable life. In 1977, UNIX was ported to the VAX computer system and a new version was independently developed at the University of California, Berkeley. The late 1970s and early 1980s have seen further proliferation of UNIX and C on diverse machines from micros to mainframes. Moreover C has become independently supported outside UNIX context, and compilers were made available on many machines under their own operating systems. For instance, powerful programming environments are available on IBM PC family of computers and compatibles under DOS operating systems. An excellent standard reference test for C is the C *programming Language* written by Kerningham and Ritchie.

References

1. Besant,C.B. and Lui,C.W.K.,(1988), Computer-Aided Design and Manugacturing, 3rd ed., East-West Press Pvt. Ltd., New Delhi.
2. Chorafas,D.N., (1986), Fourth and Fifth Generation Programming Languages, McGraw-Hill Book Co., USA.
3. Davis, W.S., (1983), Operating Systems, 2nd ed., Addison-Wesley Publishing Co., Reading Mass., USA.
4. Ellzey,R.S., (1987), Computer Systems Software, Science Research Associates Inc., Chicago, USA.
5. Encarnacao,J. and Schlechtendahi,E.G.,(1983), Computer Aided Design, Springer Verlag, Berlin, Germany.
6. Gear, W.C., (1980), Computer Organisation and Programming, 3rd ed., McGraw-Hill Book Co., New York, USA.
7. Graham,R.M.,(1975), Principles of Systems Programming, John Wiley & Sons Inc., New York, USA.
8. Knuth, D. E., (1969), The Art of Computer Programming, Addison-Wesley Publishing Co., Reading, Mass., USA.
9. Lister N.M., Fundamentals of Operating Systems, 2nd edition., Springer-Verlag, New York, USA.
10. Tucker, A.B., (1986), Programming Languages, McGraw-Hill Book Co., Singapore.
11. Wexelblat,R.L., (1981), History of Programming Languages, Academic Press, New York, USA.
12. Yates, J.L. and Emerson, S.L.,(1984), The Business Guide to UNX System, Addison-Wesley Publishing Co., Reading, Mass., USA.

Review Questions

1. What are the different tasks involved in engineering design? Explain each one of them in detail.
2. What are the roles played by the designer and computer in a Computer aided Design process?
3. What are the advantages of using computer as a design medium in Engineering Design?
4. Explain the role of various software tools in Computer Aided Design.
5. Write a detailed note on impact of CAD on Engineering Design Profession.
6. What are the essential components of a computer system? Explain the functions of each component.
7. Define the following terms.

    ROM, RAM, microcodes, secondary storage, bus, floating point processor

8. What is an operating system? What are its main functions? Give examples of different types of operating systems.

9. Make a comparative study on the command languages of different operating systems like VAX/VMS, UNIX and DOS.

10. Write short notes on the following:

      Procedural Programming

      Logic Programming

      Functional Programming

      Object Oriented Programming

11. Define the term *Programming Environment*. What are its advantages over traditional batch process? Describe various components of a Programming Environment.

12. Describe the various evaluation criteria for programming languages. For computer Aided Design software development, evaluate the programming languages FORTRAN, Pascal, BASIC and C.

CHAPTER 2

C Programming Language

2.1   INTRODUCTION

The C language has been described by its developer Ritchie(5) as a relatively low-level language. It is also called a middle-level computer language (2). The above two definitions actually describe its position lying between the high-level language like FORTRAN and the languages like assembly languages that are closer to the machine. The C language has several advantages over other languages as has been pointed out in chapter 1. It is a highly portable language resulting in enormous savings in efforts while porting a package developed on one particular type of computer to the other. Being a low-level language, normally the programs coded in C runs faster than the ones written in higher-level languages. All these advantages point out that it provides a powerful software tool for CAD system developers.

The data types, control structures, variety of operators, the use of pointers and structures which make the C language suitable for developing application software are described in this Chapter. Examples from engineering discipline are included to illustrate the carious language features discussed here.

2.2   AN OVERVIEW OF PROGRAMMING IN C

The C language is built on the concept of functions. Similar to a function subprogram or subroutine subprogram used in FORTRAN, the function in C has a name and a list of arguments, and performs a specified task. The program that activates the execution is also called a function but called specifically as main().

Example 2.1

```
/* This is the first example in C            */
main()
```

```
        {
        Printf (" I am anxious to learn C for CAD. \n");
        }
```

Output:

```
        I am anxious to learn C for CAD.
```

The following features of C may be noted through the above example.

1. In a C program the description that begins with /* and ends with */ will be treated as comment. Thus, the first line /* This is the first example in C */ is a comment.

2. The function main is followed by the opening and closing parentheses () signals the beginning of the execution.

3. Unlike other programming languages, we can begin typing the program from any position on a line.

4. Functions are usually written in lower case letters. Traditionally upper case letters are used for symbolic names and constants, and everything else is written in lower case letters.

5. The opening brace, {, marks the beginning and the closing brace, }, indicates the end of the function body. Braces are used within a function to indicate a block of statements to be executed and will be described later. As a good programming style the opening and closing braces are aligned along the function name as above. It is good practice to give suitable indentations to statements and this can be noticed in the programs presented in this chapter.

6. A semicolon marks the end of a program statement.

7. The printf(……..) used in the above example is a standard library function to print the description within the quotation marks" ". The last two characters, namely / n, called back-slash n, are collectively known as a new line character. This is similar to carriage control character used in FORMAT statement in FORTRAN and it makes the cursor to move to the extreme left in the next line.

Before we take up the study of the C language, presented in the following sections, it may be noted that running a source program written in C is similar to that of a FORTRAN program. The source code is to be compiled by the C compiler available on a particular machine. In the next step the linker has to be invoked and it resolves all the external references and memory addresses and also links all the standard library functions called by the program. The executable module produced after this link edit step is ready for running on the machine. Thus, the four steps viz., creating the source file, compiling it, linking the compiled file and finally executing the load module are involved in running a C program.

In addition to compilers, interpreters are also available for C language similar to BASIC. The interpreters may be used for learning the features of the language and running small sized programs. However, for practical problem solving and large sized programs usually met with in CAD environment, compilers are preferred.

2.3 VARIABLES AND DATATYPES

The C language gives scope to name the variables in a meaningful way compared to the restrictions we have in FORTRAN. C also provides four basic data types. These are explained in the following sections.

2.3.1 Variables

The first character of a variable should begin with a letter or underscore and may be followed by any combination of letters (upper or lower-case) or digits 0 to 9. A variable can have any number of characters. However, it is necessary to check with a particular system since some of the compilers retain only the first eight characters. Certain words are reserved by C and should not be used.

Examples:
The following are valid variable names:

```
Load
Node_number
I
Elements
```

The following are invalid variable named:

```
5thload (starts with a number)
stiff matrix (blank in between)
int (C reserved word)
```

It must be noted that in C, lower and upper case letters are distinct. For example, load, Load, LOAD, each refers to a distinct variable.

The following words are reserved by C to indicate specific tasks as part of the language. For example, int is used to declare that the variable is integer, float for floating point variable.

auto	else	int	switch	break
entry	long	typedef	case	enum
register	union	char	extern	return
unsigned	continue	float	short	void
default for	sizeof	while	do	
goto	static	double if	struct	

2.3.2 Datatypes

There are basically four data types in C. They are character, integer, floating and double precision floating point. These data types are specified in C as, char, int, float and double respectively. A fifth data type valueless, called void is proposed in the ANSI standard. In order to meet the range or accuracy requirements of the values that the variables may be assigned in different situations of programming, the data types especially integers may have modifiers preceding them. The list of modifiers is **signed, unsigned, long** and **short**. The number of bits used and range of values of data types depend on the processor of the computer and in the case of floating point types the number of digits of precision depends also on the method used to represent floating point numbers. The range and precision of various data types on a micro-computer using 16 bit word length are given in the following Table 2.1.

Table 2.1   Data Types and Range of Values

Date Type	No. of bits	Range or Precision
Char	8	ASCII characters
Unsigned char	8	0 to 255
Signed char	8	-128 to 127
Int	16	-32768 to 32767
Unsigned int	16	0 to 65535
Signed int	16	same as int
Short int	8	-128 to 127
Unsigned short int	8	0 to 255
Signed short int	8	same as short int
Long int	32	-2147483648 to 2147483649
Unsigned long int	32	0 to 4294967296
Signed long int	32	same as long int
Float	32	Approximately 6 digits of Precision
Double	64	Approximately 12 digits of Precision
Long double	128	Approximately 24 digits of Precision.

It should be noted that in C, the data types of all the variables must be explicitly declared by the programmer unlike the case of FORTRAN wherein the default option sets the data type of variables using the first character, like variables starting with I, J, K, L, M and N are treated as integers etc.

2.3.3 Declaration of Variables

The general form of declaration of variables is given below:

```
type variable_list;
```

Here, the variable_list contains the names of variables each one of them separated by a comma.

```
int node;
int node, element_number;
float load, x_coord, y_coord, z_coord;
double stiffness, stress;
char sup_type;
```

It may be noted that character constants are specified within quotes. Thus, for sup_type declared as char variable in the above, the value can be assigned as,

```
sup_type='f';
```

2.3.4 Initialization of Variables

In C the variables can be given initial values at the same time they are declared. The general form of initialization is,

```
type variable_name = constant;
```

The following assignments illustrate the process of initialisation of variables.

```
char sup_type      =      ' f ' ;
int node           =          25 ;
float load         =       28.56 ;
```

2.4 OPERATORS

An operator is a symbol that tells the compiler certain mathematical or logical operation that has to be performed on a data value called operand. C is very rich in having a number of different operations. Generally the operators can be classified as arithmetic, relational and logical, and bitwise operators. In addition, C has special operators for performing certain specific tasks. Table 2.2 lists of C operators.

2.4.1 Arithmetic Operators

The arithmetic operators are +, -, *, /, modulus operator % and a unary minus -. The first four operators +, -, *, / and unary minus – are of the same type as in FORTRAN and other languages. The modulus operator % is used in integer division and it produces the remainder. For example, 5%3 yields 2, 3%5 yields 3 and 6%6 yields 0.

The unary operator minus, -, negates the value of the operand.

2.4.2 Precedence and Associativity

FORTRAN programmers are aware that there is heirarchy of operations while evaluating an expression. In C, the order in which operators are evaluated is referred to as precedence and the way in which operators having the same Precedence are evaluated is referred to as associativity.

Table 2.2 gives the precedence and associativity of various C operators. It may be noted that the arithmetic operators *, /, %, + and – are evaluated in this order from left to right. However, the order of evaluation can be altered by using parentheses. Parentheses are treated in C as in FORTRAN and what is inside the innermost pair of parentheses is evaluated first, followed by what is inside the next innermost pair of parentheses and so on.

Table 2.2 Summary of C Operators

Operator	Description	Associativity
( )	Function call	Left to right
[ ]	Array element reference	
— >	Pointer to structure member reference	
	Structure member reference	
—	Unary minus	Right to left
++	Increment	
– –	Decrement	
!	Logical negation	
~	Ones complement	
*	Pointer reference (indirection)	
&	Address	
Sizeof	Size of an object	
(type)	Type Cast (conversion)	
*	Multiplication	Left to right
/	Division	
%	Modulus	
+	Addition	Left to right
-	Subtraction	
<<	Left shift	Left to right
>>	Right shift	
<	Less than	Left to right
<=	Less than or equal to	
>	Greater than	
>=	Greater than or equal to	
==	Equality	Left to right
!=	Inequality	
&&	Logical AND	Left to right
I	Logical OR	Left to right
?:	Conditional expression	Right to left
=	Assignment operators	Right to left
*= /= %=		
+= -=		

2.4.3 Arithmetic Expressions, Assignment Statement and Assignment Operators

Arithmetic expressions are evaluated following the precedence rules described in the earlier section. Thus the arithmetic expression b/c * d is evaluated first dividing b by c and then multiplying the results by d. The general form of assignment statement is,

```
variable name    =        expression;
```

Like FORTRAN, a single equals sign is used to indicate assignment. The expression on the right hand side of the equals sign is evaluated first and the value is assigned to the variable name appearing on the left hand side. Consider the statement,

```
t_load = w1+w2+(ud1 * (x2- x1);
```

The expression on the right-hand side is evaluated as follows. The terms within the innermost parentheses, $x2 - x1$ is calculated and then the result will be multiplied by ud1. The expression will be again scanned from left to right and evaluated by adding w1 and w2, to the result of the expression within the parentheses evaluated first. The result will be assigned to the variable t_load. Consider another statement

```
f = (a = b/ (c * d)) + e;
```

The expression on the right-hand side is evaluated as follows. First: c is multiplied by d; second; b is divided by the above result; third; assign the result of the previous step to a; fourth; ass e to the result of the previous step three; fifth; assign the result of the previous operation to f.

2.4.3.1 *Assignment Operations of C's shorthand*

Statements like n = n+5; in which the left-hand side is repeated on the right can be written in a short form as,

```
n + = 5;
```

Using an assignment operator +=. The assignment operators are formed by listing the binary operator immediately followed by equals sign (see Table 2.2). Thus, $y / = (y + c)$; is equivalent to $y = y / (y + c)$;.

There are three distinct advantages in using assignment operators. First the statement becomes easier to write since what appears on the left-hand side need not be repeated on the right-hand side. Second the resulting expression is easier to read. Third, the use of assignment operators may speed up execution.

2.4.4 Type Conversions

When different data types are mixed in an arithmetic expression one of the operands will be converted to the other type so that both of them are of the same type. Reading from right to left the conversion order is as follows.

```
char< int < long < float < double
```

1. if the ranking operand is double, the other operands (regardless of the type) are converted to double and the result will be double,

2. if the ranking operand is float, the other operands will be converted to float and the result will be a float,

3. if the ranking operand is a long, the other operands will be converted to long the and the result will be long,

4. if we are left with only ints and chars, all the chars be converted into ints and the result will be an int.

In the case of arithmetic statement, whatever is the type on the right of the assignment operator (=) it is converted to the type on the left.

2.4.5 Increment and Decrement Operators

C has two useful operators for adding 1 to the operand and subtracting 1 from the operand. These are called increment and decrement operations, denoted by ++ and —. These operators may precede or follow an operand but note that their difference in their usage which is illustrated below.

Consider the statement n = ++i; this is same as

```
i= i + 1 ; n=i;
```

If i= 10, the values of n=11 due to the above statement.

Consider now, n =i++ ; this has the effect as,

```
n = i ;
i = i + 1 ;
```

That is, in this case the statement results in a value of n = 10 and then i is incremented by 1 and set as i = 11.

Thus, the expression ++i (pre-increment) increments i before its value is used in an assignment operation or any other expression containing it. The expression i++ (post-increment) does the incrementing after the value of i is used. The decrement operator also works in the same way. Thus, N = — I ; is equivalent to

```
I = I - 1 ;
N= I ;
```

And, N =I — ; is equivalent to

```
N = I ;
I = I - 1 ;
```

Thus, the expression - - I (pre-decrement) decrements I before its value is used in an assignment operation or any other expression containing it. The expression I—(post decrement) does the decrementing after the value of I is used.

2.4.6   Relational and Logical Operators

In order to compare values and to take logical decisions, the relational and logical operators are used. The are <, <=, >, >=, ==, ! = and & &, and the meanings of these operators are given in Table 2.2. It may be noted that these operators have lower precedence compared to arithmetic operators.

The expressions that compare operands using a relational operator are called relational expressions. Like all expressions in C, the relational expressions are evaluated to yield a numerical result and the value can only be an integer value of 1 or 0. A condition that we would interpret as true corresponds to an integer value of 1 and a false condition would result in a value of 0.

In addition to the relational operators, logical operators, && (AND), ¦ (OR) and ! (NOT, negation) are used to construct more complex conditions.

When the AND operator, && is used with two simple expressions, the condition is true, if both the expressions are true. For example,

```
length > 3500           &&        depth < 500
```

is true (and has value of 1) only if length is greater than 3500 and depth is less than 500.

In the case of OR operator ¦ , the condition is satisfied if either one or both of the two expressions is true. Thus, the expression,

```
length > 3500           ¦        depth < 500
```

Is true if either length is greater than 3500, the depth is less than 500, or both conditions are true.

The NOT operator, !, is used to change an expression to its opposite state; that is if the expression is true (non zero value) ! expression produces a zero value (false). If an expression is false (zero value), ! expression makes it true by evaluating it to 1. Since the Not operator, !, is used only with one expression, it is a unary operator.

2.4.7   Bitwise Logical Operators

Since C is also used for system programming, it supports many of the operations connected with testing, setting or shifting of the actual bits in a byte or word that correspond to char and int data types. These operators are not listed in table 2.2 and for more detailed information, readers may consult references [1,2,3].

2.4.8   Conditional Expression Operator (?)

The conditional operator ? takes the general form,

```
exp1?exp2:exp3;
```

Where exp1, exp2 and exp3 are expressions. The exp1 is evaluated and if it is true, then exp2 is evaluated and becomes the value of the expression. If exp1 is false, then exp3 is evaluated and its value becomes the value of the expression. This is illustrated below.

```
x = 20;

y = (x>10) ? 100 : 200;
```

The value of y will be assigned 100 in the above example. Note the parentheses are used in exp1 to add clarity to reading though not required since the precedence of ? : is very low.

2.4.9 Address (&) and Pointer (*) Operators

The address operator, &, is a unary operator that returns the memory address of its operand. For example, the statement

```
m = @node;
```

places the memory address of the variable node into m. Suppose the variable node is stored at a location 6010 in memory, then after the above assignment, m will have a value 6010. The operator & has a meaning address of.

The other operator is pointer operator *. Pointers are very important and useful in C. A brief description of the pointer operator is given below.

The pointer operator * is a unary operator that returns the value of the variable stored at the address indicated by the variable that follows it. In the above example, m contains the address of the variable and the statement,

```
k = *m;
```

places the value of node into k. The pointer operator * has a meaning at address. In the above assignment k receives the value at the address m. As indicated earlier, pointers are powerful operators in C and a more detailed description on pointers is given in section 2.8.

2.4.10 The Compile-Time Operator – sizeof

The operator sizeof is a unary compile time operator that returns the size in bytes of its operand. The operand could be variable or data type. For example,

```
float a;
printf("%d" , sizeof(a));
```

This returns a value 4 on the display, as the sizeof the operand which in this case is a. Consider now, printf("%d" , sizeof(int));. This will return a value 2 or 4 depending on the computer. This will facilitate to make programs machine independent.

The sizeof operator can also be used with arrays. For example, if an array is declared as, int node[10]; the expression sizeof(node); returns 20 ro 40 depending on the size of int is 2 or 4.

2.4.11 Comma Operator

This operation finds its use in for statement discussed in section 2.6.3. A pair of expressions separated by a comma is evaluated from left to right and the type and value of the result are the type and value of the right operand. Consider the following two statements.

```
n = 15 ;
m = (n = n + 5, 100/n);
After execution, m will have a value 5.
```

2.4.12 Dot (.) and Arrow (- >) Operators

These are operators that are used in structures and unions and are described in section 2.11 and 2.13.

2.4.13 Parentheses and Square Brackets

Parentheses are operators and they increase the precedence of operators inside them. Square brackets are used for array indexing and will be discussed in section 2.8.

2.4.14 Cast Operator

The construct called case is used to force an expression to a specific data type. The general form is,

```
(type) expression
```

and the expression is converted to the named data type. For example, consider the statement shown below.

```
sqrt ((double)x)
```

Here the cast operator (double) converts x into double-precision float before passing it as argument to *sqrt* function. The cast is unary operator and has same precedence as any other unary operator.

2.5 INPUT AND OUTPUT

Unlike FORTRAN, READ and WRITE statements are not defined as part of the language in C. All the I/O operations are carried out through functions. Before explaining a few of the important I/O functions in this section, it may be necessary to point out that a special program statement given below may be required to include standard I/O function library.

```
#include < stdio.h >
```

Please refer your c compiler for more details

2.5.1 Character I/O

A simple function getchar( ) reads a character from the standard input (usually the key board). Repeated calls to the getchar( ) function will return successively single characters from the keyboard. The putchar( ) will write the character argument to the screen. Thus, a statement

```
putchar(c);
```

will display the character contained in c at the terminal, where c is the char type variable.

2.5.2 Formatted Output printf( )

The function printf( ) has been referred to in section 2.1 and this is used to get formatted output. The general form of printf( ) is given below:

```
printf("control string", aargument list);
```

The control string consists of two types of items. The first type is made of characters that will appear on the screen. The second type (called conversion specifications) contains format commands that define the way the arguments are displayed. A conversion specification (format) begins with a percent sign (%) and is followed by a conversion character. The conversion characters are listed in Table 2.3.

Table 2.3 Conversion Characters for printf( )

Character	Action
c	The value expected is a single character, the corresponding argument should be a character pointer
d	The value expected is a decimal integer, the corresponding argument should be an integer pointer
e	The value expected is a floating point number expressed in exponential form, the corresponding argument should be a pointer to float
f	This is similar to e, a floating number is expected
o	The value to be read is an octal integer, the corresponding argument should be an integer pointer
s	The value expected is a sequence of characters; the sequence begins with the first non-white space character and is terminated by the first white-space character; the argument is a pointer to a character array.
	[see section 2.8 for description on character array]
note:	Some compilers require double to the specified as if.
	Please check the concerned compiler manual.

There are few optional specifiers that can be used in the conversion specifications and they are given below.

```
   - (minus sign)  for left-justified print out,
                   otherwise by default all output
                   is right-justified
   dd              digits specifying field width.
   . (period)      separates field width from precisic
   dd              digits specifying precision.
   L ('ell')       for long integer arguments.
```

The following example illustrates the various formats and use of conversion characters and optional specifiers.

Example 2.2

/* Example for printf statements */

```
main()
{
int grade;
float a;
double b;
char c;
a=123.456;
b=0.577350269186;
c='M';
grade=15;
printf("Grade of concrete is %c %2d\n", c, grade);
printf("Value of a= %10.2f \n",a);
printf("Value of a in 'e' specification =%12.4e\n",a);
printf("Value of b in double precision= %14.12 f\n",b);
}
Output:
Grade of concrete is M 15
Value of a= 123.46
Value of a in 'e' specification = 1.2346 e+02
Value of b in double precision = 0.577350269186
```

It may be worthwhile to explain some of the important points to be noted in the output. Consider the first line. The characters within the quotes will be printed as it is in the printf statement along with the white (blank) space until the conversion specifier % is encountered.

Thus the string, Grade of concrete is is printed and then it matches %c, with c, the value of character variable c, in this case M is printed. Then it matches %2d with the integer variable grade and prints its value 15. Note the white space between M and 15 which is the same as specified in the printf statement. Then, \ n takes the cursor to the beginning of the next line.

For the second line of the output, Value of a = is printed including the white spaces given in printf statement and then the conversion specifier %10.2f is matched with the float variable a. The total field length for printing the value of a is 10 and the number of digits beyond the decimal point is 2. Thus, when the value is printed, it is right justified and four white (blank) spaces may be noted after = sign.

In the case of line three, two white space are left beyond the = sign. For the last line, the specification %14.12f for the double precision variable exactly fills the value.

2.5.3 **Formatted Input** `scanf( )`

The function scanf( ) allows user to enter data from the standard input and provides the conversion facilities similar to scanf( ) in the opposite direction. The general form of scanf( ) is given below:

```
scanf("control string", argumentlist);
```

The control string contains conversion specification and tells, *scanf( )* what kind of input to expect. The *scanf( )* expects every character is control string to match a character from the standard input. When the control string contains whitespace (ie., a blank or tab or new line), scanf( ) takes that white space as a signal to read input to read an integer or a floating point number or a string until it gets a non-white space character. The conversion specification begins with a percent sign (%) and is followed by a conversion character that indicates the interpretation of the input field. The corresponding argument must be a pointer to indicate where the converted input should be stored. Table 2.4 gives the various conversion factors and they are similar to table 2.3 except that in this case the action is reversed.

Table 2.4 Conversion Characters for scanf( )

Character	Action
c	The argument is taken to be a character
d	The argument is converted to a decimal integer
e	The argument is taken to be a float or double and is expressed in exponential form; One digit is always displayed before the decimal point. The number of decimal point defaults to six unless specified by precision
f	The argument is taken to be a float or double* and converted to decimal notation form
g	use e or f, whichever is shorter
o	The argument is converted to unsigned octal notation, without a leading zero.
s	The argument is a string, the string is terminated by a null character, or the number of characters indicated by the precision is exhausted.
u	The argument is converted to unsigned decimal number
x	The argument is converted to unsigned hexa-decimal notation
note:	Some compilers require double to be specified as lf. Please check the concerned compiler manual.

There are other specifiers used and one of them is the field width specifier. The other is the assignment suppression character * which tells *scanf( )* to ignore a field specification.

The following examples illustrate the use of *scanf( )* with different specifications.

Example 2.3

```
#include<stdio.h>
/* example for scanf statement */
main()
{
char con_grade, steel_type;
int fc; float fy;
scanf("%c %d %c %f",&con_grade,&fc,&steel_type, &fy);
printf("\n %c %d %c %f", con_grade,fc,steel_type,fy);
}
```

Input:
```
M 15 H 415.0
```
Output:
```
M15 H 415.00000
```

The control string of scanf() "%c %d %c %f" with a blank in between tells the function to look for the first character in the input stream i.e. terminal in this case and put its value into con_grade which may be any character such as a number, a blank, non-new line (i.e non white space) character in the input stream, and at that point look for integer value to assign it to the integer variable fc; next read a character following the integer value and if it is not a white space then assign it to the value of steel_type, if it is a white space then move on to the next character, and assign it to steel_type. Irrespective of whether it is a blank or newline or tab. This skipping of one character is due to the fact that there is one blank space between the second and the third conversion specifiers. If there is no such blank space, the character immediately following the integer value will be assigned to the variable steel_type. Then it moves on to the next non-white space and look for floating point input for the variable fy.

The conversion specifier %c in the scanf() is different from the other conversion specifiers %d and %f due to the fact that it takes any character from the keyboard as its value. So one has to be careful while entering the input for any character variable with the %c specification. To avoid such a situation, it is always better to use %1s specification(used for reading a string) for reading a character variable.

The scanf() sees all the input as a stream of characters that includes the final new line. Suppose the input for the abive problem is keyed as follows:

Input:
```
M
15 H
415.0
```

Then the scanf() sees the above input as
M\n15 H\n 415.0\n and assigns them appropriately to the variables.

The output is the same as before, i.e.,

```
Output:
        M  15     H        415.000000
```

2.6 CONTROL STRUCTURES

The control structures in C, like any other language, enable us to specify the order in which the computations are to be carried out. They rely upon a conditional test that determines the course of action.

It has been pointed out in Section 3.1, that in C a statement may consist of a single statement or a block of statements grouped within the braces ({ }) called compound statement or block.

2.6.1   if Statement

The general form of if statement is

```
        if(expression)
            Statement;
        else statement;
```

Where the else is optional. The expression is evaluated and if it is true the statement following if is executed ; if the expression is false and if there is an else part, the statement following it will be executed.

The general form of if with blocks of statements is as follows.

```
        if (expression)
        {
            statements
        }
        else
        {
            statement
        }
```

The following is an example for if statement.

Example 2.4

```
/*  Using 'if' stataement to check the minimum area of reft in a column and to find the no. of
bars required */

                main()
                {
                float area_reft, dia,breadth, depth;
                int no_bars;
                scanf("%f%f%f%f", &area_reft,&dia,&bredth,&depth);
                if(area_reft<0.008*breadth*depth)
                printf("Area of reft less than minimum reqd    \n");
                else
                {
                no_bars= area_reft/(3.1415*dia*dia/4)+1;
                printf("Area of reft = %f \n \n Number of bars dia %f required = %d \n",
                   \n area_reft, dia, no_bars);
                }
```

Input:

```
                1200        20      300      400
```

Output:

```
                Area of reft = 1200.000000
                Number of bars of dia 20.000000 required = 4
```

2.6.1.1 Nested if statement

If an if statement forms part of either if or else, it is referred to as nested if statement.
Consider,

```
                If(a>b)
                        If(c>d) printf("case 1");
                        else printf("case2");
```

In this example, the else is associated with if (c > d). Always in C, an else is linked to the
closest if that does not have an else statement associated with it. To make this else associate
with the first the above program segment can be written as,

```
                if(a>b)
                {
                        If(c>d) printf("case 1");
                }
                        else printf("case2");
```

2.6.1.2 If-else-if statement

The general form of if-else-if construct is as follows.

```
if (expression)
        statements;
else if (expression)
        Statement;
        . . . . . . . .
        . . . . . . . .
else
        statement;
```

The above program statement is evaluated from top and as soon as condition becomes true, the statement associated with it is executed and the rest of the chain is by passed. If none of the conditions is true, then the final else is executed. If the final else is not present and if all the conditions are false, no action is done.

Example 2.5

```
/* An example for nested – if statements. This program prints the integer category number
corresponding to the weight measurement as follows:
        Category            Weight
        1  <= 25 Kg
        2  25< weight <= 60
        3  60< weight <= 100
        4  200<weight                           */

main()
{
flaot weight;
int category;

scanf("%f",&weight);

if (weight <= 25)
category = 1;
else if (weight <= 60)
   category=2;
     else if(weight <= 100)
            category=3;
else category=4;
printf("catgory= %d \n", category);
}
```

```
Input:
            35
Output:
         Category=2
```

2.6.2 Switch Statement

C language provides a special multi-way decision maker that tests whether the expression matches one of a number of constant values and branches accordingly. The general form of switch statement is,

```
            switch(expression)
            {
            case constant1:
                        statements
                        break;
            case constant2:
                        statements
                        break;
            case constant3:
                        statements
                        break;

                        ........

                               .........

            default:
                        statements
            }
```

The switch evaluates the integer expression in parentheses and compares it s value one by one against constant values or labels that follow the case statements. When a match is found the program executes the statement(s) following that case and all subsequent case(s) and default statements as well until a break statement is encountered. If no match is found, only the statement following the default will be executed.

If no default statement is there and no match is found, no action takes place. However, it may be noted that the break statement causes an immediate exit from the switch.

Example 2.6

/* An example to illustrate the use of switch statements. The following program returns span to depth ratio depending on the code value.

Code	Type of Beam	Span/Depth ratio
1	Cantilever	7
2	simply supported	20

```
                    3                              Continuous 26       */
        main()
        {
            int ratio,code;
            scanf("%d", &code);
            switch(code)
            {
                case 1:
                        ratio=7;
                        break;
                case 2:
                        ratio=20;
                        break;
                case 3:
                        ratio=26;
                        break;
                default :
                        printf(" Incorrect data           ");
                        exit(0); /* return to OS */
                        }
                Printf(" Span to Depth ratio for code %d is %d, \n code,
                        ratio);
        }

Input:
        2
Output:
        Span to Depth ratio for code 2 is 20
```

In the above example a function *exit( )* is used to terminate the program. The *exit( )* is found in the standard library and it causes the immediate termination of the program. The function is usually called with an argument o to indicate the termination is normal; other arguments are used to indicate some sort of error [8].

2.6.3 Loops – while and for

The general form of while loop is,

```
        while (condition)
            statement;
```

while will continue to execute the statement as long as the condition remains true. When the condition becomes false, the control passes on to the first statement that follows the while loop. It may be noted that the statement to be executed may be one statement or a block of statements enclosed within the braces.

Example 2.7

/* An example for while loop with pre increment ++i   */

```
        main()
        {
        int i=0;
        while(I<6)
        printf("%d \n", ++i);
        /* value of I is incremented before printing */
        printf("We are out of the loop. \n");
        }
```

Ouptut:

```
        1
        2
        3
        4
        5
        6
            we are out of loop.
```

Example 2.8

/* The above example with post increment i++ */

```
        main()
        {
        int i=0;
        while(i<6)
        printf("%d \n",i++);
        /* value of i is incremented after printing */
        printf(("We are out of the loop. \n");
        }
```

Ouptut:

```
        1
        2
        3
```

```
        4
        5
            we are out of loop.
```

The for statement in C provides flexibility and power in looping and its general form is,

```
        for( initialisation ; condition ; increment)
        {
            statements
        }
```

The initialisation is usually an assignment that is used to set the control variable. The condition is a relational expression that determines when the loop has to exit. The increment defines how the loop control variable is to be changed each time the loop is repeated. In general, it is an expression that is evaluated each time after the body of the loop is executed. In summary, the execution of for statement is as follows:

1. First initialisation of the loop variable is carried out, either through an expression or statement. Usually the variable, referred to as an index variable, is set to 0 or 1.
2. The looping condition is evaluated. If the condition is not satisfied (the expression is FALSE) then the loop is immediately terminated. Otherwise the execution is continued with the program statement that immediately follows the loop.
3. The program statement(s) that constitutes the body of the loop is executed.
4. The increment is usually an expression which is generally used to change the value of the index variable. Usually the variable is incremented or decremented by certain value.
5. Return to step 2.

Example 2.9

```
/*An example to illustrate the 'for' loop */
        main()
        {
                int n, n_square;
                for(n=1;n<=10;n++)
                {
                        n_square = n*n;
                        printf(" %2d        %4d \n", n, n_square);
                }
                printf(" Out of for loop. \n");

        }

Output:
        1        1
        1        4
```

```
2        9
3        16
4        25
5        36
6        49
7        64
8        81
9        100
Out of for loop.
```

In the above program, n is initially set to 1. Since n is less than 10, the two statements in the body of the for loop are executed. Then n is incremented by 1 and the looping process is continued until n is less than or equal to 10.

Example 2.10

```
/* This program finds the largest integer of a set of positive numbers. */

main()
{
int number, largest, no_in_set, I;

largest=0;
scanf("%d", &no_in_set);

for(I=0; I<no_in_set;++i)
{
scanf("%d", &number);
if(number > largest)
largest=number;
}
printf("Largest integer of given set of %d numbers \n =%d \n",
   no_in_set, largest);
}
```

```
Input:
5
123        - 464     876      9843     - 595
Output:
Largest integer of given set of 5 numbers = 9843
```

Example 2.11

```
/*   Example for nested for-loops :
This program evaluates x² + y² for various values of y (-1,0,1) for each value of x (0,2,4) i.e.
at all points of grid in x-y plane */
```

This program evaluates $x^2 + y^2$ for various values of y (-1,0,1) for each value of x (0,2,4) i.e. at all points of grid in x-y plane

```c
        main()
        {
        float x,y,z;

        for(x=0;x<5;x+=2)
            {
                    printf("\n");
                    for(y=-1;y<2;y+=1)
                        {
                                z=x*x+y*y;
                                printf(" x= %6.2f y= %6.2f z=%6.2f \n", x,y,z);

                        }

            }
        }
```

```
Output:

X = 0.00y = -1.00 z = 1.00
X = 0.00y = 0.00 z = 0.00
X = 0.00y = 1.00 z = 1.00

X = 2.00y = -1.00 z = 5.00
X = 2.00y = 0.00 z = 4.00
X = 2.00y = 1.00 z = 5.00

X = 4.00y = -1.00 z = 17.00
X = 4.00y = 0.00 z = 16.00
X = 4.00y = 1.00 z = 17.00
```

It should be noted that in a for loop the conditional test is always performed at the top of the loop. This means that the code inside the loop may not be executed at all if the condition is false to begin with as shown in the following program segment.

```c
        x=20;
        for ( y=20; y!= x; ++y)
                printf ("%d", y);
                printf ("%d", y);
```

This loop will never be executed because x and y are equal when the loop is entered. Hence, the value of y will be 20 and the output will be 20 printed only once on the screen.

When the break statement is encountered inside a loop, the loop is immediately terminated.

There are a few additional points that may be mentioned about for loop. We can include multiple expressions separated by a comma operator. For example, in

```
for(i=0,j=1;i<10;++i)
```

The values of i and j are set to zero and one respectively before the loop begins. As another example, in

```
for(i=0,j=50;i<20;++i, j=j-5)
```

The values of j and j are initialised to 0 and 50 respectively. Each time after the body of the loop is executed, the value of j is incremented by 1 and the value of j is decremented by 5. In a for loop it is admissible to omit desired field by placing a semicolon. For example, in

```
for(i=0,i!=20;++i)
```

The initial value of I is omitted and is supposed to have been defined before the loop is entered.

2.6.4 do-while

The third loop construct in C, the do-while checks the condition at the bottom of the loop; the loop, therefore, is executed at least once. The statement is executed and the condition is evaluated. If it is true, the statement is evaluated again and so on. If the condition is false, the loop terminates. The general form of do-while loop is,

```
do
{
        statement;
} while (condition);
```

Example 2.12
```
/* An example to show the difference between while loop and do-while loop */
        main()
        {
        int x,y,z;
        x=20;
        y=10;
        while(++x<y)
```

```
        {
                z=x*x;
                printf((“I am in the while loop z= %d \n”, z);
        }
        do
        {
        z=x*x;
        printf(“I am in the do=-while loop z= %d \n”,z);
        }while(++x<y);
        }
Output:

        I am in the do-while loop z=441
```

The condition x < y is never true, so while passes control to do-while without executing the statements. But do-while does not test it until it executes the two statements.

2.6.5 Continue Statement

The continue statement makes the next iteration of the loop (for, while, do) i.e it helps to jump immediately to the top of the loop again. At the point that the continue statement is executed, any statements in the loop that appear after the continue statement are automatically skipped. Execution of the loop otherwise continues as normal. The general form is,

```
        continue;
```

Example 2.13
/* Example to illustrate the continue statement */

```
        main()
        {
        int I=0;
        while(++I<=9)
        {
        if(I==5)
        continue;
        printf(“%d \n”,I);
        }
        }
```

```
Output
        1
        2
        3
        4
        5
        6
        7
        8
        9
```

2.6.5 goto statement

One of the criticisms against FORTRAN programmers is the tendency to use goto statement which makes the programs unreadable or unstructured. C provides a rich set of control structures, described in this section, and hence the need to use goto statement for branching may not be necessary. However, there may be a few situations where goto may find a place. The general form of goto statement is,

```
goto label;
```

The goto statement thus requires a label for operation. A label is a valid C identifier chosen according to the rules for creating variable names and this must be followed by a colon. The label must be in the same function as the goto that uses it as shown below.

```
for(.......)
{
    for(......)
    {
            while(.......)
            {
                if(..........) goto error;
                    ..........
                    ..........
                ..........
            }
    }
}
error:
    printf("\n Error encountered in program.");
```

In this example the use of goto enables one to exit from the inner most loop without additional tests.

2.7 FUNCTIONS AND STORAGE CLASS

Similar to subprograms viz., function subprograms and subroutine subprograms used in FORTRAN, functions occupy an important place in C programming. Functions help to break a large computing task into smaller ones. C programs usually contain a number of small functions. Thus, functions provide the building block of C. The general form of a function is,

```
type_specifier function_name(argument list)
argument declarations
{
        variable declarations;
        C statements;
}
```

The type specifier specifies the type of value the return statement of the function returns. If no type is specified, the function returns an integer value. A function may be without an argument list and in that case, however, parentheses are still required. The general form of return statement is,

```
return(expression);
```

And the value of the expression is returned to the calling function.

Example 2.14
/* The program given below illustrates the use of a function that cubes a given number and is called by the main */

```
main()
{
int I=2;
while(I<512)
        printf("%d \n", I=cube(I));
}
/*function to cube an integer*/
cube(x)
int x;
{
return(x*x*x);
}
Output:
        8
        512
```

It may be noted that the calling function in this case *main( )* does not require the type declaration of the function if it returns an int or char. However, if we rewrite the function to cube a float or double variable, it is necessary to declare its type as given below.

Example 2.15

```
main()
{
float I=2.1;
double xcube(); /* note function type declared */
while( I< 800.0) printf("%f \n", I= xcube(i));
}
/* Function to cube a float or double */
double xcube(x)
double x;
{
return(x*x*x);
}
Output:
9.260999
794.279719
501095414.870886
```

However, if the called function (i.e double_xcube(x)) is given above the definition of the calling function (i.e main( )) in the same source code file, the type declaration in the calling function can be omitted. This may lead to some confusion. This can be avoided by declaring all the non_int functions in all the functions that call them.

2.7.1 Arguments

Every function is a black box to every other function. The communication between functions is established through arguments, the returned values or the side effects. The side effects refer to changes it produces to variables outside the function, possibly external variables which will be discussed in section 2.7.2.

The function values are passed by value, that is, the called function receives a temporary copy of each argument, not its address. Thus the function does not affect the original argument in the calling function. Within a function each argument is in effect a local variable initialised to the value with which the function was called.

The type of the actual argument in the calling function should normally match the type of argument in the called function.

In the case of arrays, the location (address) of the beginning of the array is passed, elements are not copied. The function can alter elements of the array by subscripting from this location. Thus arrays are passed by reference and not by value.

2.7.2 Storage Class

There are four storage class specifiers in C and they are: automatic, register, static and external. These tell the computer how the variable should be stored. The general form is,

```
storage_specifier type variable - name;
```

2.7.3 Automatic variables

The C compiler assumes that any variable defined inside a function is an automatic local variable and the storage_specifier auto is seldom used. An auto variable is created each time the function is called and disappears when the function is exited.

2.7.4 Register variables

Register variables in C are normally used when execution speed is important. The idea behind the register storage class is to tell the compiler to reserve one of the CPU registers for a variable. The data manipulation is faster in memory and execution speed is enhanced. The register storage class is used for variables that will be used heavily.

There are some restrictions on register variables as they are hardware dependent. One has to check with the manual of a particular system regarding the number of register variables allowed on that system.

2.7.5 Static Variables

Static variable is a third class of storage and it may be internal or global. Internal static variables are similar to automatic variables in that they are local to the function in which they are defined, but unlike automatic variables they remain alive even after a function is completed. When the specifier static is applied to a local variable, it causes the compiler to create permanent storage for it and hence, it retains the value between the function calls. The following example illustrates the difference between automatic and static variables.

Example 2.16
/* program to illustrate auto and static variable */

```
        auto_static()
        {
        int a=0; static int s=0;
        printf("automatic 'a' = %d, static 's' = %d\n", a ,s);
        ++a;
        ++s;
        }
        main()
```

```
        {
        int I;
        for(i=0;I<4;++i)
        auto_static();
        }
Output;
        Automatic 'a'=0, static 's'=0
        Automatic 'a'=0, static 's'=1
        Automatic 'a'=0, static 's'=2
        Automatic 'a'=0, static 's'=3
```

It may be noted from the above example that the initial value of static variable is done at the compilation time whereas the initialisation of automatic variable is done at the run time. The compiler assigns a space in memory for the static variable and stores its value there.

Static variables may also be external to the function ie. Global if it is used to define variables outside the function. This type of usage is discussed below in connection with global and external variables.

2.7.6 Global and External Variables

Similar to COMMON in FORTRAN, it is possible to define variables which are common to all functions, that is global variables which can be accessed by name by any function. Because these variables are globally available, they can be used instead of argument lists to communicate data between functions. The global variables are declared outside of any functions.

Example 2.17
```
/* program to illustrate external and global variable */

        int x=360;
        float y= 426.52;
        main()
        {
        printf("x= %d, y=%f \n", x,y);
        }
Outptut:
        X=306, y= 426.519989
```

As can be observed from the above example that values of x and y are available to the main(). Consider another example.

52

Example 2.18

```c
/* 2nd example to illustrate use of global variables */

flaot span,load; /* global variables*/
main()
{
float bm,deflection;   /*local varaiables*/
float mfunc();
float defunc();
priintf("Beam span = ");
scanf("%f", &span);
printf("udl on beam = ");
scanf("%f",&load);
bm=mfunc();
printf("The bending moment =%f \n" , bm);
deflection = defunc();
printf("The deflection = %f \n ", deflection);
}
float mfunc()
{
float moment; /* lovcal variable*/
moment= load * span* span* / 2.0;
return(moment);
}
float E,b,d;    /* global variables with scope to functions that follow */

void beam_prop()
{
printf("\n The breadth of the beam=");
scanf("%f", &b);
printf(" The depth of the beam=");
scanf("%f",&d);
printf("\n young's modulus E= ");
scanf("%f",&E);
return;
}
float defunc()
{
void beam_prop();
float m_intertia;       /* local variable*/
```

```
    float deflection;        /*local variable different from the same named
            variable in main()*/
    beam_prop();
    m_inertia = b * d * d * d / 12.0;
    deflection= (load*span*span*span) / (8.0* E * m_intertia);
    return(deflection);
    }
Input:
    7.0
    3000.0
    0.25
    0.45
    2.0e10
Output:
    Beam span=7.0
    udl on beam=3000.0
    The bending moment = 73500.000000

    The breadth of beam = 0.25
    The depth of beam = 0.45

    Young's modulus E= 2.0 e10
    The deflection = 0.003388
```

In the above example 2.18 span and load are global variables. The variables E, b and d declared above the function beam_prop( ) along with the global variables. Now it is necessary to know the scope rules of the C language.

The scope of a variable means the range within a program over which that variable has meaning or it is known. A variable can have a local scope or a global scope. Variables like m_inertia and deflection defined in function defunc( ) are local variables and are known within this function only, i.e. their scope is local and they are not known outside this function. This also implies that the same variable name can be declared and used in more than one function. For example, the local variable deflection in main( ) is different from the variable deflection declared in function defunct( ).

The scope of a global variable extends from the position at which they are declared. Thus the global variable is known or can be used by all functions in a program that are physically placed after the global variable declaration. Thus in the above example, the scope of the global variables span and load extend to main( ) and functions m_funct( ), beam_prop( ) and defunc( ). But the scope of the global variables E, b and d extend only to functions beam_prop( ) and defunc( ).

It may be observed that a data type called void precedes the function beam_prop( ). This signals the computer to the fact that the function will not return any value to the calling function. The use of this data type is recommended for functions that do not return a value to the calling function.

Global variables that are declared outside any function exists until the execution of the program in which they are declared is finished. Hence, these variables can not be declared as auto or register variables. However, the global variables can be declared as belonging to storage class of types static or extern. This is explained below.

Consider a program that is created and stored in two files, FILE1 and FILE2 as shown in example 2.19.

The three functions main( ), anal1( ) and anal2( ) are stored in one file and the two other functions beam( ) and column( ) are stored in another file. The global variables fy, fc, length and load declared in FILE1 can only be used by the functions main( ), aral1( ) and aral2( ) in this file. Similarly, the global variable Ec can be used by functions beam( ) and column( ) in FILE2. In addition, placing the declaration extern float Ec; the scope of the global variable Ec, created in FILE2 is extended to aral1( ) and aral2( ). Notice that Ec is not variable to main( ) in FILE1.

Similarly, placing the statement extern float length; in column( ) extends to scope of the global variable length created in file1 into the function column( ).

A declaration by extern to a global variable does not cause the creation of a new variable by reserving a new storage and it simply informs the system that the variable already exists and can now be used. The actual storage for the variable will be created somewhere else in the program where the variable has been declared as a global variable without using the class specifier extern. Initialisation of the global variable can be made with the original global declaration statement. Initialisation with extern declaration statement is not allowed and will cause a compliation error. Thus the declaration statement, with storage_specifier extern does not create a new storage area; it only extends the scope of the existing global variables.

Example 2.19

```
FILE1                               FILE2

float fy,fc;                        float Ec
float length;                       extern float fy,fc;
static double load;                 beam();
        main()                      {
        {
        anal1();
        anal2();
        beam();
        column();
        }                                   }
```

```
        extern float Ec;                column();
        anal1();                        {
        {
        ....... .
        ....... .
        }
        anal2();
        {
        ....... .
        ....... .
        }                                                       }
```

The other storage class static is used to present the extension of a global variable into another file. Thus in the above example the scope of the variable load can not be extended to file 2 since has been declared as static global class. Static global variable is known and can only be used in the file in which it is declared.

2.8 ARRAYS

An array is a collection of variables of the same type referred by a common name. We can have array of ints, of floats and doubles, and chars. A specific element in an array is accessed by an index. In C all arrays consist of contiguous memory locations. Arrays may have from one to several dimensions.

2.8.1 One Dimensional Arrays

The general form of declaration is,

```
type - specifier varaiable-name [size];
```

In C all arrays have zero as the index of their first element.

Example 2.20
/*This program computes the total load on a beam subjected to five concentrated loads whose values are stored in an array   */

```
        main()
        {
        float load[5], total_load;
        int I = 0;
        load[0]=5;
        load[1]=12.5;
```

```
load[2]=13.5;
load[3]=25;
load[4]=30;

total_load =0;
while(I<5)
{
total_load=total_load+ load[I];
++I;
}
printf("Total load on the beam = %f \n", total_load);
}
```
Output:

```
        Total load on the beam= 86.00000000
```
Initialization of Arrays

In C language, only static or extern (global) arrays can be initialized with a list of values. So if we wish to initialise an array of elements, the array must be declared static. Using the initialization concept, the above example can be rewritten as,

Example 2.21
```
/* Intialising an array */
main()
{
static float load[5] = {5,12.5,13.5,25,30};
float total_load = 0; int I=0;
while(I<5)
{
total_load=total_load+load[I];
I++;
}
printf("Total load on the beam= %f \n", total_load);
}
```
Output:
```
Total load on the beam= 86.000000
```

The compiler goes from left to right, assigning each value inside the braces to a particular memory location, depending on its position in the array. Thus, load [0] is initially assigned the value of 5.0, load [1] the value of 12.5 and so on.

2.8.2　Two-Dimensional Arrays

C allows use of two-or multi-dimensional arrays. For example, a two-dimensional array is defined as, float nodal-load[3][6] ;. This refers to a two-dimensional array with three rows and six columns. In C, the first row of the matrix is designated by row 0 and the first column by column 0. As an example, a typical set of values for this array and, the row and column designations are shown below.

Row Number (i)	Column Number (j)					
	0	1	2	3	4	5
0	15.5	-16.2	-8.6	0.0	86.0	10.5
1	20.6	10.5	0.0	5.5	25.0	14.0
2	40.5	80.5	12.5	20.5	0.0	8.0

Any element in the array is denoted by,

```
nodal_load[i][j]
```

The first index refers to the row number and the second index to the column number. Thus, the expression

```
sum = nodal_load[0][4] + nodal[2][5];
```

Would make the program to add the value contained in row 0, column 4 which is 86.0 to the value contained in row 2, column 5 which is 8.0 and the sum would be assigned a value of 94.0

Two-dimensional arrays may be initialized similar to one-dimensional arrays. However, it should be noted that the values are to be listed by rows. The array nodal_load[3][6] can be initialized using the following statements.

```
static nodal_load[3][6] = {
                          {15.5, -16.2, -8.6, 0.0, 86.0, 10.5},
                          {20.6, 10.5, 0.0, 5.5, 25.0, 15.0},
                          {40.5, 80.5, 12.5, 20.5, 0.0, 8.0}
                  } ;
```

Notice the syntax of the above statement. Commas are required after each set of braces that mark the end of a row, except in the case of last row. Braces are optional, but they improve clarity. If braces are not supplied, then initialization is done by row. Thus, the above statement could be written as,

```
static float nodal_load[3] [6] = {
                              {15.5, -16.2, -8.6, 0.0, 86.0, 10.5},
                              {20.6, 10.5, 0.0, 5.5, 25.0, 15.0},
                              {40.5, 80.5, 12.5, 20.5, 0.0, 8.0}
                   }   ;
```

It is not necessary to initialize the entire array. A statement such as,

```
static float nodal_load[3] [6] = {
              {15.5, -16.2, -8.6 },
              {20.6, 10.5, 0.0 },
              {40.5, 80.5, 12.5 }
        }   ;
```

would initialize the first three elements in each row of the matrix to the values indicated within each pair of parentheses. The remaining values will be set to zero. In this case, the inner parentheses are required to ensure correct initialisation.

It must be added here that C stores the values by row-wise unlike FORTRAN which stores values column-wise.

Example 2.22

```
#include<stdio.h>
#include<math.h>
/* Function 'mam' for multiplication of two matrices */
mam(a,b,c,m,n,p)
float a[10][10], b[10][10], c[10][10];
int m,n,p;
{
int I,j,k;
for(I=0;I<m;++I)
    for(j=0;j<p;++j)
       {
           c[I][j]=0;
           for(k=0;k<n;++k)
              c[I][j]=c[I][j]+a[I][k]*b[k][j];
   }
   }
/* main() calling the matrix multiplication function*/
   main()
```

```c
{
float mat_A[10][10], mat_B[10][10], mat_C[10][10];
/*note that the maximum
value m,n p can take is 10 */
int m,n,p,i,j;
printf("Enter the value of m,n and p \n (order of the matrices) :");
scanf("%d%d%d",&m, &n, &p);
printf("\n enter thr matrix a row wise :\n");

for(I=0;I<n;++I)
     for(j=0;j<p;++j)
          scanf("%f", &mat_A[I][j]);

printf("\n Enter the matrix B row wise : \n");

for(I=0;I<m;++I)
     for(j=0;j<n;j++)
scanf("%f", &mat_B[I][j]);
mam(mat_A,mat_B,mat_C,m,n,p); /* calling 'mam' fn*/
printf("\n\n The resultant matrix       : \n");

for(I=0;I<m;++I)
{
printf("\n");
for(j=0;j<p;j++)
printf("%f ", mat_C[I][j]);
}
}
```

Input and output:

    Enter the values of m,n and p
    (order of the matrices);
    2   2   2
    Enter the matrix A row wise :
    3   4
    4   7

    Enter the matrix B row wise :
    5   6
    6   8
    The resultant matrix :
    43.000000   50.000000
    74.000000   86.000000

2.9 POINTERS

One of the most useful features of C language is pointers. Pointers enable us to efficiently represent complex data structures, to change the values passed as arguments to functions, to dynamically allocate memory and, to deal with arrays more concisely and efficiently. A brief introduction to pointers has been given in section 2.3.9. The operations associated with pointers are described in this section.

A pointer is a variable that contains the memory address of another variable in memory. If one variable contains the address of another variable, then the first variable is said to point to the second. The general form of declaring a pointer variable is,

```
type * name;
```

This will create a pointer variable as named pointing to a data object of type the pointer can point, i.e. it declares a pointer to a particular data type. It is the asterisk perfacing the variable name that indicates that the variable is a pointer. As a matter of style pointer variable name may be so chosen like following it with an underscore and ptr (e.g. char *c_ptr; int *node_ptr;).

The declaration of the pointer variable tells the compiler to do three things.
1. *Create an address for the pointer*
2. Create a scalar for the pointer equal to the number of bytes associated with the data type being pointed to, and
3. Mark the variable as a pointer.

For example, the declaration statement int *node_ptr; tells the compiler that it is pointer variable, its name is node_ptr and it needs a memory address to reside and create it with a scalar that is associated with a data type int variable. The third item makes it distinctly different from other declarations.

2.9.1 Pointer Operators

There are two special pointer operators & and *. The & is a unary operator that returns the memory address of the operand. The other operator * is also unary operator that returns the value of the variable located at the address that follows.

In example 2.23, the node_ptr is declared as a pointer variable and it has been initialised with a value of the memory address of the variable number. In the printf statement for *node_ptr, the compiler takes the value stores in node_ptr (which is the memory address of the variable number, assumed as 4.54) and using the scalar bytes of the data type (in this case int) prints the value (25) stored in that memory address (4054). It may be noted that in this case the value of the variable number is obtained through indirect addressing (or indirection).

Example 2.23

```
/* Program to illustrate pointers and operators */

    main()
    {
    int number;
    int *node_ptr;
    number=25;
    node_ptr = &number;
    printf("The value %d is stored at address %u \n", number, &number);
    printf("The value %d is stored at address %u \n", node_ptr, &node_ptr);
    printf("The value %d is stored at address %u \n", *node_ptr, node_ptr);
    }
Output:
    The value 25 is stored at address 4054
    The value 4054 is stored at address 4338
    The value 25 is stored at address 4054
```

2.9.2 Pointer Arithmetic

There are only four arithmetic operators that may be used with pointers; +,-,++,—. Consider a pointer called node_ptr and that it points to an integer data type that is 2 bytes long. Assume that the variable node_ptr has been initialised with a value of 4054 which will be the memory address of the variable it points to. If the following expression is executed,

```
node_ptr + +;
```

node_ptr would contain a value of 4056 and not 4055. Each time a pointer is incremented it points to the memory location of the next element of its base data type. Similarly, each time it is decremented it points to the location of the previous element. That is, if the following expression is executed,

```
node_ptr - -;
```

node_ptr would contain a value of 4052. We can add or subtract integers to or from pointers.

Thus, node_ptr = node_ptr + 4 ; makes node_ptr point to the fourth element of node_ptr type beyond its current position. For this example of int data type it will point to the element at 4062 memory address.

It may be noted here again that the construction ptr + n means the nth object beyond the one ptr currently points to. The compiler scales n according to the size of the objects the ptr points to, which is determined by the declaration of ptr. The scale factors on a PC are 1 for char, 2 for int and short, 4 for long and float, and 8 for double.

Because of the above nature of operations, we should not add or subtract type float or type double to pointers. A pointer can also be used in the right-hand side of an assignment statement to assign value to another pointer as illustrated in the following example.

Example 2.24

```
main()
{
int element_num;
int *ptr1, *ptr2;
ptr1= &element_num;
ptr2=ptr1;
printf("The value of ptr1= %U and the value of ptr2= %u \n", ptr1,ptr2);
}
Output:
    The value of ptr1=4050 and the value of ptr2=4332.
```

2.9.3   Pointers and Arrays

There is a strong relationship between pointers and arrays. Any operation which can be achieved by array subscripting can also be done with pointers. The pointer approach will in general be faster. The declaration,

```
float load[100];
```

defines an array load of size 100, that is a block of 100 consecutive objects named load[0], load[1],..........., load[99]. The notation load[i] means the element of the array i position from the beginning. If load_ptr is a pointer declared as,

```
float * load_ptr ; then the assignment
load_ptr = &load[0] ;
```

sets the load_ptr to point to the zeroth element of load vector; that is, the load_ptr contains the address of load[0]. Since the name of an array is a synonym for location of the zeroth element, the above assignment can be written as,

```
load_ptr = load;
```

Now the assignment, x = *(load_ptr + 1); will copy the contents of load[1] into x.

Example 2.25

/* Function to sum the elements of an array */

```
int a_sum(a,n)
int a[];
int n;
{
int sum=0, *a_ptr;
int *aend_ptr= a+n;        / same as *int a_end;
            a_end=a+n; */
for(a_ptr=a; a_ptr< aend_ptr; ++a_ptr)
sum+= *a_ptr;
return(sum);
}
main()
{
static int x[10] = {2,3,-9,12,14,-1,-8,5,6,8};
printf("The sum of the array x is %d \n", a_sum(x,10));
}
```

Output:

```
The sum of the array x is 32
```

Pointers can be used in character arrays as illustrated in the following function which copies the string to the string s.

Example 2.26

/* Program for pointers to strings*/

```
stringcopy(s,t) /* function for copying a string*/
char s,t;
{
while((*s++=*t++) != '\0')
;
}
main()
{
char new_string[9];
char string[9] = "2D TRUSS";
stringcopy(new_string,string);
```

```
            printf("using pointers string %s \ has been copied to new_string.
            \n.\t \t new_string = %s \n", string,new_string);
            }
```
Output:
```
            Using pointers string 2D TRUSS has been copied to new_string.
            new_string = 2D TRUSS
```

2.9.4   Pointers to Functions

A very useful feature of pointers is the function pointers. To understand working of the function pointers, it is necessary to know how a function is compiled and called in C. When a function is compiled, the source code is transformed into object code and an entry point is established. When a call is made to the function in a program, a machine language reference is make to this entry point. Therefore, if a pointer contains the address of a function's entry point, it can be used to call that function.

The address of a function is obtained by using the function's name without any parentheses or arguments and this is shown in the following program.

Example 2.27
```
/* Getting the address of a function */
        main()
        {
        int tdof();
        printf(" Function tdof's address is %u \n", tdof);
        }
        tdof()
        {
        }
```
Output:
```
        Function tdof's address is 32
```

Since main() will be scanned first, we have to specify that tdof is a function and that it returns a value of type int. The above example can be modified to show how a pointer to a function can be used to invoke the function.

Example 2.28
```
/* function invocation through pointers */

        main()
        {
        int tdof();
        int n;
```

```
              int (*tdof_ptr) ();

              printf(" Function tdof's address is %u. \n",tdof);
              tdof_ptr=tdof;
              printf( " tdof_ptr value is also %u, \n", tdof_ptr);
              printf("input number of nodes(+ve integer):";
              scanf("%d", &n);
              tdof(n), (*tdof_ptr) (n);
              }
              tdof(a)
              int a;
              {
              printf(" Total degrees of freedom: %d. \n", 6*a);
              }
Output:
              Function tdof's address is 96.
              tdof_ptr value is also 96.
              input number of nodes (+ve integer) :5
              Total degrees of freedom:30.
              Total degrees of freedom:30.
```

It is necessary to use parentheses to indicate the pointer function as (*tdof_ptr). The assignment statement

```
              tdof_ptr = tdof;
```

assigns to the pointer the address of the function tdof(). In this example, the last two statements show different ways of invoking the same function.

In the above example, obviously nothing is gained. However, there are situations when several number of functions are kept and we do not know before hand which function is to be executed. In table driven programs, the flow of control depends on the input. At a given point in a program execution we need to call one of the several functions but there is no way of telling in advance which function it will be. But if we know how to invoke functions indirectly via pointers we can store the pointers to the functions in the table that drives the program.

2.9.5 The malloc **function**

There are many programming situations in engineering analysis and design in which it is not possible to know how large an array will be needed as the elements in the array are computed during problem solving process. In addition, there are many cases in which the programmer wants to run a program on machines with only minimal memory for a smaller sized problem. Thus it is desirable to be able to start a program with the smallest amount of memory necessary and then allocate extra memory as the need arises. This capability to dynamically allocate memory is provided in the C language through a library function malloc().

The parameter for the malloc() function is an integer that specifies the number of bytes needed. This function allocates memory and returns a char *pointer to the start of a contiguous memory of the size specified. It may be noted that the function returns a pointer of type char but it can be cast into any other type as appropriate.

When the array is no longer required, we can release the previously allocated memory by passing the pointer to the function called free().

```
char *a;
a = malloc(100);
free(a) ;
```

This program segment allocates 100 bytes of memory and a points to the first of 100 bytes of memory. The following example illustrates the use of pointers and malloc().

Example 2.29

```
#include<stdio.h>
/* program for matrix multiplication showing the use of pointers and malloc
function */
float *mat_A, *mat_B, *mat_C;
int m,n,p;
main()
{
int I,j,k;
scanf("%d%d%d",&m,&n,&p);
mat_A=(float *) malloc(m*n*sizeof(float));
mat_B=(float *) malloc(n*p*sizeof(float);
mat_C=(float *) malloc(m*p*sizeof(float);

/* Reading matrix A */
printf("\n Enter the elements of matrix Row wise \n");
for(i=0;i<m*n);++i)
scanf("%f", (mat_A+i);

/* Reading matrix B */
printf("\n Enter the elements of matrix Row wise \n");
for(i=0;i<n*p);++i)
scanf("%f", (mat_B+i);

/*calling function matmult */
matmult();
```

```c
/*printing the matrix A */
printf('\n matrix A");
for(i=0;i<m;++i)
{
printf('\n");
for(j=0;j<n;++j)
printf("%10.2f", (mat_A+i*n+j));
}

/*printing the matrix B */
printf('\n matrix B");
for(i=0;i<n;++i)
{
printf('\n");
for(j=0;j<n;++j)
printf("%10.2f", (mat_B+i*p+j));
}

/*printing the resultant matrix C */
printf('\n the resultant matrix C");
for(i=0;i<m;++i)
{
printf('\n");
for(j=0;j<p;++j)
printf("%10.2f", (mat_C+i*p+j));
}
}
/* function for multiplication of two matrices */
matmult()
{
int i,j,k;
for(i=0;i<m;++i)
{
for(j=0;j<p;j++)
{
(mat_C+i*p+j)=0;
for(k=0;k<n;++k)
(mat_C+i*p+j)+= (mat_A+i*n+k) * * (mat_B+k*p+j);
}
}
```

```
        }
Input and Output
     2   2   2
Enter the elements of matrix Row wise
     2   12
     3   6
Enter the elements of matrix Row wise
     4   4
     12  3

matrix A
     2.00     12.00
     3.00      6.00
matrix B
     3.00      4.00
     12.00     3.00
The resultant matrix C
     150.00   44.00
     81.00    30.00
```

2.10 STRINGS

A string is an array of characters terminated by an unseen null character, represented by '\0'. A string variable can be declared and initialised using statements like,

```
char *greet_ptr = "Hello!";
char greet_arr[] = "Hello!";
```

The first statement declares a string pointer variable. This would result in the string constant "Hello!" being stored at some location in the memory and the variable greet_ptr getting the starting address of this location. On the other hand, the second statement which declares an array variable, would be treated equivalent to the statement,

```
char greet_arr[7] ={'H','e','l','l','o','!',\0};
```

and the variable greet_arr is treated exactly like any other C array. Note that an extra location has been used to hold the null character, hence if we are explicitly giving the array size, we should take care of this.

```
char greet_arr[7] = "Hello!";
```

Since a string is an array of characters, we can directly manipulate the individual elements of a string. For example, in the above declaration,

```
greet_arr[0] would contain 'H'
greet_arr[4] would contain 'o' and
greet_arr[6] would contain '!'
```

There is another difference between string pointers and string arrays. While string pointer variables can be reassigned to different strings using the direct assignment statements, the string array variables can point to only one location in the memory. That means, the only way to make a string array variable to point to a different string is to copy the new string to the location where the variable points (see example 2.26). The following examples illustrate this point.

Example 2.30

```
main()
{
char *beam_type[4]={"sab","cantilever","propped","continuous"};
char *current_beam;
int I;
for(I=0;I<4;I++)
{
current_beam=beam_type[I];
printf("current value: %s \n", current_beam);
}
}
Output:
Current value: sab
Current value: cantilever
Current value: propped
Current value: continuous
```

In the above program, depending upon the value of i, the string pointer variable current_beam is assigned to a string value which is the beam_type.

On the other hand, if a string array variable is used, such an assignment is not possible. For example, the following code will not work.

```
main()
{
char greet_arr[]="Hello";
printf("Greeting: %s \n", greet_arr);
greet_arr= "byte";
printf("Greeting: %s \n", greet_arr);
}
```

2.10.1 Reading Strings

The scanf() function uses the space character ' ' as a delimiter. On the other hand, a space is also a legal part of a string. Hence, scanf() cannot be used to input strings which contain spaces.

Example 2.31

```
        main()
        {
        char string[10];
        scanf("%s",string);
        printf("%s",string);
        }
Input:
        Good Day!
Output:
        Good
```

C provides us with an alternative – the gets() function to input strings. The delimiter for gets() is the newline character or the Enterkey. The newline character in the string is replaced by the null character when the function returns the string. The corresponding output function is puts() which prints the contents of a string on the screen and terminates by printing a new line. The following example illustrates these functions.

Example 2.32

```
        main()
        {
        char string[10];
        gets("%s",string);
        puts("%s",string);
        }
Input:
        Good Day!
Output:
        Good Day!
```

2.10.2 sscanf and sprintf functions

These functions are similar to scanf() and printf() functions. Sscanf() reads from a character array instead from keyboard. Similar to that sprintf() writes to a character array instead of to the screen.

Example 2.33

```
main()
{
char buffer[100]; float num;
printf("Enter a number:");
scanf("%f", &num);
getchar();
sprintf(buffer, "you entered : %10.5f",num);
puts(buffer);
printf("Enter another number:");
gets(buffer);
sscanf(buffer,"%f", &num);
printf("you entered: %10.5f", num);
}
Output:

Enter a number: 23
You entered: 23.00000
Enter another number: 4566
You entered: 4566.00000
```

It may be noted that the format string of the sscanf() and sprintf() statements is exactly like that of the scanf() and printf() statements and buffer is a programmer-selected variable name that must be declared as, either an array of characters sufficiently large to hold the resulting string or as a pointer to a string. In this case, buffer has been declared as a character array.

There are number of library functions available for string manipuplation and a few of them are listed in Table 2.5

Table 2.5 Library Functions for String Processing

Function Name	Description
strcat (string1, string 2)	Concatenates string2 to string1.
strchr (string, character)	Locates the position of the character within the string. Returns the address of the character.
strcmp (string1, string2)	Compares string2 to string1. Returns the address of the first nonmatching character.
strcpy (string1, string2)	Copies string2 to string1.
strlen (string)	Returns the length of the string.

2.11 STRUCTURES

The data type array permits us to group elements of the same type like all integers, all characters etc. into a single logical entity. To refer an element in an array we give the name of the array with the appropriate subscript. But when we handle real world data we deal with entities that are collections of things, each having its own attribute. For example, an entity date is a collection of things such as day, month_name and year, each of which has its own attributes. In the case of finite element analysis, a node may have attributes such as node_number, x, y, z coordinates and degrees of freedom. For dealing with such collections, C provides a compound data type called structure. Structures help to organise complicated data as a unit instead of as separate entities. The data example mentioned above can be put in a structure like this:

```
struct date{
int day;
Char *mon_name;
int year;
};
```

The keyword struct tells the compiler that we are declaring a structure. An optional name called structure tag may follow the word struct and in the above example, the tag is date. The elements defined inside the structure are called members, like date, mon_name and yea are members of the structure in the above example. Each member is declared to be of a specific data type.

It is important to note that structure declaration does not tell the compiler to reserve any space in memory to its members. The declaration only acts as template that describes the characteristics of the variables defined by this particular structure. Normally, structure declarations will appear at the top of the source code file, before any variable or function is defined.

2.11.1 Structure Variables

Analogous to other data type like int, char etc., structure data type can be used to declare variables. The syntax of this declaration is,

```
struct struct_name variable list ;
```

For example, if we want to describe three dates using the structure template date defined earlier, the three variables can be added as,

```
struct date{
        int day;
        char *mon_name;
        int year:
        } d1, d2, d3;
```

Alternatively, if the structure has been defined as in the earlier section, the variables can be declared as,

```
struct date d1, d2, d3 ;
```

The above declaration defines each of the variable d1, d2 and d3 to be of structure of type date. A member of a particular structure is referred through the use of the dot operator as,

```
structure_variable_name.member_name
```

For example, the following code assigns the value 1987 to the member year,

```
d1.year = 1987;
```

The following program illustrates the use of the features mentioned above.

Example 2.34

```
/* An example for structures */
struct date {
int day;
char *mon_name;
int year;
};

main()
{
struct date d0,d1,d2;
d0.day=2;
d0.mon_name="Jan";
d0.year=1987;
d1.day=7;
d1.mon_name="Aug";
d1.year=1987;
d2.day=15;
d2.mon_name="May";
d2.year=1987;

printf("The date of d0 is %d \n", d0.day);
printf("The month name d1 is %s \n", d1.mon_name);
printf("The year of d2 is %d \n", d2.year);
}
```

```
Output:
            The date of d0 is 2.
            The month name d1 is Aug.
            The year of d2 is 1987.
```

2.11.2 Arrays of Structures

One of the most common usage of structures is in arrays of structures. For the example given in the previous section, the three variables d0, d1 and d2 can be thought of as three elements of the array [d] and can be declared as follows:

```
            struct date d[3];
```

The following example illustrates the use of structure data type for representing nodal data in finite element analysis.

Example 2.35

```
/* An example for arrays of structures*/
struct node {
int node_num;
double x;
double y;
int dof[3];
}; /* structure node contains node no, its x & y coordinates and an array for
the degees of freedom of the joint */
main()
{
int I,j;
struct node joint[2];
/* joint is an array of structures of type node */
joint[0].node_num=1;
joint[1].node_num=2;
joint[0].x=0;
joint[1].x=3;
joint[0].y=0;
joint[1].y=0;

joint[0].dof[0]=0;
joint[0].dof[1]=0;
joint[0].dof[2]=0;
joint[1].dof[0]=1;
```

```
joint[1].dof[1]=1;
joint[1].dof[2]=1;

printf("\n joint no.      X coor.           Y coor.          D.o.f.  \n");
for(I=0;I<2;++I)
{
printf("\n %6d %15.2f %15.2f", joint[I].node_num, joint[I].x, joint[I].y;
for(j=0;j<3;++j)
printf("%3d", joint[I].dof[j]);
}
}
Output:

Joint no.        X coor.          Y coor.            d.o.f.
1                0.00             0.00          0    0    0
2                3.00             0.00          1    1    1
```

2.11.3 Pointers to Structure variables

Structure pointers are used to create linked lists and other dynamic data structures by using C's allocation system. When pointers are used the arrow operator [- >] is used to point to a particular member of a structure variable. The general form is,

```
name_of_pointer_to_structure_variable- > member_name
```

The use of pointer is illustrated through the simple example given below:

Example 2.36

```
/* program showing the similarity between the arrays and pointer */
struct node {
int node_num;
float x,y;
int dof[3];
};
main()
{
struct node *joint, origin_node;
int I,n;
printf("Give no. of joints in the structure \n \t (no restriction over the
number) ....>");
scanf("%d",&n);
```

```
joint=(struct node*) malloc(sizeof(struct node) *n);
printf("\n Enter following data for every node \n");
printf("Node no. x-coord. Y-coord. dof[0], dof[1] dof[2] \n");
for(I=0;I<n;I++)
scnf("%d %f%f%d%d%d", &joint[I].node_num, &joint[I].x, &joint[I].y,
&joint[I].dof[0],&joint[I].dof[1],&joint[I].dof[2]);
printf("\n OUTPUT \n");
printf("Node no. x-coord. Y-coord. dof[0] dof[1] dof[2]");
for(I=0;I<n;++I)
printf("\n %4d %10.2f %6d %6d %6d", jioint[I].node_num,joint[I].x,joint[I].y,
joint[I].dof[0],joint[I].dof[1],joint[I].dof[2]);
/* To find out the node lying in the origin */
for(I=0;I<n;++I)
if(!(joint+I)->x && !(joint+I)-> y)
{
origin_node=*(joint+I);
printf("\n\n Node %d is at origin", origin_node.node_num);
}
}
```

Input and Output:

```
Give no. of joints in the structure
(no restriction over the number).....>4
Enter following data for every node
Node no.   x-coord.        y-coord.         dof[0]  dof[1]  dof[2]

1     0     0     1     1     1
2     0     4     0     0     0
3     4     4     0     0     0
4     4     0     1     1     1
```

Output

Node no.	x-coord.	y-coord.	dof[0]	dof[1]	dof[2]
1	0.00	0.00	1	1	1
2	0.00	4.00	0	0	0
3	4.00	4.00	0	0	0
4	4.00	0.00	1	1	1

Node 1 is at origin

2.12   DATA FILES

In programming for CAD applications, quite often we come across situations in which we need to store large amount of data created during problem solving for use during the execution of the program or for passing the data to another program. The data is usually stored in the form of data files in secondary storage devices like floppy diskette, hard disk or magnetic tape. A data file is any collection of data that is stored under a user defined file name. In this section the basic operations connected with creating, reading and writing data files are described.

2.12.1   Basic Operations

Each data file is stored using a unique file name and most computers require that the file name consists of no more than eight characters followed by an optional period and an extension of upto three characters. The following are valid data file names:

```
pfem.ist   passfem.dat    passfem.ndx    ndaray
```

In a C program a file is referenced by a variable name that must be declared within the program. For files, the variable is actually a pointer to a special file structure called FILE as indicated below:

```
FILE*istres
FILE*ndaray
FILE*input
```

In the above examples, the file pointer names are selected by the programmer and the name will be used to refer to the concerned file. This name need not be the same as the external name used by the computer to store the file.

The term FILE used in the above declarations is the tag name of the special data structure used by C for storing all the information about a file. The actual declaration of a file structure with the symbolic name FILE is contained in the stdio.h, standard header file. Attention is invited to the readers to section 2.4 and it is to be reemphasized here that in order to make full use of I/O functions of the standard C library the programmer should include it at the beginning of the program:

```
#include<stdio.h>
```

Usually the .h suffix to a file name indicates that the file is a header file, meaning that it is included at the head of a program for the purpose of defining certain values and symbols. Many functions found in the standard library work with their own data types and variables to which the particular program that needs to use them must have access. These variables and types are defined in the header file. In the above case, the header file stdio.h supports file I/O operations.

2.12.1.1 *Opening a File*

There are two purposes accomplished in opening a file; first it opens a disk file and establishes a physical communication between the program and the data file; second, it relates the file's external computer name to the pointer name used in the program. The function which does the above operations is called fopen(). The function fopen() returns the starting address of a FILE structure that is needed for reading data from the file and writing data on to it and is declared as

```
FILE*fopen();
```

It must be included in any function that calls fopen(). The function fopen() contains two arguments, fopen(filename, mode). The first argument is the computer name of the file and the second argument is the mode in which the file is to be used. Permissible modes are "r" for reading, "w" for writing, "a" for appending to a file. The following example illustrates the statements required to open a file.

Example 2.37

```
#include<stdio.h>
main()
{
File *fopen(), *file_inp;
File_inp=fopen("passfem.dat", "r"); /*open file*/
If(file_inp==NULL)
{
printf("\n The file can not be opened.");
printf("\n check that the named file exists");
}
else
printf("\n File has been successfully opened");
}
```

In the above example the internal file name used in the program is file_inp. The computer name of the file that is stored in a disk is passfem.dat. The intention of the programmer is to get the passfem.dat and assign it to file_inp. If the file passfem.dat does not exist, the fopen() function returns the NULL address value and this is checked for successful opening of the file.

It may be mentioned here that C provides a special pointer value called NULL that acts as a flag and has a numerical value of zero. The NULL pointer is frequently used to indicate the last record in the case of linked lists described in the next chapter.

2.12.2 Reading and Writing Files

Reading and writing on a file is supported through several standard library functions similar to reading input from a terminal and writing data to a display screen. Table 2.6 gives the description of some of the frequently used functions. The reader may refer to other manuals and books for information on additional functions [1,2].

Table 2.6 Selected File I/O Functions

Function	Description
fopen ("file name", "mode")	Open or create the file
putc (c, filename)	Write a single character to the file
fputs (string, filename)	Write a string to the file
fprintf (filename, "format", arguments)	Write values of the argument to the file according to the format
getc (filename)	Read a character from thhe file
fgets (string name, n, filename)	Read n-1 characters from the file and store the characters in the given string name
fscanf (filename, "format", & arguments)	Read values for the listed arguments from the file, according to the format
rewind (filename)	Resets the current position to the start of the file
fseek (filename, offset, origin)	To move to a position in the file indicated by the offset (see description under random access file)
ftell (filename)	Returns the offset value of the next character
fclose (filename)	Close the file

The following examples illustrate the use of some of the functions for reading and writing on to a file.

Example 2.38

```
/* Program to demonstrate file writng*/
#include <stdio.h>
main()
{
FILE *results_file;
int I, beam[3];
float bm[3],sf[3];
analysis(beam,bm,sf);
results_file=fopen("passfem.res", "w");
for(I=0;I<3;++I)
fprintf(results_file, "Beam_NO %d bending_moment= %5.2f shear_force= %5.2f
\n", beam[I],bm[I],sf[I]);
fclose(result_file);
}
analysis(beam_no,bm,sf)
int beam_no[3];
{
```

```
int I;
for(I=0;I<3;++I)
scanf("%d%f%f",&beam_no[I],&bm[I],&sf[I]);
return;
}
```

Input Data

```
1       2000     234
2       3455     312
3       4456     778
```

contents of PASSFEM.RES
Beam_No 1 bending_moment= 2000.00 shear_force=234.00
Beam_No 2 bending_moment= 3455.00 shear_force=312.00
Beam_No 3 bending_moment= 4456.00 shear_force=778.00

Example 2.39

```
/* program to demostrate reading from files*/
include<stdio.h>
main()
{
FILE *inp_file;
Iit I,beam[3];
float bm[3],sf[3];

char descript1[20], descript2[20], descript3[20];
Inp_file=fopen("passfem.res", "r");
for(I=0;I<3;++I)
{
fscanf(inp_file, "%7s %d %15s %f %12s %f",
&descript1, &beam[I], &descript2, &bm[i], &descript3, &sf[I]);
printf("%7s %d %15s %f %12s %f \n", descript1, beam[I], descript2, bm[i],
descript3, sf[I]);
}
fclose(inp_file);
}
ouput
Beam_No 1 bending_moment= 2000.00 shear_force=234.00
Beam_No 2 bending_moment= 3455.00 shear_force=312.00
Beam_No 3 bending_moment= 4456.00 shear_force=778.00
```

Example 2.40

```c
/* Program to write to a file, uses ftell() */
#include<stdio.h>
main()
{
FILE *results_file;
int I,beam[3];
float bm[3],sf[3];
long position;

analysis(beam,bm,sf);
results_file=fopen("passfem.res", "w");
fprintf(results_file," ");
for(I=0;I<3;++I)
fprintf(results_file, "Beam_NO %d BM= %5.1f SF= %5.2f \n",
beam[I],bm[I],sf[I]);
if(I==0)
{
position=ftell(results_file,
rewind(results_file);
fprintf(results_file, "%41d", position-4);
fseek(results_file, position , 0);
}
}
fclose(results_file);
}
analysis(beam_no,bm,sf);
int beam_no[3];
float bm[3], sf[3];
{
int i;
for(i=0;i<3;++i)
scanf("%d%f%f",&beam_no[I],&bm[I],&sf[I]);
return;
}
```

Input Data

```
1     2000      234
2     3455      312
3     4456      778
```

```
contents of PASSFEM.RES
Beam_No 1 BM = 2000.00 SF=234.00
Beam_No 2 BM = 3455.00 SF=312.00
Beam_No 3 BM= 4456.00 SF=778.00
```

Example 2.41

```
/*program to demonstrate reading from files using fseek()*/
    #include <stdio.h>
    main()
    {
    FILE *inp_file;
    int I,beam[3];
    float bm[3],sf[3];
    long record_size;
    char descript1[20], descript2[20], descript3[20];
    inp_file=fopen("passfem.res", "r");
    fsacnf(inp_file,"%ld", &record_size);

    for(I=2;I>=0;–i) /* Reads them in reverse to demonstrate random access */
    {
    fseek(inp_file,(record_size*I)+4,0);
    fscanf(inp_file, "%7s %d %15s %f %12s %f",
    &descript1, &beam[I], &descript2, &bm[i], &descript3, &sf[I]);
    printf("%7s %d %15s %f %12s %f \n", descript1, beam[I], descript2, bm[i],
    descript3, sf[I]);
    }
    fclose(inp_file);
    }
Ouput

    Beam_No 3 bending_moment= 4456.00 shear_force=778.00
    Beam_No 2 bending_moment= 3455.00 shear_force=312.00
    Beam_No 1 bending_moment= 2000.00 shear_force=234.00
```

2.13   ADDITIONAL CAPABILITIES

The C programming language provides facilities for string replacement and inclusion of files through a pre-processor. Also in many programming situations the user would like to specify the data types and these are supported through typedef and enum statements. In addition, the data type defined as union will help the programmer to reserve the same area in memory for two or more variables, each of which can be a different data type. These features are briefly discussed in the following section.

2.13.1 The C Preprocessor

The C preprocessor is a program that processes the source code before it passes through the compiler. Its most often used features are: simple string replacement, macro expansion and file inclusion.

2.13.1.1 Simple string replacement

The replacement of a string by another string is accomplished through #define statement. Consider the following program.

```
#define PI 3.141593
double area (radius)
double radius;
{
    return (PI * radius * radius);
}
```

In the above program the preprocessor replaces PI wherever it occurs by the value 3.141593. This replacement is made by the C preprocessor just prior to program compilation. The general form is,

```
#define string1 string2
```

Please note that there is no semicolon in the define statement. It is a common practice to use upper case letters for named constants. Once a name has been #defined it can be used in subsequent #define statements. Thus,

```
#define PI 3.141593
#define PISQARE PI*PI
```

2.13.1.2 Macro Expansion

In addition to using #define statements for simple string replacements, we can also use it to equate symbolic names to either partial or complete expressions. When the equivalent text consists of more than a single value, operator, or variable, the symbolic name is referred to as a macro, and the substitution of the text in place of the symbolic name is called a macro expansion or macro substitution. The word macro refers to the direct, in-line expression of one work into many words. The following example illustrates the macro definition.

```
#define CUBE(X)   (X*X*X)
main ( )
{
    printf ("%f \n", 81.0/CUBE (3.0);
}
```

The preprocessor scans the source code. Whenever it finds the four characters CUBE followed by the actual argument inside the parentheses (which makes the macro call look like just like a function call), it replaces the macro name with its macro expansion, at the same time replacing the formal argument with the actual argument. After the code has passed through the preprocessor, the compiler gets the following code to work with:

```
main ( )
{
    printf ("%f \n", 81.0/ (3.0*3.0*3.0));
}
```

Consider now the same example with the difference in macro definition

```
#define CUBE (x) x * x * x
main ( )
{
    printf ("%f \n", 81.0/CUBE (3.0));
}
```

Output

```
162.000000
```

In this case the processor expands the macro definition as,

```
printf ("%f \ n", 81.0/3.0 * 3.0 * 3.0));
```

and hence the result becomes different from the earlier one.

The advantage of using a macro such as CUBE (X) is that since the data type of te argument is not specified, the macro can be used with any data type argument. Since the macro is directly expanded and included in every expression or statement using it, there is increase in execution speed compared to the call and return procedures required by a function. However, there is disadvantage in the increase in required program memory space when a macro is used repeatedly. A function is stored in memory only once no matter how many times the function is called, whereas in the case of macros the expanded text version is included every time it is used.

2.13.1.3 File Inclusion

In section 2.4 it was brought to the attention of the reader that in-order to include standard I/O function library the following statement must be inserted as the first statement of the program.

```
#include <stdio.h> , or
#include "stdio.h"
```

In general, C supports inclusion of any file through a statement,

```
#include "filename"
```

and it simply causes the entire contents of the file, with that filename, to be inserted in the source code at that point in the program.

2.13.1.4 *User-Specified Data Types*

The C programming language permits a developer to create new data types and are briefly described below:

Enumerated Data Type

An enumerated data type is a user created data type in which the values appropriate to the data type are specified in the user defined list. This data type is identified by the C reserved word enum, followed by the user selected name of the data type and a listing of acceptable values of the data type. A few examples are given below:

```
enum time {am, pm};
enum color {red, green, yellow};
enum support {hinge, roller, fixed};
```

The first specified data type is time and any variable subsequently declared to be of this type can take value of am or pm. Similarly, the second and third data types color and support used to defined variables that would belong to this data type can take any one of the values listed in the enum definintion. For example, the statement

```
enum support boundary;
```

declares the variable boundary to be of type support. Similar to other data types such as int, char etc., the enumerated data type may be assigned values or compared to variables or values appropriate to their type. Thus the following statements are valid:

```
boundary = fixed;
if (boundary == fixed) printf (" \ n The support is fixed");
```

It is now necessary to know how the acceptable values are handled internally. The C compiler assigns sequential integer values beginning with 0. For example, for the user defined data type support, the C compiler assigns 0 to hinge, 1 to roller and 2 to fixed. These equivalent numbers are required when inputting values using scanf( ) or printing values using printf( ). Consider the following example:

Example 2.42

```
main()
{
```

```
            enum support { hinge,roller,fixed};
            enum support boundry= hinge;
            printf("\n Enter a value:");
            scanf("%D", &boundry);
            if(boundry==hinge)
            printf("\n The support is hinge.");
            else if(boundry == roller)
            printf("\n The support is roller.");
            elseif (boundry==fixed)
            printf("\n The sipport is fixed."); else
            printf("\n The support condition is not defined.");
            }
sample session:
            The support is 0
            Enter a value: 2
            The support is fixed.

            typedef statement
```

The C language allows the programmer to create new names for existing data types. The statement, typedef float REAL; makes the name REAL a synonym for float. The name REAL can now be used in place of float anywhere in the program after the above declaration like,

```
            REAL span
```

is equivalent to float span;

Consider another example:

```
            typedef struct
            {
                    int node_num ;
                    float x, y ;
                    int dof [3] ;
            }       NODE_DATA ;
```

In this case NODE_DATA is declared as a struct datatype. The subsequent declaration NODE_DATA joint [10] is equivalent to the declaration:

```
            struct  {
                    node_num;
                    float x, y ;
```

```
                         int dof [3] ;
            }      joint [10];
```

The use of such typedef statements is illustrated in the next chapter in more detail.

Unions

A union is a data type that reserves the same area in memory for two or more variables, each of which can be of different data type, such as character, integer, float, double etc. The declaration of a variable as a union data type is illustrated in the following example.

```
union  {
                int int_number;
                float float_number;
        }      value ;
```

The above declaration creates a union variable named value. As a union, value contains a single member that can be either an integer or a float. On the other hand, if this variable is declared as a structure, it would have two members.

In effect, a union reserves sufficient memory location to accommodate its largest member's data type. The same locator is referenced by different variable names depending on the data type of the individual member which is referred similar to that of a member of a structure, for example, value.int+number.

This chapter described the C programming language with a number of example to illustrate the capabilities of the language. One cannot write good programs just with the knowledge of syntax and semantics of a language. The major portion of programming activity involves design of the program, which includes proper organisation of information for its effective handling during processing and appropriate modeling of various solution techniques. Coding of translating the data organisation and manipulating techniques into a particular programming language is only one of the many steps involved in programming. The features of C programming language described in this chapter provide mechanisms for different programming tasks. To design and develop programs for any application one has to know various Programming Techniques for efficient organisation of data and algorithms. The next chapter presents the concepts of and methods for programming and data structures with a number of illustrative examples.

References

1. Baker Louis, (1989), C Tools for Scientists and Engineers, McGraw Hill Publishing Company, New York, USA.
2. Bronson, G.J. and S.J. Menconi, (1988), A First Book of C-Fundamentals of C Programming, West Publishing Company, Minnesota, USA.
3. Cooper, H.L., (1987), The Sprit of C – An Introduction to Modern Programming, West Publishing Company, Minnesota, USA.

4. Hancock, Les and Krieger, M., (1986), The C Primer, McGraw Hilll Book Company, New York, 2nd Edition.

5. Kernighan, B.W. and Ritchie,D.M., (1986), The C Programming Language, Prentice Hall of India Limited, New Delhi, India.

6. Kochan, S.G., (1988), Programming in C, Hayden Book Company, New Jersey, USA.

7. Pren, W.H., Flannery, B.P., Tenkolsky, S.A. and Vetterling, W.T., (1988), Numerical Recipes in C – The Art of Scientific Computing, Cambridge University Press, Cambridge.

8. Schildt,H., (1987), C:The Complete Reference, Osborne McGraw Hill, Berkeley, California, USA.

Exercises

1. Write a program to compute and print area and perimeter of a triangle and a trapezium and volume of a sphere.

2. Write a program to compute the overall resistance of four resistors connected in parallel.

3. A 25 kg. projectile is fired vertically upward from the ground to a height of H meters with an initial velocity of V m/sec. Write a C program to compute the maximum height it will reach for ten different input values of V, neglecting the atmospheric resistance.

4. Write a square root function using Newton-Raphson method.

5. Given the diameter of the gear, torque to be transmitted, pressure angle and helix angle, write a program to compute the gear forces.

6. A simply supported beam is loaded with partial uniformly distributed load. Write a program to compute the shear force and bending moment values, at 10 equidistant points on the beam.

7. Write a program in C to compute coefficient of discharge, coefficient of contraction, velocity coefficient, head loss per unit head and power loss in flow through an orifice given the following parameters: Diameter of orifice, head, discharge and the trajectory is given by a drop H at distance X.

8. The diameter of a shaft can be computed for a given load, the distance of load from bearing, yield strength of the shaft and the factor of safety. Write a function to read in the neccssary data and compute the diameter of the shaft.

9. The analysis of a group of weight measurements involves representing a weight value into a string as shown below. Write a program which will put the correct string value depending on the value of input entered.

Category	Weight (Kg.)
Low	weight < 100.0
Medium	250.0 < weight < 500.0
High	weight > 500.0

10. The principal stress components for a three dimensional finite element is stored in a two dimensional array stress [][3], the row representing the element number. Write a function to find the maximum stress for a given set of elements and also print the corresponding element number.

11. Given the diameter of a gear, torque to be transmitted, pressure angle and helix angle, write a function to compute the gear forces. Test the function with a suitable main program.

12. Write a complete program to convert a Julian date, which is the year followed by the number of the day in the year, into Gregorian date, which is month-day-year form. For example, 89012 should be converted to 011289. The program should take leap years into account.

13. Write a program to compute an n x n determinant.

14. Write a program to create an array of 100 elements, and then interchange 1st and 100th elements, 2nd and 99th elements, and so on.

15. Write a program to read two vectors A and B and compute the dot product.

16. Write a program to compute the following for any conformable matrices A, B and C.
    (i) (A + B).C,
    (ii) A.C + B.C,
    (iii) (A.B).C

17. Write a function to solve a set of simultaneous equations using Gauss elimination method.

18. Write a program that will compute the approximate area under the given curve f(t) for $0 = t = T$, where f(t) can be any user defined function.

19. Write a function to compute the tip speed of a propoller whose shaft speed varies from 1000 to 10,000 rpm in increments of 1000. Pass the diameter of the shaft D as an argument to the function.

20. Write a program to create an array of coordinates for a set of points. The total number of points should be read as input and the memory should be dynamically allocated. The array element should be declared as a structure. Write another function, which arranges the elements of the array in the ascending order of the z-coordinate of points.

21. It is required to compute a linear equation to fit a set of data. Write a program which reads the x and y values of points into an array, computes the estimated values of y and residual sum to determine the goodness of the fit. Declare the array element as a structure of four members for original values of x and y, estimated value of y and the residual.

22. Write a function which reads one page full of text matter and then returns the total number of words in the text.

23. A function input, which reads student grade data from the keyboard and creates a data file. Another function process_data reads the file created by the function input and assigns a letter grade to the students as shown below, and adds this information also to the file. Write the function input and process_data and validate them with suitable data.

$$\begin{array}{ll}
\text{marks} \geq 90 & \text{S} \\
90 > \text{marks} \geq 80 & \text{A} \\
80 > \text{marks} \geq 70 & \text{B} \\
70 > \text{marks} \geq 60 & \text{C} \\
60 > \text{marks} \geq 50 & \text{D} \\
\text{marks} < 50 & \text{U}
\end{array}$$

24. Rainfall data of a region collected from five different rain-gauge stations are stored in a file in a format, where each record consists of year, date, guage_no, rainfall. The data file contains the rainfall data for 10 years. Write a program to read the data from the data file, compute the average yearly rainfall and write it onto an output file.

CHAPTER 3

Object Oriented Approach to CAD

3.1 NEED FOR PARADIGM SHIFT IN PROGRAMMING

Normally CAD deals with engineering entities which are real and most of the times physical in existence. These entities form the goal of realization of any CAD process and as such are constructed or fabricated to result in components, sub-systems and systems. But from computer usage point of view, these entities appear as data and any program or software operates on the data. This had been the trend as the role of computers was confined only to number crunching initially; later when the computers attained significant sophistication in terms of graphics, multitasking and parallel programming with very large data storage resources, it was felt that there is a need for a change in integrating computers in a design process. This shift came primarily from looking at the data as part of programming from 'inside' rather than treating data 'outside'. Very soon the realization came that the data can completely control a design process rather than the procedures involved in design and thus led to a paradigm shift from procedures –rather the 'how' of – to objects –rather the 'what' of- making the role of data invaluable in the context of engineering designs. A simple example of a design of a beam is shown with both procedure and object orientation in Fig. 9.1.

As may be seen Procedure requires data whereas Object tries to fit the data to the performance, bringing in lot of flexibility in using different sections, materials and systems. Even a change system from beam to truss model or arch model can be tried for the problem shown in Fig.3.1 To get a better understanding we should see the basics of both approaches.

3.2 POP VS. OOP – BASICS

Computer programming has been a major area of activity particularly in engineering design since the rigor of solving equations and functions is best handled by computers rather than by humans and this justifies the adage 'to err is human'! Large voluminous and complex calculations are done reasonably well – as the accuracy of computing plays a vital role

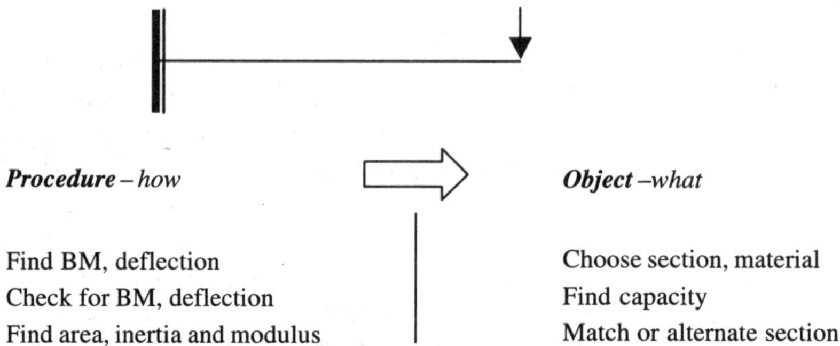

Fig. 3.1 Paradigm shift in beam design

depending on bit representation – by the computers and this led to development of programs mainly to pose the method of solution to the computers. With the introduction of hardware and software sophistications at affordable financial investments, more and more powerful programs and well tailored software for analysis started to appear. All this development has a procedure for solving the function or equations defining the performance of the analytical model, emphasizing the goal of programming or development of software is in implementing a procedure or algorithm. Many times these programs may not 'know' "what for " they are solving. Many finite element and finite difference software fall in this category. But these can only be used if *a-priori* information about the analytical model in terms of some data input is given. This clearly indicates that engineer/designer should model the system or component – which he intends to realize as a physical object – with proper inputs and he cannot get any help from the procedure or the software. Typically solving an equation of the type given in eq.3.1 with given values for

$$BM - k*d*d*b = 0 \qquad\qquad eq.3.1$$

BM, b and k to find d, requires a method without the need to know what BM, b and k stand for. But the same equation becomes the design requirement for a beam with given values of b, d and k so that given BM is matched as shown in

$$BM - k*b*d*d <= 0 \qquad\qquad eq.\ 3.2$$

3.2 where an object of size b and d has a capacity given by k*b*d*d, can match the given value of BM or greater. Here we are choosing a design and evaluate its performance whereas in eq.3.1 the equation is solved to find data, d which may or may not be realistic. Thus OOP rather Object Oriented Programming is involved in matching a data with performance while POP, Procedure Oriented Programming, is involved in solving the performance equation to get a data. One can easily see here that engineering and system design approaches rely on objects and components making OOP more relevant for programming and this aspect has added more features in OOP, which we will see now.

3.3 FEATURES OF OOP

Conventional programming methods have to be raised to a different level as some inherent features of any object or component or a group of objects called 'class' are expected to be carried on software-wise also and these features are discussed now with some simple examples for highlighting them.

3.3.1 Encapsulation

The basic feature of OOP lies in integrating data with functions or procedures and this is called encapsulation as one cannot think of any object without data. A simple 'beam' object has span, material, support conditions, shape etc as basic data and one cannot talk about or develop programs without these. The functions help to instantiate the status of the object like the function in eq.3.3 for bending moment instantiating the beam as beam_simply_supported rather simply 'beam_SS' under center load,W

$$W*span/4 \hspace{6cm} eq. 3.3$$

Thus functions can be used to instantiate different objects in a group of beam objects called 'beam' class.

3.3.2 Data hiding

This feature in OOP merely permits the object to have different usages depending on the application interests of the user. Extending the case of the beam object 'beam_SS' given the earlier section, the data needed for this usage are span if bending moment is the intention or span, inertia I, modulus E for calculating deflection. The other data like shape of the beam, area of the beam, color or material of the beam are not needed for this usage and thus get 'hidden' so that they do not get changed or corrupted.

3.3.3 Polymorphism

This is very powerful and needed feature of OOP as it reflects the possibility of the same object to be used in different ways without changing its basic characteristics. Reflecting on the beam object, one can polymorph it as a cantilever or a fixed beam keeping the basic material, geometrical and response attributes in tact. This gives wonderful design innovations like the suitability of the object for different applications. Even one can think of using the beam as a column implying that axial effects besides bending.

3.3.4 Overloading

This is an extension of the feature of polymorphism by exploiting the functions that can be made to act or simple mathematical or logical operators that convert the object for an extended usage. Using the beam object, one can polymorph it by adding a function for taking in axial effects or by suing a simple operator like '+' to convert to a continuous beam with two spans. The power of polymorphism is to be properly taken care of in programming and software development as it might lead to wrong use of objects.

3.3.5 Dynamic binding

This feature is related to loading and unloading of all objects in a class while execution of an application. Many times in an application consisting of many number of different types of beams of a class, execution of a particular phase of activity might need one beam at a time. In stead of loading all beams during execution time, a dynamic binding feature helps to load one at a time only thus saving in time and memory. At the same time the features of each object are maintained.

All the above features lead to a new development wherein reusability, integrity and expandability of all software objects are guaranteed. Towards this one should look at the language for development.

3.4 LANGUAGE FOR OOP

Higher level languages – HLL – in the context of programming and software development serve to bridge the gap between normal human communication language like English and the basic binary form of computer communication and understanding in providing a pseudo English form which is the one used in Basic, Cobol, Fortran and C. If one has to include features of OOP mentioned earlier in HLLs it should be able to operate at the core – bits and bytes – level of the computer and at the same time use high level scientific computing terms like matrices, trigonometric functions and literal terms like 'input'. Among the languages mentioned earlier, C provided the right basis and hence OOP features are introduced in C with an extension C++. This is popular even though other developments like 'smalltalk' were there mainly because of its adaptability with complex scientific computing and at the same time elementary data-based computing. A brief review of C is given which can easily update the other C programs given in other chapters.

3.5 BRIEF OVEREVIEW OF C++

Since C++ is an extension of the language C, basic features of C are retained. Conventionally FORTRAN had been the language of engineers as it can take care of scientific and algorithmic part of engineering analysis and design very easily. But, with the power of graphics and data access to BIT level of the computers became possible in PCs, the sophistication available in FORTRAN has to give way to the simple and down-to-earth approach of C. C language can handle both graphics and scientific processing casily, by making any program an assemblage of series of functions. This function approach coupled with integration of data through provisions of derived data types, enhanced C to an incremented level called C++. All the features of object orientation are available in C++ to a reasonable level and as C++ compilers are available both in MS-DOS and Windows operating systems, the coverage in this chapter is aimed to provide the reader enough scope to develop OOP concepts. Here some basic needs of programming for engineering problems will be presented and the demonstration programs follow in the same order in chapter 5, where source codes are given with explanations. Readers familiar with any kind of programming experience may skip this.It should be noted that all C++ commands, operators, keywords and programme statements are given with a special font like '**main()**'.

3.5.1 Display

Any program development calls for displaying information or data either in alphanumeric form or in graphic form through an output device or an interactive device. In the context of C++ this is handled by a set of library functions and streams under '**iostream.h**' and operators like '**cout**'. Display forms a very good part of user interface as the user of any programme can get an idea of the performance of the programme and possible interactions with it.

3.5.2 Constants and Variables

Any programme requires data for processing, representing and developing objects and this necessitates knowing ways and means of representing data. Basic data is normally represented as constants and variables with both numeric and non-numeric adaptations. Young's modulus, yield stress are some of the constant data types for defining materials. Here again, Young's modulus can be integer or floating point depending upon whether it is declared or generated. Hence, the two types of representations are constants and variables belonging to either an integer type or a floating point type or a non-numeric type like character or boolean (meaning 0 or 1 or 'true' or 'false'. In C++, '**int**', '**float**', '**char**' are some of the terms used to represent constants and variables.

3.5.3 Strings

Strings are used to provide identification of the different stages of working of a program, of the types of the representations being used with names or for displaying structured and well informed outputs. A string constant is a sequence of characters enclosed between double quotes. Strings need to be distinguished form characters in that characters are enclosed in single quotes, like **'beam'** and **"beam"**.

3.5.4 Simple Operations

All scientific manipulations in a programme are effected through generic simple operations like addition, subtraction, multiplication, division and exponentiation. C++ has definite operators for these simple operations and an additional feature for incrementing and decrementing through '++' and '− −' for effective manipulation of algebraic operations. There is also an operator precedence indicating the priority of different operators.

3.5.5 Input Operations

Both keyboard and file manipulations using any input device like floppy or CD are possible and this again uses built-in libraries and commands and operators like **cin** and >>. Usage of input particularly in the context of object oriented programming is mostly in terms of manipulation objects by modifying their states and linkages. This would necessarily mean that keyboard input or mouse input should be an inherent feature of OOP to perform and study different classes and objects.

3.5.6 Functions

A major feature of C and also C++ is the organization of all activities of programme development and class development into smaller modules called functions. In fact functions play a vital role in reflecting OOP features and particularly modifying features in terms of data to generate new objects and classes. Some of the functions needed for normal code development or file handling are available through built-in libraries like '**iostream.h**' for input/ output operations and '**graph.h**' for graphic usage and these can be accessed as header files.

3.5.7 Decision Making

Even though C programming and its enhancement C++ have functions as the basic building blocks, there are certain features in handling these functions through controls for decision making at a particular stage of the programme. Similarly, certain operations or even functions need to do repeatedly done again with and without control and these aspects are covered briefly here.

3.5.7.1 Unconditional Control

Many times, in a sequence of operations of developing Classes and Objects, it is necessary to identify features with specific reference to an application and this is where the flow of programme or the flow of development of Objects should have decision making streams to cater to different applications. One can easily visualise how the features of OOP like Polymorphism or Inheritance can be used in decision making to check or initiate the flow of the code. Unconditional control normally fall in the category of 'go to' in earlier languages, where segments are skipped initially and later used with no controlling statements. For example if a beam object is developed with provisions of functions to calculate resisting moment, axial force, shear or torsion, sometimes only bending moment may be needed, in which case all other functions are skipped. Normally '**switch**' or '**break**' are some of the keywords for this type of operation.

3.5.7.2 Conditional Control

Conditional control in any code or object development permits features of object to be generated only under certain conditions, which may be logical or numerical comparisons of certain quantities developed during the course of the programme. In the beam example, given earlier, if bending moment and shear functions are to be included if the beam object is to serve as a simple beam. But the same object is to serve in a frame it should have axial forces also and the conditions change now. Common keywords are '**if**' '**if..else**' etc. are used in C++ to have conditional control in addition to operators like '**&&**' , '**||**' etc.

3.5.7.3 Repetitive Operations

During the course of any class or object development , certain functions may have to be repeated a certain number of times which is a predefined number or a variable developed earlier. A simple example is if one wants to calculate the bending moment is beam under load for drawing the diagram, the function for bending moment may have to be repeatedly done at 10 or 20 stations within the beam length with position of station only varying.

3.5.8 Derived Data Types

In addition to data types like integer, floating point etc., OOP needs derived types like putting a set of related information of different types as is available in C language as '**struct**'. These data types help in storing a series of objects or data related to an object or class and should contain features of OOP. C++, besides having C features like '**struct**', '**strings**' '**pointers**' and '**arrays**', have '**class**' as one of the major derived data types specific for OOP applications. A brief explanation of each of these will noe be given.

3.5.8.1 Structures

This has been part of C language and as such helps in putting related information –data or functions- in one name along with keyword '**struct**'. A simple example could be '**struct wall**', which contains data on size, material and functions to calculate volume and display it.

3.5.8.2 Strings

Storing file names, titles, characters or combinations into one entity is possible through this derived data type and here, some built-in library functions in '**string.h**' provide some features for calling or passing.

3.5.8.3 Pointers

An excellent feature in C and C++, permitting one to go to the core of the computer that is address locations of variables and functions. Pointers also permit one to traverse sets of data or data types without actually loading the complete contents in the memory or RAM of the computer, thus making efficient utilization of the memory. As pointers are data types only all advantages of data representations are available.

3.5.8.4 Arrays

Storing data in a multi-dimensional form is a basic need for class and object definitions. A set of steel sections will have properties relating to their shape, size, name and derived properties like area or weight and if one has to use them for designing all these can be stored in array form. Further if objects are generated based on application as a beam or column relevant objects can be grouped and stored as arrays.

3.5.9 Classes

A distinct feature of C++ language to reflect OOP features is the derived data type '**class**' and as organization of any application into sets of classes and objects is the major step in OOP paradigm, the importance of this feature of C++ needs hardly any emphasis. One important point to be noted here is that there is no definition of objects in C++ and this is avoided mainly with a view to generate new classes as object virtually is the end of any development. In the engineering context this is very useful as classes can be used in different applications after suitably modifying them suitably depending on their functions and needs. This is the reason to distinguish between basic class and derived classes.

3.5.9.1 Basic Class

As explained earlier, an object contains both data and functions integrated into it and thus the basic definition of **class** in C++ should have the feature of having data and functions built into it –defined earlier as encapsulation—and this forms the basic class in C++. All basic classes can have data in different forms open or closed or partially closed –data hiding- to pave way to develop new classes without affecting the base class. Some examples in base class could be 'beam' 'plate' or 'analysis'.

3.5.9.2 Derived Class

Having defined the base class, exploitation into various derived ones should be possible through simple operations and this feature is also a departure from C towards object orientation in C++. Here derived classes can inherit some or all properties of one or more base classes or polymorphed suitably to reflect usage of the base class in an application. The example of '**SS_beam**' as a derived class of '**beam**' serves to highlight the implications.

3.5.9.3 Classes and Objects

The combination base class and derived classes make a powerful setup for tackling different applications with reusability as the main advantage in saving time and validation. Examples of beam class having **SS_beam** as derived classes and **rect_RC_SS_beam** as objects bring home the potentials of OOP vis-à-vis AOP as here what object is to be selected for application is the major focus. In the process it is taken for granted that all objects are validated, physically realizable products.

3.5.10 OOP Features

Since C++ is an enhancement of C language, implementation of OOP features has been done more as an extension of C rather than a new development. A brief mention of each of the features mentioned earlier will be made mainly from C++ point of view for the sake of completion. The demonstration examples give complete idea as each aspect is presented by one C++ programme.

3.5.10.1 Encapsulation

Both '**struct**' and '**class**', which are derived data forms have capabilities of integrating data and procedures to reflect encapsulation with corresponding data access provisions.

3.5.10.2 Inheritance

This feature is enabled through derived classes and data grouping so that certain properties can be passed across a class of objects and through scope operators to different classes for multiple inheritance features.

3.5.10.3   Polymorphism

Operator and function overloading – declaring various operations through one operator or function depending on the object or class – enable this feature of morphing objects depending on their applications.

3.5.10.4   Data Hiding

This is a major feature of C++ enabling other features like inheritance or polymorphism to be effected easily and three types – private, public and shared – permit different possibilities.

3.5.10.5   Overloading

Operators and functions can be made to perform differently depending on the type of class and objects in various applications, bringing tremendous advantages in reusing an object suitably.

3.5.10.6   Dynamic Binding

Pointers and array features help in bringing group of objects dynamically depending on applications so that memory of the system is used prudently and at the same time different applications can have on-line access to the same group of objects.

3.6   APPLICATION EXAMPLE

Here a simple C++ code is given to demonstrate that different shapes of a polygon class are treated as objects and their properties derived using OOP and C++ features. The class is 'shape' and the objects are 'circle' and ' rectangle' and private and public data are declared and functions for area are encapsulated.

```cpp
#include<iostream.h>
class shape
{
public:
virtual double area()=0;
};
class Circle : public shape
{
    private:
        double X,Y,R;
    public:
        Circle(double x,double y,double r)
        {
            X=x;Y=y,R=r;
        }
```

```cpp
double area()
{
    double A;
    A=(22.0/7.0)*R*R;
    return A;
}
void move(double x, double y)
{
    X=x;
    Y=y;
}
};
class rectangle : public shape
{
    private:
        double length,breadth,lcx,lcy;
    public:
        rectangle(double l, double b, double x, double y)
            {
                    length=l;
                    breadth=b;
                    lcx=x;
                    lcy=y;

            }
        double area()
        {
            double area;
            area= length*breadth;
            return area;
        }
        void move(double x, double y)
        {
            lcx= x;
            lcy= y;
        }
};
void print_area(shape * s)
```

```cpp
{
    double area;
     area = s-> area();
     cout<<"area of the given shape is "<<area<<"\n";
}

void main()
{

    double X, Y, R, L, B, LCX, LCY;
    cout <<"Circle.. \n";
    cout << "X "; cin>>X; cout << "Y"; cin>>Y; cout <<"R"; cin>>R; cout <<"\n";
    Circle c(X,Y,R);
    print_area(&c);
    cout <<"Rectangle.. \n";
    cout <<"L" ; cin>>L; cout<<"B"; cin>>B; cout <<"LCX"; cin>>LCX; cout <<"LCY";
    cin>>LCY; cout <<"\n";
    rectangle r(L,B,LCX,LCY);
    print_area(&r);
    c.move(30.0,30.0);
    r.move(5.0,9.0);
    }
Sample Inputs:
    Circle..
    X 12
    Y 22
    R 4
Sample Outputs:
    area of the given shape is 50.285714 with centre x=12 y=22
```

CHAPTER 4

Programming Techniques

4.1 INTRODUCTION

The term Programming is quite often used in computer related activities. To solve a given problem using a computer, one has to write a program. The art of writing a program is generally called programming. To write programs, one must know a programming language. The problem to be solved is first reduced into a set of sequential steps called algorithms and then this algorithm is translated into a programming language. The first step of reducing the problem into a set of sequential operations is simple in the case of small sized problems. But in the case of large real world problems, it becomes very difficult to reduce the problem into different steps. In such cases organising the data to be handled by the program is very important, so that the steps to solve the problem can be defined and specified precisely based on the data organisation.

In large engineering problems, where the data items are many and one has to carry out many operations on the data items at different stages of processing, the problem statement as well as the algorithm development becomes complex. In order to make the programming simple and efficient, it is necessary to represent the data items that the program will handle in an organised or structured manner.

There is a common belief in the case of engineering problem solving that the numerical computations are predominant compared to data management. This is not true. Input data in an engineering program may be very less, but during computation large amount of data is generated and that has to be handled properly to achieve best results. To achieve this the programmer has to fully understand the data items that have to be handled by the program. Only then a better and efficient data organisation can be done for effective manipulation. This chapter presents the concepts of Programming and Data Structures with the help of a wide variety of illustrative examples. First the term data is defined along with its few essential properties. Then the concept of data structures is described with a number of programming examples. Design of data structures and development and refinement of algorithms are illustrated for a number of engineering applications.

4.2 DATA

We have used the terms program and data many times in the previous section. The terms program and data are dependent on each other. A data is anything that a program manipulates and program is anything that manipulates the data. Before discussing more about structuring the data, a brief description on a few essential properties of data is given below.

1. Data requires some space for its storage. This space, where the data resides can be either in main memory, disk, magnetic tape or the register of a micro-processor.
2. The value of the data may be as small as the value of a bit or as big as the contents of a huge database.
3. Every data is uniquely identified by the program by its address
4. Even though data is an internal object that only programs can understand, like displaying characters on screen or a printer.
5. A data can logically be interpreted in many ways. For example, a numeric data 4.50 can be the weight of a rolled section, can be the diameter of a shaft or the length of a cylinder, depending on the context or application.
6. Every data has a structure and a format. It can be a string of bits or a contiguous array or scattered over a space in memory.

We have defined the program as one, which manipulates the data. Hence, once the data on which a program will manipulate is clearly defined, and organised, the major part of programming is completed. In many of the problems, it is not as simple as it seems since the actual problem may be complex and ambiguous. There may be many assumptions, inconsistencies and conflicts is the problem. All of this have to be structured and formatted, so that it can be moulded into a shape that can be stored in a data space. This is the real problem that a programmer faces. The data has to be organised into bits without losing its properties. Such data objects are the computer models of real physical problems to be solved. The computer models encode the data into proper forms that the programs can interpret, decode and manipulate.

At the machine level all computers work with bits. It is practically impossible for anyone to organise the complete data in the form of bits. Programming languages provide facilities to use numeric values or character strings as data. The language compilers appropriately transform this form of data into binary form, which a machine can interpret and act upon. All the programming languages define various data types that a programmer can directly use. The language compiler converts the programmer's representation into the machine level instruction. To understand this concept more clearly, let us try to analyse an assignment statement in a typical programs.

float a, b, c ;   is a declaration statement and

a = b + c ;   is an assignment statement is a programs

The declaration statement allocates each 32 contiguous bits in the computer memory and assigns it to variables a, b and c. Each group of these 32 bits can uniquely be identified by an unique address. When the assignment statement a = b + c is executed, the program has to fetch the contents of the bits corresponding to variables b and c; send them to the arithmetic logic unit to get them added; receive the result of the addition and store the result into the bits corresponding to the variable a. Here the facility of datatyping provided by the language compiler enables to group the required number of bits and make them act together to be identified as a single entity. Along with the datatyping, the language also defines a set of operations that can be applied on the data types. This facility helps the programmers in grouping their data into the various available data types in the language, so that the functions and operations provided by the language can directly be used while programming the algorithm for solving the problem.

4.3 DATA STRUCTURES

The first step in solving any problem using a computer is to properly represent the problem in the computer. The physical problem has to be translated into a form which the computer can process. The computer processes only bits at machine level. But programming languages accept characters and numbers, and translate them into corresponding bits. Hence, if the problem can be modelled in the form of numbers and characters, then the language compiler does the required operations. Hence, the programmer should first numerically model the problem, for the purpose of solving it using computers. The numerical model is a collection of numbers, to be precise, an organised collection of numbers, logically divided into one or more groups, which describe completely the physical properties of the problem. This numerical model has to be then transformed in the form of data, to have the representation of the physical problem in the computer. When the numerical model is transformed into such a computer model, the properties of the physical problem should not be lost. To achieve this, one has to logically group the data items and relate them exactly the way the mathematical model or the algorithm would require for solving the problem numerically. Such organisation of data items for the purpose of solving problems is generally known as data structuring. Many real world problems are so complex, that considerable amount of effort is required to effectively generate a proper computer model and to organise all the data related to the problem efficiently.

The language compilers offer limited data structuring capabilities like grouping bits into different data types viz., character, integer, real or float types. The compilers also offer basic operations on these data types for manipulating them. A programmer requires some higher level data objects or data types, which group the basic data types into different data objects depending on the types of operations to be carried out on the group of data. Such programmer defined data types are called Abstract Data Types (ADTs). List, Stack, Queue, Tree, Graph etc. are some such abstract data types, which along with their representative operations defined on them, serve as powerful tools for computer modelling of many engineering problems. A few of these abstract data types, operations that can be defined on them and their implementations are discussed in the subsequent sections of this chapter along with illustrations showing their use in solving engineering problems.

4.4 LISTS

A List is an abstract data type, where one or more elements of any basic or derived data type are arranged in an order. Depending on the type of problem the length of the list can either be fixed or flexible. One has to carefully study the situation before deciding on the implementation of the abstract data type list. For example, if the number of items to be represented as list is known beforehand, it can be designed as a contiguous one. On the other hand, if the items are to be inserted into or deleted from the list during the processing, i.e., the length of the list varies, the list has to be implemented as a scattered one but logically linked together. In a particular problem if several lists are to be used, it will be easier for one to define an abstract data type list and a set of operations on it, so that the same functions can be used for processing any list.

Mathematically, a list is a sequence of zero or more elements of a given data type. The data type of an element is nothing but the structure of the element in the list. It can be of any basic data type or derived data type. For example, if the data related to members, in the case of a frame analysis is represented as a list, then an element in the list can be represented as given below:

```
struct memb_data
{
        int back_node ;
        int fore_node ;
        float area ;
        float moment_of_inertia ;
        int material_type ;
} ;
```

Every element in the list has five members and the derived data type structure is used to represent the element in a list. Another example of a list element is given below.

```
struct pipe_data
{
        int pipe_no ;
        float pipe_dia ;
        float pipe_thickness ;
} ;
```

Similar to the mathematical operations and functions that can be operated on the basic data types, representative operations can be defined and functions can be written for these operations on the abstract data types.

The abstract data type list can be implemented either as a contiguous data object or as a linked data object. The main advantage of contiguous data object is that it is easy to process at the element level. A contiguous implementation of list leads to direct access, i.e, the ability to determine the position of any element by a simple computation. The major disadvantages of this type of implementation are that it needs a single chunk of connected and addressable space and its relative inflexibility. The array is an example of contiguous implementation of list and it is helpful when the length of list remains constant during processing. To insert a new element in the middle of a contiguous list, one has to shift aside all elements on one side or the other. But in the case of linked implementation, the list elements are scattered all over the place; the links logically connect the elements into a single object. The linked objects store data wherever space is available and use the address pointers to link the scattered data into a single data object. In those applications, where the number of list elements vary during processing, linked representation is a powerful and efficient method.

The abstract data type list with its representative operations can be implemented either using arrays or using pointers as linked lists. The essential details of array and linked representation are described below.

As has already been defined, a list is a collection of zero or more elements, placed sequentially. Every element in the list is identified by its position viz., 1stt, 2nd, 3rd, ... nth etc. To form an abstract data type (ADT) list; one must define a set of operations on list. These set of operations are to be defined based on the type of application, in which the ADT list is to be used. But in many cases, a few general operations can be applied and only such operations are discussed here in detail.

1. create_list (L)   :   This function created an empty list L.
2. insert (L,p,x)   :   Inserts a new element with value x, at position p in list L.
3. delete (L,p)   :   Deletes the element at position p from L.
4. locate (L,x)   :   searches for the given element x in L.

When list is implemented as an abstract data type, one can use it similar to any other basic data types. Many lists can be used in a program, for storing different data. In one case the list element can be an int type or float type. In another case, the list element can be char type and in the third case, it may be a derived data type structure, with many members within it. The operations one would like to do on these different lists may be different. The above stated operations are common to all types of lists. However, if the list elements are of different data types, one has to write the same function many times. To avoid this, an element in a list is declared to be of type element_type and this element_type can be integer, float, char or a structure depending on the application. This is achieved using the typedef declaration facility offered by C-programming language. Typical typedef declarations for list elements are shown below:

```
i)   typedef float element_type ;

     Here the element type refers to float

ii)  struct node
     {
             float x ;
             float y ;
```

```
              int quantity ;
              char label [3] ;
         } ;
         typedef struct node element_type ;
iii)   typedef struct node
         {
              float x ;
              float y ;
              int quantity ;
              char label [3] ;
         } element_type ;
```

In this case every element in the list is not a single item. It is a structure containing two float quantities, one int quantity and one char quantity. The derived data type structure allows to address these four quantities as a single entity. Every element in the list will have these four quantities. The struct declaration defines a type for every element of the list, which is referred to as element_type.

Functions written for many of the representative operations, with element_type as the data_type of list element can be applied to any lists. In the subsequent sections on implementation of lists and various operations on the list, it is assumed that the list element is of element_type.

4.4.1 Contiguous Implementation of Lists

This section briefly describes the implementation details of lists as a contiguous data object. Either arrays or pointers can be used to implement them. In array implementation, a type list_type can be defined to be a structure with two members, the first member is an array of elements and the second is an integer last, indicating the position of last list element in the array. The schematic diagram is shown in Fig. 4.1.

The declaration statements for this implementation are given below.

```
#define max_length 100

typedef struct arylist
```

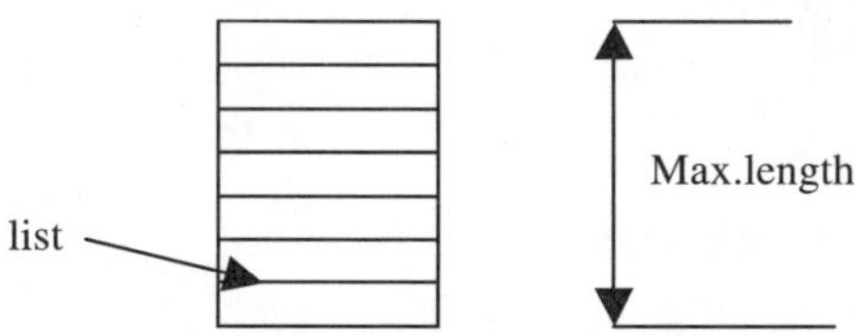

Fig. 4.1 Array Implementation of List

```
{
        element_type elements [max_length] ;
        int last ;
} list_type ;

typedef int position ;
```

Every list element is identified by its position. Eventhough, the int data type can be used to define position, a type position is defined using the typedef statement, because literally it makes more sense in the case of an abstract data type list. It can directly be used in the functions defining various representative operations on abstract data type list.

These declarations define the structure of the list. Along with the actual elements in the list, the length of the list is also stored. This facilitates easy insertion and deletion of elements from the list. The following function end(L) returns the next position to the last element.

```
position end(L)
list_type L ;
{
    return (L.last+1) ;
}
```

Here the type of the function is defined as position. The value returned by the function is the array index of the first empty position in the list. The other two important operations on the list are insert and delete. To insert an element at location p, the elements at locations p, p+1, p+2…..last have to be moved into locations p+1. P+2, p+3, ….., last +1 respectively, and then the new element has to be inserted at location p. The function delete removes element at p, by moving the elements at positions p+1, p+2, p+3, …., last into positions p, p+1, p+2, …. , last-1. The following are the functions insert and delete, for array implementation of contiguous lists.

```
/* function to insert an element in list L */
insert (L,p,x)
list_type L;
position p; element x;
{
position I;
if(L.last >= max_length)
printf("the list Lis full \n");
elseif(p> L.last+1 || p<0)
printf("position does not exist \n");
else
{
```

```
                for(I=L.last; I>=p; I-)
                    {
                        L.elements[I+1]=L.elements[I];
                        L.last=L.last+1;
                    }
                L.elements[p]= x;
                    }
            }
/* function to delete an element from list 1 */
delete (L,p)
list_type L;
position p;
{
position i;
if(p>L.last || p<1)
     printf("position does not exist \n");
else
{
L.last=L.last-1;
For(I=p; I<=L.last; I++)
L.elements[I]=L.elements[I+1];
}
}
```

It can be seen that for the insert and delete functions, all the elements after the position p, have to be either pushed down or pushed up, thus wasting a good amount of computer time. The linked implementation completely avoids these operations and also eliminates the use of contiguous memory for storing lists. However, in this case, extra space is required for storing pointers to the next element.

4.4.2 Linked Implementation of Lists

In the linked implementation, the list is made up of cells, each containing an element of the list and an associated pointer to the next cell of the list. If a list contains n elements $a_1, a_2, a_3...a_n$, the cell with element a_i has a pointer to the cell with element a_{i+1}, for i = 1,2 … n-1. The last cell, ie., the one with an has a NULL pointers, i.e. the pointer does not point to any object. When linked lists are implemented, it is a common practice to have a header cell, which is again of list_type, and has a part for data and pointer. The data part of the header contains nothing. The pointer part points to the first element of the list, which has a_1. Representation of a linked list with a header cell is shown in Fig. 4.2.

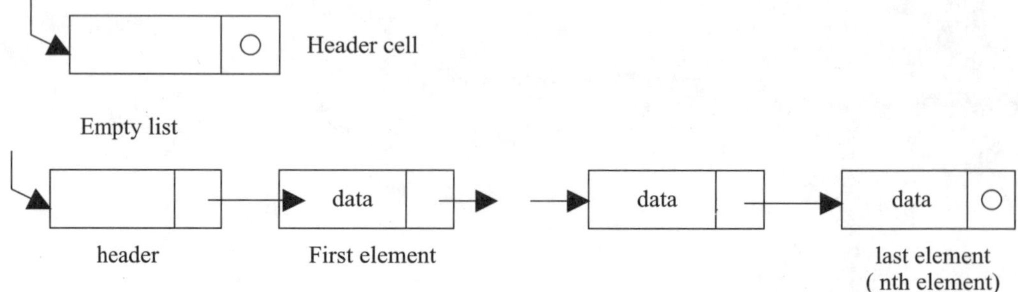

Fig. 4.2 Linked implementation of list with a header cell

An empty list is represented by a header cell with a NULL pointer. There is no strict rule that a header cell has to be there for every list. Instead, a pointer pointing to the first element is sufficient. Both these variations in implementations have their own advantages and disadvantages, depending on the context.

Because the cells containing list elements are connected together using pointers as links, this representation is called a linked list. Here the concept of position is different from that of the array implementation. In this case, position i, is a pointer to the cell containing the pointer to a_i ; where i = 1,2,3…n, i.e., position 1 is a pointer to the first element in the list. In the implementation with the header cell, the first element in the list is the one next to the header cell. Hence, the position 1, is nothing but the pointer pointing to the header cell. In the implementation without a header cell, the pointer pointing to the list itself is treated as position 1. Whenever elements are to be inserted to or deleted from a list, the parameter position, which is of integer type, has to be properly transformed into corresponding pointer. Typical declaration in the case of linked implementation is given below.

```
typedef struct list        {
    element_type data ;
    struct list *next ;
} list_type ;
```

If one compares this declaration with the previous one of the array implementation, a distinct difference can be seen. In the linked implementation, every element of the list contains two items, viz., data and a pointer to the next element. The data again can be of either a basic data type like int, float or character or a derived data type like an array or a structure itself. Consider a case where a list element contains the x, y and z coordinates of a point. Then there are two ways by which the list element can be declared as shown below. The first one has only one struct statement, while the second one has two. In the second one, a structure is defined first for the data portion of the element. Both the ways of declarations serve the same purpose, but the second one has some advantages, which are described below.

```
 i)    typedef struct list {
       float x; float y; float z;
       struct list *next;
       } list_type;

ii)    typedef struct element
       {
       float x;
       float y;
       float z;                  } element_type;

       typedef struct list
       {
            element_type data;
            struct list *next;
       } list_type;
```

In both the cases there are three float values and a pointer to the next element of the type struct list. In the second case the three float items x, y and z can be handled as a single entity data, whereas in the first case it is not possible. The second representation makes the linked list implementation more general compared to the first. The advantages of the second representation will be illustrated in more detail later, when the insert function is discussed. The functions described here are for linked lists with header cells. The functions create_list, insert and delete, are general operations on the abstract data type list implemented as a linked list. These functions will work irrespective of the structure of the list element. The working of the functions are described below.

```
create_list ()
        /* function to create list */
        list_type *create_list()
        {
        list_type *L;
        L= (list_type *)malloc(sizeof(list_type));
        L->        next = NULL;
        return(L);
        }
```

This function creates a header for the linked list and stores the address of the header element list in the pointer variable L. As discussed earlier, the data part of the header element contains nothing and the next pointer points to the first element in the list. But when the list is created, as there is no element in the list, the next pointer points to nothing, i.e., the value of the pointer will be NULL. After creating the header for the list the function returns the address of the header to the main program.

insert (L, p, x)

The function insert inserts an element x into the list at position p. The position p is an integer, but defined as a data type position in the function.

```c
/* function to insert an element to the list */
insert ( L, p, x)   .
list_type *L;
position p;
element_type x;
{
list_type *s, *q;
int i;
s=L;
for(i=1; i<p; i++)
s = s ->   next;
q=(list_type *)malloc(sizeof(list_type));
q ->      data = x;
q ->      next = s -> next;
s -> next = q;
return;
}
```

Initially a temporary pointer variable s is assigned to the value of list header L [Fig.4.3(a)]. The statement s=s - >next inside the for loop modifies the value of s such that, s points to the element which is just before the position p. If the position is 1, then the for loop is skipped and s points to the list header, i.e., the value of pointer variables L and s are equal. Then memory is allocated to store the element with data x. The newly allocated memory is pointed to by variable q. The data is put into the newly allocated space by the statement q - >data = x [Fig.4.3(b)]. Here x is a variable of type element_type. The two statements q - >next = s - >next and s - >next = q connect the new element at the proper place. I.e., the next pointer of q will now point to the element previously pointed to by s - >next and the next pointer of the element pointed to by s is made to point to the new element [Fig.4.3(c)]. This completes the insert function.

delete (L, p)

This function deletes an element at the position p in the linked list with list header pointed to by L. Deleting an element in a linked list is quite simple. Only pointers are to be rearranged here to delink the element from the list and the memory space occupied by the element is freed.

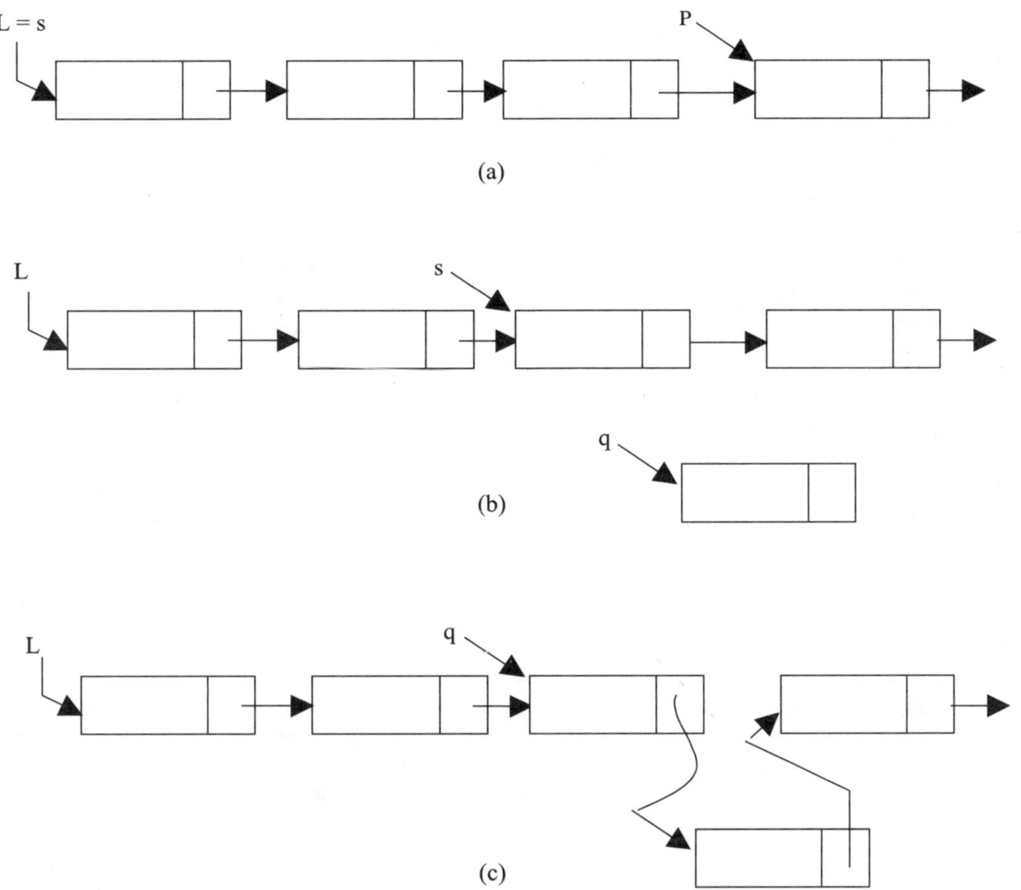

Fig. 4.3 Insert Operation in Linked

```c
/* function to delete an element in the list */
delete (L, p)
list_type *L;
position p;
{
        list_type *temp, *s;
        int i; s= L;
        for(i=1; i<p; i++)
        s = s ->   next;
        temp = s -> next;
          s -> next = temp -> next;
        free(temp);
        return;
}
```

Similar to the function insert, it is necessary to transform the position information p to a corresponding pointer information s. The for loop and the previous statement s = L achieves this. s points to the element just before the one to be deleted [Fig. 4.4(a)]. Now the address of the element to be deleted is stored in a temporary pointer variable temp; by the statement temp=s - >next. Now the pointer s - >next, i.e., the one pointing to the element to be delinked has to be assigned the address of the element after the one to be deleted. This is equivalent to delinking the element from the list. This is achieved by statement s - >next = temp - >next [Fig. 4.4(b)]. Now the delete operation is complete, but the memory space occupied by the delinked element has to be freed, so that it can be used again. The temporary pointer temp now pointes to this delinked element. The function free (temp) frees this memory and completes the delete operation [Fig.4 .4(c)].

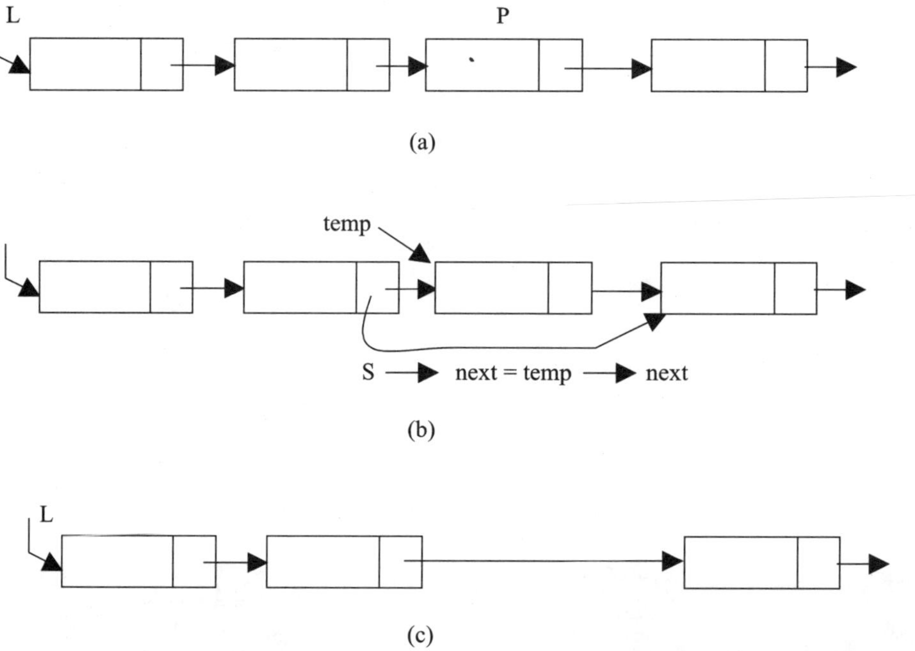

Fig. 4.4   Delete Operation in Linked List

The flexibility of a linked implementation of list, compared to the contiguous one is obvious. In applications where list elements are to be deleted or inserted during solution process, organising the data in the form of linked list is very helpful. In situations where the length of the list is known beforehand and it remains constant during the solution process, the contiguous implementation either using arrays or pointers are better as they offer a direct access to any list element in contrast to the sequential access in the case of linked lists. Example 4.1 illustrates the use of the above functions in processing linked lists.

Example 4.1

```c
/* List processing program */
#define max_size 5
typedef struct element
{       /*declarations */
int number;
float value; /* list data*/
} element_type;
typedef struct list
{
element_type data ; /* structure defining*/
struct list *next;
} list_type;
typedef int position ;

main()
{
        list_type *list_header, *s;
        int I,j,posit ;
        element_type x;

        /* create list header */
        list_header = create_list ();
        j=1;
        while (j < 4)
        {
        printf("Enter 1 to insert an element
                2 to delete an element
                3 to print contents of the list \n");
        scanf("%d", &j);
        switch (j)
        {
case 1:
{
printf("position to insert ?");
scanf("%d" , &posit);
puts("value to insert ?");
scanf("%d %f" , &x.number,&x.value);
insert(list_header,posit,x);
```

```c
break;
}
case 2:
{
puts ("position to delete ?");
scanf("%d", &posit);
delete(list_header, posit);
break;
}
case 3:
{
print_list (list_header);
break;
}
default;
{
puts ("exit from program \n\n\n ");
exit(0);
}/* end switch */
}/* end while */
}/*end program */
}
/* function to print the contents of list */
print_list(L)
list_type *L;
{
list_type *s;
s=L;
printf("following is contents of list \n");
while(s ->next != NULL)
{
s= s ->        next;
printf("number = %d value = %f \n", s ->        data.number, s ->
data.value);
}
return;
}
```

In example 4.1, the initial declaration specifies the structure of the list element. The first element is declared as a structure with two members. They are data of element_type and a pointer to the next element in the list of list_type. In the present example, the element_type is again declared as a structure with two members. The first, being number of integer data type and the second, the value of float data type.

The variable list_header of list_type points to the header of the linked list. The value is assigned in the function create_list. The insert function is used to create the list with five elements. A for-loop is used to increment the position from 1 to 5. Here the elements get appended to the list. To check whether the list has been created successfully, a function print_list is written, which prints the contents of the data part of the list. To print the contents of the list one need not know the number of elements that a list has. Because the next pointer of the last element points to nothing, the value of the pointer is assigned NULL. Hence, to print the contents of all the list elements, one has to start traversing the list from the header, print the contents of the data items of every element, till a NULL pointer is encountered. The next part of the program illustrates insertion of an element at 3rd position. And finally delete function is called to delete the element at 4th position in the linked list. At every stage print_list function is called to print the contents of the linked list. A sample session with the above list processing program is shown below.

```
Enter   1 to insert an element
        2 to delete an element
        3 to print contents of the list
1
position to insert ? 1
value to insert ? 18 23.5
position to insert ? 2
value to insert ? 40 12.8
position to insert ? 3
value to insert ? 32 67.3
position to insert ? 4
value to insert ? 45 94.3
position to insert ? 5
value to insert ? 51 21.2
Enter 1 to insert an element
        2 to delete an element
        3 to print contents of the list
3
number = 18   value = 23.5
number = 40   value = 12.8
number = 32   value = 67.3
number = 45   value = 94.3
```

```
        number = 51    value = 21.2
    Enter   1 to insert an element
            2 to delete an element
            3 to print contents of the list
    2
    position to delete ? 3
    Enter   1 to insert an element
            2 to delete an element
            3 to print contents of the list
    3
    number = 18    value = 23.5
    number = 40    value = 12.8
    number = 45    value = 94.3
    number = 51    value = 21.2
    Enter   1 to insert an element
            2 to delete an element
            3 to print contents of the list
    5
    exit from program
```

Using the insert and delete operations, elements can either be inserted or deleted anywhere in the list. But in some applications, it is seen that the insert and delete operations are done only at the ends of the list. In one case insertion takes place at one end, while deletion at the other. Such lists are called queues. In the second case both the insertion and deletion takes place at the same end. Such lists are called stacks. Stacks and queues are powerful data objects which can be used for organising the data generated during the problem solving. Even though the same list representations can be used for stacks and queues, they are defined as separate abstract data types with typical representative operations and are discussed in the following sections.

4.5 STACKS

A Stack is a particular form of data abstraction, which can be implemented either using arrays or pointers. Implementation of stacks as a linear linked lists is discussed in this section. Stack has access restricted tot he head of the list, which is generally called the top. Insertions or deletions of elements takes place only at top. The last inserted element is first deleted. A schematic diagram of stack is Fig. 4.5. The common representative operations on a stack are listed below.

1. create_stack ( )	:	creates the stack and returns the pointer of stack header
2. push (s,x)	:	inserts the element x at the top of the stack s
3. pop (s)	:	deletes the element at the top of the stack s
4. top (s)	:	returns the element at the top of the stack s

```
/* function to create stack */
stack_type *create_stack()
{
s= (stack_type *) malloc (sizeof(stack_type));
s -> next = NULL ;
return(s);
}
```

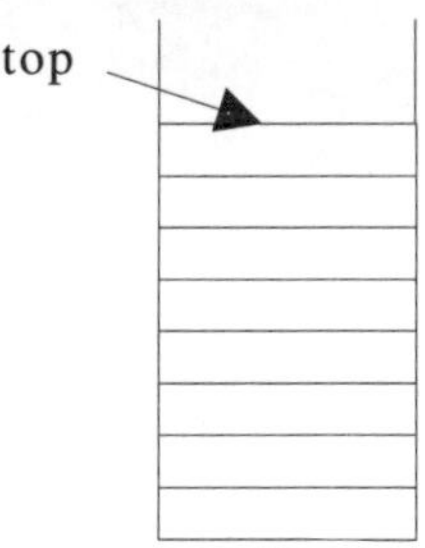

Fig. 4.5   A Schematic Diagram of a Stack

The create_stack function is similar to create_list. It creates a header cell pointed to by s. The address of the header cell is finally returned to the main program.

```
push ( s, x)
stack_type          *s;
element_type        x;
{
stack_type *p, *q;
p=(stack_type *) malloc(sizeof( stack_type));
p ->       data = x;
p ->       next= NULL;
q = s -> next;
s ->       next = p;
s ->       next -> next = q;
return;
}
```

This function push (s,x) adds an element x to the stack s. Here the stack is organised in such a way that always the element next to the header is the one top of the stack. Then the push operation is exactly similar to the insert in a linked list and is shown in Fig. 4.6 (a), (b) and (c).

```c
/* function to delete an element from stack */
pop (s)
stack_type *s;
{
stack_type *q;
q= s ->    next;
s ->       next = s ->    next -> next;
free (q) ;
return;
}
```

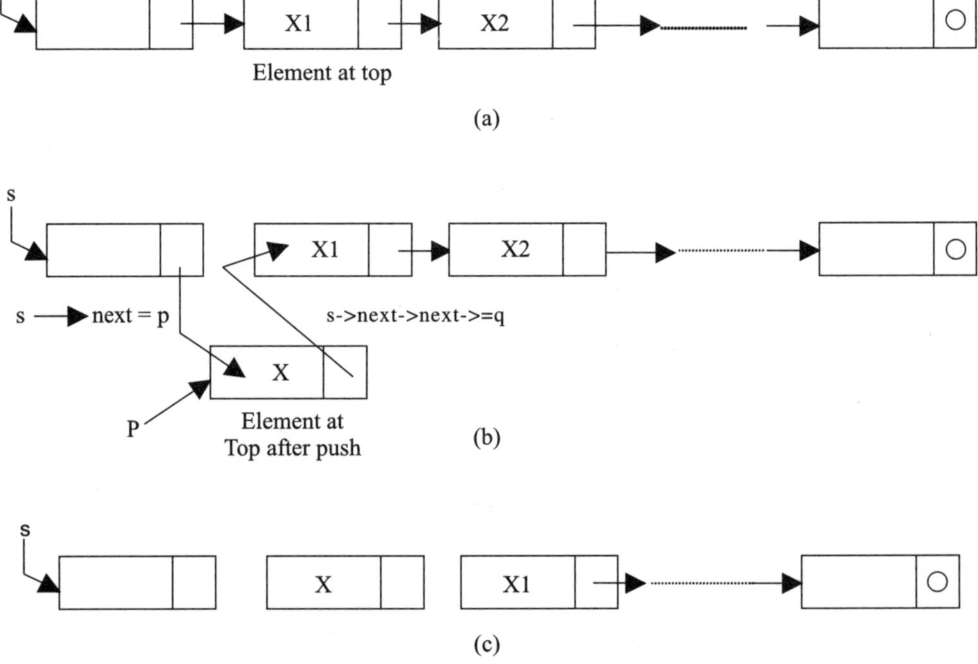

Fig. 4.6 Push Operation on a Stack

Function pop (s) is similar to the delete function for a linked list. Here the positional parameter is not required as the element to be deleted is always the one at the top. In the present organisation of stack, the next pointer of the header cell points to the element at top. That means the delete operation is nothing but assigning the next pointer of the element at top to the next pointer of the header cell, and then freeing the memory occupied by the delinked element. Fig. 4.7 illustrates the pop operation on a stack.

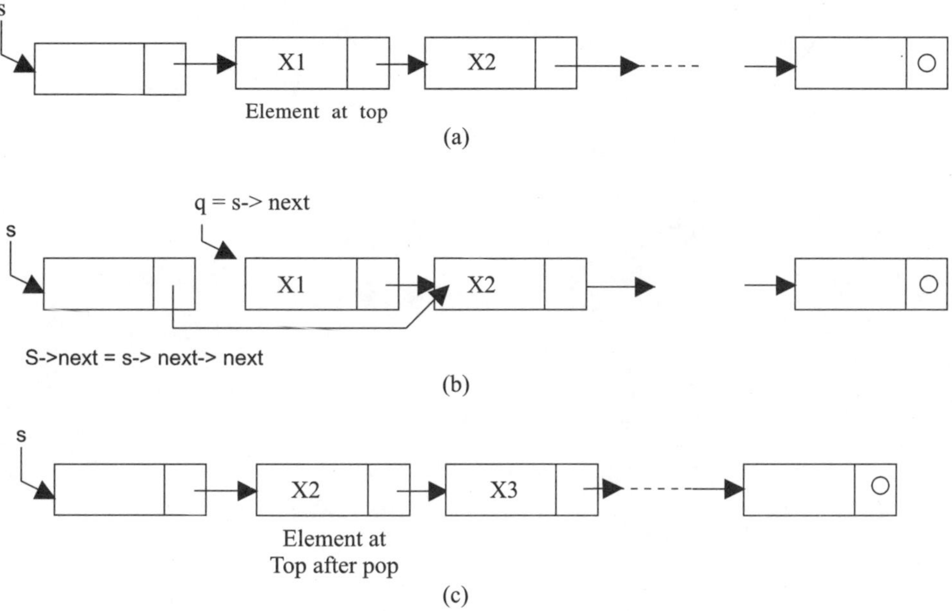

Fig. 4.7 Pop Operation on a Stack

The function top(s) just returns the value of the element at top of the stack. In many applications it may be necessary to get the element at the top of the stack. The function has nothing to do but to return the data of the element next to the header cell. The following function achieves this.

```
/* function to return element at top of stack */

element_type top (a)
stack_type *s ;
{
    return( s -> next -> data );
}
```

Example 4.2

The following is a program which uses the above functions for stack processing. The program is self explanatory and can be used directly. Here only one integer value is used as data.

```
/* stack processing program */

include <stdio.h>
typedef struct element
```

```c
{
        int number ; /* structures for data*/
}       element_type ;
{
        element _ type data; /* stack structure */
        struct stack *next ;
}       stack_ type;
main()
{
stack_type *s;
element_type x, *y ;
int i;
int j=1;
s = create_stack();
while ( j < 5 )
{
        puts(" To push a value        [enter 1];
        to pop a value           [enter 2];
        to find top value        [enter 3];
        to print stack           [enter 4];
        to exit                  [enter > 4 \n");
scanf("%d", &j);
switch(j)
{
case 1:
{
puts("element to push ? \n");
scanf("%d", &x. number);
push(&s, x );
print_stack(s);
break;
}
case 2;
{
pop(s);
print_stack(s);
break;
}
```

```
case 3:
{
printf("top element is %d \n",top(s));
break;
}
case 4;
{
print_stack(s);
brak;
}
default:
{
puts("exit stack processing program \n")
exit(0);
}
}
}
}
/*function to print stack */
print_stack(s)
stack_type *s;
{
        stack_type      *p;
        p= s -> next;
        while (p != NULL)
        {
printf( "%d \n", p ->data.number);
p= p -> next;
}
}
```

Here the structure stack_type has a significant difference as compared to the list_type declaration of linked list implementation. In the present case, data is declared as a pointer, whereas in the case of the list it was not. Either of the two approaches can be adopted. But when a structure is to be returned it may contain more than one member. A function in C can return only one value. Because a structure can contain more than one value, one can return a pointer which has the address of the variable of a structure type. To facilitate this type of operation, data is specified as a pointer variable in the declaration struct stack.

There are many engineering problems in practice, where the processing of data follows such a sequence that, it fits into the abstract data type stack. A few problems, where stack data object can be used are discussed at the end of this chapter.

4.6 QUEUES

Queues are also lists, where the elements are inserted at one end and deleted from the other. The end where insertion takes place is called the rear and the other end where deletion takes place is called front. A queue can be referred to by two pointers rear and front. Again queues can be implemented using arrays and pointers. The representatives operations that can be defined on the abstract data type queue are the following.

create_queue ( ) : creates an empty queue with pointers f for front and r for rear

enqueue (r, x) : adds an element with data value x to the queue

dequeue (f) : deletes an element at the front of the queue

When arrays are used to implement queues, circular arrays are most preferred. In the circular array implementation of queues, the length of the array is fixed in such a way that at any time the length of the queue will not exceed the length of the array. Fig. 4.8 shows the schematic representation of the circular array implementation of queues.

Consider a queue Q as shown in Fig. 4.8. The first element is referred to by the array index [0]. If the maximum length of Q is limited to max_length, then the last element can be referred to by the array index [max_length-1]. Let at any stage the element corresponding to the index n be the element at the front and the one corresponding to the index m be the element at the rear. The elements Q[n] to Q[m] are in the queue. Now the value of front will be equal to n and that of rear, m. Now to insert an element in Q, i.e., to carry out the operation *enqueue,* one has to only reset the value of m. i.e., the new value of m becomes m+1. Similarly *dequeueing,* i.e., deleting an element in the queue means making n = n+1 (or n++). That means, when insert and delete operations are carried out, the queue moves always in clockwise direction in the circular array. One important thing to be taken care of is to set the value of the index to 0, when it exceeds max_length.

One disadvantage with the circular array implementation is that the maximum length the queue may take at any time must be known before hand. On the other hand linked implementation does not require this information, because memory is allocated and freed as and when the elements are inserted into or deleted from the queue. Functions create_queue, enqueue and dequeue are explained in detail below.

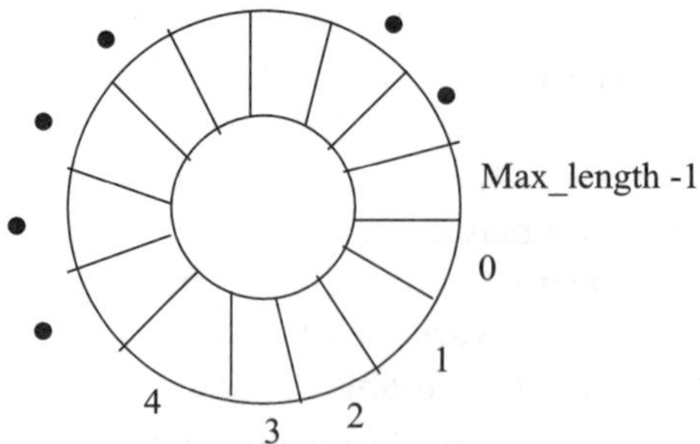

Fig. 4.8 Circular Array Implementation of Queue

Function create_queue creates the queue header. As discussed earlier, two positional parameters must be defined for a queue. They are front and rear. When there are no elements in the queue, both front and rear point to the queue header, as shown in Fig. 4.9.

```
queue_type *Create_queue()
{
        queue_type *f ;
        f=(queue_type *) malloc(sizeof(queue_type));
        f -> next = NULL;
        return(f);
}
```

The create_queue allocates the memory for the queue header and returns the pointer to it. When there is only one element in the queue, the rear and front - >next points to the element. In the case of more elements, front - >next points to the first element and rear points to the last element, i.e., the first element is the element at the front and the last element is the element at the rear. Fig. 4.10 illustrates this.

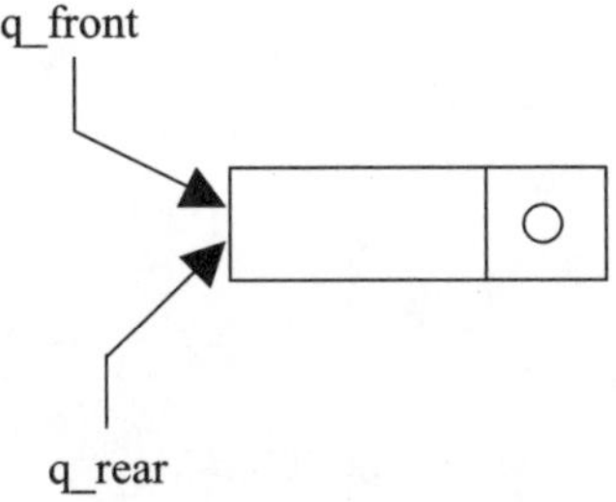

Fig.4.9 Empty Queue

```
/* function to add an element to queue */
queue_type *enqueue ( rear, x)
queue_type *rear;
element_type x;
{
        queue_type *p ;
        p=(queue_type *) malloc(sizeof(queue_type));
        p -> next = NULL;
        rear ->   next = p;
rear = rear ->       next;
return(rear);
}
```

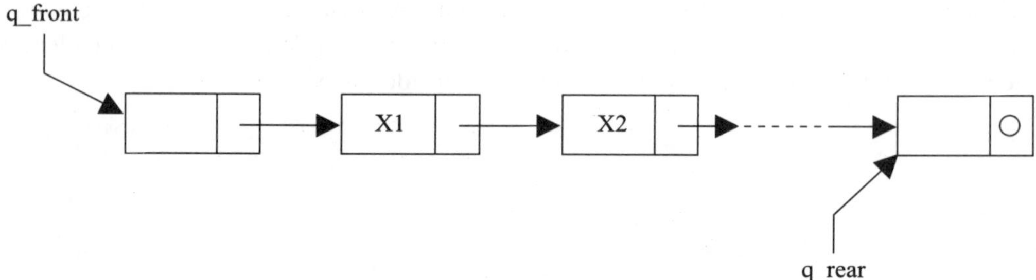

Fig. 4.10 Linked Implementation of Queue

Only the rear pointer and the data value x is passed onto the function enqueue. The process is similar to that of inserting an element in a linked list. As the pointer variable rear points to the last element in the queue, a search for the last element need not be carried out to find the position at which the element is to be added. The statement rear - >next – p connects the new element pointed to by p at the end of the queue. Now the pointer must point to the newly added element. This is achieved by the statement rear = rear - >next. As the value of the pointer variable rear is changed, it has to be returned to the main program.

```
/* delete an element from queue */
dequeue (front)
queue_type   *front ;
{
          queue_type  *q;
q= front ->  next;
front ->next = front ->       next -> next;
free (q) ;
}
```

Always the element at the front of the queue, i.e., the 1st element is deleted from the queue. The first element is pointed to by front - >next. The dequeue operation is again exactly similar to that of deleting the first element in a linked list. Delinking of the first element is done by the statement front - >next = front - >next and free(q) frees the memory occupied by the element just deleted.

Example 4.3

The following program illustrates the working of the functions create_queue, dequeue and enqueue. The program first creates a queue with five elements. The element type defined has only one member item of integer data type. Then one element is deleted from the queue and then one element is added. The print_queue function, which is given at the end of the main program is used to check the contents of the queue at every stage, by printing the data items in the queue.

```c
/* program for queue processing */
#include <stdio.h>
typedef struct_element {
          int item ; /* declaration of data */
} element_type;
typedef struct queue
{
          element_type data ; /* queue structure */
          struct queue *next;
} queue_type;
main()
{
queue_type *front , * rear ;
element_type x;
int i;
int j=1;
front = NULL;
front= create_queue();
rear = front;

while ( j<3)
{
puts (" to enqueue [enter 1] \
to dequeue [enter 2] \
to exit [enter 3] \n " );
scanf("%d",&j);
switch(j)
{
          case 1:
          {
                    puts("value to enqueue ? \n");
                    scanf("%d", &x.item);
                    enqueue(rear, x);
                    print_queue(front);
                    break;
          }
          case 2:
          {
                    dequeue (front);
```

```
                    print_queue(front);
                    brak;
            }
        default:
        {
        puts("exit from program .....\n \n");
        exit(0);
        }
}
}
}
print_queue (f )
queue_type *f;
{
 queue_type *q;
q= f ->    next;
printf("contents of the queue are : \n");
while ( q!= NULL)
{
printf ( " %d \n", q ->      data.item);
        q=q -> next;
        }
        return;
        }
```

4.7 TREES

Tree is an abstract data object, which can be used to organise data, where there is a hierarchical structure on a collection of items. There are many problems in engineering, where a tree organisation of data items can be effectively used, to efficiently solve problems. A tree can be defined as a collection of elements called nodes, one of which is uniquely identified as root, with a hierarchical relation on the nodes. A schematic diagram of a tree is shown in Fig. 4.11.

In Fig. 4.11, the node number is given in circle. Altogether, there are fourteen nodes in the tree; with node 1 being the root. Here every node has a parenthood relationship attached to it. Node 1 is parent of nodes 2,3 and 4. Or in other works, nodes 2, 3 and 4 are children of node 1. Nodes 5,7,8,11,12,13 and 14 have no children, and they are called leaf nodes. The height of a node in a tree is the length of the longest path from the node to a leaf. For tree is the length of the longest path from the node to a leaf. For instance, the height of node 2 is 2, i.e., while traversing from node 2, one has to cross only two more nodes to reach the leaf node lying on the longest path. The height of a tree is the height of the root. The children of a node is generally ordered from left to right.

Trees can be implemented in many ways. One simplest implementation is using an array. Let the nodes of a tree are named 1, 2, 3, …n. Then a linear array A can be created such that, A[i] points to the parent of the node i. Consider the tree shown in Fig. 4.11. The entry corresponding to A[3] in the array is 1. That means, the parent of node 3 is 1. This representation of tree does not contain necessary information on the tree that are required for problem solving, and hence generally not used.

A very useful way of representing trees is to attach a list of children to every node. This is very much similar to an adjacency list kind of representation discussed earlier in the case of networks. Fig. 4.13 shows the implementation of the tree shown in Fig. 4.11 by list of children.

In this representation, the root, leaf and parenthood relationships are built in. Also, ordering of children of any node can easily be achieved by the order in which the elements are added to the linked lists. The first element in the linked list is the left-most-child of the corresponding node, and the next element is its right-sibling. A right-sibling of any node is the next node on the right side with the same parent. Depending on the other properties of the tree and the required processing techniques using the tree representation, the structure of linked list as well as the array elements can be decided. The structure of the array element can be decided depending on the kind of node related information to be stored in the data structure. When large trees are to be generated from smaller ones, this representation also poses large amount of difficulties. For many practical applications, the representation by list of children is quite adequate.

When the number of children of any node is limited to 2, the tree is called a binary tree. Binary trees are often used to organise data in many applications. When a large amount of data

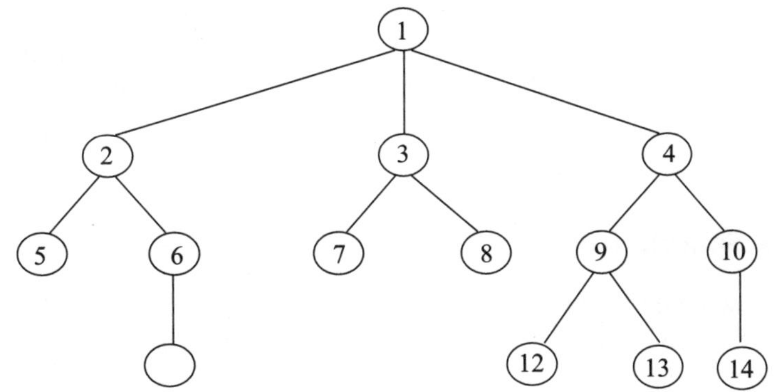

Fig. 4.11   Schematic Diagram of a Tree

i	1	2	3	4	5	6	7	8	9	10	11	12	13	14-
A	0	1	1	1	2	2	3	3	4	4	6	9	9	10-

Fig. 4.12   Array Implementation of Tree

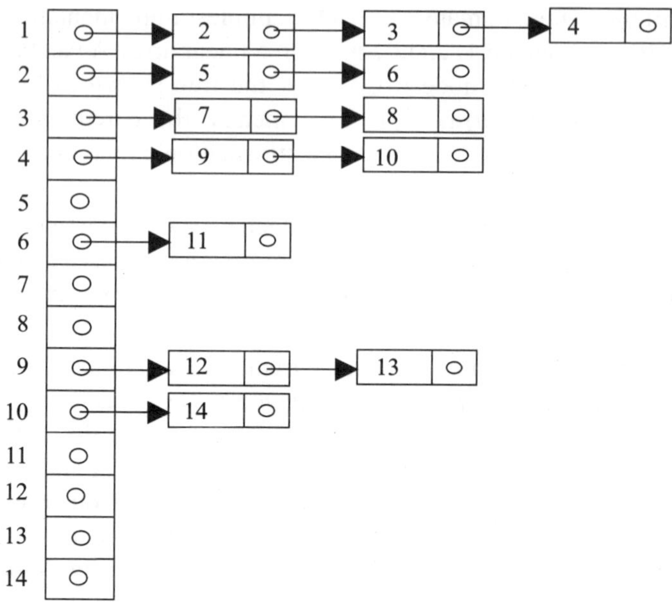

Fig. 4.13 Implementation of Tree by List of children

is to be searched for a given item many times, a binary search tree representation of the data reduces the amount of time required for carrying out the search. Organisation of data in a binary search tree is briefly described below to illustrate its use. Readers may refer to books given at the end of this chapter for more information on data structures and algorithms on abstract data object tree and operations on it. A typical example where tree representation is very helpful to solve problem is an activity network used in project management, where it is required to find out the critical path and other associated information related to it.

Example 4.7 given in next section illustrates the use of tree as an abstract data type to solve an activity network.

4.7.1 Binary Search Tree

Consider the following data which consists of a set of 10 numbers, viz., 20.8, 6.8, 15.3, 31.5, 3.12, 18.1, 92.6, 81.3, 63.5 and 71.7. The organisation of these numbers in a binary search tree form is shown in Fig. 4.14.

The first number 20.8 is placed at the root of the tree. The next number is 6.8. Since it is smaller than 20.8, it is put as the left child of 20.8. The next number 15.3 is smaller than 20.8, hence it should lie on the left hand side of the root. As already there is a left child for the root node, another left child is not possible, since a binary tree can have only a maximum of two children for every node. As the number 15.3 is greater than 6.8, it is put as the right child of 6.8. Similarly all the numbers are organised as shown in Fig. 4.14. It can be observed from the figure that, whenever a node is considered, all the smaller numbers form part of the left subtree and larger numbers form a part of the right subtree. This is true for all the nodes in the

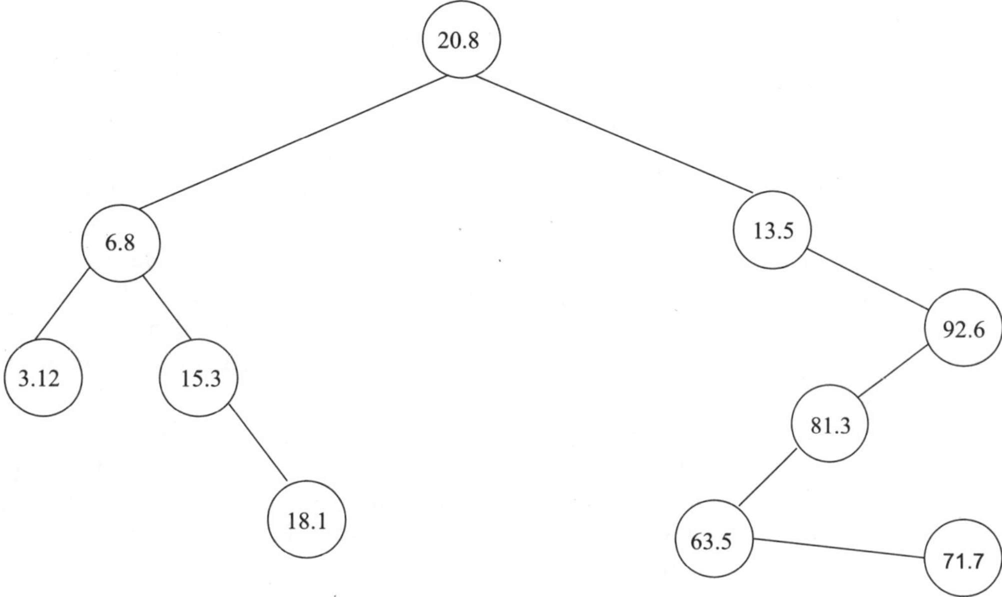

Fig. 4.14 Binary Search Tree

tree. Such a binary search tree organisation is extremely useful, when a large set of numbers are to be organised in sorted order. In the present example, there is only one item at every node. In some cases, at every node there may be more data items grouped together using derived data type struct. In that case, the organisation of the binarry search tree can be done based on any one member of the structure called key-member. Then the binary search tree can be used to search and obtain information, which depends on the order of the key-member. Once the data is organised in a binary search tree, it is very easy to get a sorted listing of the data. To get the sorted listing one has to traverse the tree following an order.

The tree can be traversed in many different orders. There are three different order of traversals, which are commonly used. They are, preorder traversal, inorder traversal and postorder traversal. Inorder traversal can be used to obtain a sorted listing of data. A binary search tree organisation of data is very useful when a large amount of data has to be added or deleted from the set of data during processing, and frequent searches have to be carried out. The inorder traversal of binary trees is described in brief below.

In order traversal follows a left-visit-right order. This means that during traversal, it first visits the left child, then the present node and finally the right child. For instance, the in order traversal of the binary search tree shown Fig.4.15 starts with the node root. As there is a left child for the root, it goes to the left child, which is the node with data 6.8. That also has a left child and hence it goes to 3.12. Now there is no left child, hence it has to visit the current node. Since our aim is to obtain a sorted listing of the data, here the visit can be interpreted as just printing the data. In the present case, first the number 3.12 is printed. Now it has to go to the right child of the current node. As there is no right child, it goes back to the previous node, of which the left child has already been visited. As the left for the current node is over, now it has to be visited. As a result the data 6.8 is printed. After visiting the current node, the right child has to be visited, which the one with data 15.3. This is continued till all the nodes are visited. The complete path of the in order traversal is shown in Fig.4.15. If one follows the path shown in the figure, the data is printed when a node is passed for second time.

The inorder traversal completely prints the data in sorted order. Programming such traversals are very easy, if the recursive feature of the traversal is made use of, which is explained in the section on recursion.

The abstract data types defined so far are the basic building blocks for data organisation. In many applications, one may have to create many lists and group of lists together and relate them properly, so as to generate a true computer model of the physical problem. Linear linked lists and contiguous lists can be combined such data object which is formed by combining lists and relating the lists properly, so that the required information for processing could be easily accessed. Tree is an another type of data object, which can be very effectively used, where data items follow a hierarchical order. The applications discussed in the subsequent sections, illustrate how physical problems are modelled for representing them in the computer, how the generated data during processing are efficiently stored using different abstract data objects, and how the abstract representations are used efficiently to solve the problems.

4.8 RECURSION

One of the very useful feature of the C programming language that help programmers is the recursive programming capability. In a programming context, recursion can be defined as calling a function within the same function. There are some mathematical functions, where,

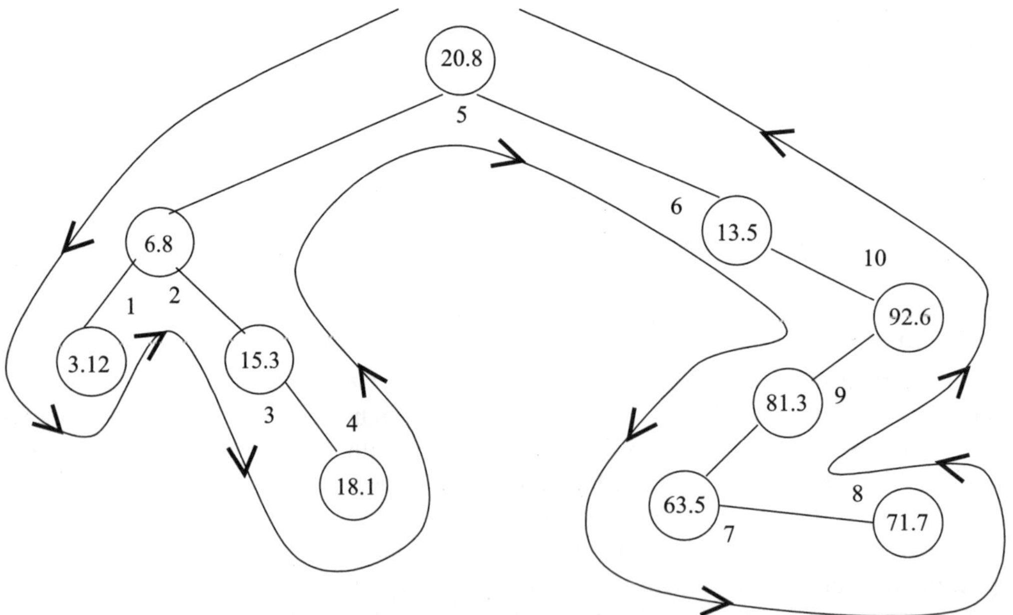

Fig. 4.15 Path for Inorder Traversal

the function itself is defined in terms of the same function. Such functions are called recursive functions. For example, the formula for factorial is factorial (n) = n x factorial (n-1). i.e., factorial(n-1), factorial(n-2) is required and so on. Finally factorial (1) is required to compute factorial (2). Factorial (1) is a trivial problem and we know that it is 1 itself, and this is the criterion for terminating the computation of factorial (n). Every recursive function should have a criterion for termination, otherwise it goes into an infinite loop. A recursive function in C for computing the factorial is given below.

```
/*recursive function for computing factorial */
fact(n)
int n;
{
if(n= =1) return (1);
else return ( n * fact (n-1) );
}
main()
{
int i;
i= fact (5);
printf ( " Factorial 5 is = %d \n", I);
}
```

In the function fact, first the termination criterion is specified. That is if n = 1, value 1 is returned. Otherwise, it is kept in a stack by the language compiler itself and finally, once the termination criterion is achieved, values are popped from the stack, and calculations are completed. This is a very useful feature of C. This feature can be applied to solve many problems, where the solution is defined recursively. Dynamic programming is a mathematical programming technique, used for the optimization of multi-stage problems. There are many engineering optimization problems, which can be formulated as dynamic programming problems, in which the optimum for the present stage is expressed in terms of optimum till the previous stage, and the optimal functions are recursive in nature. To write algorithms for such problems, the recursive feature of the programming language can be utilised, so that the programming becomes much easier. Another example where the recursive feature can be used is in programming for branch and bound search techniques. Branch and bound search techniques are represented in the form of a binary tree data structure, and the traversal of the tree can easily be programmed using recursion.

4.9 APPLICATIONS

The basic concepts in the use of data structures and the advantages of having user defined data types are illustrated in this section. One of the main steps in solving any engineering problem using computers is to properly represent the problem in the computer, so that the process of solution becomes easier and efficient. Although many engineering problems are computation oriented, i.e., number crunching type in nature, at every stage of computation, large amount of data generated have to be properly stored and later retrieved to complete the problem solving. Unless the total data related to the problem is organised in a structured manner in the computer memory, for frequently accessing the data for both storage and retrieval, the search operation become inefficient and slow. Hence, it is extremely important that one should organise all the necessary data related to the problem in a most efficient way. This makes not only the search operations efficient, but also makes further programming simpler. It is also to be noted that the representation of the problem depends very much on the kind of processing to be carried out with the data. Four simple engineering problems are considered for illustration. First one is a determinate truss problem second one a pipe network problem for storm sewer run off system, third a traffic signal design problem and fourth an activity network in a project management problem. The first three problems are discussed in detail, whereas, only salient points are discussed for the last one.

Example 3.4

A determinate truss with 12 joints and 21 members is shown in Fig.4.16. It is required to find out the forces in all the members using the method of joints for the given loading.

The above physical problem has to be numerically modelled for representing it in the computer. The problem has to be transformed into a set of numbers and value, without losing the characteristics of the problem. Let us examine the data for the truss. It has got 12 joints and 21 members connected to it. Every member is connected to two joints and the coordinate data of these joints decides the length and the orientation of the members, which is a vital information that the analysis procedure requires. The support conditions are imposed and the external loading on the joints are to be supplied as input data. This set of data can be treated as an attribute of the joint. The member connectivity information is an attribute of the member. The complete information on the truss can be divided into two sets of data, viz., data related to joints (attributes of joints) and data specify that we have to process the truss joints one after the other to find the forces in the members connected to the joint. Because the truss is determinate, the equilibrium equations can be applied at every joint to get the member forces. An algorithm for solving the problem is discussed below.

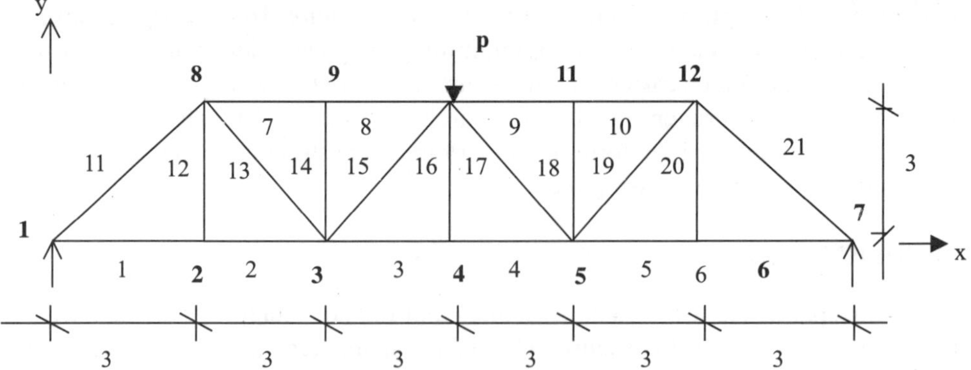

Fig.4.16 A Determinate Truss

From the given external loading, compute the reaction at supports. i.e., at the joints 1 and 7. Once the support conditions are utilized in the computation of reactions due to external loading, the loads or forces acting at all the joints are know. Now, one should find out the first joint to be processed. The first set of joints to be processed are those, which have only two members connected to them. This is so because there are only two equilibrium equations

By applying the equilibrium equations, the forces in the members connected to the joint can be computed. To find a joint with only two members, all the joints are to be searched to get the number of joints connected to each joint. For the given problem, joints 1 and 7 have only two members connected to them. Applying the law of static equilibrium of forces in horizontal and vertical directions at joint 1, the forces in the members 1 and 11 could be found out. The next joint to be processed is 7. At this stage, i.e., after processing the joint 1, and before processing 7, we can find out the joint to processed after 7. Because the forces in members 1 and 11 are already known, joint 2 can be processed because it has only two members viz., 2 and 12, connected to it with unknown forces. Similarly, after processing joint 7, we find that joint 6 is the next to be processed after joint 2. These steps are repeated till the forces in all the members are computed.

A detailed analysis of the above algorithm, brings out a few important issues regarding the computer representation of the problem and processing technique. They are summarised below:

Joints of the truss are to be searched many times to get the next joint to be processed.

When the joints are searched for members, one must know whether the force in the member is already computed or not.

Joints to be processed follow a systematic pattern in sequence, and it resembles a queue in the literal sense.

4.9.1 Design of Data Structures

One of the best mathematical models to represent the above problem is Graph or Network. A Graph or Network is a set of vertices or joints and a set of arcs connecting the vertices. There are mainly two ways in which the graphs are represented. The first way is by an adjacency matrix and the second by an adjacency list. The adjacency matrix is faster to process when the number of attributes to the joints are very less. Again if there are a large number of joints, then a large amount of space is wasted if the adjacency matrix is used, since a large number of entries in the matrix will be zero. In the case of the adjacency list representation of graph, only the required space is allocated. In the problems where a large number of attributes are there for the joints, the adjacency list representation is a better method to implement. The adjacency list contains all the information related to joints. It is a combination of several lists. These can again be implemented in many ways. One such implementation procedure is discussed here.

The basic data one enters are the coordinate information of the joints, other joint related data like external loads in the case of truss, inflow at joints in the case of pipe network and the member connectivity data. The member connectivity data is read and stored in a connectivity list. Then the connectivity list is used to create the adjacency list. A close look at both the above algorithms show that the information regarding the joint at the other end of the members connected to the current joint is required to carry out the solution process. The data structures for the problems should be designed in such a manner that all the necessary information required for solution should be readily available. Some of this information may be the input data itself. But additional information is generated using the input data. The connectivity list and the adjacency list together store all the information required for problem solving. The following sections describe the data structures designed. The algorithms as well as the C functions required to generate the data structures are also provided.

Connectivity List

A Connectivity list contains the necessary information regarding the member connectivity and other member related data. In the truss problem a list element contains the following items of data. (i) back_node, (ii) fore_node (iii) force in the member. The first two items are the input information and the third the result of analysis. Provision is made in the beginning itself to store the results related to members in the connectivity list. The structure of connectivity list for the truss problem can be declared as shown.

```c
typedef struct c_list
{
    int back_node;
    int fore_node;
    float force;
} c_element_type ;
```

This defines the data type for an element in the connectivity list. As every element in the connectivity list correspond to the attributes of every member in the truss, the length of the list is equal to the maximum number of members in the truss. As this information is already known before the start of the solution process and there is no possibility of either inserting elements into or deleting elements from this list, it can be implemented in a contiguous fashion using either arrays or pointers. The pointer implementation is discussed here in detail.

Memory can be allocated for the connectivity list as the total length of the structure of every element is known. The statement,

```c
c=(c_element_type*)malloc(max_members*sizeof(c_element_type));
```

allocates the required amount of memory for the connectivity list and the starting address of which is assigned to the pointer variable c of c_element_type. Now each member in the every element of the list can be accessed directly using pointer arithmetic. For example the back_node of nth member is (c+n-1) - >back_node. The connectivity data can be read and directly put into the list using the above syntax. The following function get_connectivity reads the data and puts it in the list.

The function reads the back_node and fore_node for every member from the console and directly puts it into the connectivity list, which is being referred to by the pointer c. It is assumed that the memory for the list is already allocated in the main program itself. It also initialises the member force in the list element to zero. The connectivity list for the truss problem is shown in Fig. 4.17.

```
        get_connectivity ( c)
        c_element_type *c;
        { int i;
              for ( i=0 ; i< max_members ; i++)
```

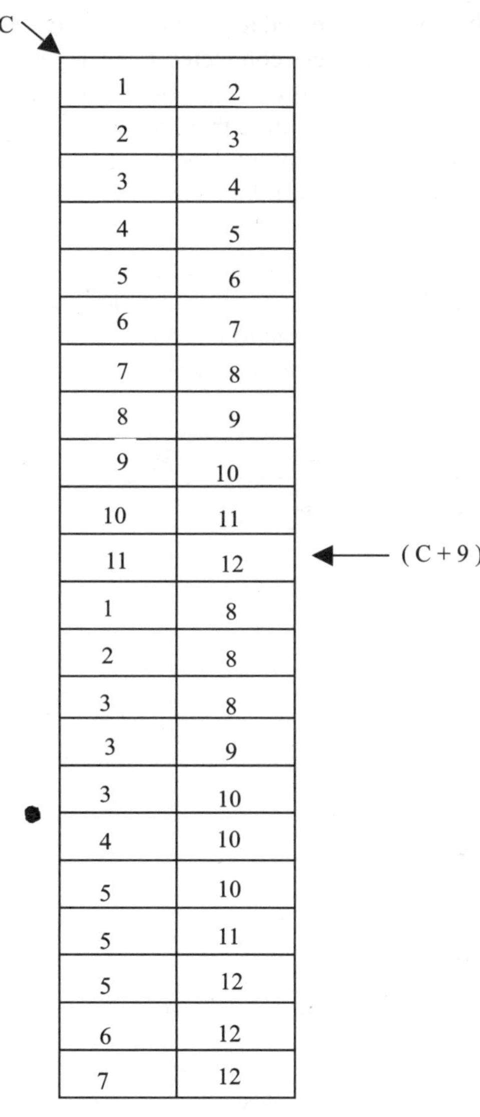

Fig. 4.17 Connectivity List for Truss

```
{     scanf ( " %d %d" , &(c + i)-> back_node,
              &(c + i) -> fore_node);
      (c+i) -> force = 0.0 ;
}}
```

Adjacency List

The adjacency list contains all the necessary joint related information organised as a set of lists connected together. Considering the truss problem, the joint related data are: x and y coordinate data, external loading data and adjacency information. The adjacency information contains the data on the members connected to each joint and the joint number of the other end of the member. The number of members connected to each joint varies and this data can be computed from the connectivity list. From the point of view of programming it is a better proposition to store the adjacency information in a linked list. i.e., a linked list is necessary for every joint in the truss. The coordinates and the external load data are the other attributes of every joint and this data can be stored similar to the one in connectivity list. The schematic diagram of the adjacency list is shown in Fig. 4.18.

Referring to Fig. 4.18, the adjacency list can be visualised to be consisting of a primary list and a set of secondary lists. The primary list stores the coordinate and the loading data and the secondary lists store the adjacency information. Every element of the primary list contains a pointer to the first element in the secondary list corresponding to the joint. As the primary list

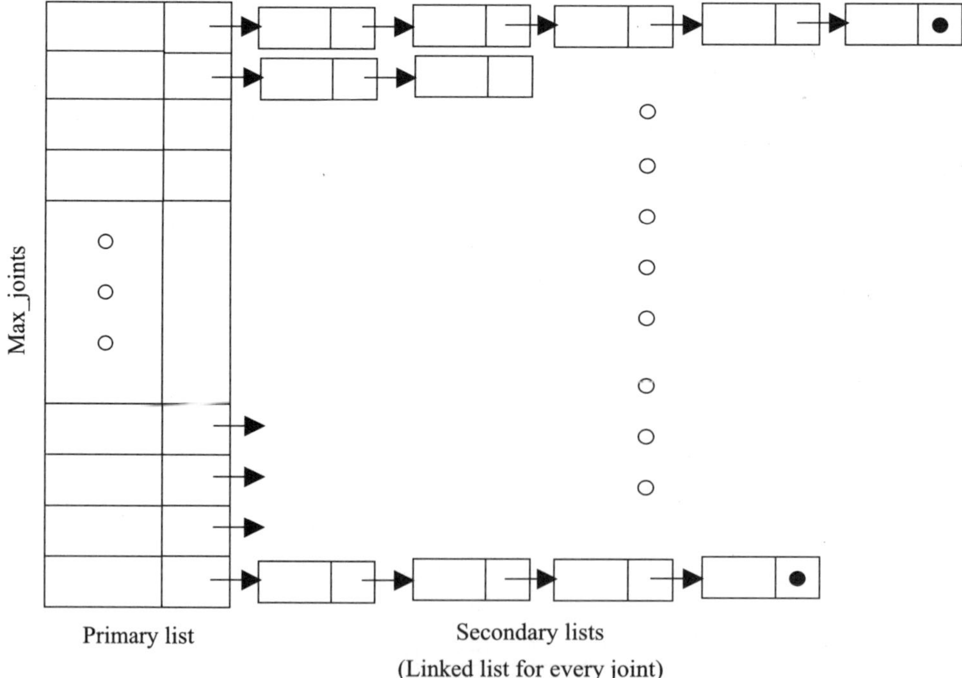

Fig. 4.18 Schematic Diagram of Adjacency List

contains the pointer to the first element of the secondary list, the structure of the elements of the linked lists are written first. In addition to adjacency information, a data item called force_flat is also included in the structure m_data. This force_flag indicates whether the force in the corresponding adjacent member is computed or not.

```
typedef struct m_data
{
        int adj_member ;
        int adj_joint ;
        int force_flag;
} m_data_type ;
typedef struct m_element
{
        m_data_type data;
        struct m_element        *next;
} m_element_type ;
```
Now the structure of an element in the primary list can be defined.
```
typedef struct  a_list
{
        float x , y , Fx, Fy ;
        int no_adj_members ;
        m_element_type *m_ptr ;
} a_element_type ;
```

Here a_element_type defines the structure of a primary list element and m_element_type defines the structure of a secondary list element. In addition to coordinates, external loading and pointer to secondary list, one more member has been included in the primary list, i.e., no_adj_members. This takes the value of total members connected to the joint. This is computed at the time of creating the adjacency list from the connectivity list. As the number of joints is already known, the memory for the primary list can be allocated. The following statement allocates the memory for the primary list.

```
a=(a_element_type*) malloc(max_joints *(sizeof(a_element_type))
```

The pointer variable a of a_element_type is assigned the address of the first memory location of the allocated space. Now any member of any element in the list can be accessed using pointer arithmetic. For example, the x and y coordinates of mth joint can be obtained from (a+m-1) - >x and (a+m-1) - >y respectively. The following function get_data, reads the coordinate information and external loading on the truss and puts it in the adjacency list. Address a of the adjacency list is passed on to the function as a parameter. The function does not return any value.

```
get_data ( a)
a_element_type *a;
{
int i, j ;
int no_load ;
float   tx, ty ;
for( i=0; i< max_joints; i++)
{       scanf( "%f %f" , & ( a+ i ) -> x, & (a + i ) -> y ) ;
}
{

        ( a+ i ) -> Fx = 0;
        ( a+ i ) -> Fy = 0;

}
printf ( "How many joints are loaded ? " );
scanf ( "%d" , &no_load );
printf ( " Enter joint, Fx , Fy \n \n" );
for(i=0; i< no_load; i++)
{
scanf (" %d %f %f " , &j, &tx, &ty);
( a+ j - 1 ) -> Fx = tx ;
( a+ j - 1 ) -> Fy = ty;
}
}
```

The algorithm for creating the secondary linked lists of the adjacency list is discussed below.

As a first step, consider the joint 1. There are two members connected to it. They are member 1 and member 11. That means the secondary list connected to the element corresponding to the joint 1 in the adjacency list will have two elements. The list is shown in Fig. 4.19.

The first data in the element is the member connected to the joint and the second the joint number of the far end of the member. This information can be obtained from the connectivity list. To get these data the elements corresponding to members 1 and 11 are scanned. In both the cases the back_node is 1. The fore_node corresponding to member 1 is 2 and that of

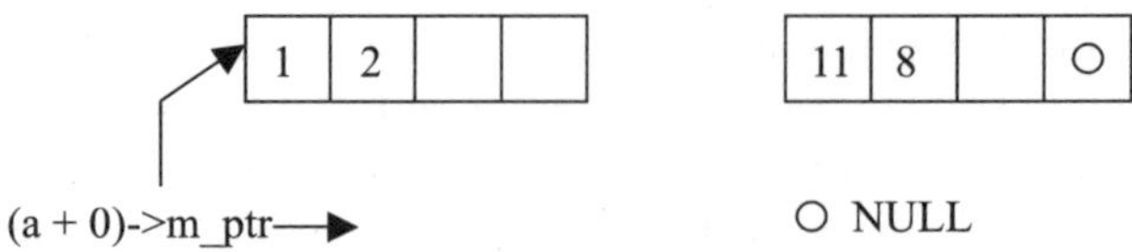

Fig. 4.19   Linked List for Joint 1

member 11 it is 8. But it is difficult to create the secondary lists jointwise, because the data pertaining to the members connected to every joint is not explicitly available. Hence the connectivity list is scanned from the beginning and elements are added to the secondary lists wherever possible. And when the end of the connectivity list is reached, all the secondary lists corresponding to all the joints in the truss are completed. The algorithm is as follows:

Start scanning the connectivity list. The first element corresponds to member 1, and its back_node is 1. i.e., member 1 is connected to joint 1. Now the first element in the secondary list of joint 1 can be created. The data values in the m_list element are: adj_member is 1 and adj_joint (far end joint of member 1) is 2, i.e., the fore_node of member 1. Create an element with this data and link it with the primary list through m_ptr corresponding to joint 1. Now take the fore_node. Its value is 2. That means the member 1 is connected to joint 2 also. Now an element can be connected to the secondary list corresponding to joint 2. Its data values are adj_member is 1 and adj_joint is the back_node of member 1, i.e., 1. The newly created element is connected to the primary list through m_ptr corresponding to joint 2. This process is continued for every entry in the connectivity list, to complete the formation of all the linked lists corresponding to all the joints. When the data of member 2 is used, then also we get an element to be connected to joint 2, which is the second element in the linked list. Hence the new element is appended to the list at the end. The following is the algorithm written in pseudo-code for better understanding.

```
create_adj_list ( c, a )
    {    i = back_node of current member
        If ( no elements in secondary list of joint i in a)
            ptr = m_ptr corresponding to joint i
        else
            ptr= next pointer of the last element in the secondary linked
                list of joint i in a
        allocate memory for new list element
        adj_member = current member
        adj_joint = fore_node of current member
        connect new element to ptr
        i= fore_node of current member
            if (no elements in secondary list of joint i in a)
                ptr= m_ptr corresponding to joint i
        else
                ptr= next pointer of the last element
                    in the secondary linked list of joint i in a
        allocate memory for new list element
        adj_member = current member
        adj_joint= back_node of current member
```

```
                connect new element to ptr
        }
        } end of function created_adj_list
```

The above algorithm clearly explains the method of creating the adjacency list from the connectivity data. The adjacency list has all the necessary data to systematically process all the joints of the truss to obtain the forces in all the members. The following program is a translation of the above algorithm to C programming language.

```c
/* function to create the adj_list from connectivity data */
create_adj_list (c, a)
c_element_type   *c ;
a_element_type   *a ;
{
int i,j,k,l,n;
m_element_type *ptr, *pl;
get_data (a); /* read nodal coordinates and forces */
for ( n=0; n< max_joints; n++)
{
(a+n)-> no_member = 0; /* initialisation */
}
for ( i=0; i< max_members; i++)
{
        j= (c+i) -> back_node;
        ptr = (a + j - 1) -> m_ptr;
        pl=(m_element_type *) malloc \
                (sizeof ( m_element_type ));
        pl -> data. Adj_member = I+1;
        pl ->   data.force_flag = 0;
        pl ->   next = NULL;
        if((a+j-1) ->       no_member == 0 )
{

        (a+j-1) ->   m_ptr = pl;
}
else
{
for(k=1 ; k < (a+j-1) -> no_member; k++)
{
ptr= ptr -> next ;
```

```c
}
ptr= ptr -> next ;
}
(a+j-1) -> no_member += 1;
/* now do the same for the fore node */
j= (c+i) ->   fore_node;
ptr = (a+j-1) -> m_ptr;
p1 = ( m_element_type * ) malloc ( sizeof(m_element_type));
p1 -> data. Adj_member = I+1;
p1 -> data.adj_joint= ( c+ I) ->          back_node;
p1 -> data.force_flag = 0;
p1 -> next = NULL;

if(a+j-1) ->  no_member == 0)
(a+j-1)           -> m_ptr = p1;
else
{
 for( 1 = 1; 1< (a+j-1) -> no_member; 1++)
{
ptr = ptr ->  next;
}
ptr ->next = p1;
}
(a+j-1) -> no_member +=1;
}
return;
}
```

The above function creates the adjacency list for the truss. The complete adjacency list for the truss is shown in Fig. 4.20

Now the data structures for the truss problem are complete. All the necessary data for computing the forces in the truss members are represented in the computer. Now it is quite easy to carry out various search operations efficiently. The first thing to be searched is to find joints with only two members connected to it. The following code will get those joints and put them into a queue. As it has already been discussed that the order in which the joints are to be processed can be simulated to a queue. Hence, whenever a joint to be processed is obtained it is put into a queue. The joint at the front of the queue is processed and the forces in the members connected to the joint are computed. Then the joint is deleted from the queue by a dequeue operation.

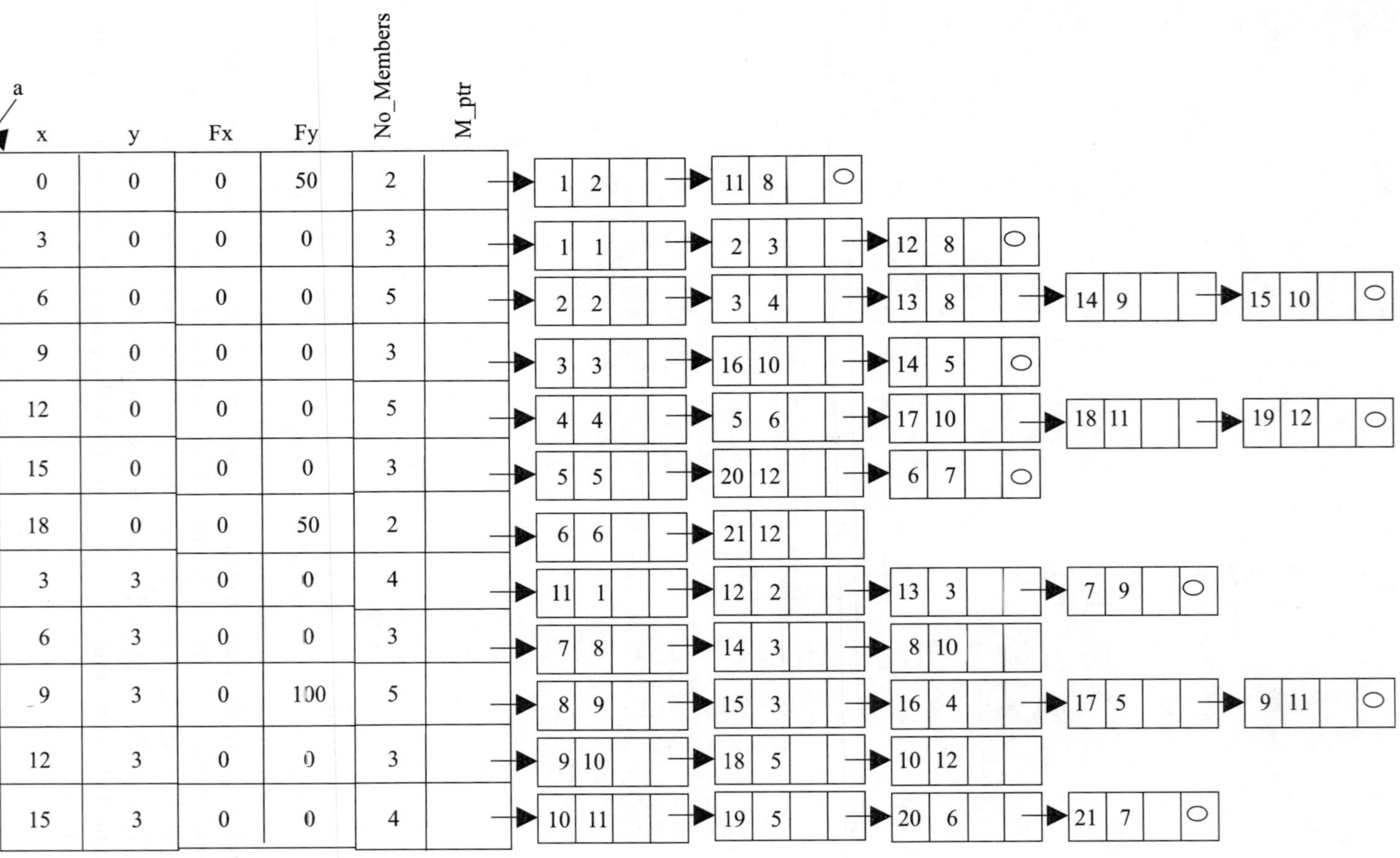

Fig. 4.20   Complete Adjacency List of Truss

```
for ( i=0 ; i < max_joints ; i ++)
{ if ( (a+i) ->        no_adj_members = = 2 )
           q_rear_ptr = enquee (q_rear_ptr , i+1);

}
```

The lines shown above search the no_adj_members in the adjacency list and those joints that have only two members connected to it are put into a queue by the enqueue operation. Now by making use of this representation of the truss, an algorithm can be written to solve the problem. Here, a queue will be used to store the joint information as explained in the beginning of this section. The algorithm is described below. The algorithm given is a very crude one. It has to be further refined and then translated into a programming language. The algorithm gives an overall idea as to how to go about solving the problem using the data structures designed.

```
/*algorithm to analyse determine truss by method of joints */
{
          search adj_list to get first joint to be processed and enqueue joints
          in queue ;

while ( force in all members not computed )
{
          current_joint = front ( queue) ;
process_joint ( current_joint) ;
dequeue (queue) ;

          search adj_list and get next joint to be processed and enqueue joint
          in the queue;

}
}
```

Let us examine the above algorithm in little more detail. The first part, i.e. searching for the first set of joints to be processed and enqueing them is already explained. The next part is the logical expression of the while loop. At very stage it is necessary to find out whether the force in all the members have been computed or not. It can be done by searching in many ways. One method is described here. Whenever a joint is processed, and the member forces are computed, the data force_flag in the linked list element corresponding to those is set to 1, and the corresponding entry in the no_adj_members is decremented by 1. Now the search for a joint with only two members with unknown forces becomes simple, as only the no_adj_members in the primary list has to be searched, as explained for the first search.

For processing a joint first it checks for any external loads on the joint, [support reactions are represented here as external loads with proper signs] computes the inclination of the members with the x and y axes, and applies the laws of static equilibrium to compute the forces in the members connected to the joint. The forces are then stored in the connectivity list. If a joint has more than two members and forces in a few members have already been computed, these member forces are retrieved from (c+i) - >force of the connectivity list.

Such operations are very easy to code, as the data structures for the program are well designed. Now these operations are to be repeated till forces in all the members are computed. The complete listing of the function analyse_truss is given below.

```c
/* function to analyse the truss */

analyse_truss ( a, c, q_rear, q_front)
a_element_type *a;
c_element_type *c;
queue_type *q_rear;
queue_type *q_front;
{
int i, joint, member, c_joint, kount, mb1 ;
int mb2, point1, m1, count1=0, count2=0;
m_element_type *ptr, *ptr1;
float x1, y1, x2, y2, sigma_fx, sigma_fy ;
float c1, c2, c3, c4, c5, c6, f1, f2;
float h, v, theta, fx, fy ;

for(i=0; i<max_joints; i++)
{
    if(( a+i) ->no_member = =2 )
    q_rear = enqueue ( q_rear, i+1);
}
while ( q_front     -> next != NULL )
{
    c_joint = q_front ->     next -> data.joint;
    x1 = ( a+ c- joint - 1) -> x;
    y1 = (a+c_joint - 1) -> y;
    ptr = (a+c_joint - 1) -> m_ptr ;
    sigma_fx = 0.0 ;
    sigma_fy = 0.0 ;
    kount = 1;
    while ( ptr != NULL)
    {
        member = ptr     -> data.adj_member ;
        joint = ptr -> data.adj_joint ;
        x2 = (a+joint - 1) ->      x;
        y2 = (a+joint -1) ->      y;
        h = x2 - x1 ;
```

```c
        v = y2 - y1;
        c5= ( h> 0.0 ) ? - 1.0 : 1.0 ;
        c6 = ( v > 0.0) ? - 1.0 : 1.0 ;
        if ( h == 0) theta = pi /2.0 ;
        else
        if( v= = 0) theta = 0.0 ;
        else theta = atan ( ( double) ( v/h) );
        theta = absolute((double) theta) ;
        if ( ptr -> data.force_flag = = 0)
        {
            if (kount = = 1)
            {
                c1= cos ( (double) theta) *c5;
                c3= sin ( (double) theta * c6;
                mb1 = member ;
                kount = kount + 1;
                count1 =1;
            }
            else
            {
            c2 = cos ( (double) theta ) * c5 ;
            c4 = sin ( (double) theta) * c6 ;
            mb2 = member ;
            count2 = 1;
            }
        }
        else
        {sigma_fy += ( c + member - 1 ) ->force * sin((double) theta) * c6;
        sigma_fx += ( c + member - 1 ) ->  force * cos((double) theta) * c5;
}
ptr data.force_flag = 1;
(a + joint - 1) ->no_member -=1 ;
point1 = ptr ->data. Adj_joint;
m1 = ptr ->data.adj_member ;
ptr1 = (a + point1 - 1) -> m_ptr;
while ( ptr1  data.adj_member != m1)
    ptr1= ptr1 ->  next;
ptr1 ->  data.force_flag = 1;
if ( ( a+ joint - 1) ->no_member == 2)
```

```
{
q_rear = enqueue (q_rear, joint);
}
ptr = ptr    next ;
}
if ( kount = = 2)
{
 fx = sigma_fx + (a + c_joint -1) ->        Fx ;
fy= sigma_fy + (a+c_joint - 1) ->    Fy;
if ( count1 * count2 = )
{
f2 = -1 * ( c3 * fx - c1 * fy ) / (c2 * c3 - c1 * c4);
f1= -1 * (c4*fx- c2*fy)/ (c1*c4- c2* c3);
}
else if ( count = 1 )
{
if ( c1 = 0.0 ) f1= -1*fy;
else f1= -1 * fx / c1 ;
}
else
{
 if(c2 = 0.0 ) f2 = -1 * fy;
else f2 = -1 * fx / c2;
}
if ( count1 = 1 ) (c + mb1 -1) ->force = f1;
if ( count2 = 1 ) ( c+ mb2 - 1) ->force = f2 ;
count1 = 0.0 ;
count2 = 0.0 ;
dequeue ( q_front ) ;
}
}
```

A main program can be written to call the above functions to analyse a truss. The declarations and the main function for calling the function analyse_truss is shown below.

```
/* main program to analyse truss */
# define pi 3.14159
#include <stdio.h>
#include <math.h>
```

```c
#define absolute(x) ((x)<0 ? (-(x)) : (x) )

File *out ;

typedef struct c_element
{ int back_node ;
int fore_node ;
float force ;
} c_element_type;

typedef struct m_data
{int adj_member;
    int adj_joint;
    int force_flag;
} m_data_type;

typedef struct m_element
{   m_data_type data ;
    stuct      m_element *next;
} m_element_type ;

tyepdef struct a_element
{   float x;
    float y;
    float Fx;
flaot Fy;
int no_member;
m_element_type *m_ptr;
} a_element_type ;

typedef struct element
{   int joint ;
} element_type ;

typedef struct queue
{   element_type   data;
    struct    queue *next;
} queue_type ;

int max_joints, max_members;
FILE *inp; /* file where input data for truss is stord */
main()
{
    c_elemet_type   *c;
```

150

```c
    a_elemet_type    *a;
    queue_type       *q_rear, *q_front;
int i,j;

inp = fopen ( " truss.dat" , "r");
out = fopen (" truss.out" , "w");
fsacnf = (inp, "%d%d", &max_joints, &max_members);

c = (c_element_type *) malloc (max_members * sizeof(c_element_type));
a = (a_element_type    *) malloc(max_joints * sizeof(a_element_type));
get_connectivity(c);
create_adj_list(c,a);
print_adj_list(a,max_joints);
q_front = create_queue();
q_rear = q_front ;
analyse_truss (a,c,q_rear,q_front);
print_results (c, max_members);
}
 /* function to print results */
print_results ( c, j)
c_element_type *c;
int j;
{
int i;
fprintf(out, "\n members nodes forces \n");
for(i=0; i<j; i++)
    fprintf(out, " %3d %3d %3d %6.0f \n" , i+1,(c+i) -> back_node,
        (c+i) ->fore_node, (c+i) ->force);
}

/*function to print the adjacency list */
print_adj_list (a,j)
a_element_type *a;
int j;
{
int i;
m_element_type *ptr;
fprintf(out, "\n output: \n adjacency list: \n");
fprintf(out, " x          y      fx      fy       no       \n");
for(i=0; i<j ; i++)
{
```

```c
fprintf(out, "%2.0f %2.0f    %2.0f   %5.0f   %2d",
(a+i)->  x, (a+i) ->y, (a+i) ->     Fx, (a+i) ->Fy, (a+i)->no_member);
ptr = (a+i) ->     m_ptr;
while (ptr != NULL)
{
    fprintf(out, "-> | %2d %2d %2d |" , ptr->data.adj_member,
        ptr ->     data.adj_joint, ptr ->    data.force_flag) ;
ptr = ptr -> next;
}
fprint(out, "-       > NULL \n");
}
}
```

The illustration of the above problem shows the various steps involved in problem solving. First study the problem from programming point of view and design data structures by keeping in mind the solution techniques. Write down the algorithm for solution and keep refining the algorithm till it reaches a stage where it can be translated into a programming language and finally transform the algorithm in the programming language chosen.

One important point to be kept in mind at the time of designing the data structures is the capabilities of the language chosen for programming. As the data structuring capability of different languages vary one from the other, it is essential that the programming language to be used is decided before starting the design of the data structure.

In the above example, first the solution technique was finalised. It has been observed that the joints to be processed follow a sequence and it resembles a queue. Hence, a data structure queue was used to store the necessary data, so that the sequence to be followed for processing the joints can be achieved easily. Based on the kind of search operations to be carried out the truss with all the details was represented as a network, in the form of two lists, viz., connectivity list and adjacency list.

Example 4.5

Fig. 4.21 shows a pipe network for storm-water sewer runoff system. The nodes of the network represent catch basins or grate openings. Water may enter or leave the system at these points. It is required to determine the flow through each pipe for the purpose of design and outflow at the sink node. For the time being, time dependent effects and other flow parameters are ignored. The flow in all branches is towards the sink node.

In the present problem, there are 7 nodes and 6 pipes, and node 7 is the sink node. Flow of water through each grate opening (node) is also known. To begin with the processing, one should find out the first node to be processed. The criteria for selecting the first node is that the node should have only one pipe connected to it, which is an outgoing pipe from the node. Here it can be either node 1,2,4 or 6. Once we get the first node to be processed, then an algorithm can be evolved for further processing. Here the processing of each node is as

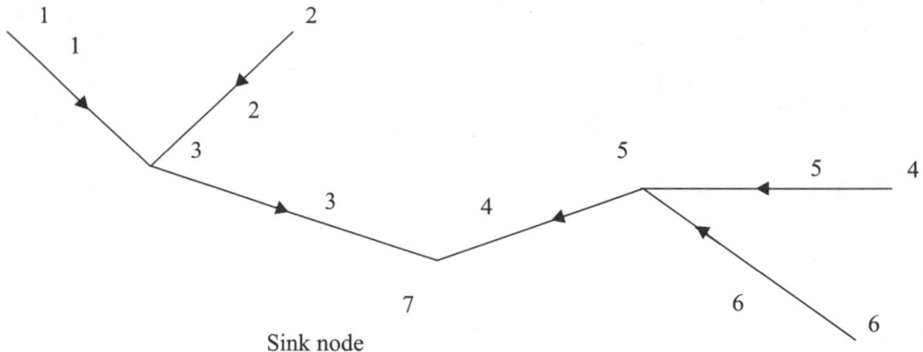

Fig. 4.21 A pipe Network

follows. Let us assume that node 1 is to be processed first. The only member connected to node 1 is pipe 1. Then

$$Q_1 = P_1$$

i.e., flow Q in pipe 1 is equal to the inflow P from joint 1, and the inflow at joint 3 is increased by Q_1.

i.e., $P_3 \Rightarrow P_3 + Q1$

Then process joint 2. Similar to above

$$Q_2 = P_2 \text{ and } P_3 \Rightarrow P_3 + Q_2$$

Now all the incoming members at joint 2 have been processed, hence the flow in outgoing member 3 can be computed.

i.e., $Q_3 = P_3$ and $P_7 \Rightarrow P_7 + Q_3$

Once the sink node is reached, one should find out whether all the incoming pipes to the sink node has been processed. If not, again repeat the process from a node where there is only one outgoing member. This has to be repeated till all the incoming members at the sink node is processed.

As there may be many nodes with no incoming member, the selection of node to begin the solution process is arbitrary. Also since the joints to be processed do not follow any order, it will be slightly difficult to efficiently automate the solution process.

An alternate method to tackle this problem from the programming point of view is to start processing from the sink node itself. As there will be only one sink node in a problem no search is to be carried out to find out the node to be processed first. In the present problem node 7 is the sink node. Put this node into a stack. Take one of the members connected to the present node under processing and get the joint at the other end of the pipe member. In the present problem, the pipe member is 3 and the other end node is 3. Push node 3 into stack. Search for any incoming members to node 3. Push node 3 into stack. Search for any incoming members to node 3. There are two members. They are 1 and 2. Take one of the members, say

1 and push the joint at the other end of member 2 to the stack. Now there are three elements in the s tack. The data of the elements being 7, 3 and 1 in order. The element at top of the stack is the one with data 1. As there is no incoming pipe member at node 1, compute the flow in the outgoing member from 1, i.e., pipe member 1, and update the inflow at joint 3 and pop the stack. Now the data of the element at top of stack is 3. Find out whether all the incoming members at joint 3 are processed or not. If not get one unprocessed member and push the node 2 at the other end of the member into the stack. As there are no incoming members at node 2, compute the flow in the outgoing member, i.e., member 2, and update the inflow at joint 3 and pop the stack. Now element with data 3 is at the top of the stack. i.e., node 3 becomes the current node to be processed. Find out whether all the incoming members to the current node have been processed or not. As all the incoming members are processed, compute the flow in the outgoing member 3 and update the flow at node 7 and pop the stack. Now the stack has only one element with data 7. Now check the sink node for any unprocessed incoming members. If there are any, repeat the above mentioned process to compute the flow in all the remaining pipe members and the total outflow at the sink node. At the end of the process, there will be only one element in the stack, which will have the data 7 (sink node).

The algorithm processes the pipe network in a systematic manager, starting from the sink node and after processing all the members come back to the sink node. Similar to the truss problem here also joints and members are to be searched many times to get various information related to the joints and members. The data structures to represent the problems are to be designed by taking into account these points.

Back_node	fore_node	Q
1	3	
2	3	
3	5	
4	5	
5	6	
6	6	

Fig. 4.22 Connectivity List of Pipe Network

The pipe network is of a tree type network. The method of solving the problem has already been described. It may be noted that the kind of data retrieval during solution process is more or less the same as that of the truss, i.e., the same kind of representation in the form of connectivity and adjacency lists can be used here also. One major difference being, in the truss problem, one can give any of the node as the fore_node and the other as the back_node, but in the pipe network problems, the direction of flow in the pipes have to be represented for correctly solving the problem. Hence, the back_node and fore_node has to be properly given so that the direction from the back_node to the fore_node is the direction of flow. The direction of flow is represented in the adjacency list by adding a negative sign to the adj_member in the member lists in the adjacent list. The back_node and fore_node information is interpreted properly while generating the adjacency list. The connectivity and adjacency lists for the pipe network problem are shown in Fig. 4.22 and Fig. 4.23.

In the discussion of the problem earlier, it was described that the order in which the joints are to be processed could be achieved using a stack data structure. The processing starts from the sink node and also gets terminated at the sink node. All the joints are traversed many times depending on the number of pipe members connected to them. Finally when the sink node is reached all the necessary computations are also completed. The following is a complete program for analysing the pipe network of the type shown.

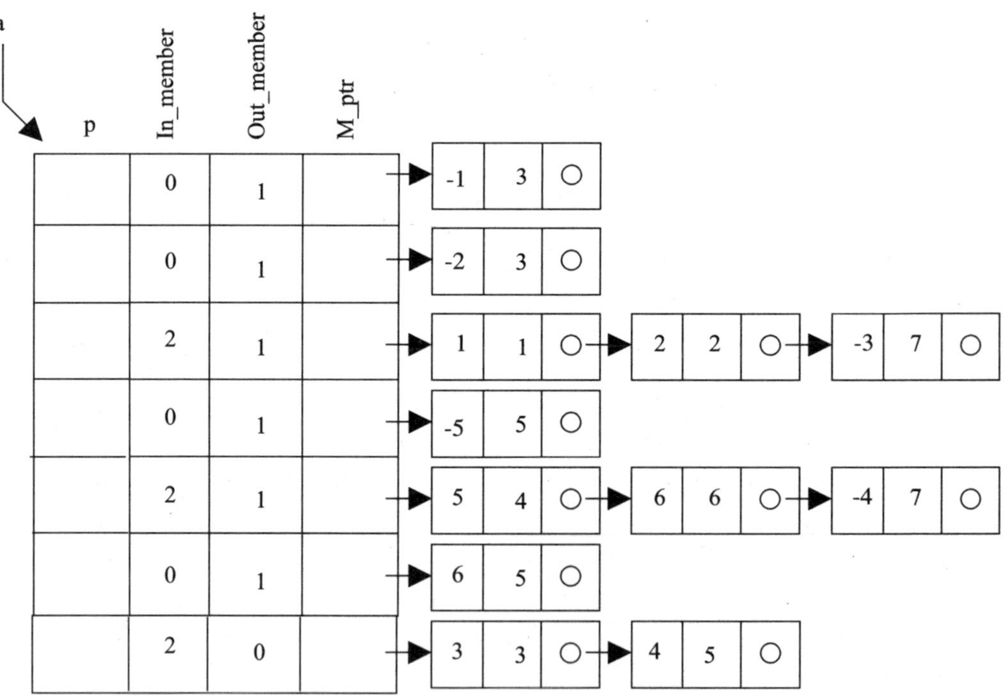

Fig. 4.23 Adjacency List for Pipe Network

```c
/* program for analysing tree type network */
#include <stdio.h>
#include< math.h>
typedef struct c_element
{
    int fore_node ;
    int back_node ;
    float q;
} c_element_type ;

typedef struct m_data
{
    int adj_member;
    int adj_joint;
} m_data_type;

typedef struct m_element
{
    m_data_type data ;
    stuct     m_element *next;
} m_element_type ;

tyepdef struct a_element
{
    float p;
    int in_member;
    int out_member;
    m_element_type *m_ptr;
    int count;
} a_element_type ;

int max_joints, max_members;
main()
{
    c_element_type *c;
    a_element_type *a;
    int I,j ;
    printf("Enter max_joints and max_members: ") ;
    scanf("%d %d", &max_joints,&max_members);
    c = (c_element_type*) malloc \ (max_members * sizeof(c_element_type));
    a = (a_element_type *) malloc \ (max_joints * sizeof(a_element_type));
```

```
        get_connectivity_list(c);
        print_connectivity_list(c);
        create_adj_list(c,a);
        print_adjacency_list (a);
        analyse_network (c,a);
        }

        /* Function to input connectivity data */
        get_connectivity(c);
        c_element_type *c;
        {
            int I;
            for(I=0; I<max_members; I++)
            {
                    printf("\n Enter fore node and back node of pipe %d \n", I+1);
                    scanf("%d %d , &(c+I)-> fore_node, & (c+I)-> back_node);
                    (c+I) -> q = 0;
}
return;
}
create_adj_list(c,a)
c_element_type *c ;
a_element_type *a;
{
m_data_type value;
int iin, iout, sum, k, I, j ;
m_element_type *pte, *p ;
get_flow ();
for(I=0; I<max_joints;I++)
{
    (a+I)->    in_member = 0;
    (a+I)->    out_member = 0;
    (a+I)->    count = 0;
    }
for (I = 0; I<max_members;I++)
{
    j = ( c+I ) -> fore_node;
    ptr = (a+j-1) -> m_ptr;
iin= (a+j-1) -> in_member;
```

```c
iout= (a+j-1) -> out_member;
sum= iin + iout;
p= ( m_element_type *) malloc (sizeof(m_element_type));
p -> data.adj_member = I+1;
p -> data.adj_joint= (c+I)-> back_node;
p -> next = NULL ;

if(sum== 0)
(a+j-1)    -> m_ptr = p;
else
{
for( k=1; k<sum; k++)
ptr= ptr ->     next
ptr ->     next = p;
}
(a+j-1) ->       in_member += 1;
j = (c + I )-> back_node;
ptr = (a+j-1)-> m_ptr;
iin= (a+j-1) ->      in_member;
iout= (a+j-1)-> out_member;
sum= iin + iout;
p= ( m_element_type *) malloc (sizeof(m_element_type));
p -> data.adj_member= -(I+1);
p -> data.adj_joint= (c+I)-> fore_node;
p -> next = NULL ;
if(sum== 0)
(a+j-1) -> m_ptr = p;
else
{
for( k=1; k<sum; k++)
ptr= ptr -> next
ptr ->     next = p;
}
(a+j-1) -> in_member += 1;
}
return;
}
/* Function to input values of nodal flow */
get_flow(a)
```

```c
a_element_type *a;
{
    int I ;
    float d;
    for(I=0; I<max_joints; I++)
{
printf( "\n Enter the value of nodal flow at node %d \n", I+1);
scanf("%f", &(a+I) ->      p);
(a+I) -> m_ptr = NULL ;
}
return;
}

/* Function to print the connectivity list */
print_connectivity_list (c)
    c_element_type *c;
    {
        int I;
        printf(" Fore node, Back node, Flow | \n");
        for(I=0; I<max_members; I++)
        {
            printf("%d %d %6.2f \n" , &(c+I)-> fore_node,&
            (c+I) -> back_node
        (c+I) -> q = 0);
    }
    return;
    }
/* Function to print the adjacency list */
print_adjacenc_list (a)
a_element_type *a ;
{
    int I;
    a_element_type *ptr ;
    m_data_type val;
    printf("\n \n \n) ;
    for(I=0; I<max_joints; I++)
    {
    printf( " %6.2f              %d        %d",
        (a+I)->      p, (a+I)->  in_member, (a+I)->     out_member);
```

```
        ptr=(a+I) ->   m_ptr;              while ( ptr != NULL)
    {
    val = ptr -> data;
    printf(" ->   [%d, %d]", val.adj_member, val.adj_joint);
    ptr = ptr ->   next;
    }
    }
    return
    }
```

The function analyse_network (c, a), which makes use of these computer representation of the pipe network problem can be written in two different ways. One way is to define a stack data structure, as described earlier in this section, and second way is to make use of the recursion feature of C programming language. The following section explains a recursive algorithm for solving the problem. At the end of the section, a recursive algorithm for the function analyse_network, is given.

Recursive Algorithm for Pipe Network Processing

One interesting point that can be noted in the pipe network problem is that, the same criterion is applied for e very joint in the pipe network during the analysis. That is, every joint is checked for the number of incoming members to be processed, so as to take a decision on the next joint. To begin with, first the sink node is tested to find whether all the incoming members have been processed or not. As they have not, the next joint is selected. It can be either 3 or 4. Let us assume that joint 3 is selected. The joint is tested for whether all the incoming members are processed. As they have not, joint 1 is selected as next joint [it can be 2 also]. Now at joint 2, since there are no incoming members unprocessed, it computes the flow in pipe 1 and joint 3 and joint 3 as next joint. It continues this check until the sink node is reached and all the incoming members at the sink node have been processed. This is the criterion for terminating the solution process. Because of this nature of the problem recursion feature can be used in programming to solve the problem.

The following function process_joint is written using the recursion. From the comparison of the two functions, one with the explicit stack data structure and other with the recursive feature, it is evident that the recursive feature of the language can very well be utilised to write simple and efficient programs, wherever it is possible to use it.

```
/* Recursion function to calculate the flow through each pipe and the total flow
 at sink node*/
    process_joint (joint)
    int joint ;
    {
    int pipe_member, I , next_joint ;
    m_element_type *temp, *ptr ;
```

```
   if(joint == sink_node && (a+joint-1)-> in_member == 0 )
 return ;
 else
 {
 ptr = (a+joint-1)->      m_ptr ;
 if(ptr -> data.p_flag == 1)
 ptr= ptr->          next;
 if ( a+ joint - 1) ->    in_member == 0)
 {
 pipe_member = -(ptr -> data.adj_member);
 next_joint = ptr -> data.adj_joint;
 ptr ->    =data. P_flag = 1;
 (a+joint - 1)->    out_member -= 1 ;
 (c+pipe_member -1)->q = (a+joint-1)->   p;
 (a+next_joint-1)->        p+= (c+ pipe_member - 1)->      q:
 process_joint ( next_joint) :
 else
 {
 while ( ptr->     data.adj_member < 0 || ptr -> data.p_flag==1)
 ptr = ptr ->      next;
 next_joint = ptr ->        data.adj_joint;
 ptr ->    data.p_flag =1;
 (a+joint -1 ) -> in_member -= 1;
 process_joint (next_joint);
 }
 }
 }
```

To use this function, first call the process_joint function with the joint as sink node. The program recursively calls the same function again and again and completes the solution when all the incoming pipes at the sink node are processed. It can be noticed that the first execution statement in the function is the termination criterion. i.e., To terminate the solution process, the joint should be the sink node and (a+joint − 1) - >in_member, i.e., the unprocessed incoming members must be zero. The main program has to be written to call this recursive function and is given below.

```
/*function analyse_network which calls the recursive function process_joint */
analyse_network ( c, a)
c_element_type *c;
a_element_type *a;
```

```
{
        int sink_node, I;
        for(I=0; I<max_joints; I++)
        {
            if( ( a+I ) -> out_member = = 0)
                    sink_node = I+1 ;
        }
        process_joint ( sink_node ) ;
}
```

The above two example problems illustrate the use of data structures in program design and implementation. Only simple problems are selected here for the purpose of illustrating the use of data structuring in problem solving using computers. The determinate truss is a very simple engineering example, where the fundamental equations of forces of statics are used for solution. But the solution process depends on a sequence. The queue data structure properly simulates the required sequence in programming. The truss analysis problem illustrates the use of this data structure.

The second example problem, the pipe network for a storm sewer runoff system requires another kind of sequence, which is different from the truss problem. This is achieved either by using stack processing techniques or by using recursion. Stacks are powerful data structures that can be used to simulate this kind of sequence, which is very common in many engineering problems. The same problem also brought out the use of another interesting and very useful feature viz. Recursion. FORTRAN has been the conventional language used by engineering programmers, and it does not have the recursion capability. Hence, long programs were written for many applications, which can now be written in a more efficient way using the recursive techniques. Another interesting point that is observed here is the same numerical and computer model for representation of both the problems. The Graph or Network model is used to represent the truss as well as the pipe network problem. In both the cases, two lists, viz., connectivity and adjacency lists are used to completely represent the problem in the computer. The only difference in the second problem was that the direction of flow has to be represented. This is achieved by putting a negative sign to the adjacent_member. This once again illustrates the use of abstract data types and their use in program design and implementation. List, Stack and Queue are the three abstract data types used in the two example problems. The problem as a whole is represented as a graph or network data object, in the form of a set of lists. Graph is not explicitly used as an abstract data type with representative operations like create_graph( ), creaet_connetivity_list (c), create_adjacency_list(a) etc. In the above two examples, two totally different physical problems are represented using the graph model. There are many problems in engineering where modelling can be achieved using this model. The truss as well as the pipe network problem physically look like a network, with nodes and arcs or members. Many other problems which do not look like a network can also be modelled using a graph. To illustrate this statement consider the following problem, where it is required to design a signal system for the traffic junction shown Fig. 4.24. [1]

162

Example 4.6

This is a five legged junction with constraints of one way traffic on two legs namely B and D as shown in Fig. 4.24. There are 13 turns possible at this intersection. Some pair of turns can be carried out simultaneously, while others cause turns to cross and therefore cannot be carried out simultaneously. There are conflicts like crossing, diverging and converging ones. The traffic engineers are asked to study this problem and propose an optimum signalling system for the traffic intersection. Even though the physical problem does not look like a network as in the case of the truss and pipe network, the mathematical model graph (network) can be used to obtain an optimum phase diagram to design the signalling system. The problem can be modelled as explained below. The graph representation of the problem is shown in the Fig. 4.25

The vertices (nodes) represent the turns and the edges (similar to members in the truss problem). Connect pairs of vertices whose turns cannot be performed simultaneously. First assume that, AC and CA will be operated simultaneously. Now, AC and AD cannot operate at the same time, hence connect AC and AD. Similarly, AC and BD cannot operate simultaneously, connect them.

This figure has vertices and edges and hence can be called a graph. As we know that there are many ways that the graph can be represented in the computer. Either similar to the truss problem i.e., in the form of connectivity and adjacency lists or in the form of an adjacency matrix. This will be decided by the solution process. Let us analyse the present problem and find out which graph representation is ideal for this. Colouring algorithms can be used in the present case to obtain an optimum phase diagram from the given graph. A colouring algorithm assigns a colour to each vertex of the graph so that two vertices connected by an edge will not have the same colour. The graph is to be coloured using as few colours as possible to get an

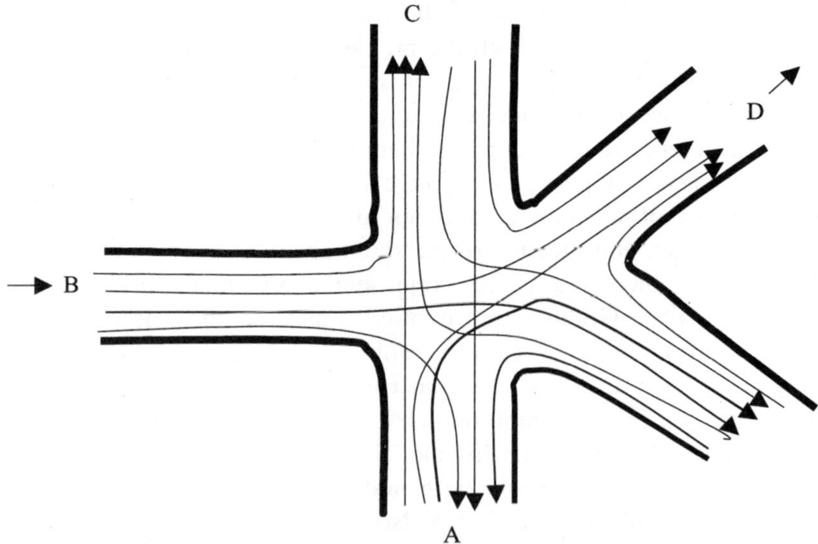

Fig. 4.24 A Five Legged Traffic Intersection

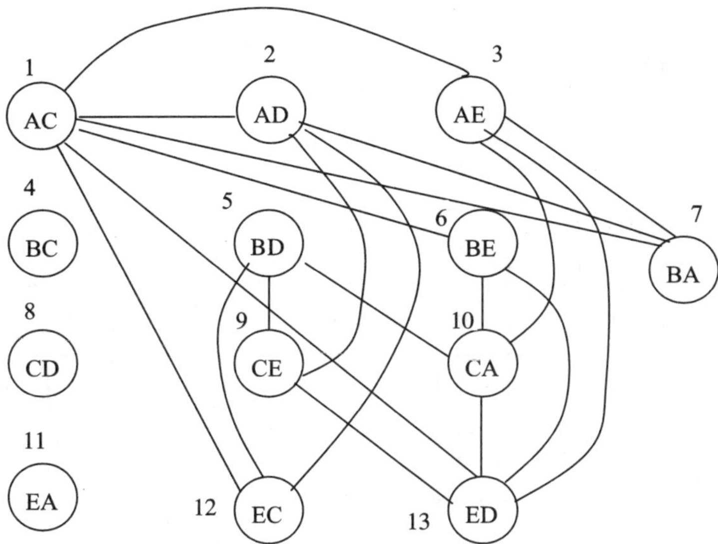

Fig. 4.25   Graph Representation of Signal Design Problem

optimum solution. In the present problem the information that is required of the graph is only the connectivity. An adjacency matrix can be used to represent this problem. An adjacency matrix is a square matrix with a number of rows and columns, where n is the number of vertices in the network. A non-zero entry in the matrix indicates an edge between the vertex corresponding to the row and vertex corresponding to the column in the matrix. The adjacency matrix for the present graph is shown in Fig. 4.26. The matrix contains only zeros and ones as entries. A 1 in row i and j. The matrix is a square matrix with size equal to number of turns.

```
greedy_coloring ( a, clr)
{

        for ( each uncoloured vertex in the graph)
            if ( vertex v is not adjacent to any vertex in clr)
                colour the vertex v;

}
```

The greedy's colouring algorithm shown above is used to arrive at a solution to the signal design problem. The algorithm initially colour as many vertices as possible with the first colour, then as many as possible of the uncoloured vertices with the second colour, and so on. But depending on which vertex is coloured first the number of phases and the turns in each phase may vary. Given a colour, the algorithm searches the adjacency matrix and carries out colouring depending on the entries in the matrix. The program can be refined and finally written in C programming language and implemented. The following is a complete program which creates the adjacency matrix, and completes the colouring. The program can be

	1	2	3	4	5	6	7	8	9	10	11	12	13
1	0	1	1	0	1	1	1	0	0	0	0	1	1
2	1	0	0	0	0	1	1	0	1	1	0	1	1
3	1	0	0	0	0	1	1	0	1	1	0	1	1
4	0	0	0	0	0	0	0	0	0	0	0	0	0
5	1	1	1	0	0	0	0	0	1	1	0	1	1
6	1	1	0	0	1	0	1	0	0	1	0	0	1
7	1	1	1	0	1	1	0	0	1	1	0	0	0
8	0	0	0	0	0	0	0	0	0	0	0	0	0
9	0	1	1	0	1	1	1	0	0	0	0	1	1
10	0	1	1	0	1	1	1	0	0	0	0	1	1
11	0	0	0	0	0	0	0	0	0	0	0	0	0
12	1	1	1	0	1	1	0	0	1	1	0	0	0
13	1	1	1	0	1	1	0	0	1	1	0	0	0

Fig.4.26 Adjacency Matrix for Signal Design Problem

followed easily, hence a detailed explanation is not given. One solution for the above problem is given at the end of the program.

```c
/* program to apply Greedy coloring algorithm to resolve conflicts at an
intersection */
#include<stdio.h>
typedef struct color_list
{
int stream ;
```

```c
struct color_list *next ;
} color_list_type ;
int * adjacency ;
int * stream;
int max_streams;
int stream_count = 0;
color_list_type *front, *color_list_ptr;
FILE *inp;
main(0
{
int I;
inp = fopen ( "greedy.in", "r");
printf("Give total no of traffic strams:");
fsacnf(inp, "%d", &max_streams *max_streams * sixeof(int));
get_adjacency();
stream = (int * ) malloc(max_streams * sizeof(int));
create_stream_list();
do
{
for( I=0; I< max_streams && *(stream + I) != 0 ; I++);
if(I< max_streams)
{
            greedy_coloring(I) ;
            print_color_list();
}
while(I < max_stramms);
}
get_adjacency()
{
int I,j;
for(I=0; I<max_streams ; I++ )
{
            printf(" Enter row %d of Adjacency matrix : \n", I+1);
            for(j=0; j < max_strams ; j++)
                fscanf(inp, "%d" , adjacency + I * max_streams +j);
}
return;
}
create_stream_list()
```

166

```c
{
int I;
for(I=0 ; I < max_streams ; I++)
*(stream + I) = 0;
return;
}
color(1)

int 1;
{
 *(stream + 1) = 1;
 return;
}
gredy_coloring(I)
int I;
{
int j;
create_color_list();
for ( j=0 ; j< max_streams ; j++
{
          if (* (adjacency + I * max_streams + j) == 0)
          {
            append_list(j) ;
            color(j) ;
          }
}
return;
}
create_color_list()
{
          color_list_ptr = (color_list_type * )
          malloc (sizeof(color_list_type)) ;
color_list_ptr-> next = NULL ;
front = color_list_ptr ;
}
append_list (j)
int j;
{
color_list_ptr-> next = (color_list_type * )
```

```
malloc ( sizeof(color_list_type));
color_list_ptr-> next-> strem = j+1;
color_list_ptr          -> next -> next = =NULL;
color_list_ptr = color_list_ptr-> next;
return;
}
print_color_list()
{
color_list_type       * ptr;
printf ( "\n Traffic streams in phase %d :\n", ++stream_count);
ptr = front -> next;
do
{
printf(" %d " , ptr -> stream);
ptr = ptr -> next;
}
while( ptr != NULL);
printf("\n\n");
}
```

The input data for the program is the adjacency matrix and the output is the list of turns in different phases. The output for the problem shown is shown below.

Traffic streams in Phase 1	:	1	4	8	9	10	11
Traffic streams in Phase 2	:	2	3	4	5	8	11
Traffic streams in Phase 3	:	3	4	6	8	9	11
Traffic streams in Phase 4	:	4	7	8	11	12	13

This solution may not be the optimum one. The idea here is only to illustrate the use of computer models for problem solving. Eventhough, the physical problem does not look like a network or graph, still it can be modelled as a graph for the purpose of easy and efficient solution. This problem also illustrates the implementation of graph data object in the form of adjacency matrix instead of adjacency list and connectivity list.

Example 4.7

Fig. 4.27 shows an activity network with nodes numbered. Such an activity network can be represented in a computer in many ways. An activity network is primarily used to find out the longest path from the start node to the finish node, which is nothing but the critical path. In the process of computing critical path, many other associated information like early start time, early finish time, late start time, late finish time, slack of different activities etc. can also be computed. Also the same computer representation can be used for further processing like resource allocation, resource leveling etc.

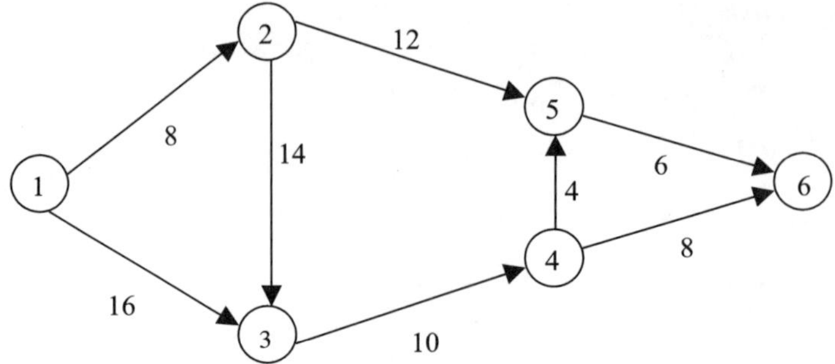

Fig. 4.27   An Activity Network

The idea of the present description of the activity network problem is only to illustrate the different representation schemes that can be adopted to solve the problem. One of the easiest and obvious representation scheme is using the graph or network model. All the data pertaining to the activity network can be represented in adjacency and connectivity lists. The way these lists are formed is exactly similar to that discussed in examples 4.1 and 4.2. A tree model also can be used to represent this problem. Fig. 4.28 shows the representation of the activity network in the form of a tree.

It can be seen from Fig. 4.28 that the root node is the start node and all the terminal nodes are the finish node, i.e, 6. There are five leaf nodes in the tree, which implies that there are altogether five possible different paths from start to finish. To find out which is the longest path, one can search through the tree and compare various lengths. In that case same part of the tree is traversed many times, which is a waste. To avoid it a stack can be used to search the tree. A typical stack element can be written as shown below.

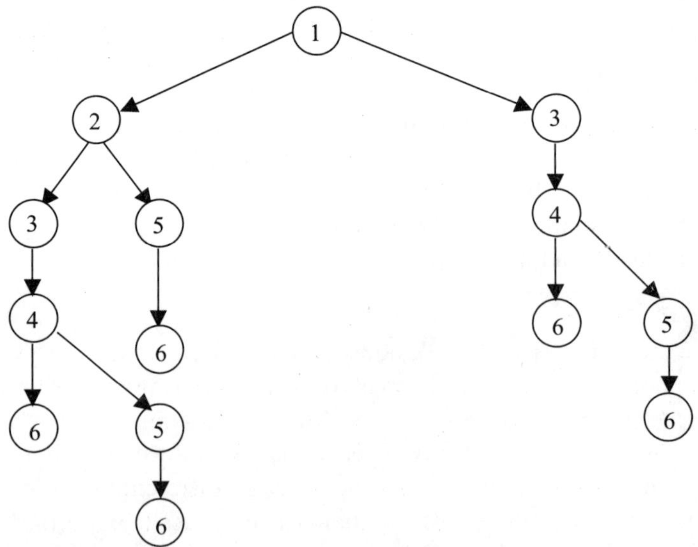

Fig. 4.28   Tree Representation of Activity Network

```
struct stack_element
{          int node;
           int length;
};
```

Here node is the current node and length, the current length of the path from the root. A recursive algorithm also can be written to find the critical path and related information from the activity network. The details of the algorithm and program are not included here, and it is left as an exercise to the readers.

This chapter described the concepts of data structures and programming techniques. Just like any engineering product, computer programs are also end products, which are used by consumers for carrying out computations and other engineering or commercial activities. The programs developed for Computer Aided Engineering are used as design tools by engineers, researchers and designers. Just like the amount of care that is put into for the design and manufacture/construction of design tools, it is very much essential that extreme care is exercised during design and implementation of a computer program, to get the desired results from them. Also the performance of the programs very much depends on the way they are designed and implemented. Whenever computer programs are designed, the design should be kept as open and modular as possible such that any future modifications and additions can be carried out without much difficulty. The techniques described in this chapter to organise and manipulate data provide the readers an introduction to the subject. For more details, other books may be referred, which are enumerated below.

References

1. Aho, A.V., Hopcroft, J.E. and Ullman, J.D., (1985), Data Structures and Algorithms, Addison-Wesley Publishing Company, USA.
2. Berry, J.T., (1986), Advanced Programming, A Brady Book, Prentice Hall Press, New York, USA.
3. Horowitz, E. and Sahni, S., (1983) Fundamentals of Data Structures, Galgotia Book Source, New Delhi, India.
4. Lipschutz,S., (1986), Theory and Problems of Data Structures, Schaum's Outline Series, McGraw-Hill, New York, USA.
5. Roski, S., (1985), Data Structures on IBM PCs, Brady Communication Company Inc., New York, USA.
6. Tremblay, J.P. and Sorenson, P.G., (1984), An Introduction to Data Structures with Applications, 2nd Ed., McGraw-Hill Book Co., Singapore.
7. Van Wyk, C.J., (1988), Data Structures and C Programs, Addison – Wesley Publishing Co., Reading, Mass., USA.

Exercises

1. What are the properties of data? Explain the term Abstract Data Type.

2. What are the circumstances in which linked implementation of list is more desirable compared to an array implementation?

3. Rewrite the function create_list, insert and delete for linked list without header cell. Write also the main program to test the above functions.

4. What are the basic differences between the abstract data types stack and queue? Describe with at least two examples the use of these abstract data types in engineering problem solving.

5. Write the functions create_queue, enqueue and dequeue for a circular array implementation of queue. Write a main program to test these functions written.

6. Network or graph model can be used to represent many problems in Engineering. Explain with neat sketches, the data structures to represent a network model in a computer. Illustrate the above representation with any one engineering problem of your choice. Write necessary functions to read the input data for the above problem.

7. Explain the abstract data type tree. Name two problems in engineering where the tree representation of the problem is very helpful in efficiently solving it. Write an algorithm in pseudo language first and then corresponding function in C programming language to solve the problems.

8. Explain with neat sketches the three different representations of abstract data type tree. Also write functions for a few representative operations in each of the above.

9. Using any one of the three representation schemes write a program to determine the height of a given node in a tree.

10. What are binary trees? Explain how binary search trees are created. Write an algorithm and corresponding function to create a binary search tree, delete a node from and locate a given element in a binary search tree.

11. Write a complete program to represent a three dimensional frame as a network incorporating all the necessary data to analyse the frame to compute the deformation of all the joints and forces in all beam and column members.

12. A truss is represented as a network in the form of connectivity list and adjacency list. Write a function to delete a joint and a member in the truss so that the corresponding lists arc simultaneously updated.

13. To find out whether the solution obtained using the greedy's colouring algorithm for the traffic intersection problem is optimum or not, it is necessary to compute the k-clique of the network. Write a program to compute the k-clique for the network representation in the form of adjacency matrix.

14. A transportation network is given with one-way constraints on a few selected road segments. Write a program to represent the road network in the form of a tree for finding out the minimum path from given origin to destination.

15. A pile foundation for a large structure consists of many piles and they are interconnected. The vertical loads from the structure are transmitted to the foundation through the pile caps. It is required to analyse the pile system. Design a suitable data structure to represent the pile foundation system with the structural as well as soil data.

16. In a finite element analysis program it is required to have a combination of element and joint load cases. A structure load case specifies factored combination of an element load case and a joint load case. The factors for element and joint load case can be different. Design a suitable data structure to represent the element loads and joint loads which is to be used properly forming a load vector for specific structure load cases. Write an algorithm in pseudo language to form the load vector for every structure load case.

17. The floor system of a multistoried building is of beam and slab type. All the slab panels are rectangular and the position of cross beams vary from one bay to another. A typical such system is shown in figure 3.29. It is required to compute the load coming on the beams from the slabs. Design a suitable data structure to represent the problem and develop an algorithm to compute the loads on beams.

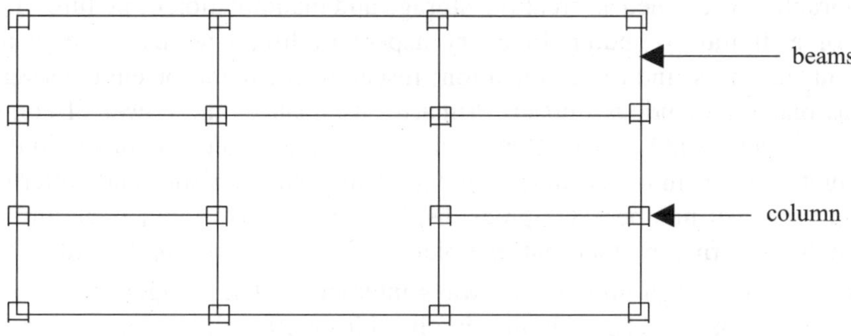

Fig. 3.29   Exercise 17

18. A plate is to be analysed using finite difference method. Represent the descretized plate model as a network. Develop an algorithm to generate the simultaneous equations by finite difference technique. Assume the plate to be simply supported on all the edges.

19. The Bala's additive algorithm for zero-one integer programming consists of generating a tree structure for solving the problem. Write a recursive program for integer programming using Bala's additive technique.

20. Dynamic programming is a technique to solve multistage problems. It consists of specifying the optimum value at any given stage in terms of the optimum value till the last stage. Use the recursive feature of C programming language to write a program to compute the shortest path in a network using dynamic programming technique.

CHAPTER 5

Computer Graphics

5.1 INTRODUCTION

Computer Graphics is defined as creation, storage and manipulation of pictures and drawings by means of a digital computer. In every aspect of life, whether it be in advertising, entertainment, business, industry, education, research, medicine or engineering, computer graphics has made tremendous impact. Primarily it enhances the power of communication between the computer and its users. Representation of a huge set of numbers in the form of a graph or a picture helps in better understanding of the characteristics and pattern of the data contained in the set of numbers. Graphics displays also improve understanding of complex systems, which reaffirms the fact that one picture is worth a thousand words.

The engineering design process is always interactive. The designer first puts down his idea on a sheet of paper, and keeps improving it till it satisfies all the necessary requirements. During the process of improvement, the designer may have to do a large amount of computation and the effects of the results of computation on the model have to be evaluated, so that the improvement could be well suggested. The traditional tools for design like paper, pencil and calculators, which act as an extension to the brain of the designer, are passive in nature. A computer with a good amount of graphics capability helps the designer in developing his ideas, carrying out complex computations, presenting the results of computation for the designer to take decision on improvement, and immediately presenting the modified model for evaluation. Interactive computer graphics helps the designer a great deal in his design process. In a computer aided design environment, the traditional tools of design are replaced by computer systems with interactive graphics capabilities, that are more active and dynamic, so that the designer can carry out experiments with the computer model of his ideas, towards search for better designs.

Computer graphics is used at every stage of design process, whether may it be for preliminary design, analysis, evaluation, detailed design or drafting. As one cannot think of CAD without graphics, knowledge of computer graphics is essential to carry out CAD. This chapter presents a comprehensive overview of computer graphics with a brief introduction to the essential hardware requirements, basic principles of computer graphics, manipulation of images, geometric modelling and finally programming for computer graphics. Programming examples are given in C to demonstrate the concepts of graphics programming using Graphical Kernel System (GKS), which is now the international standard for graphics functionality.

5.2 GRAPHICS DEVICES

The graphics capabilities of a computer system basically depend on the hardware attached to it and also on the support software available. Even alpha-numeric display units and letter printers can be used to generate images. The quality of such images is sufficient in some applications. But engineering design applications demand high quality graphics images. Additional devices are required to produce such high quality images. Many graphics output devices are available now with varying capabilities to display images and produce engineering drawings.

As engineering design is an activity, where the model generated based on the ideas of the designer, has to be modified often to improve the quality of design, it is very important to have a good communication between the graphics systems and the designer. Most of the time, the interaction that the designer needs, is either locating, selecting, or picking in nature. To do such operations suitable hardware devices are necessary. A variety of graphics input devices are available, which can be attached to graphics systems.

5.2.1 Output Devices

These are devices on which the images generated by computer graphics are displayed, so that the designer can examine them. Four different types of graphics output devices are generally used. They are:

1. CRT displays
2. Pen Plotters
3. Ink-jet Plotters
4. Dot Matrix Printers

CRT displays are softcopy devices, whereas the other three devices are hardcopy devices. Displays are of temporary nature in a softcopy device. The image that is presented on a CRT display can be dynamically modified, erased or regenerated. On hardcopy devices images are generated on paper and dynamic modification of images drawn is not possible. But a drawing displayed on a hardcopy device can be used for further activities.

5.2.1.1 CRT displays

This display device works on the principle of Cathode Ray Tube (CRT). In a cathode ray tube, there is a cathode, which when heated emits continuous stream of electrons. The flow of these electrons is controlled by a grid surrounding the cathode and this grid focusses these electrons into a beam. This electron beam sweeps across the phosphor, so as to retain the display till the next time the beam is focussed. To control the brightness of the pictures generated, the current of the electron beam is regulated and varied.

Basically there are two types of CRTs available, based on the techniques with which images are generated. They are vector drawing (stroke writing) and raster scan. The vector drawing technique generates images by drawing lines connecting two given points. In raster scan techniques a matrix of closely spaced dots is used to form images. Images generated using line drawing technique will be sharper compared to the one with the raster scan. In the case of raster scan technique a line is formed by making bright those dots in the matrix, which lie very close to the shortest path connecting the two end points of the line. Depending on the number of dots available in the matrix and the size of dots that can be displayed, it will not always be possible to get all the dots in a line to lie exactly on the shortest path. Some dots may lie exactly on the line, while some dots will have only part of the dot on the line. This will make the line look like a stepped line instead of a sharp straight line.

Once the pictures are generated either by vector drawing or raster scan techniques, it has to be retained on the screen's phosphor coating. The duration of time that a phosphor continues to glow after it is excited by the electron beam is called persistence. As the persistence is very short, it is necessary to retain the images generated for more time. A storage tube physically retains the image generated until it is erased, whereas a refreshed tube continuously regenerates the image at some frequency.

CRT displays made of direct view storage tubes (DVST) create images by drawing vectors or line segments. During the initial years of development of computer graphics, i.e., in the early 1960s, displays made of DVSTs were very popular. A major disadvantage of DVSTs in interactive computer graphics is its inability to selectively erase parts of image from the screen. To erase a line segment from displayed image, one had to first erase the complete image and then redraw it, by omitting the line segment to be erased. This technology brought down the popularity of DVSTs in interactive computer graphics. The resolution of a display with storage tube was very high and up to 4000 displayable points on an 19 inch screen was possible. As it was also a vector drawing device, and had high resolution, the images were sharp and had crisp edges. And also, the images were retained till they were erased, hence the displayed images were generally flicker free.

Raster scan displays are more popular in computer graphics, and is the present *de-facto* standard for CRT displays. The viewing surface of a raster scan display unit has a matrix of tiny picture elements. Every display has a finite number of picture elements in both horizontal and vertical directions. The size of these picture elements is the size of the smallest dot that can be displayed on the viewing surface. These picture elements are often referred to as pixels. Every pixel on the viewing surface can be uniquely addressed by referring to its position in the matrix by specifying the row and the column. Brightness or colour of each one of these pixels can be controlled by using a hardware device, called display controller.

The number of picture elements or pixels that are available on the viewing surface of a display unit gives a qualitative idea on the sharpness of the image generated. This measure of pixels is called the resolution. The resolution of a viewing surface can be specified in two ways; either by giving the number of pixels in horizontal direction, number of pixels in vertical direction and the diagonal size of the screen or by giving the number of pixels per unit length in horizontal direction and the number of pixels per unit length in vertical direction. Typically the display surfaces commonly used in CAD workstations now-a-days has the range of about 640 x 480 pixels on a 14" diagonal monitor to 1280 x 1024 pixels on an 19" diagonal monitor. CRT displays with resolution as high as 4096 x 4096 on a 19" monitor are also available, which are used for some specialised applications. The resolution mentioned in the previous discussion gives only one kind of measure, i.e the sharpness of the image generated. There is another measure, which gives an idea of the number of colours or different levels of brightness that can be generated. It is also required to know about the quality of the image generated. The number of memory bits that are associated with every pixel is a measure of this quality. The measure of pixels on a display surface is called spatial resolution and the measure of number of bits associated with every pixel is called tonal resolution. The spatial and tonal resolutions together give a clear indication on the quality of images generated.

As already discussed earlier, the raster scan displays are of a refresh type, i.e., the image is regenerated many times in a second display surface from left to right. The colour or intensity of a pixel is controlled by the momentary intensity of the beam, which continuously changes depending on the information stored in the memory bit associated with the pixels. When the beam completes scanning one line, it is turned off and quickly brought to the beginning of the next line, and then turned on to continue scanning as before. Once all the lines are scanned from top to bottom, again the beam is turned off and returned to the beginning of first scan line. The frequency at which the scanning of raster lines are to be carried out is decided by the persistence of the phosphor coating on the display surface. Generally, it so happens that the refresh rate and the persistence of the phosphor coating may not match. Then the top parts of the images get faded, while the beam scans the bottom part of the image. This gives rise to flickering of images. To overcome this difficulty a technique of interlaced scanning is used, where the beam scans all the odd numbered lines from top to bottom first and then the even numbered lines. i.e. During every refresh cycle, the screen is scanned twice. To prevent flickering, the screen is scanned anywhere between 30 to 65 times a second. Higher frequency scanning produce less flicker of images. The spatial resolution of raster scan CRT displays are relatively low when compared to the displays with DVSTs. This makes the diagonal lines in the image generated appear jagged or stepped on refresh tubes, as these are point plotting devices. Every image in raster scan displays is composed of a set of dots and lines, which are displayed by making those dots bright which lie as close as possible to the shortest path between the end points of the line. Fig.5.1 shows a typical CAD workstation with a high- resolution color graphics monitor.

5.2.1.2 Pen Plotters

Pen plotters are hard copy devices. Once an image is generated on a pen plotter, it cannot be erased. Plotters are the most popular kind of hard copy devices. Two types of plotters are quite common. They are: flat bed plotters and drum plotters. In flat bed plotters, the drawing surface, i.e., the paper is stationary and the pen moves in both x and y directions. The paper is fixed on a flat bed. A moving arm carrying the pen moves in one direction and the pen moves along the arm in the other direction. These two movements make it possible for the pen to move anywhere on the paper fixed on to the plotter. Most of the flat bed plotters have facilities

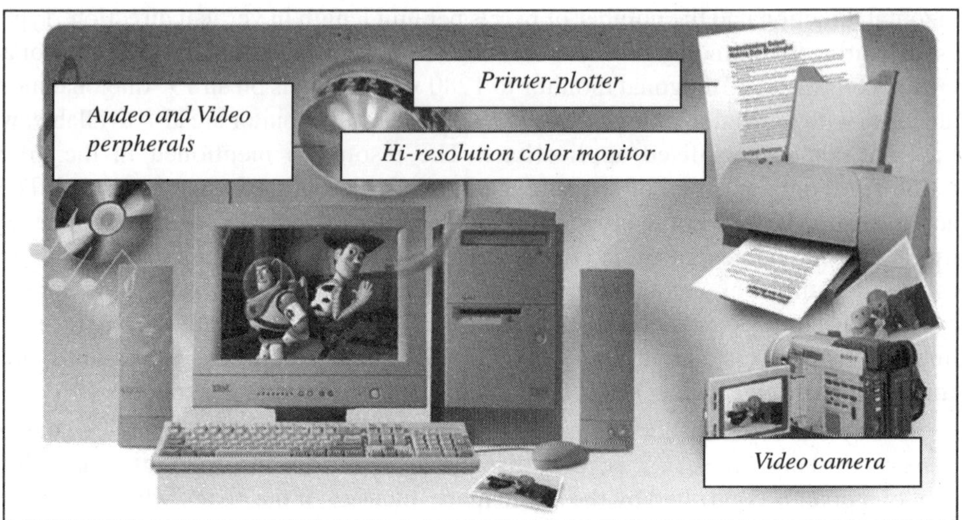

Fig. 5.1 Graphic Workstation and Peripherals

to use more than one pen. The pens are fixed on the plotter in the slots made for it and the moving arm picks one pen at a time. After completing the drawing with the pen currently in use, it is put back in the respective slot and another pen is taken to continue drawing. These plotters are generally intelligent and can be programmed for different graphics actions, like drawing lines, circles, splines and selecting pens etc. Depending on the requirements of the drawing, either pens with different colours can be used or pens with different line thicknesses can be used. Electrostatic means are generally employed to hold the paper down while plotting. Flat bed plotters are generally costly compared to drum plotters. Flat bed plotters are preferred to drum plotters, as they resemble the manual drafting table. With recent developments these flat bed plotters are mostly of the ink-jet type with two or three color tanks manipulating colours and shades. Fig. 5.2 shows a typical ink-jet plotter. Ink-jet plotters are hardcopy devices, where images are produced by combining dots instead of lines. i.e., these are point plotting devices. When drawings with large number of lines are to be prepared, the speed at which the pen plotters generate the drawing is very slow. The ink-jet plotters produce drawings at a faster rate at the expense of the quality of the drawing produced. The quality of drawings is reduced due to the point plotting nature of the ink-jet plotters. Drawings with different colours can be generated by using inks of different colours.

In a drum type plotter, a roller or a drum is rotated by a stepper motor and the paper which is fixed on to the drum moves in one direction in a reciprocating manner, as shown in Fig. 5.3. A pen fixed on to a pen carriage moves in a perpendicular direction to that of the paper. Both these movements together make it possible to position the pen anywhere on the plotter. Multiple pens can be used in these plotters also as in the case of flat bed plotters. Paper is held down to the drum by generally mechanical means. Drum plotters are inexpensive compared to the flat bed plotters. They occupy less floor area.

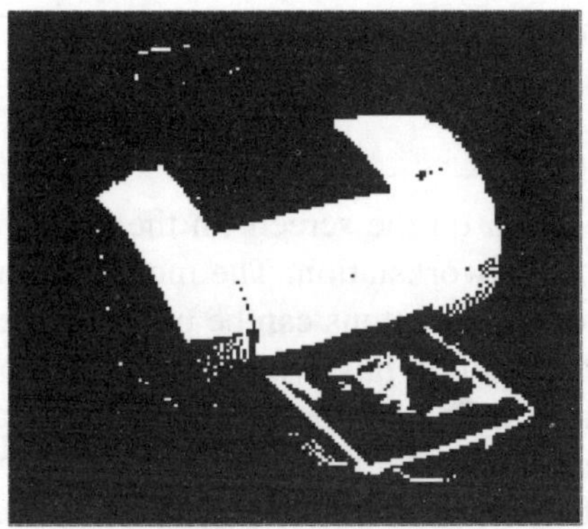

Fig. 5.2   Ink-jet plotter

Fig. 5.3   Drum Plotter

Pens used in both types of plotters are similar. Different types of pens are available for use with plotters. Some are discarded when the ink gets exhausted, whereas, some other type of pens can be refilled and reused. The cost of production of drawings can be brought down if reusable type of pens are used.

5.2.1.3 Dot Matrix Printers

Dot matrix printers are also used to prepare graphics output. Similar to the ink-jet plotters, dot matrix printer is also a point plotting device. The mechanical operation of a dot matrix printer is similar to that of an ink-jet plotter. The paper is fixed onto a roller by mechanical means and the roller is rotated, so that the paper moves in vertical direction. A print head consisting of an array of needless hit against the paper through an inked ribbon produces dots on the paper. The print head moves horizontally to position the dots anywhere on the paper fixed on to the roller. Dot matrix printers are relatively cheap graphics output devices, compared to plotters. Nowadays, ribbons with different colours are available so that hardcopies of images with colours can be produced using dot matrix printers.

5.2.2 Input Devices

Graphics input devices help users to input information to graphics programs running in the computer system. One can interact with the images displayed on the screen using graphics input devices: Commonly used graphics input devices are:

1. Keyboard
2. Mouse
3. Digitizer
4. Light pen

5.2.2.1 Keyboard

The most commonly used input device is the key board. Many keyboards have special programmable keys over and above the regular alpha-numeric keys. These special keys can be programmed for some standard input data, thus improve the user interface of the CAD system.

5.2.2.2 Mouse

Mouse is a locator device used to control cursor location on the screen. In the photograph shown in Fig. 5.1 a three button mouse is connected to a workstation. The mouse generally comes with a varying number of buttons. Each one of these buttons can be programmed for different input values. Mouse works on any smooth table top. It has two rollers located on its base, one fixed perpendicular to the other. When it is rolled on the table top the relative positions of the rollers are converted to electronic signals and the position of a cursor associated with the mouse on the screen is moved. The movement of a mouse on the table top thus moves a cursor on the screen for drawing and menu selection. As only the movement of rollers make the cursor to move, picking up the mouse and relocating it on the table top will not affect the position of the cursor on the screen.

Another type of mouse generally used with many CAD systems have a base plate. In this case the base of the mouse will not have any rollers. The base generates a magnetic field and circuitry in the mouse interprets its relative position on the base and position the cursor on the screen. The mouse provide better coordination between the eye and hands of the user of the CAD systems to input data to graphics programs.

5.2.2.3 Digitizer

A digitizer is an input device used for inputting a series of x-y coordinate pairs. In a CAD environment, digitizers are mainly used for two functions, viz., inputting maps and drawings into the system and for creating tablet menus. Sometimes these are used just as locating devices like mice. The stylus of the digitizer acts as the mouse. Typical accuracies of digitizers vary from 0.005" to 0.05". Digitizers are available in different sizes.

5.2.2.4 Lightpen

A light pen is a pen like input device, which works on the principle of photoelectricity. It is activated by depressing its tip against the screen. On activation, it sends back to the computer the location of the illuminated pixel in its field of view. A pixel must be lit up in order to pick it up using a light pen.

5.2.2.5 Scanner

A present day popular input device used for inputting directly images is the scanner, which converts a page into an array of dots depending on the resolution of the scanner. These dots are converted to pixels by a software so that they can be used as inputs.

5.2.2.6 Touch screen and voice input

Sophistications in technology have brought in human interaction through touch and voice Means. In touch screen mode the monitor has touch sensitive material coated on it and any word or icon or image on the screen can activate a programme by physically touching it.

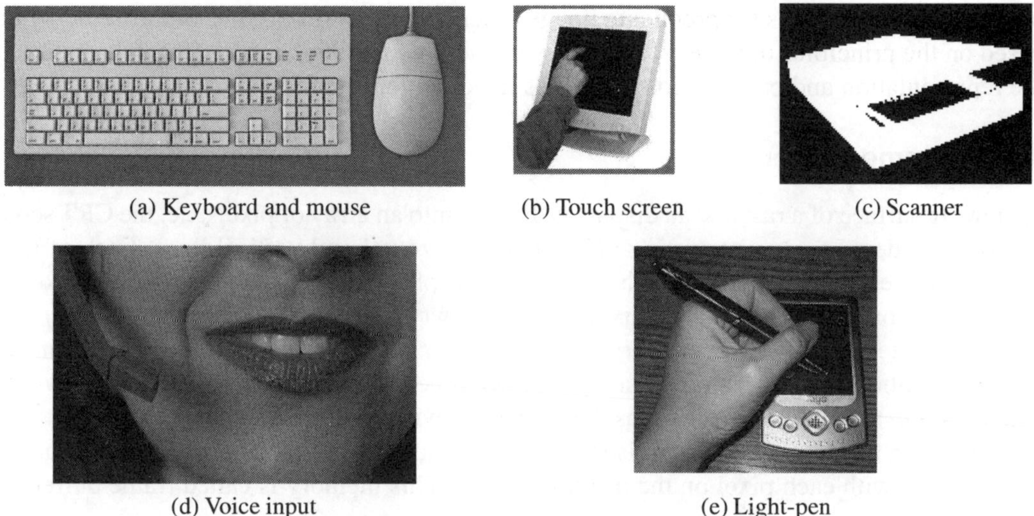

(a) Keyboard and mouse (b) Touch screen (c) Scanner

(d) Voice input (e) Light-pen

Fig. 5.4 Typical Input Devices

Similarly oral commands can be given through mike and a voice recognition software helps in translating the command as inputs. Fig. 4.4 shows typical input devices.

5.3 REPRESENTATION OF IMAGES IN COMPUTERS

For better understanding of computer graphics, it is necessary to know more about the representation of images in computer graphics. It may be observed that an image is finally represented in computers only in the form of bits. Now let us examine how pictures can be transferred into a form that can be represent in binary digits, so that they can directly be stored in a computer.

5.3.1 Converting Images into Binary Form

Any image, say an engineering drawing can be visualised as a collection of straight lines, curves and text matter. A proper combination and layout of the above three entities produces pictures. Going one step further, a line, arc or an alpha-numeric text can be formed by a collection of dots. A line consists of a set of dots lying on the shortest path connecting its end points. Similarly an arc is also a collection of dots lying on the trajectory of the arc. The position of the dots can be found out using the parameters associated with the arc. The parameters can be a combination of one or more of the following: radius, initial angle, ending angle, three points lying on the arc. The parameters associated with the line are the x-y coordinates of the two end points of the line. Similarly, any alpha-numeric text can be constructed by combining lines and curves. The above discussion leads to the conclusion that any image – an engineering drawing or a picture – can be represented as a set of dots put at appropriate locations. Now it is sufficient to understand how a dot can be represented in the computer, to know about image representation. Most of the present day CAD systems use only raster scan displays for producing images. Hence, further discussion on this topic will be based on the principles of raster scan display units, which will give sufficient information on the representation and presentation of images in computer graphics.

5.3.2 Frame Buffer

A viewing surface of a raster scan display is divided into an array of pixels. i.e. the CRT screen can be considered as one consisting of a grid of horizontal and vertical lines. Each of these horizontal lines are made up of pixels. Consider a display surface, where a pixel can take two states, either bright or dark. As the pixel takes only two states, it is quite easy to represent this in the computer memory. The memory of the computer is a collection of bits and a bit can take any value either 0 or 1. 1 can be assigned for brightness and 0 for darkness. To achieve this every pixel in the viewing screen must be associated with one bit of memory. Generally a part of memory in the computer system is reserved for graphics. In this graphics memory, one bit is associated with each pixel on the display surface. This memory is called frame buffer.

5.3.3 Scan Conversion

If a line has to be represented, one has to first find out those pixels to be made bright, to display the line, and make the state of the bits corresponding to those pixels in the memory to 1. The operation of finding out the location of pixels to be made bright and then making the value of corresponding bits in the graphics memory to 1 is called conversion. Once an image is scan converted, a display controller scans the graphics memory and makes those pixels bright corresponding the bits with value1 in the frame buffer. The sequence of steps are shown in figure 5.5.

Location of each pixel on the viewing surface and the corresponding memory location in the frame buffer is accessed by an (x,y) coordinate pair. The coordinates are integers as they refer to pixel locations. The origin of this coordinate system is generally fixed at bottom-left corner. In some computer systems, the origin is set at the top-left corner. This may create some inconvenience to the programmers. Either the device driver or the application program should take care of such difficulties.

As there is one bit corresponding to every pixel on the display surface, a display unit with 512 x 512 pixels require 262, 144 bits in the frame buffer, which is equivalent to 32 kilo bytes. The pixel can either be made bright or dark, depending on whether the value of the corresponding bit is 1 or 0. If the image to be displayed is composed of colours, or with many different brightness levels, it is necessary to store more information about the attributes of the pixels. This can be achieved only by associating more bits with every pixels. If there are two bits associated with each pixel, then four different combination of information is possible. These four combinations are given below.

combination 1	0	0
combination 2	1	0
combination 3	0	1
combination 4	1	1

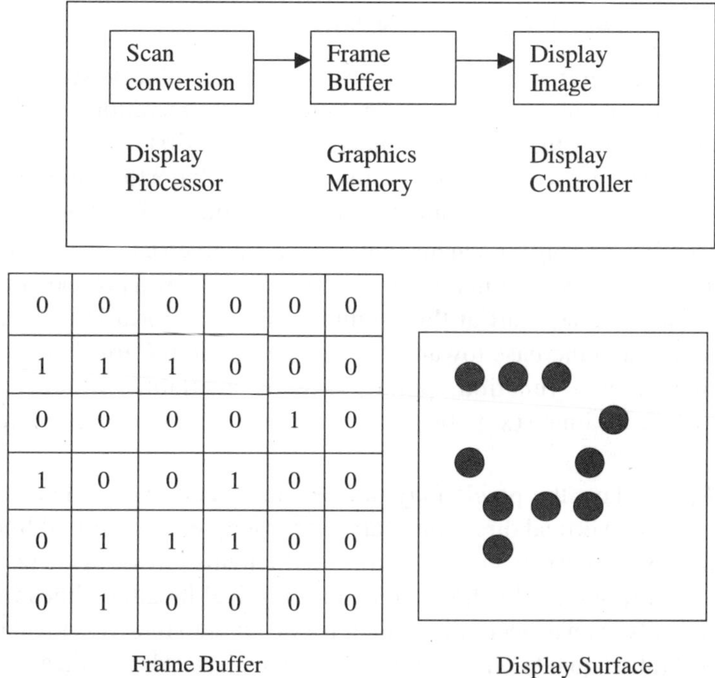

Frame Buffer

Display Surface

Fig. 5.5 Sequence of steps in Scan Conversion

Each of these combinations can be assigned either a colour or brightness level. The number of colours that can be displayed simultaneously is equal to 2n, where n is the number of bit planes. A display system with 8 bit planes require 256 kilo bytes of memory (with a resolution of 512 x 512) in the frame buffer and can display 28, i.e., 256 colours simultaneously. The present day technology offers graphics systems with 24 planes and a resolution of up to 4096 x 4096 pixels. In these systems, a group of 8 bit planes is attached to one primary colour. Such graphics systems are used in only highly specialised applications. For engineering design applications, a resolution of approximately 1280 x 1024 with 8 bit planes will be good enough. Many engineering workstations offer graphics screens with such capabilities. Many design applications can be carried out with systems with still less capabilities. Personal computers offer different graphics adapters with varying graphics facilities. An enhanced graphics adapter (EGA) on personal computers give a resolution of 640 x 350 pixels with 16 colours. Much better graphics adapters are available now for use with personal computers which give very good tonal and spatial resolutions.

We have briefly discussed representation of images in computers. Recapitulating, it is observed that complex images are broken down to lines and curves and they in turn are represented as a collection of points. These points are represented in computer memory in the form of bits. The following section describe algorithms for scan converting primitive objects.

5.3.4 Scan Conversion of Primitive Objects

Complex images are generated on computer using primitive objects such as points, straight lines, circles, text etc. and also using some graphics screen operations. In the last section, it has been shown that to draw the primitive objects, one has to first scan convert the object. i.e., The pixels to be made bright to display the primitive objects have to be found out. This section discusses few scan conversion algorithms for primitive objects, i.e., lines and circles.

Assume that both frame buffer and display surface are given a two dimensional coordinate system with origin at lower left corner. Each pixel is accessed by a non-negative integer (x, y) coordinate pair. The x values start at the origin and increase form left to right, while the y values start at bottom and increase towards top as in a standard Cartesian coordinate system. It is also assumed that a function, point (x, y) is available, which makes the pixel corresponding to the coordinate (x, y) bright, where x and y are non negative integer constants or expressions.

In many CRT displays the pixels may not be square and the number of pixels per unit length in horizontal and vertical directions vary. For example, a horizontal line with 10 pixels and a vertical line with 10 pixels may have different lengths physically. This may distort the image displayed on the screen. Such difference in physical length of lines in horizontal and vertical direction leads to an aspect ratio, which is not equal to one. It is ideal to have a square pixel and an aspect ratio equal to one. The present trend is towards this ideal situation, in many CAD workstations.

As discussed earlier, the lines are drawn on a raster scan display by turning on the pixels which lie either on or very close to the shortest path between the end points of the line. The lines drawn on displays with lower resolutions will have more gaps between the pixels compared to the one with high resolution display. It is quite easy to draw vertical and horizontal lines. The following algorithm draws a horizontal line from xstart to xend at a constant y.

```
for (x = xstart, x<=xend ; x++)
    point (x, y) ;
```

If xstart > xend, then x - - can be put instead of x + + in the for loop. Similarly vertical lines can also be drawn. There are many problems to draw lines with arbitrary slopes. Since the pixels are arranged in the form of a grid on the display surface, it is very difficult to obtain pixels lying exactly on the line. Hence a decision has to be taken to choose the pixels which are to be turned on. Many algorithms have been developed to find out different pixels to make up the approximating line. Digital Differential Analyzer (DDA) algorithm is a line drawing procedure, which is very easy to program. It produces reasonably good lines.

Assume that a line is to be drawn connecting (xstart, ystart) and (xend, yend). Let the slope of the line be m.

$$\text{slope of the line, m} = \frac{\text{yend} - \text{ystart}}{\text{xend} - \text{xstart}} \tag{5.1}$$

Any two consecutive points (x_1, y_1) and (x_2, y_2) lying on this line should satisfy the following equation.

$$\frac{y^2 - y^1}{x2 - x1} \qquad (5.2)$$

For a line in first quadrant with absolute value of slope < 1, the line can be generated by incrementing the previous x and by one unit, until xend is reached and then solve for y. Then we have

$$x2 = x1 + 1 \ or \ x2 - x1 = 1 \qquad (5.3)$$

Substituting (4.3) in (4.2) will yield

$$(y2 - y1)/1 = m \ or \ y2 - y1 = m \ or \ y2 = y1 + m \qquad (5.4)$$

This equation (5.4) can be used to compute the successive values of y from the previous value. i.e. a constant is added to the previous value of y to get the new value of y. This is an incremental calculation. The DDA algorithm is given in detail below:

```
line ( xstarrt, xednd, ystart, yend)
int xstart, xend, ystart, yend ;
{
        slope = (yend - ystart) / (xend - xstart);
        point ( xstart, ystart );
        yn = ystart ;
        for ( xn = xstart + 1; xn <= xend - 1; xn++)
        {
                yn = yn + slope ;
                point ( xn, round - off (yn) );
        }
}
```

The above function line draws a line from (xstart, ystart) to (xend, yend), with xstart < xend and abs (slope) > 1.

This algorithm can be generalised to draw lines for any values of xstart, xend and ystart, yend with any slope. This simple algorithm does a floating point addition and rounds off float to int to find out every pixel position. Several good line-drawing algorithm have been developed where only integer arithmetic is done, which is much more efficient and takes less time. Such ways of minimizing even a single arithmetic operation is so important, because every drawing or image generated will have large number of line segments in it and every line segment will have many pixels. So saving of one computation per pixel will save number of computations in generating an image, which in turn minimizes the time required to generate the whole image on the screen. Integer DDA and Beshenheim's algorithms are the other two efficient algorithms used to scan convert lines.

Circles are the most used curves in graphics. This section describe one scan conversion algorithm for circle drawing. A circle can be represented mathematically by the equation,

$$(x - x_c)^2 + (y - y_c)^2 = r^2 \tag{5.5}$$

where (x_c, y_c) is the centre of the circle and r the radius.

The equation (4.5) can be solved for 'y' .

$$y = yc + sqrt (r^* r - (x - xc)^\wedge 2) \tag{5.6}$$

To draw a circle, the value of x is incremented in units of one from –r to +r, equation (5.5) is used to solve for two values of y for each step, the resulting locations are converted from float to integer type and points are plotted. This method is inefficient in many respects. If the advantage of symmetry is made use of, time taken for scan conversion can be reduced greatly. The circle generated by the above method will be dense and flat near the y-axis, and have large gaps and steep near the x-axis as shown in Fig.5.6.

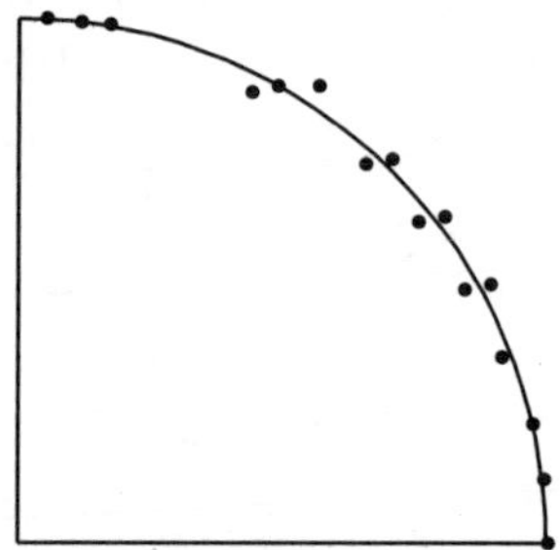

Fig. 5.6   Effect of scan Conversion of Circle

Making use of the parametric polar representation of the circle will eliminate this problem. This representation helps to overcome both the difficulties viz., non-uniform distribution of pixels along the circle and unnecessary computations, which could have been omitted, if the property of symmetry is used. The parametric polar representation of a circle is given as below.

$$x = x_c + r \cos(\theta) \; ; \; y = y_c + r \sin(\theta)$$

Where θ is measured in radians from 0 to 2π. As arc lengths are proportional to θ, equal increment of θ result in equal in equal spacing between successively plotted points.

Method of incremental drawing can be adopted here also to develop the algorithm for drawing the circle. The incremental equations are to be developed to obtain the next point to be displayed in terms of the previous point. Let (x_1, y_1) and (x_2, y_2) be two consecutive points on a circle and they are related by:

$$x1 = r \cos(\theta) \; ; \; y1 = r \sin(\theta)$$

$$x2 = r \cos(\theta + d\theta) \; ; \; y2 = r \sin(\theta + d\theta) \tag{5.7}$$

Here d θ is an angular step size, which is fixed. From trignometry, we get

$$x2 = r \cos(\theta) \cos(d\theta) - r \sin(\theta) \sin(d\theta)$$

$$y2 = r \sin(\theta) \cos(d\theta) + r \cos(\theta) \sin(d\theta) \tag{5.8}$$

$$x2 = x1 \cos(d\theta) - y1 \sin(d\theta)$$

$$y2 = y1 \cos(d\theta) + x1 \sin(d\theta) \tag{5.9}$$

Once the step size angle increment d θ is fixed, to draw the complete circle, cos (d θ) and sin (d θ) has to be calculated only once, and it can be used for all the points. Once the location of one pixel on the circle is found out, using the property of symmetry, seven other points can be obtained without carrying out any computations.

The following function circle (x_1, y_1, r) will scan convert a circle, where cos (d θ) and sin (d θ) are calculated only once and the property of symmetry is made use of. To make the spacing between adjacent points equal to approximately one unit, the arc length for every step has to be taken as one unit (i.e) r. d θ = 1. Then d θ becomes 1/r. A variable ar is used to specify aspect ratio. The y coordinates of every point is multiplied by this aspect ratio so that a circle looks exactly like a circle on the display surface. Otherwise a circle will look like an ellipse, if the aspect ratio of display surface is not 1.

```
/* algorithm to scan convert circle */

circle( xc, yc, r)
int xc, yc, r;
{
/* a variable 'ar' defined for aspect ratio */

dtheta = 1/r ;
ctheta = cos (dtheta) ;
stheta = sin (dtheta) ;
x = 0; /* these are the initial */
y = r; /* points */
while ( y >= x)
{
        point ( round-off ( xc + x), round-off (yc + y * ar)) ;
        point ( round-off ( xc - x), round-off (yc + y * ar)) ;
        point ( round-off ( xc + x), round-off (yc - y * ar)) ;
        point ( round-off ( xc - x), round-off (yc - y * ar)) ;
        point ( round-off ( xc + y), round-off (yc + x * ar)) ;
        point ( round-off ( xc - y), round-off (yc + x * ar)) ;
        point ( round-off ( xc + y), round-off (yc - x * ar)) ;
```

```
                point ( round-off ( xc - y), round-off (yc - x * ar)) ;

                xtemp = x ;
                x = (x * ctheta - y * stheta) ;
                y = ( y * ctheta + xtemp * stheta) ;
                }
        }
```

Another method of drawing a circle is by using many small line segments. Depending on the required smoothness one can set the number of line segments to draw the full circle. Most of the arcs used in graphics are generally circular arcs. By specifying the centre, initial angle and final angle, arcs can be drawn by slightly modifying the above function.

5.3.5 Text in Graphics

Drawings will not be complete without proper dimensions and notes. Generation of these require text in conjunction with lines and curves. In computer graphics two methods are adopted to generate text primitive. They are vector generated text and raster generated text.

A vector generated text is created using a series of line segments. This is exactly similar to the way how other objects were created using line segments. Fig. 5.7 shows vector generated characters.

A character A is generated with five vectors and character B with ten vectors. The vector generated text can be displayed in any size and at any angle by applying modelling transformations on the characters. Section 4.4 describes modelling transformation used in graphics.

A raster generated text defines characters by rectangular patterns of dots called raster cells. The cell size vary from one system to another. Consider a character cell of size 7 – dot wide and 7 – dot high, shown in Fig.5.8.

Here each character is represented by 7 x 7 = 49 bits. For each character, some rasters in the dot matrix are made bright and others dark. The raster information to generate characters are generally stored in Read Only Memory (ROM) of the display units. By changing the rasters to be made bright different text fonts can be generated in raster text. It is difficult to apply modelling transformations on raster generated characters to scale or rotate the text. All the micro computers have built-in raster generated characters. Special softwares are to be written to get vector characters on them. Modern CAD systems offer a wide variety of text fonts generated using vectors.

Depending on the capabilities of the display units, the scan version is done either at the software or at the hardware level. These display units, where the scan conversions and other graphics actions are done at the hardware level are called intelligent display devices. Image generation will be many times faster on such devices, compared to those where all the graphics actions and scan conversions are done using software. Most of the present day personal computers need separate software for scan conversion. In personal computers all the scan conversions are done at the device level with the device coordinate system specified in pixels.

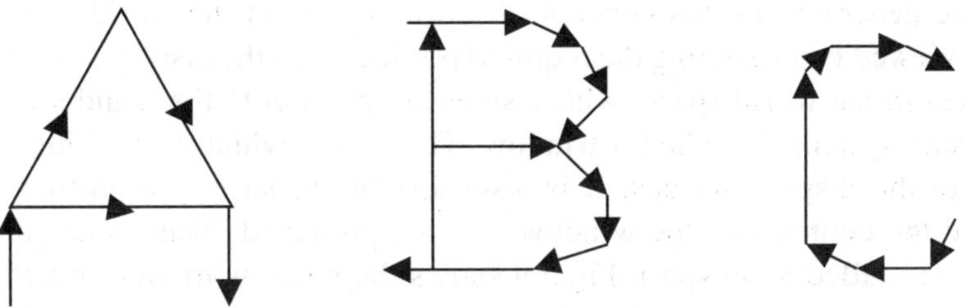

Fig. 5.7   Vector Generated Text

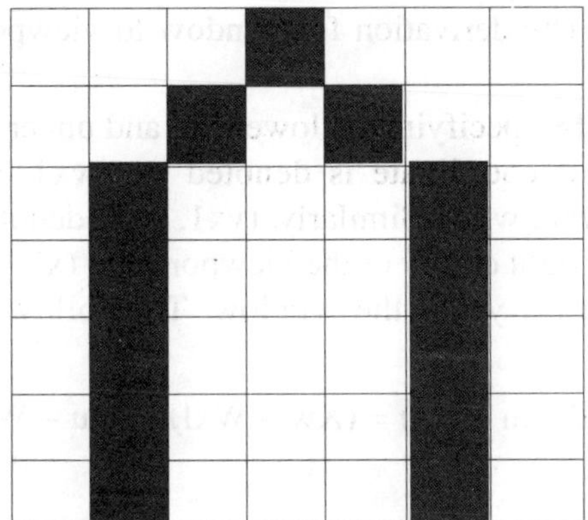

Fig. 5.8   Raster Generated Text

5.4   TRANSFORMATIONS

If a real drawing has to be produced using a computer, the limitation on the size of display surface poses a problem. There are only fixed number of pixels on the display surface. It is very difficult to accommodate the drawing as it is in the limited space available on the monitor. The coordinate values in the actual drawing may vary from one drawing to another. The device coordinate system in pixels is too restrictive for many applications.

A programmer can adopt transformation techniques to overcome such difficulties. These transformation techniques employed for the purpose of viewing the image generated on the display surface are called viewing transformations.

5.4.1   Viewing Transformations

Viewing transformations define a device-independent Cartesian coordinate system called world coordinate system. In the world coordinate system, the units are the user units which can be anything like mm, m, km, foot etc. Theoretically, the world space extends from -8 to +8 in both x and y directions. As infinity cannot be represented in any computer system, the limits are governed by the maximum and minimum number that can be represented in the computer, which is being used.

Images are generated in this conceptual world space, in the world coordinate system. Then they are viewed by projecting the required portion on to the display surface. The selected rectangular area in the world space, whose sides are parallel to the x and y directions of the world coordinate systems is called a window. The image which lies within this window is projected on to the display surface. It is also possible to specify a portion of the display surface, where the contents of the window is to be projected. This rectangular area on the display surface is called a viewport. Fig.5.9 shows the window to viewport transformation.

In practice, a line is represented in the world space by the x and y coordinates of its end points. These points (coordinate pairs) are transformed to the device units, using the size and position of the window and viewport defined. Then the line is scan converted using the device coordinates and displayed. The derivation for window to viewport transformation is given below.

The window is defined by specifying its lower left and upper right coordinates as shown in Fig.5.10. The lowest left coordinate is denoted by (wx1, wy1) and the upper right coordinate is denoted by (wxu, wyu). Similarly, (vx1, vy1) denote the lower left corner and (vxu, vyu) denote the upper right corner of the viewport. Let (x', y') be the point on viewport corresponding to the point (x, y) on the window. The following are the conditions for transformation.

$$(Xv - vxl)/(vxu - vxl) = (Xw - Wxl)/(Wxu - Wxl)$$

Solving for x' , we get

$$Xv = [(vxu-vxl)/(Wxu - Wxl)] (x - Wxl) + vxl \qquad (5.10)$$

Solving for Yv, we get

$$Yv = [(vyu-vyl)/(Wyu - Wyl)] (y - Wyl) + vyl \qquad (5.11)$$

Equations (5.10) and (5.11) together makeup the viewing transformation. Once the size of the window and viewport is fixed, the ratios,

$$[(vxu - vxl) / (Wxu - Wxl)] \text{ and } [(vyu - vyl)/(Wyu - Wyl)]$$

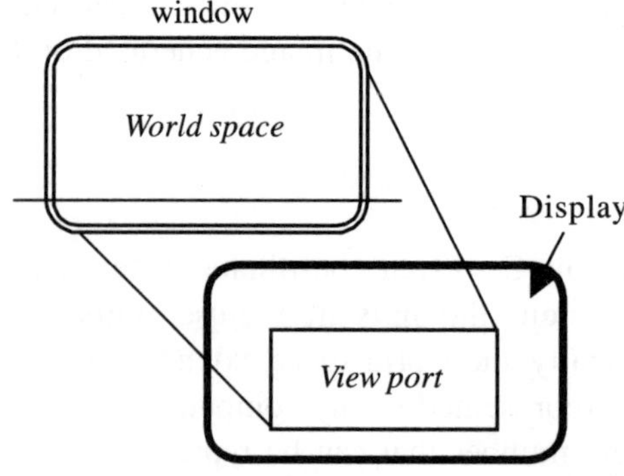

Fig. 5.9 Viewing Transformation

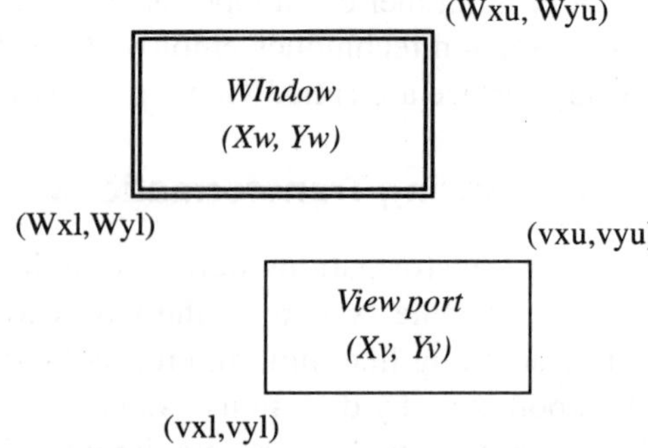

Fig. 5.10 Points in window and viewport

can be computed and this computation need not be repeated for every point as this is constant for one set of window and viewport. This need be changed only when either the window or viewport is changed. Few points are to be kept in mind when the window and viewport is fixed. If the height to breadth ratio of the window and viewport is not kept the same, the image displayed gets distorted. A circle drawn in the world space will be displayed as an ellipse and a square as a rectangle. Hence, the programmers have to keep the aspect ratios of window and viewport the same, to avoid distortion of the displayed images. This window – to – viewport transformation can be made use of to enlarge or reduce the image on the screen by properly selecting the size of window.

5.4.1.1 Clipping

Before drawing any primitives in the world space, first the window is fixed. It is possible that some part of the image being drawn may be outside the rectangular portion specifying the window. It is not desirable to have these parts of image lying outside the window displayed on screen. This process of removing those part of images lying outside the window is called clipping.

Fig.5.11 shows the effect of clipping. The portion of the image shown with dotted lines will not be visible on the display surface. Since complex images are composed of thousands of line segments, efficient clipping procedures are necessary to effectively reduce the time required to generate images. Several line clipping and polygon clipping algorithms have been developed by many researchers. Readers may refer to any book on computer graphics to know more about clipping and clipping procedures.

5.4.2 Modelling Transformations

To generate complex images in computer graphics, modelling transformations provide powerful techniques. The figure shown in Fig. 5.12 is a simply supported beam with two concentrated loads.

The above picture can be generated in many ways. It is made up of five objects A, B, C, D and E. Object A is a straight line and all the other four objects are the same but placed at different locations and also with different orientations. First the objects A and B can be drawn. Then to draw C, the object B can be copied by moving (translating) it to the other end of the line. To draw the object D, the object B can be first rotated by 180 degrees about the point

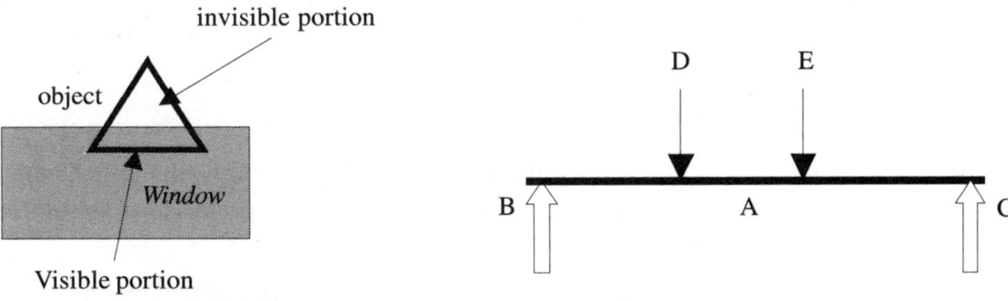

Fig 5.11 Clipping   **Fig.5.12** Beam with loads

where it touches the line A and then translating it to the required position. Similarly E also can be drawn by translating the object D. That menas to draw the objects C, D and E, we are making use of two transformations, viz., translation and rotation of object B. Instead of explicitly computing all the coordinates of other objects, they were obtained by simply transforming the coordinates of a previously drawn object. Any number of such transformations can be defined mathematically to generate graphics models of objects. Some of them are translation, rotation, scaling, mirroring and shearing.

5.4.2.1 *Translation*

A point (x, y) in world coordinate system is transformed to another position by modifying its x and y coordinates. In Fig.5.13 (x, y) is the original point which is translated to (x', y').

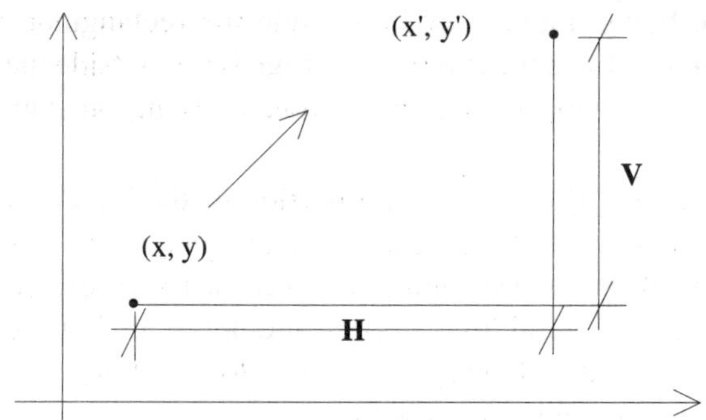

Fig. 5.13 Translation

$$\text{Where } x' = x + H \text{ and } y' = y + V \tag{5.12}$$

where H and V represent the horizontal and vertical displacement of the original point. H and V can take negative values also. To translate an object made up of several line segments, it is necessary to translate all the line segments defining the object.

5.4.2.2 *Rotation*

This transformation is used to rotate objects or images about any point in the world space either in the clockwise or anticlockwise direction.

The point about which the image is rotated is called pivot point. Consider a trial case, where the pivot point is the origin as shown in Fig. 5.14. Then the point to be rotated (x, y) can be represented as

$$x = r \cos (\Phi) \qquad\qquad y = r \sin (\Phi) \tag{5.13}$$

where r is the distance between the origin and the point (x, y) and 0, the angle which the line joining origin and the point (x, y) makes with x axis. When the point (x, y) is rotated the new points (x', y') becomes

$$x' = r \cos (\theta + \Phi) \qquad\qquad y' = r \sin (\theta + \Phi) \tag{5.14}$$

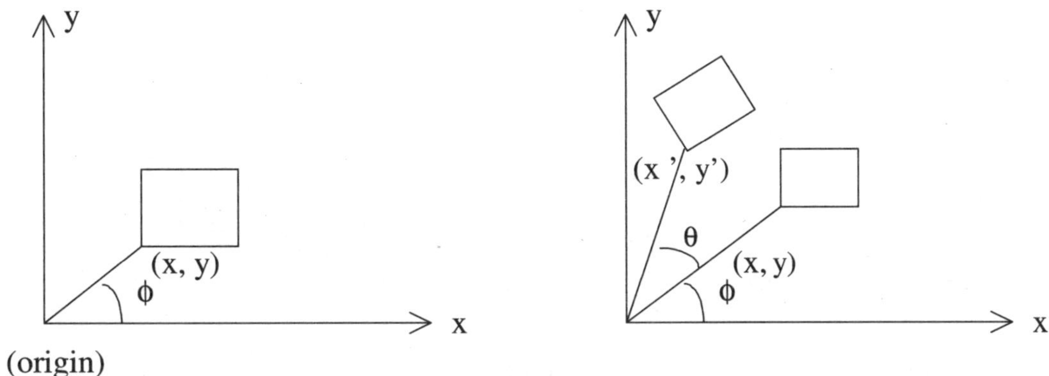

Fig. 5.14 Rotation Transformation

Rewriting the above equations, using laws of sines and cosines from trignometry,

$$x' = r \cos (\theta) \cos (\Phi) - r \sin (\theta) \sin (\Phi)$$

$$x' = r \sin (\theta) \cos (\Phi) + r \cos (\theta) \sin (\Phi) \tag{5.15}$$

Simplifying these we get,

$$x' = x \cos (\theta) - y \sin (\theta) \qquad y' = y \cos (\theta) + x \sin (\theta) \tag{5.16}$$

Equations 5.16 are applicable only for rotation about origin. But in many applications, the pivot point will not be the origin. It may be any point (xp, yp) in the world space. A generalised transformation for rotation is derived to rotate a point about the pivot point (xp, yp). Three steps are required to perform this operation. They are:

1. translate the pivot point (xp, yp) to the origin

2. rotate these translated points by è degrees about the origin and

3. translate the centre of rotation back to the pivot point.

These sequence of operations are shown in Fig.5.15. Fig.5.15 (a) shows the translation, (b) rotation and (c) translation back to the pivot point. In the first step the point (x, y) gets transformed to (x', y'). In the second step to (x", y") and in the third step to (x"', y"'). All the line segments on the objects has to be transformed to get the complete image rotated about pivot point (xp, yp). The derivations of obtaining (x"', y"') from (x, y) is given below.

Step-1

Translating pivot point (xp, yp) to origin, we get,

$$x' = x - xp; \ y' = y - yp$$

Step-2

Rotating the point (x', y') about origin using equations (4.16)

$$x'' = x' \cos (\theta) \ 2 \ y' \sin (\theta)$$

$$y'' = y' \cos (\theta) + x' \sin (\theta)$$

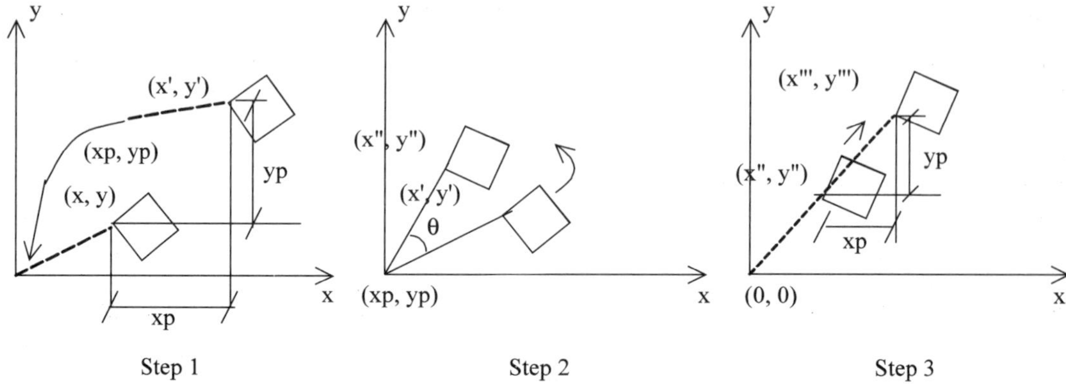

Fig. 5.15   Rotation about a pivot point (xp, yp)

Substituting for x' and y' and rewriting we get,

$$x'' = (x - xp) \cos(\theta) - (y - yp) \sin(\theta)$$

$$y'' = (y - yp) \cos(\theta) + (x - xp) \sin(\theta)$$

Step-3

Translate the centre of rotation back to the pivot point (xp, yp)

$$x''' = x'' + xp$$

$$y''' = y'' + yp$$

substituting for x'' and y'', we get,

$$x''' = (x - xp) \cos(\theta) - (y - yp) \sin(\theta) + xp$$

$$y''' = (y - yp) \cos(\theta) + (x - xp) \sin(\theta) + yp \tag{5.17}$$

Here the counter clockwise rotation is considered to be positive. To rotate in clockwise direction, make the value of the angle negative.

5.4.2.3 *Scaling*

It has already been seen that, the image displayed can be reduced or enlarged using the viewing transformations. But, the whole image within the window gets scaled up or down, when these transformations are used. To scale an object within the image, a scaling transformation can be applied. Scaling can be done either in x or y direction or in both directions simultaneously. Scale factors can be specified in x and y direction to carry out scaling.

Whenever a scaling transformation is applied, one point remains the same and this is the fixed point of the scaling transformation.

Fig. 5.16 shows the scaling transformation applied to an object. Every point lying on the object gets transformed. Take the object shown in Fig.5.16. All the four sides of the square got enlarged, i.e., the end points of the lines gets shifted. The point in world space which does not undergo any transformation while scaling is the fixed point associated with the scaling. If the fixed point is kept on the origin and S_x and S_y be the scaling factors in x and y directions respectively, then the transformed points (x', y') are

$$x' = x \times S_x \qquad\qquad y' = y \times S_y \qquad\qquad (5.18)$$

Values of S_x and S_y should be the same to have the scaling in both directions same. Otherwise, the objects gets distorted after scaling. A scaling factor greater than one enlarges the object and less than one reduces the size of the object after scaling. Scaling transformation can be applied with a different fixed point. In this case, three transformations have to be applied in sequence to obtain the transformed points as in the case of rotation about a pivot point. If (xf, yf) is the fixed point and S_x and S_y the scaling factors in x and y directions respectively, then the transformed point (x', y') becomes

$$x' = (x - xf) \times S_x + xf$$
$$y' = (y - yf) \times S_y + yf \qquad\qquad (5.19)$$

Many other transformations can be performed, depending on the requirements, while generating images. Mirroring and shearing are the other two modelling transformations generally used. Expressions can be derived for these transformations also on similar lines as that of translation, rotation and scaling. Derivations of these transformations are not dealt here in this book. Readers may refer to any one of the book on Computer Graphics given in reference at the end of the chapter to get more details on various transformations.

Looking at the expressions derived for the above transformations, it is seen that in some cases we have to apply addition, in some cases multiplication and in some other cases both. To generate complex images, different modelling transformations have to be applied many times. If all these transformations can be represented in a homogeneous manner, it will be easy to use them quite frequently. Matrix representation of these transformations is thus very useful from the point of view of programming.

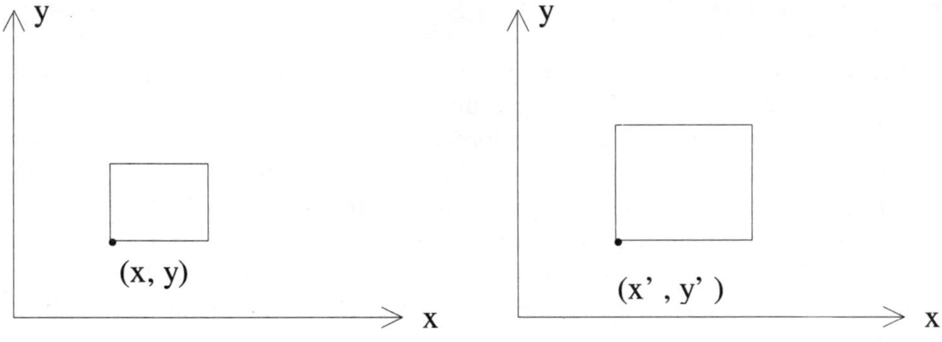

Fig. 5.16 Scaling

5.4.2.5 *Matrix Representations of Modelling Transformations*

Scaling and Rotation can be represented in 2 x 2 matrix as shown below:

Scaling:

$$(x', y') = (x, y) \begin{bmatrix} Sx & 0 \\ 0 & Sy \end{bmatrix} \tag{5.20}$$

Rotation:

$$(x', y') = (x, y) \begin{bmatrix} Cos(\theta) & Sin(\theta) \\ -Sin(\theta) & Cos(\theta) \end{bmatrix} \tag{5.21}$$

Translation cannot be represented in this matrix form, as only an addition is involved there. To have all the three transformations represented uniformly, a homogeneous coordinate system is adopted, where a dummy coordinate is added, i.e., (x, y) becomes (x,y,1) where the third coordinate is dummy. This is done to have a uniform representation of all the transformations. In the homogeneous system, the transformations can be represented as follows:

Translation:

$$(x', y', 1) = (x, y, 1) \begin{bmatrix} 1 & 0 & 0 \\ 0 & 1 & 0 \\ H & V & 1 \end{bmatrix} \tag{5.22}$$

Rotation:

$$(x', y', 1) = (x, y, 1) \begin{bmatrix} Cos(\theta) & Sin(\theta) & 0 \\ -Sin(\theta) & Cos(\theta) & 0 \\ 0 & 0 & 1 \end{bmatrix} \tag{5.23}$$

Scaling:

$$(x', y', 1) = (x, y, 1) \begin{bmatrix} Sx & 0 & 0 \\ 0 & Sy & 0 \\ 0 & 0 & 1 \end{bmatrix} \tag{5.24}$$

Another important advantage of having matrix representation is the ability to combine different transformations. The transformations can be combined by multiplying the corresponding matrices. Since all the transformation matrices are of size 3 x 3, they are conformable for multiplication. The order in which the transformations are to be applied is very important as different order of multiplication of matrices will result in different effects. Fig.5.17 shows two different effects of applying translation and rotation on an object in different order. In Fig.5.17 (a) first rotation is applied and then translation, whereas in Fig.5.17 (b) translation is applied first and then rotation. This happens because matrix multiplication is not commutative.

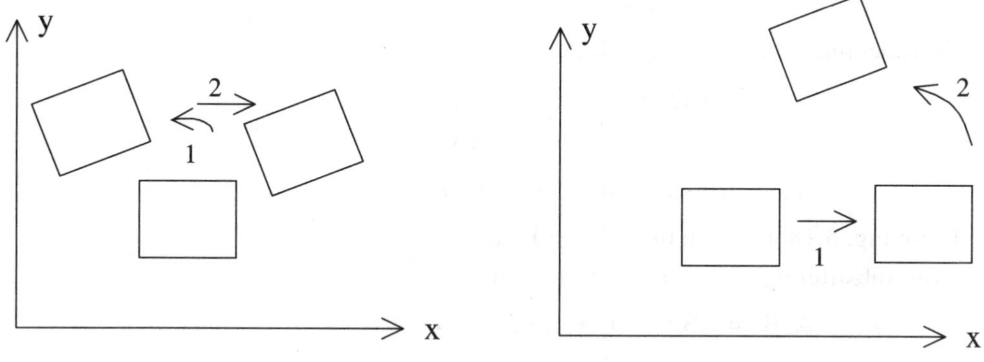

First Rotation and then Translation   First Translation and then Rotation

Fig. 5.17   Effect of Order of Multiplication on Transformation

Inverse transformations can be applied to nullify the effects of already applied transformations. In many of the intelligent display units most of the transformations are provided in low level codes in the special hardware. This makes such transformations very fast. On personal computers, it is necessary to code these in software systems. The following algorithm illustrates the use of scale, translation and rotation transformations to draw the spiral shown in Fig. 5.19. The algorithm to draw the spiral is as given below.

The spiral is generated by drawing squares successively by enlarging and rotating it at each stage. Refer to Fig. 5.18. The squares ABCD is drawn first. Then it is rotated by an angle 5o about the centre after enlarging it in such a way that the corners of the first square just touches the second square A' b' C' D'. The side AB is transformed into A' ' after scaling and rotating it as described above. The new length A' B' is obtained by multiplying AB with a scale factor. The scale factor can be obtained as follows.

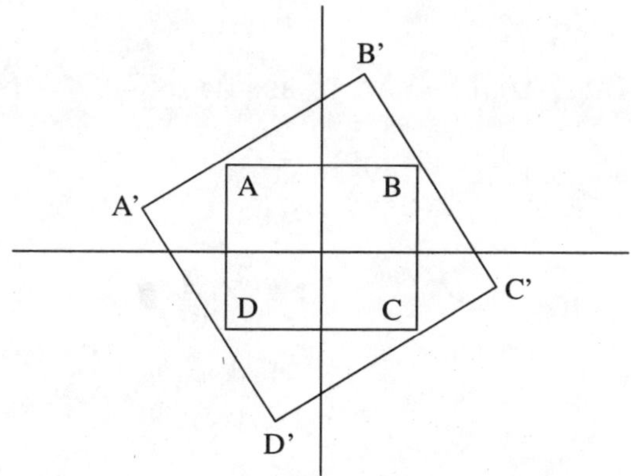

Fig. 5.18   Original Square ABCD and Transformed Square A' B' C' D'

$$A'B' = AA' + AB' \tag{5.25}$$

Consider the right angled triangle ABB'

$$\sin 5° = \frac{BB'}{AB} \text{ and } \cos 5° = \frac{AB'}{AB}$$

i.e., $$BB' = AB \sin 5° \text{ and } AB' = AB \cos 5° \tag{5.26}$$

From Fig. 5.18 it is seen that A' A = B' B

Now substituting (5.26) in (5.25) we get

$$A'B' = AB (\sin 5° + \cos 5°)$$

i.e., scaling factor $$= \frac{AB'}{AB} = (\sin 5° + \cos 5°) \tag{5.27}$$

As the angle through which the square is rotated is fixed as 5o , scaling factor remains constant at every stage. This property is used in writing the algorithm for generating the spiral. It is assumed that two functions moveto and lineto are available. Function moveto (x, y) moves the current cursor position to (x, y) and lineto (x, y) draws a line from the current cursor position to (x, y). A window is suitably assumed in such a way that the origin is displayed at the centre of viewport.

```
draw_spiral
{
        side = 10.0 /* assume the side = 10 */
        that = 5.0          /* angle of rotation 5 degrees          */
        sf = cos(that) + sin(that)        /* const scale factor */
        moveto(0.0, 0.0)  /* move cursor position to origin */
        do 37 times         /* as there are 37 square to draw */
        {
                draw_square (side)
                rotate (that) /* it is assumed that the rotation and scaling
gets accumulated */
                scale (sf) /* at every stage */
        }
}
function draw_square (side)
{
        moveto (-side/ 2, -side/ 2 )
        lineto ( side/ 2, -side/ 2 )
        lineto ( side/ 2, side/ 2 )
        lineto ( -side/ 2, side/ 2 )
```

```
lineto ( -side/ 2, -side/ 2 )
moveto (0.0, 0.0)
return( ) ;
}
```

The above algorithm illustrates the advantages of having transformation functions like rotate and scale to generate complex images.

Real world objects are always three dimensional images. Many applications in engineering demand display of three dimensional objects on graphics screen. Three dimensional graphics provide techniques to generate three dimensional objects and display them on two dimensional display surfaces. The following section briefly explains transformations and viewing in three dimensions.

5.4.3 Three Dimensional Viewing

All the real world objects are not just plane objects, but are solid objects. In the previous section, viewing of two dimensional objects is described where images generated on a two dimensional world space are projected onto a two dimensional display surface. When 3D objects are to be generated in world space, the world coordinate system must have all x, y and z axes. In this world coordinate system, images can be generated by defining lines or points with values for x, y and z coordinates. For the purpose of viewing this 3D image on a display surface, it has to be transformed from a 3D representation to a 2D representation, because finally the image is viewed on a 2D plane of the display device. This section describes the viewing transformations for a three-dimensional viewing pipeline. Basically there are two

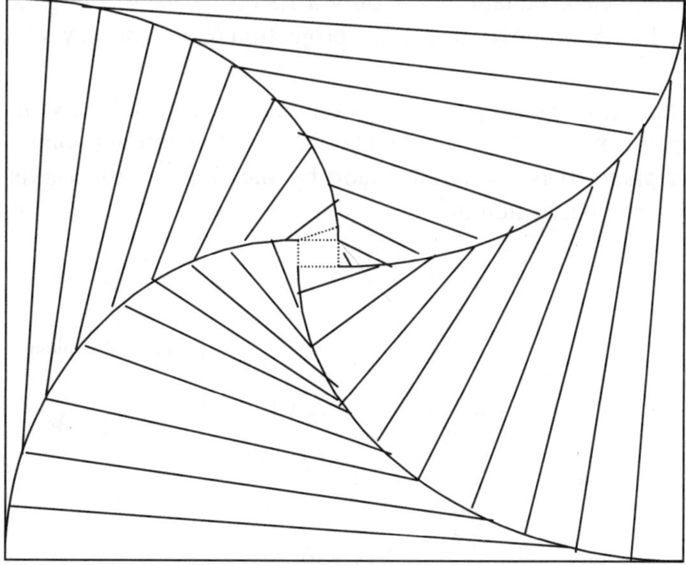

Fig.5.19 Spiral Drawn by applying Transformations on a square

methods for projecting a 3D image onto a 2D plane. In the first method, all points defining the object are projected to the surface along parallel lines. This is called parallel projection. In the second method, points are projected along lines that converge to a point. It is called perspective projection. Parallel projection is used to prepare views like plan, elevation, side view etc. of the three dimensional objects. In general, parallel projection does not give a realistic picture of the object. On the other hand, perspective projection of an object is more realistic, but it does not maintain the relative dimensions. This section briefly describes the essential principles of three dimensional viewing.

5.4.3.1 *Parallel Projection*

In parallel projection, the projection plane can be either perpendicular to the projectors or it may make an angle other than 90 degrees. The projection with plane perpendicular to the projectors is called orthographic projection. When the projection plane is oblique to the projectors, it is called oblique projection. Engineering drawings are generally produced by employing orthographic projection, where plans, elevations and side views of objects are generated. Orthographic projections can also be formed to show more than one face of an object. Isometric projection is one such commonly used projections. In an isometric projection, projection plane intersects each coordinate axis at the same distance from the origin.

It is very easy to form transformation equations for orthographic parallel projection. Consider a point (x, y, z). This has to be transformed for getting the projection of this point on a plane parallel to x-y plane. If the projection point is denoted by (x_p, y_p, x_p), then

$$x_p = x; \; y_p = y \quad \text{and} \quad z_p = 0$$

The above equations are the transformation equations for parallel projection on a plane parallel to x-y plane. These equations are only a specific case of the general equations for oblique projection. Fig. 5.20 shows an oblique projection of a point (x, y, z) on a plane lying in x-y plane.

In Fig.5.20, (x_p, y_p) is the projection of the point (x, y, z) and (x, y) is the orthographic projection of the point (x, y, z). Let 1 be the length of the line joining points (x, y) and (x_p, y_p) on the projection plane, θ is the angle made by the line 1 with x-axis. The projection coordinates (x_p, y_p) can be written as

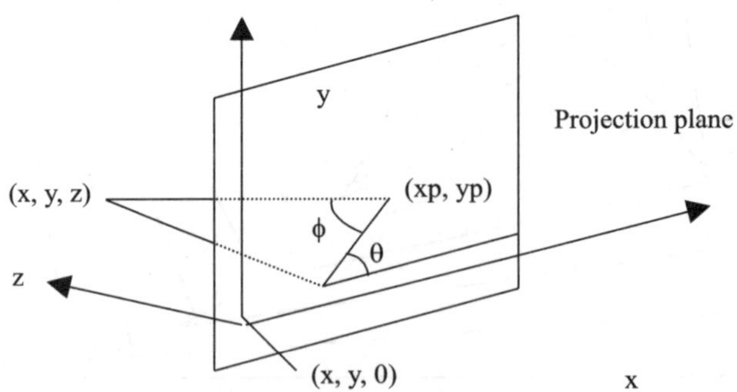

Fig. 5.20 Oblique Projection

$$xp = x + 1 \cos(\theta) ; \qquad\qquad yp = y + 1 \sin(\theta) \qquad\qquad (5.29)$$

Here the length l is a function of z coordinate. If Φ is the direction of projection, i.e., the angle made by the proj ector with the projection plane, then

$$\tan(\Phi) = z / 1 \qquad\qquad (5.30)$$

Assume that $l = l_1$, when $z = 1$; i.e., $l = z.l_1$. Now rewriting the equations (4.24) in terms of l_1, we get

$$x_p = x + z(11 \cos(\theta)) \qquad\qquad y_p = y + z(11 \sin(\theta)) \qquad\qquad (5.31)$$

Representing these equations in a matrix form, we obtain

$$[\, x_p, y_p, 1, 1\,] = [\, x, y, 1, 1\,] \begin{bmatrix} 1 & 0 & 0 & 0 \\ 0 & 1 & 0 & 0 \\ 1_1 \cos(\theta) & 1_1 \sin(\theta) & 1 & 0 \\ 0 & 0 & 0 & 1 \end{bmatrix} \qquad (5.32)$$

When $l_1 = 0$, it becomes parallel projection and for all other values of l_1 it becomes oblique projection.

5.4.3.2 *Perspective projection*

A perspective projection is obtained by projecting points along projection lines that meet at centre of projection. Fig. 5.21 shows the perspective projection of a point (x,y,z) to $(x_p, y_p, 0)$ on a projection plane, which lies on x-y plane.

Here the centre of projection is chosen, on the z-axis at a distance d from origin, in z-direction. It is easier to derive the transformation equations for perspective projection by expressing the projection equations in parametric form as shown below:

For any position (x', y', z') on the projection line,

$$x' = x - x.c \quad y' = y - y.c \text{ and } z' = z - (z + d).c \qquad\qquad (5.33)$$

where c is a constant, and varies between 0 and 1. $c = 0$ and $c = 1$ represent the end points of the projection line; i.e., $c = 0$ corresponds to the point (x, y, z) and $c = 1$ corresponds to the centre of projection (0, 0, -d). The point of intersection of the projection line with the projection plane is (x_p, y_p) and can be obtained by putting z' = 0, and solving for the constant c.

$$\text{i.e., } c = z/ (z+d) \qquad\qquad (5.34)$$

Substituting this in equations (5.33), we get

$$x_p = x (z/(z+d)) \text{ and } y_p = y (z/(z+d))$$

$$\text{i.e., } x_p = x [1/((z/d)+1] \text{ and } y_p = y [1/((z/d)+1]$$

$$\text{and } z_p = 0 \qquad\qquad (5.35)$$

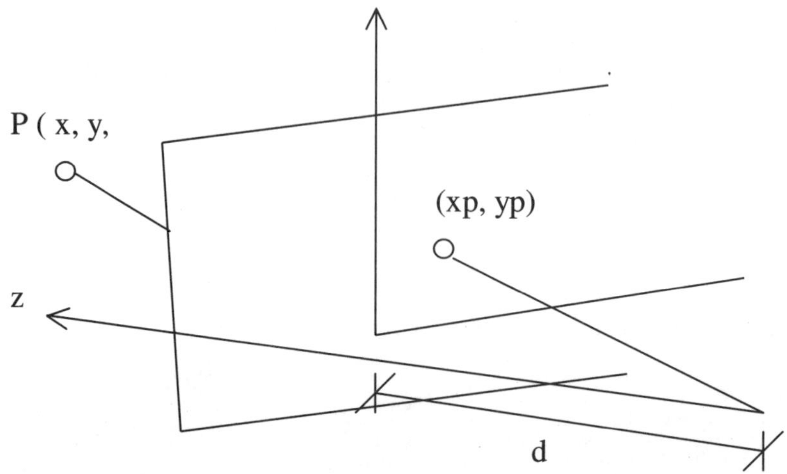

Fig. 5.21   Perspective Projection of a Point

These transformation equations can be represented in a homogeneous matrix form as

$$[x_h, y_h, z_h, 1] = [x, y, z, 1]\begin{bmatrix} 1 & 0 & 0 & 0 \\ 0 & 1 & 0 & 0 \\ 0 & 0 & 1 & \dfrac{1}{d} \\ 0 & 0 & 0 & 0 \end{bmatrix} \tag{5.36}$$

Now the projection coordinates on the projection plane can be computed as

$$[x_p, y_p, z_p, 1] = [xh/w, yh/w, zh/w.1] \tag{5.37}$$

where $w = (z/d) + 1$

when parallel lines that are not parallel to the plane of projection, are projected onto a plane using perspective transformation, it is observed that these parallel lines appear to converge at some point. This point is called a vanishing point. Each set of projected parallel lines will have separate vanishing point. The vanishing points corresponding to set of lines parallel to coordinate axes are called principal vanishing points. The number of principal vanishing points are controlled by appropriately orienting the projection plane. The number of coordinate axes intersecting the projection plane determines the number of vanishing points. Depending on number of vanishing points, perspective projections are classified as one-point, two-point and three-point projections.

To define viewing transformations in three dimensions, it is required to specify the following parameters, viz., the orientation of view plane, the point from which the object is viewed and the portion of the image to be projected. The 3D image is projected onto a view plane for the purpose of viewing. A viewing coordinate system has to be defined to establish the viewplane. Viewing coordinate system is a Cartesian coordinate system, with view reference point as its origin. The viewing plane is nothing but the x-y plane of the viewing coordinate system. The z and y directions of the viewing coordinate system is defined by two vectors, view panel normal (N) and view-up (V) respectively. Fig.5.22 shows the viewing coordinate system with respect to the world coordinate system.

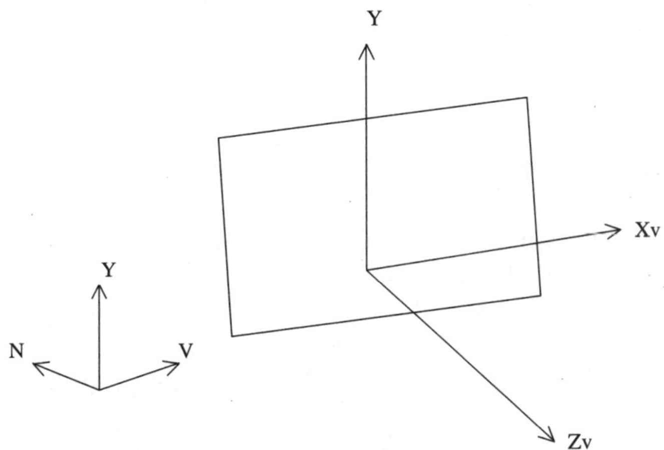

Fig. 5.22   Viewing Coordinate System

The vectors N and V are established by specifying coordinate positions in world coordinate system. The viewing coordinate system can either be a left handed one or a right handed one. For the purpose of illustration a left handed system which is more natural is used here. To generate a view from a point specified relative to the origin of the world coordinate system, the coordinates defining the image has to be transformed from the world coordinate system to the viewing coordinate system. This transformation can be achieved with a sequence of translations and rotations, that map the viewing system axes to the world coordinates axes. The details of which are not described here.

5.4.3.3   View Volume

In two dimensional graphics, the image lying within a rectangular area in world space (window) is projected onto the viewport. Similar to this in three dimensional graphics, a view volume is defined, such that only those objects lying within the view volume are projected and displayed on view plane. The shape of the view volume depends on the type of projection. In the case of a parallel projection, the view volume is a parallelepiped, whereas, in perspective projection, the shape of view volume is a truncated pyramid, with its apex at the centre of projection.

In parallel projection, the orientation of view volume is defined by the direction of projection. To overcome some difficulties in projecting objects in an infinite parallelopiped, two more planes are used, which produces a finite view volume bounded by six planes as shown in Fig.5.23. These planes are called the near plane and the far plane.

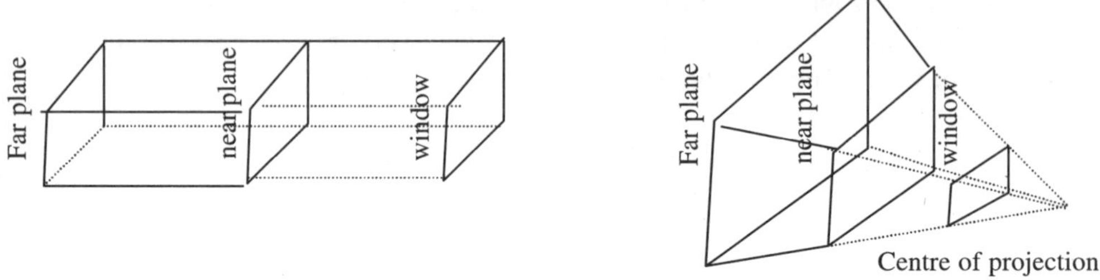

Fig.5.23 View Volume in Parallel and perspective Projection

Once the objects lying within the view volume are identified by clipping algorithms, they are projected onto the view plane. All the objects in the view volume will fall within the projection window. Now the rest of the actions are similar to those in two dimensional graphics. The contents of the projection window from the view plane are mapped onto a specified viewport on the display surface. Fig.5.24 shows the logical flow of processes in three dimensional viewing.

5.4.4 Modelling Transformations in 3D

Modelling transformations in three dimensions are just an extension of those in two dimensions. Transformation equations for translation, rotation and scaling represented in homogenous system in presented in matrix form here.

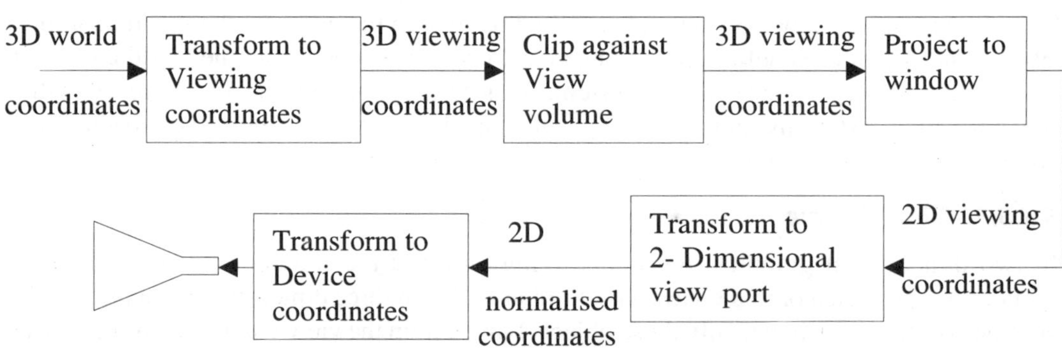

Fig.5.24 Three Dimensional Viewing Pipeline

Translation :

$$[T] = \begin{bmatrix} 1 & 0 & 0 & 0 \\ 0 & 1 & 0 & 0 \\ 0 & 0 & 1 & 1 \\ Tx & Ty & Tz & 1 \end{bmatrix} \qquad (5.38)$$

where Tx, Ty and Tz are the translations in x, y and z directions respectively.

Rotation

In three dimensional graphics rotation has to be carried out about any axis or any arbitrary line. If the rotation is carried out about the z-axis, the z-coordinates remain unchanged, while x and y coordinates behave exactly the same way as in two dimensions. The rotation matrix for rotation about z-axis is shown below. Fir. 4.25 shows the rotations about x, y and z axes.

$$[Rz] = \begin{bmatrix} Cos(\theta) & Sin(\theta) & 0 & 0 \\ -Sin(\theta) & Cos(\theta) & 0 & 0 \\ 0 & 0 & 1 & 0 \\ 0 & 0 & 0 & 1 \end{bmatrix} \tag{5.39}$$

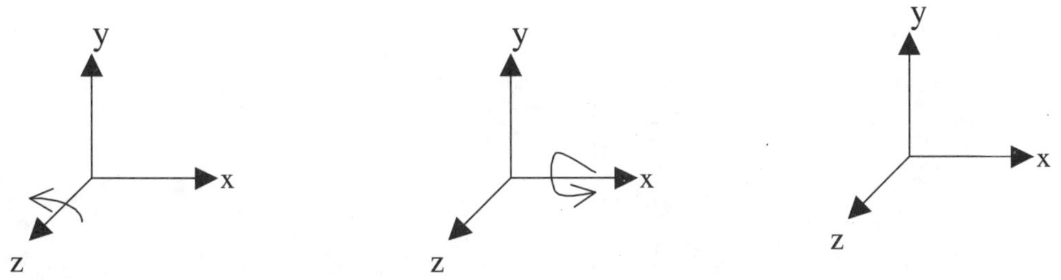

Fig. 5.25 Rotation about z,x and y axes

Transformation matrix for rotation about x and y direction is also similar and is given below.

$$[Rz] = \begin{bmatrix} 1 & 0 & 0 & 0 \\ 0 & Cos(\theta) & Sin(\theta) & 0 \\ 0 & -Sin(\theta) & Cos(\theta) & 0 \\ 0 & 0 & 0 & 1 \end{bmatrix} \tag{5.40}$$

$$[Ry] = \begin{bmatrix} Cos(\theta) & 0 & -Sin(\theta) & 0 \\ 0 & 1 & 0 & 0 \\ Sin(\theta) & 0 & Cos(\theta) & 0 \\ 0 & 0 & 01 & 1 \end{bmatrix} \tag{5.41}$$

The above transformation matrices are for rotation about the coordinate axes. However, in practice it may be necessary to rotate an object about an arbitrary line. This transformation can be achieved by following the sequence of steps given below:

Translate the line to the origin.

Rotate it about the x axis until the axis of rotation is in the zx plane.

Rotate it about the y axis until the z-axis corresponds to the axes of rotation.

Rotate it about the z-axis instead of fixing the object and rotating the axes.

Reverse the rotation about y axis.

Reverse the rotation about x axis.

Reverse the translation carried out in step 1.

Derivation of the transformation matrix for rotation about any arbitrary line is left to the readers as an exercise.

Scaling

Scaling transformation is similar to that in two dimensions. The transformation matrix for scaling is given below.

$$[S] = \begin{bmatrix} S_x & 0 & 0 & 0 \\ 0 & S_y & 0 & 0 \\ 0 & 0 & S_z & 0 \\ 0 & 0 & 0 & 1 \end{bmatrix} \tag{5.42}$$

Graphics packages supporting graphics in three dimensions provide functions to set viewing parameters and modelling transformations.

Readers may refer to books on Computer Graphics, to know more about these transformation. It is not the aim of this book to give a comprehensive theoretical description on computer graphics. An overview of graphics from a users' point of view is presented here. More details on each one of these topics may be obtained from the reference books given at the end of this chapter.

5.5 SEGMENTATION

In many applications, it may be required to manipulate parts of images. For example, on a machine drawing, one view of a bolt has to be drawn at many places. Let the view look like a hexagon. The hexagon consists of six lines and to draw the bolt at many places, these six lines forming the hexagon are to be drawn many times at appropriate proportions. It is easier to treat this view of the bolt – the six lines – as a single entity, and reproduce the entity, wherever necessary. This process of grouping primitives or objects together and treating it as a single entity for the purpose of further manipulation is called segmentation in computer graphics.

5.5.1 Segments in Graphics

Segmentation play a very important role in computer graphics. Complex images can be generated by applying modelling transformations on segments. Segmentation helps a great extent in creating animated images. Animation is the process of dynamically moving images on the display screen. Segmentation helps in generating animation sequence in a much better way. Consider a case, where a line has to be moved from one position to another. One way of doing it is first redraw the line with the back ground colour, and redraw it again by moving it by one pixel. This operation has to be repeated many times. If this line crosses any other part of the image, during every redraw, in background colour, it erases those parts of the image, which, are being overlapped or crossed by the line. i.e., the animation sequence creates hole on the other parts of the image. If the concept of segmentation is used properly in programming this drawback of forming holes in image can be avoided.

5.5.2 Display Files

Images are generated in computers using programs, which has many graphics commands to draw lines, curves, text etc. Whenever calls are made to these graphics commands, they invoke scan conversion functions either in the software or in the hardware to find out the correct pixels to be made bright. This collection of graphics commands, that represent the image displayed or to be displayed is called a display file. There are many ways how a command is represented in a display file. Some software use standard specifications to store the commands and associated parameters, whereas some other software use their own data structures. A generalised linked list data structure is an appropriate data structure to store the commands and their operands. The number of operands generally varies from one command to another. Hence, the structure of a list element has to be designed in such a way that any valid command and its parameters can be stored in that. Because the linked list is a flexible data structure, it can grow depending on their number of commands to be accommodated. As different segments will have different number of commands, this data structure optimizes the memory utilisation by the graphics application program, compared to an array structure. One can have as many linked lists as possible, as the number of segments. i.e., Each linked list corresponds to a display file or segment.

A good approach to graphics programming is to structure the complete image by dividing it into sub images or segments. In many application programs, there may be many segments and hence may need many display files. We have already seen that the display files are implemented as linked lists, i.e., either there will be a header cell for every linked list or a pointer pointing to the first element in the list. The application programs refer the segments by name or numbers. It is necessary to assign the names with appropriate pointers. It should be done in such a way that the time spent to search a segment is reduced to a minimum. Display file tables are implemented to assign the segment name by the appropriate list pointers. The data structures of the display file tables are designed to minimize the search time.

5.5.3 Operations on Segments

We have seen that, segments are created by grouping primitives together to treat them as a single entity for the purpose of further manipulations. The manipulations that can be carried out on segments are briefly described here.

Open segment

Whenever a new segment has to be opened, a command has to be given for the purpose, with the name of the segment. A call to this command or function creates a display file with no entry in it and associates it with the segment name, with an appropriate entry in the segment table. All graphics commands called subsequent to open the segment function, will be included in the currently opened segment.

Close segment

This command closes the currently opened segment, by doing appropriate operations on the data structure representing the display file.

Set-visibility

Any segment can be either made visible or invisible independently by the operation visibility. A visibility attribute is defined by the application program, based on which the segment is either made visible or invisible.

Transform-segment

Modelling transformations can be applied on segments to transform them by translating, rotating or scaling. This is carried out in different ways in different graphics (support) software. Some software provide separate function for each of these transformations. The present trend is towards defining a transformation matrix, in which parameters for standard modelling transformations translation, rotation and scaling are defined. Many graphics systems provide facilities to define transformation matrices in absolute or relative manner. An example program is given in the later part of this chapter, which illustrates the concept of segment transformation. This approach gives the application programmer flexibility to either do individual transformations or combine them together.

delete-segment

This operation, deletes a specified segment, by deleting the display file corresponding to it from the memory and by making appropriate entries in the display file table. Once deleted segment cannot be recalled back.

The basic operations on a segment and display files are discussed above. Many more operations can also be thought of like, combining two segments to one, associating a few segments to some specified active display devices, setting primitives of segments etc. Only the concepts of segmentation and its advantages and few operations on segments are discussed here.

5.6 GEOMETRIC MODELLING

Geometric modelling is the process of generating three dimensional objects of the real world for the purpose of analysis, design, drafting and manufacture. Geometric modelling creates a database in the computer, which represents the object generated. This object database is used to display the object, to prepare drawings of the object with different views, to prepare data for analysis and design and also to manufacture the object using CNC machines. This section briefly describes the techniques of geometric modelling.

In general, there are three types of models commonly used to represent physical objects. They are wireframe model, surface model and solid model. A brief description on the three modelling systems is given below.

5.6.1 Wireframe Modelling

Wire frame models are the simplest of the three above mentioned types of models. They are easy to create and use. Wire frame models provide sufficient information on the solid object. Wire frame modelling can be done even on an inexpensive CAD system based on personal computers.

Wire frame models are generally used to create models of simple objects. As it does not distinguish between inside and outside of the surfaces of the object, they are inadequate to be used for generating cutter paths to drive NC machines to manufacture the object. Wire frame models are generated by continuing line segments. Many commercial CAD systems provide wire frame modelling where a sequence of commands generate wire frame models of three dimensional objects, first by generating points and lines and then applying modelling transformations like translation, rotation and scaling. In older CAD systems, the commands are given in a batch form, which generates a database of the model. But present day CAD systems provide interactive facilities with friendly user interfaces.

5.6.2 Surface Modelling

Surface entities are introduced to the wireframe model in surface modelling. Surface models define part geometry more precisely, as compared to the wire frame model, and can be used directly to generate path profile data for NC machines. Many methods are available to generate surfaces. Objects with complex shapes are generated by combining planes, ruled surfaces of revolution, sweep surfaces and fillet surfaces. Many sophisticated CAD systems offer facilities to generate complex surface representations like B-surfaces and cubic patch surfaces. An object generated through surface modelling can be displayed on a screen, in such a way that it look like a solid object. Techniques like hidden surface removal and hidden line removal makes it possible to display the objects as a solid object and viewed from any point. As these models also do not truly represent the solid nature of the object, a still higher level of sophistication is introduced in geometric modelling, which makes it possible to represent the information on the solid nature of the object, which is necessary to carry out engineering analysis of the object. Solid models can associate with them properties like mass, weight, volume etc.

5.6.3 Solid Modelling

A cube is represented in a wire frame model as twelve lines and eight points with its connectivity details. In a surface model the cube is represented as six surfaces, the lines defining the surfaces and the points defining the lines. In a solid model, the cube is represented by the volume. It is easy to represent objects like cube, prism, sphere, cylinder etc. in solid modelling, because they are standard and simple objects and their representation is quite simple

The mathematical formulae to compute their properties are also simple. When complex objects are to be generated, it is cumbersome to represent its geometry and compute its properties. Solid modelling offers many techniques to generate the model of the objects as well as to compute its properties.

Two methods are generally used to construct solid models. One method uses basic shapes like cube, prism, cylinder, sphere etc.. as primitives to build the model of complex objects. The other method uses the boundary approach, where the perimeter on the boundary of the model is used to represent the solid object. Both the methods have their own advantages and disadvantages.

In the first method, which is based on Constructive Solid Geometry (CSG) approach, primitives are combined to generate complex objects by Boolean operations such as union, intersection, difference etc. The primitives are first positioned in the proper place and then the Boolean operations are carried out. Fig.5.26 shows a typical example of how objects are generated from primitive building blocks. It is required to generate a model shown in Fig.5.26 (e). For this three primitive objects are defined, viz., A, B, and C, A and B being rectangular blocks and C a cylinder. They are shown in Fig. 5.26 (a). Two Boolean operations are carried out with these primitives to get the desired object. They are:

The operation (A U B) generates the object shown in Fig.5.26 (b). The operation (A U B) difference C creates a cylindrical hole though the block B as shown in Fig.5.26 (c).

Most CAD systems provide many primitives as building blocks to generate solid objects, out of which only three or four primitives are used quite often, and are usually sufficient to generate many objects. They are plane, cylinder, sphere and cone.

Primitive modelling is more useful to generate shapes whose surfaces are more standard. Boundary modelling provides an efficient solution where the model has complex surfaces. In boundary modelling, both topology and geometry of solid models are defined and stored in databases. Consider a wedge shown in Fig. 5.27.

The solid can be visualised as a tree structure with four levels as shown in Fig.5.28. The solid is first assumed to be made of 5 surfaces then the surfaces are formed by combining edges and finally the edges are formed by combining vertices. This representation contains all

1. A U B and 2 *(A U B) difference C*

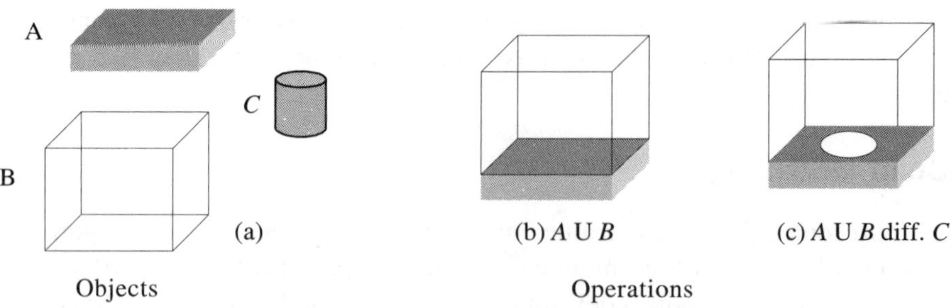

Fig. 5.26 Solid Modelling with Primitives

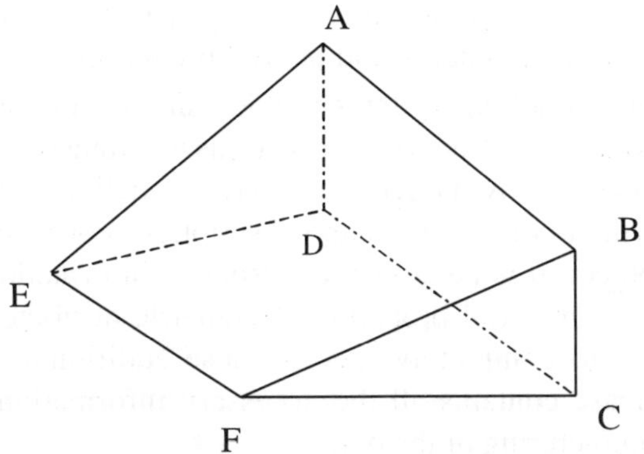

Fig. 5.27 A Solid Object - wedge

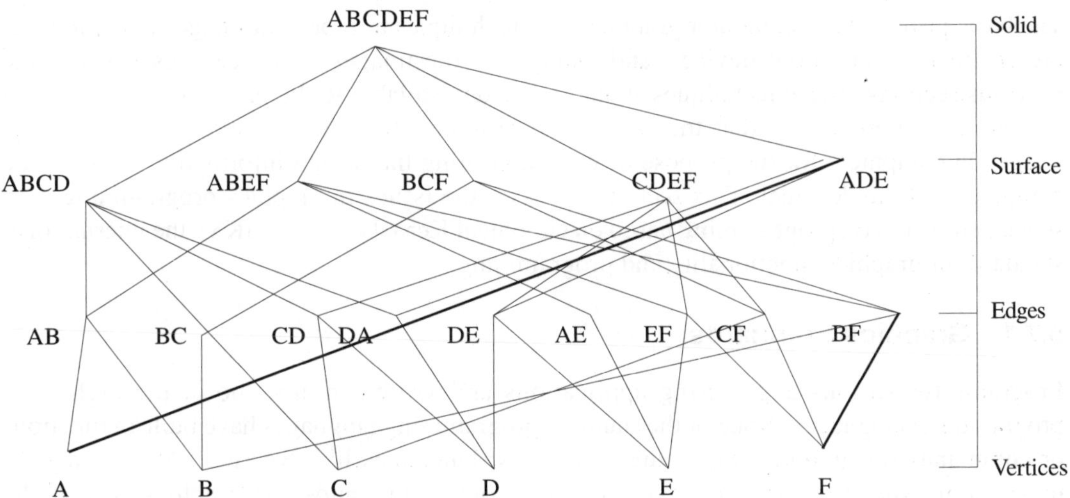

Fig. 5.28 Tree Representation of wedge

the necessary information regarding the geometry of the solid. The above tree representation is quite simple, but it takes too much time to carry out search. To avoid this, in most practical problems a winged-edge data structure is employed, where some amount of topological redundancy is built-in to reduce search time.

The shape defined in boundary modelling have to follow Euler's relationship. They are:

(i) *In a polyhedra*

number of vertices – number of edges + number of faces = 2

(ii) *In solids with holes and passages*

number of vertices +number of faces – number of edges – number of holes – 2 x number of bodies + 2 x passages = 0

The boundary representation is more suitable for generating different views of the solid model as well as for computing geometric and inertial properties.

Most of the geometric modelling systems provide simple commands to generate model with complex shapes. Modelling transformations are used extensively to create objects with standard geometrical shapes. Many modern geometric modelling systems have facilities to provide much more information than just shape description. For instance, in addition to the geometry details of an object, it is necessary to associate information on attributes such as surface finishes, tolerances, material properties, Geometric attributes etc. Many modelling systems provide facilities to completely specify these additional aspects in a consistent manner, so that the database contains all the necessary information to carry out analysis, design, detailing and manufacturing of the object.

5.7 GRAPHICS PROGRAMMING

The basic principles of computer graphics with techniques to represent images in computers, present images on output devices, and manipulate the images have been described in the previous sections. These techniques should be made available to the programmers and users of computer graphics, so that they can write programs to create, display and manipulate images in computers for the purpose of communicating the design information between the computer and the designer. This section discusses the issues in graphics programming with special emphasis on programming based on Graphical Kernal System (GKS), the international standard for graphics functionality and programming.

5.7.1 Graphics Standards

Programs for various engineering applications are written in any one of the high level programming languages. None of the standard programming languages have built-in functions or commands for graphics. Some dialects of few languages like BASIC, PASCAL and C, under some specific operating systems have some commands for graphics, which the programmers can use along with their regular program statements. Complex images can be generated and presented using these facilities. But the amount of control that a good engineering software demands cannot be achieved by those dialects, especially in graphics programming. Controlling many graphics output and input devices is also not possible through these language dialects. Also, the fast development in the hardware technology necessitates porting of application software on many computer systems with different hardware technology. All these requirements demand a standard specification for graphics functionality, so that application programs developed on one computer system can be ported on to the other computer systems with different graphics devices connected to it. These standards should have specific names for different graphics functions with specified set of arguments, so that graphics programming becomes universally standard, just like regular programming in any standard language. This requirement has led to the development of a few standards in computer graphics.

CORE is one such graphics standard suggested by ANSI a few years ago. It specified standard graphics functionality in both two and three dimensions. A large number of graphics support software were developed based on this standard to be used along with many programming languages. One of the major drawbacks of CORE graphics standard was the lack of language binding. Different software developed based on CORE graphics standard had different names for the same functionality. This put the limitation on porting of programs across different computer systems. In parallel to the development of CORE standard, another graphics standard was adopted by DIN, the West German institution for National Standards. It was called Graphical Kernal Systems, popularly known as GKS. Steps were taken by many groups seriously working in Computer Graphics to get GKS accepted as an international standard for graphics functionality by the International Standards Organisation (ISO). After many deliberations and discussions by acknowledged experts in the field of computer graphics, in 1985, GKS was accepted as a standard – ISO 7926 – for graphics functionality in two dimensions by ISO.

Graphical Kernal System is a device independent, language independent standard. To write programs for graphics actions in different languages, GKS specifies language bindings in different high level programming languages. Already the language bindings for FORTRAN and Pascal have been adopted. Working groups and committees are carrying out deliberations now to finalise the language binding for C programming language. The graphics programming is explained in this book based on the second working draft proposal for C language binding, dated August 1988.

It is not the aim of this book to give full description of GKS. The graphics functionality as specified in GKS will be explained in brief with an introduction to language binding in C language. To get more specific details, readers may refer to books on GKS, given in the reference, at the end of this chapter. A few examples written in C with GKS functions are also be discussed at the end of this section.

5.7.2 GKS-Introduction

The GKS standard document defines a set of functions acting as graphical tools in a language-independent manner. These functions are realised, in a given programming language, in an implementation. Such language-specific realisation, in which the language-independent system – kernal system – is embedded, is called the language layer. The application programmer can use the language layer to write programs for graphics tasks.

The language-independent and device-independent functions of GKS makes the graphics programs portable across a wide range of computer systems. The graphics input and output devices connected to GKS are called workstations. A device driver assigned to each workstation translates the device independent representation to a device dependent or workstation specific one. Fig.5.29 shows the interface of GKS with application programs and workstations. Initially GKS was designed as a two-dimensional system. But later, standards for three-dimensional graphics (GKS-3D) have been introduced. Only standards pertaining to two-dimensional GKS system is discussed in this chapter. Readers may refer to additional books given in the reference section for details on GKS-3D. Functionally GKS carries out the following tasks.

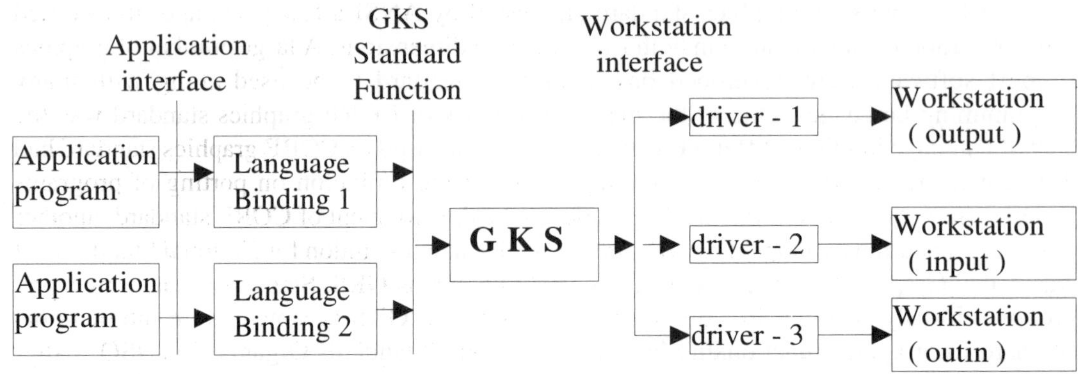

Fig. 5.29 Interface of GKS with Application Programs

- *Generation and representation of pictures*
- *Routing images or parts of images created in user coordinate systems to different workstations and transforming them into the respective device coordinate system*
- *Controlling workstations attached to the system*
- *Structuring the image into parts for the purpose of manipulation like display, storage, transformation, copying, deleting etc.*
- *Storage of images on secondary storage devices for future use.*

5.7.3 GKS - Output

GKS provides six output primitives. They are: Polyline, Polymarker, Text, Fill Area, Cell Array and Generalized Drawing Primitive.

1. Polyline: This is a line primitive. Polyline ganerates a sequence of straight lines connecting points specified as its parameters.
2. Polymarker: This is a point primitive. This primitive generates a set of specified type of symbols at given positions.
3. Text: This is the text primitive. Text generates a charcter string at a specified position.
4. Fill Area: This is a raster primitive. A polygon generated is filled with a specified style.
5. Cell Array: This is also another raster primitive. An array of reactanular cells are generated with individual colours.
6. Generalised Drawing Primitive (GDP): This is a general purpose primitive provided to make use of the capabilities of workstations attached to the system like drawing curves, circles, splines etc.

The following table gives the output primitives and a set of attributes that control their apperance. It gives an idea about the different attributes of a primitive which will modify the appearance of the primitives on output workstations, colour and pick identifier being common to al. The colour attribute is specified by the particular colour. For instance, (0,0,0) represents black, (1,1,1) white and (0,1,0) green. The pick identifier is a number assignd to every output primitve and is returned by a pick device. It has significance only with the input functions used for identification.

Primitive	Attributes
1. Polyline	line type, line width scale factor, colour, pick identifier
2. Polymarker	markertype, marker size scale factor, colour, pick identifier
3. Text	text font, text precision, character height, character up vector, character expansion factor, text path, charter spacing, text alignment, colour, pick identifier
4. Fill Area	pattern size, interior style, hatch style, pattern reference point, pattern array, colour, pick identifier
5. Cell Array	colour, pick identifier
6. GDP	dependent on the type of GDP and pick identifier

A brief description on the various attributes of different output primitives is given below.

line type:
Different line types are used to distinguish the lines from one another. For instance, a line may be solid, dashed or dotted line.

line width :
This controls the width of the line displayed factor: which is a multiple of a normal width.

marker type:
This is a number specifying a particular symbol used for identifying different markers.

marker size :
The actual marker is the normal size factor: multiplied by this scale factor.

text font:
This is a number used to select one specific character type out of the many possible on a work station.

character height :
This attribute specifies the vertical size of character.

text precision :
This attribute specifies a scale of capability of character display. The three precisions defined in GKS are string, character and stroke. String allows text to be displayed only horizontally in one of the three different character sizes. Stroke allows any direction and any size.

character up vector:
Specifies the up directions of a character. For instance, the vector specifies (0,1) gives the vertically up-ward direction, whereas, that direction (-1, 1) specifies that, a character will be rotated by 45 degrees from its normal direction.

character expansion factor :
Specifies the width to height ratio of a character display.

text path :

Defines the direction in which the subsequent characters are to be displayed. The values allowed are: left, right, up and down.

character spacing :

Specifies spacing between two adjacent characters.

character alignment :

This attribute specifies whether the text string is to be displayed left justified, right justified or centred.

interior style :

This is an attribute to the fill area primitive, which determines the style in which a closed polygon is to be filled.

pattern size :

Specifies the size of the basic pattern rectangle.

pattern reference point :

This specifies the origin of the basic pattern rectangle. The lower – left corner of the pattern rectangle is placed at this reference point.

pattern array :

This array defines a pattern. Each cell in the rectangular array is assigned a colour to it.

hatch style :

This is workstation dependent and specified by the implementers of GKS. Hatching is specified by a number for selecting one style from many available.

Fig. 5.30 shows the effect of different attributes on output primitives. These attributes can be set either in a workstation independent or workstation dependent way. Once an attribute is set, all the subsequent output primitives are displayed with these attributes. It has with, characters rotated by 45° anticlockwise can be displayed by calling the following two functions.

Set character up vector (-1, 1)

Text (point, 'GKS')

The workstation dependent attributes are set by an index associated with the primitive. This index points to a table on each workstation for different attributes. For example, the polyline_index points to a table, which is called polyline bundle table, that contains the different attributes line type, line width and a colour index. Fig. 5.31 shows the relationship between the polyline attributes for the bundled attribute binding mode.

GKS provides two modes for setting attributes for output primitives. They are individual mode and bundled mode. Generally global attributes are set in individual mode, but workstation specific attributes are set in bundled mode. In bundled mode the workstation specific attributes are grouped together and an index is assigned to it. Later to set the attributes, these predefined indices are set using set index functions of GKS. The required mode is selected by setting the aspect source flag value to INDIVIDUAL or BUNDLED.

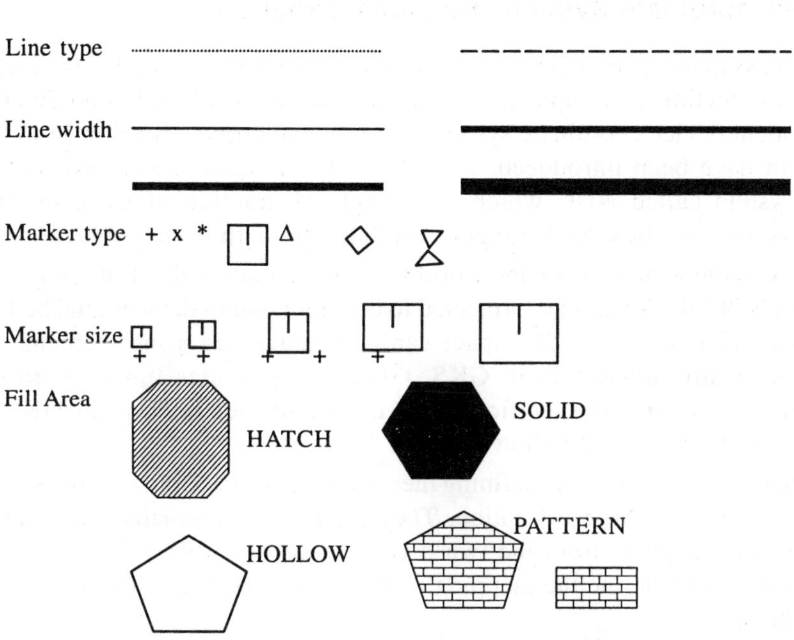

Fig. 5.30   Effect of Attributes on Output Primitives

Similar to the polyline bundle table shown in Fig. 5.31 all other attributes also have bundle tables through which workstation dependent attributes for output primitives can be set. The generalized drawing primitives have no special bundle. The attributes settings for GDP are implementation dependant.

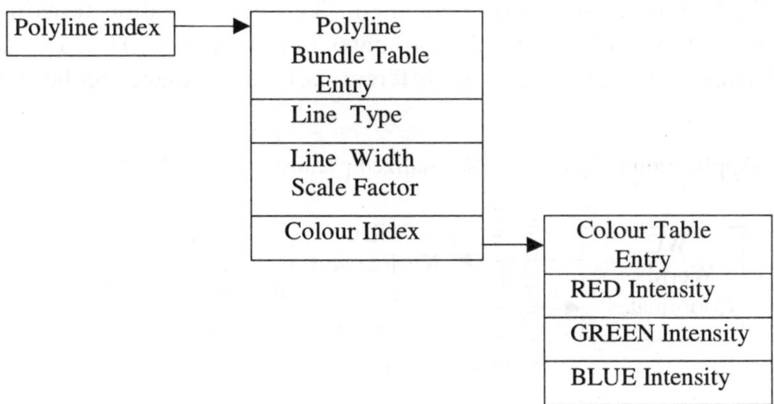

Fig. 5.31   Polyline Bundle Table

5.7.4 GKS- Coordinate System and Transformations

The coordinate system and transformations have already been discussed in the earlier sections on general introduction to computer graphics. A user defined world coordinate system, a device dependent device coordinate system and a viewing transformation from the world to device system have been introduced. In addition to the above two, GKS defines a thrid coordinate system called NDC which is a single abstraction of these different device coordinate systems. In GKS, NDC ranges from 0 to 1 in both x and y directions.

The image in the window from the world space is first normalized and projected to NDC, and then from NDC, the images are projected to different output devices attached to the GKS. The normalized picture in the NDC space can be manipulated using segmentation. Device coordinates normally are meters in GKS. GKS also provides functions to enquire the correspondence between the specific device units and meters. Typical GKS coordinate systems and transformations are shown in Fig. 5.32.

These are two transformations defining the viewing pipeline from the application program to the display surface of the workstation. They are a set of normalisation transformations, which define the mappings from the world coordinates to NDC and a set of workstation transformations, which define the mapping of NDC to every one of the active workstations attached to GKS.

Any number of normalisation transformations can be set, but only one is selected eat a time. The number of normalisation transformations allowed is implementation dependent. A normalisation transformations is defined by specifying a rectangular area on the normalised device coordinate space, called a viewport. This definition of viewport is restricted to GKS. The rectangular space.

Defining window and viewport must be parallel to the coordinate axes in world and Normalized Device Coordinate systems.

Each normalization transformation is identified by a number, ranging from 0 to a maximum, which is implementation dependent. The normalization transformation with number 0 maps (0,1) x (0,1) in world coordinates to (0.0, 1.0) x (0.0 x 1.0) in normalized device coordinates. This cannot be rest. Different parts of an image can be presented using

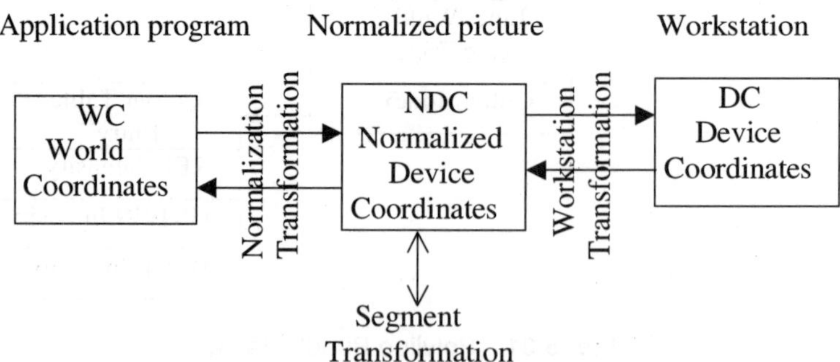

Fig. 5.32 GKS Coordinate System and Transformations

different transformations. GKS provides facility to control clipping. Clipping can be turned either on or off by the applications program, by calling appropriate functions.

The images are mapped from NDC to the workstation by workstation transformations. Before going into the details of workstation transformations, it is necessary to know a little about the workstation concepts of GKS. In GKS, workstation are abstractions of physical devices. An abstract graphical workstation has the following properties:

- It has one display surface with a fixed resolution.
- The display spaces are rectangular.
- No image is display outside the specified display space.
- It supports several line types, marker types, text fonts, character spacings etc.
- It has one or more logical input devices.
- It stores and manipulates segments.

Appearance of the same output primitives can be varied on different workstations in GKS. This is done using the attribute bundles and the indices pointing to bundle entries and workstation transformations. GKS also provides more control on different workstations by defining a deferral state. This allows one device to be driven by a buffered output, wile others will display picture changes as soon as possible. Application programs identify workstations using a workstation identifier. Connection between application programs and workstations is established by opening the workstation. Output primitives can be sent to a workstation only after it is activated. Outputs cannot be sent to a deactivated workstation. Input can be performed from all the workstations opened. GKS defines six categories of workstations. They are:

1. Output workstation : which has a display surface for displaying images.
2. Input workstation : with at least one logical input device.
3. Output/input workstation : with a display surface and at least one input device.
4. Workstation independent segment storage (WISS)
5. GKS metafile output
6. GKS metafile input.

The last three categories are some special features of GKS, for the purpose of storing images temporarily or permanently. They are treated as workstations only to have a better control on them.

An application program can select portions of images on NDC to be displayed on a specified area on the display surface of open workstations. Workstation transformation maps NDC on to the device coordinates for the workstation selected.

Normalization transformation composes the images and workstation transformation allows viewing of different aspects of composed image on different workstations. A workstations transformation is defined by specifying a rectangular area in the Normalised device coordinate system, called workstation window and a specified area of the device coordinate space called workstation window viewport. Both the workstation window and workstation viewports are defined parallel to the respective coordinate axes. GKS allows more control on workstations by allowing a workstation to delay, for a specified amount of time, the actions performed by the applications program. A workstation state variable controls this delay and is called deferred state of the workstation. Outputs can be displayed on interactive terminal screens as soon as possible and on a plotter after completing the preparation of desired image, by setting the value of the control variable deferral state.

The capabilities of output devices available vary from one to another. Many workstations will have additional capabilities like many of the advanced graphics actions at firmware level. These capabilities can be tapped using the Generalized Drawing Primitives - GDP - and ESCAPE function. Application programs with sufficient knowledge on the workstation hardware can make use of these facilities to carry out graphics actions more effectively.

5.7.5   GKS - Input

The output primitives discussed so far, along with their attributes, generate desired images on a display device. These displays are passive as long as they are not dynamic or changing in response to a user's requirement. The user interacts with the graphics images by inputting some values to the application program. This interaction with the graphics adds a new dimension to computer graphics and results in interactive computer graphics. The instantaneous system responses to these use interactions are generally pointing, sketching, selecting, dragging, erasing or picking in a direct manner. As these actions are very much similar to the way human beings react to the environment, interactive graphics is one of the most powerful instrument for human – computer interaction for proper and effective communication. There are many graphics input devices and the working of a few of those have already been discussed in previous section 5.2 of this chapter. GKS defines a set of logical input devices and which can be mapped on to the physicsl input devices like, mouse, digitizer, light pen etc. A logical input device provides a logical input value to the application program. The input class is defined as a set of input devices that are logically equivalent with respect to their function. GKS defines six distinct logical input device classes. They are locator, valutor, pick, choice, string and stroke.

Locator provides a position, i.e., one x-y coordinate pair. The position will be in world coordinates. The operator moves either the thumb wheel or a mouse to position the cursor or cross hairs on the screen.

Valuator provides a real number. A key board can be used to enter the real number. Here the keyboard which is the physical device is mapped on to the logical device valuator.

Pick provides a segment name and a pick identifier. A pick device is pointed to a segment or a specific output primitive. A light pen is a typical pick device, which is used to point images.

Choice provides a non – negative integer which represents a selection from a given number of choices. Entering a value corresponding to an item from a menu is treated as a choice.

String provides a character string. The operator enters a string of characters using a string input device, which is usually the key board. Stroke provides a sequence of positions. The positions are supplied by placing the locate device at a number of places. The action of inputting an image into the computer by placing the locator device at a number of places. The action of inputting an image into the computer by placing a locator device on closely spaced points on the lines describing the image is a stroke input action. A digitizer is used as a stroke device. All graphical as well as non-graphical interactions can be achieved by using the above logical input devices described above are not truly graphical they are included in the GKS functionality to provide all possible interactive actions, irrespective of whether they are graphical or non- graphical.

GKS defines three different operating modes for each of these logical input devices.

At any given time, one of the three operating modes, is selected to obtain input from the devices. The three operating modes are Request, Sample and Event.

When an input is sought in the request mode by the program, a break action is performed by the operator. The break action is implementation dependent and also depends on the type of logical input device. An input in sample mode does not cause the GKS to stop, but program execution continues without waiting for operator action. It returns the current logical input value set on the logical input device. Event mode, creates and maintains an input queue operator actions, asynchronously. An event report contains two information, viz., identification of a logical input device and a logical input value from the device. The application program can either remove the oldest event from the queue or flush all the event reports from the queue. In most of the CAD applications, request operating mode is commonly used.

Whenever an application program requires an input value, the user has to be informed either graphically or textually. Standard output primitives are used to display messages for the operator. The output produced is called prompt. Many different prompts can be implemented in GKS. For instance, for a locator device, a cross hair cursor, an arrow cursor or a text cursor cab be used as a prompt.

It is also necessary to notify the operator on the actions taken by the application program, by modifying the graphics output. Such an action is called an Echo. For example, input through a pick device can be echoed by blinking or highlighting the segment picked.

5.7.6   GKS – Segments

The use of segmentation in computer graphics has already been explained in section 5.5. A collection of output primitives that can be manipulated as a unit is called segment. In GKS, When a segment is created, it is stored on all active workstations. If a workstation does not have capability to store and manipulate segments, GKS does it through Workstation independent Segment Storage (WISS). Segments are uniquely, identified by an identifier, usually an integer number. The creation of a segment requires two functions, one to create a segment and another to close the segment. All the output primitives generated after a call to create segment function and before a call to close segment function become part of that segment an shown below.

```
Create segment (1)
       Output primitives
Close segment   create segment 2)
       Output primitives
Close segment
```

A new signal can be created only after the previous segment is closed. The output primitives within a segment can be given separate identification using the attribute pick identifier. GKS provide the following facilities for manipulating segments.

- Changing their positions, shape etc, by transformations
- Turning on or off the visibility, delectability or highlighting.
- Setting the primitives of segments
- Copying segments to other segments
- Associating segments with workstations
- Renaming and deleting segments

Some of the attributes that can be associated with segments are visibility, highlighting, delectability and segment priority.

Visibility is an indication of whether or not a segment is displayed on the workstations. Only visible segments can be picked using a pick input device. Highlighting makes a segment blink by modifying its visual attributes. The attribute delectability decides whether or not a segment can be picked input device. Segment priority is another segment attribute which determines the order in which the overlapping segments are displayed on screen. The same order is maintained in the case of graphics input also. If parts of segments overlap, those primitives of the segment with highest priority will be picked from overlapping segments.

Even though images can be generated without using segments, it is always advisable to group output primitives in segments. Modeling transformations can be applied on segments and these are carried out in Normalized Device coordinates. They perform translation, rotation and scaling individually or in combination. Segment transformations are defined by a transformation matrix of size 2 x 3 in which the 2 x 2 portion is for scaling and rotation and 2 x 1 for transformation. GKS provides functions to set and modify the transformation matrix. The following functions are associated with segment transformation in GKS :

- Set segment transformation
- Evaluate transformation matrix
- Accumulate transformation matrix

Evaluate transformation matrix generates a matrix from the single operations – translation, rotation and scaling – specified by its argument list. The function, accumulate transformation matrix, allows the accumulation of any number of translate, rotate and scale operations in any order and multiplicity within one transformation matrix.

On segment storage, GKS defines two concepts, first Workstation Dependent Segment Storage (WDSS) and second Workstation Independent Segment Storage (WISS). The conceptual storage of segments on a workstation, which allows for change of segment attributes including transformation and deletion, is called WDSS. WISS is defined, where segments are to be transformed from one workstation to another, or segments are to be copied or inserted into other segments. WISS is treated as a special workstations in GKS. This makes the programmers efforts minimum from the point of view of effective control of segments. Since WISS is treated as workstation, one need not remember a separate set of functions associates with it. All the workstation functions are valid for WISS also. WISS has to be opened and activated before any segment is stored in it. The function clear workstation, operated on WISS deletes all segments stored. All the primitives are transformed from World Coordinates to NDC before they are stored in WISS. The three functions that use data in segments stored in WISS are:

- Copy segment to workstation
- Associate segment to workstation
- Insert segment

The function copy segment to workstation copies all primitives in the specified segments to the specified workstation, which is already activated. Associate segment with workstation function sends a specified segment to a specified workstation. If a workstation was not activated when the segment was created, this function later associates the segment with the workstation after it has been made active. Function insert segment copies all the primitives in a segment from the WISS and applies a special transformation specified in the function arguments. After carrying out these transformations, he primitives are inserted into the viewing pipe line.

Segmentation along with WISS facility offers powerful features for image manipulation and for controlling the display of primitives on workstations. WISS is a means of temporarily storing picture data in the computer memory, for better control of segments and displays on workstations. It is also necessary to store images on secondary storage devices, to be used at a later date. They are also used to transfer images generated on one computer system to another. GKS metafile standard define a standard format for storing picture information.

5.7.7   GKS – Metafiles

A graphics metafile is defined as mechanism for the transfer and storage of graphics data, which is both application independent and device independent . the metafiles used by GKS are called GKS metafiles or GKSM. GKS metafiles are sequential files containing graphical information, which can be read and interpreted by GKS.

Now a days computer graphics metafile (CGM) is being accepted as s separate standard. GKS provides an interface to this metafile. For easy usage and for better control, metafiles are treated as separate class of workstations in GKS. GKSM – Input is one type of workstation for reading in graphical data from metafiles. Similarly, GKSM – output workstation writes image data into metafiles.

One major advantage of having graphics metafiles is that images are made displayable on a number of display devices. Also the device independent way of storing metafiles, makes it possible to store images for a long time and display on a number of devices.

5.7.8   GKS – Operating States

When an applicat6ion program, which uses GKS, is executed , at any time, the GKS will be in a definite state. The operating states of GKS is defined by a list of state variables in many state lists present in GKS. Calls to different control functions set the operating states of GKS. There are five operating states defined in GKS.

They are:

1. GKS closed
2. GKS open
3. at least one workstation open
4. at least one workstation active

segment open

Calling a specific GKS function may be valid or invalid depending on the operating state. For instance, call to functions for output primitives are not valid, when GKS is in the state GKS closed. FIG. 5.33 shows schematically the transition between operating states and allowed functions.

GKS provides many inquiry functions, which allow the application program to get the current state of GKS, and also the current status of variables in GKS state lists, workstation state lists, segment state list, error state list, workstation and pixel attributes, GKS description table and workstation description table. These information will help the programmers a great extent to design the graphics programs in a more effective manner. These functions will not be described here in detail. Readers may refer to any books on GKS mentioned in the reference.

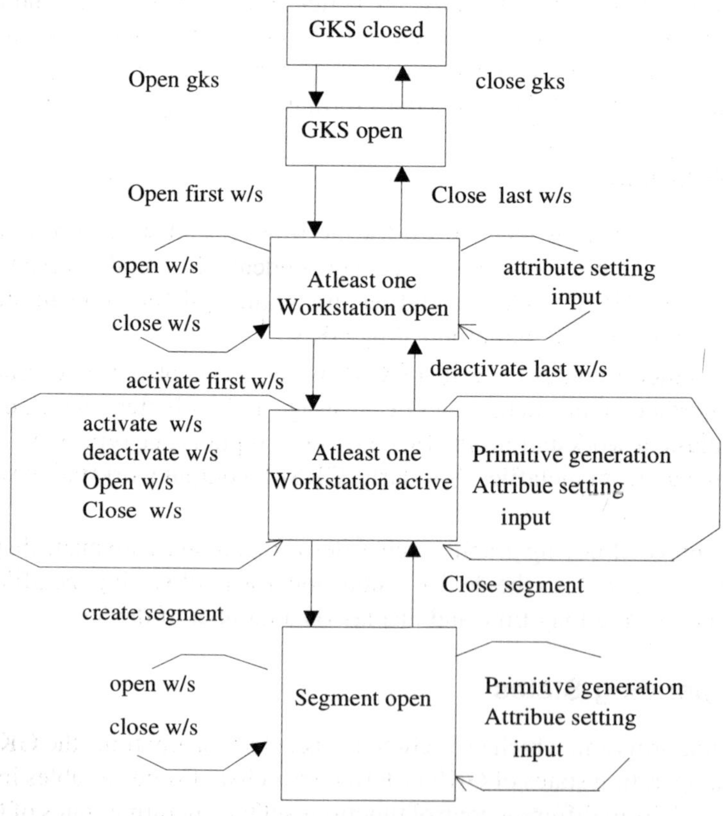

Fig. 5.33 Operating States and Allowed Functions

5.7.9   GKS – Levels

The GKS system as a whole is designed to be used in a wide range of application, right from static display of images to real time interaction. Also it is extremely difficult to incorporate all the GKS features in all implementations, since many features never be used in many applications. Hence, based on the level of functional capability of GKS implementation, with respect to input and output, different levels of implementation are defined in GKS standard. The functional capabilities of GKS are grouped into five major areas. They are:

- Output (minimal, full)
- Input (no input, request only, full)
- Number of workstations (one, multiple)
- Attributes (only predefined bundles and individual specifications, full bundle)
- Segmentation(none, basic,(without WISS), full)

An unlimited number of combinations may result, if any arbitrary combinations are allowed. Hence, GKS defines a level structure on two independent axes, input on one axis, and all the other functions on he other, summarized as output.

The input level axis has three possibilities :

     a: No input

     b: REUESAT input

     c: Full input

The output level axis also has three possibilities :

     0: Minimal output

     1: Basic segmentation with full output

     2: Workstation Independent Segment Storage and full output

At every level, three different types of capabilities are defined. They are:

1. an explicitly defined and required capability

2. an explicitly defined and non-required capability

3. a conceptually defined and non-reuired capability

Fig.5.34. shows the GKS level concept. Each box contains only these functions, which are added to the previous boxes of the same row and column. For instance, level 2b will contain everything corresponds to column 0a, 0b, 1a, and 2a, and 2b. That means it has all the capabilities except SAMPLE and EVENT input and PICK.

5.7.10   GKS – Programming

The GKS functionality independent of any programming language has been in the earlier sections. To write programs in high level programming languages GKS provide language binding specifications. So far language bindings for FORTRAN and Pascal programming languages have been accepted by ISO. Now work is in progress in ISO to publish a separate language binding standard for C programming language. The present discussion on language

Output Level	a	b	c
0	No input, minimal control Predefined bundles, Multiple normalization, Transformation with minimum settable as 1., all Output functions, metafile Optional	REQUEST input, mode setting initialise functions for logical input devices no PICK, set viewport, input priority	SAMPLE and EVENT input, no PICK
1	Full output with full bundle concept, multiple workstation(s) concept, basic segmentation (everything except WISS), metafiles	REQUEST pick, mode setting and initialize for PICK	SAMPLE and EVENT input PICK
2	Workstation Independent Segment Storage (WISS)		

Fig. 5.34 GKS - Levels

binding for C is based on second working draft of Part 4 of ISO 8651, which gives complete details on the proposed language binding in C programming language. The knowledge of basic concepts of GKS is necessary to write programs for graphics using GKS.

A number of graphics libraries conforming to GKS standard are available on a wide range of computer systems, to be used with programs written in Fortran, Pascal and C languages. Due to delay in publishing C language binding for GKS, most of these graphics libraries do not conform to the proposed c binding . In fact, most of the GKS systems available on micros and workstations use the standards stipulated in FORTAN binding for C also. Such GKS systems use only the basic data types supported by the language, whereas, the proposed C binding. Defines about 132 data types using typedef, structure, union and enumeration. The use of such GKS systems This section describes the proposed C binding standard conforming to part 4 of ISO 8651 deaft. Four example programs are given at the end of this section. The first two programs are intended to do the same task. But the first one conforms to the proposed standard C binding, Whereas, the second one uses only the basic data types for parameters similar to that of FROTRAN, which uses only basic data types, is much easier to program. Readers may refer to books by Hopgood et al [9] ad Enderele [5] to know more about FORTRAN binding standard of GKS. It is expected that, once the final document on C binding is published by ISO, number of graphics systems conforming to the standard will be a available for use on a wide variety of computers.

The function names of GKS are all mapped to C functions which begin with the letter g. For example a GKS function DELETE SEGMENT FROM WORKSTATION is gdel_seg_ws. Del, seg and ws are the abbreviations for DELETE, SEGMENT and WORKSTATION. The conjunctive FROM is mapped to the null string.

All the functions in GKS return void. i.e., all the functions are of void type. The C binding document defines different data types for different types of attributes to be associated with primitives, and other parameters to be used with many GKS functions. The header file gks.h contains declarations for all these data types. An application program has to include this header file, so that all the data types are declared in the program.

There are four different classes of data type definitions in C language binding of GKS. They are described in brief here.

5.7.10.1 Environmental Type Definitions

These allow for ease of porting GKS implementation between different environments. These type are used as the basis for other daa types defined.

> Gchar: This type is used for storing characters.
>
> These are defined as typedef char Gchar;
>
> Gint: This data type stores integer values used by GLS.
>
> This is defined as typedef int Gint;
>
> Gfloat: Variables of this type are for storing real values.
>
> This is defined as typedef float Gfloat;

5.7.10.2 Skeleton Type Definitions

These set of data types called skeleton associate with items which are subject to registration or implementation dependent. In each skeleton nnnn refers to the absolute value of the item identifies. For instance GDP is a non standard primitive in standard GKS. It varies form one workstation to another and from one implementation to another. This GDP dependent data type is defined as

```
Typedef struct {


       .......
    } Ggdp_data_nnnn;
```

For every identifier nnnn, the number of members in the structure can vary. The document on C language binding specifies a total of 18 data type definition of skeleton type. These are defined mainly for types associated with implementations.

5.7.10.3 Implementation Dependent Type definitions

Take the case of a prompt and echo type associated with one the logical input devices, say locator. An implementation can define up to six different prompt and echo type these are declared as shown below:

```
Typedef struct {

    .... .
    } Gloc_pet_1;
```

The above typedef statement defines all the parameters associated with the first prompt and echo type as members of the structure. The members can be of type Gint, Gfloat or Gchar or any other derived data type from the above. Similarly up to six different prompt and echo types can be defined. 26 different implementation dependent data types are defined in the language binding document under this category.

5.7.10.4   *Implementation Independent Type Definitions*

These are the general type definitions which are implementation independent. Eighty-five (85) different data types are defined under this class. A few important and most commonly used data types are described below, along with a few functions, which uses the data types defined.

Attributes to output primitives can be set either in an individual manner or in abounded manner. It is required to set the value of the aspect source flag to select the manner in which attributes are to be set for output primitives. The aspect source flag is set by defining a structure variable of the **Gasfs**, which has 13 members for different attributes of output primitives. Each on member of the structure can take a value either GBUNDLE OR GINDIV for bundled mode or for individual mode respectively. The typedef statements for **Gasfs** and gasf are shwon bello:

```
typedef enum {
            GBUNDLE,
            GINDIV,
} Gasf;
typedef struct (
Gasf line_type;         /* line type ASF */
Gasf line_width;        /*line withd scale factor ASF*/
Gasf line _colour;      /*polyline colour ASF */
Gasf marker_type;       /*marker type ASF */
Gasf marker_size;       /* marker size scale factor ASF*/
Gasf maker_colour;      /* poly marker colour ASF */
Gasf fontprec;          /*text font and precision ASF 8?
Gasf expan;   /*character expansion ASF */
Gasf space;   /*character spacing ASF8/
Gasf text_colour;       /* text colur ASF */
Gasf fill_int_stype; /*file area interior style ASF */
Gasf fill_colur;
            } Gasfs;
```

In the above, the first data type definition define Gasf is on enum (enumeration). I.e., any variable of type Gasf can take the vale either GBUNDLAE or GINDIV. The second one defines aspect source flags for all attributes of output primitives. I.e., The each member of the structure Gasfs can take a value either GBUNDLE or GINDIV as explained above.

A variable with type Gcoord_unit defines the device coordinate units. It can be either metre or any other user specified unit.

```
typedef enum {
            GMETRE_UNIT,
            GOTHER_UNIT,
            }Gcoord_unit;
```

The display size of the output device is declared using the data type **Gdisp_size**, which require three paramenters to be defined as shown below;

```
typedef struct {
        Gcoord_unit coord_unit; /*device coordinate unit */
        Gpt coord_unit_sized;    /*device cordinate unit size */
Gint_pt ras_unit_size;         /*raster unit size */
} Gdisp_size;
```

A variable of type Gdisp_size is used for specifiyihg device coordinate units,

Functions for point, line and text primitive reuire point information to be passed as parameteres. These are specified in terms of coordinate pairs. Gks C language binding provides two data types Gint_pt and Gpt which define an integer coordinate pair and float coordinate pair respectively.

```
typedef struct {
        Gint x_coord      /* x coordinate */
        Gint y_coord      /* y coordinate */
          } Gint_pt;
typedef sturct {
        Gfloat x; /* x coordinate */
        Gfloat y; /* y coordinate */
          } Gpt;1
```

The output primitive fill_area reuires a parameter defining the interier style of the area to be filled. GKS define four different interior styles i.e., hellow, solid, pattern or hatch. The following enum type definition is used to define this.

```
typedef enum {
        GHOLLOW,
        GSOLID,
        GPAT,
        GHATCH
        } Gfill_int_style;
```

Now a style index can be assigned to a selected interior style with a colur associated with it. This is called file area representation. The data type to define file area represntation is shown below:

```
typedef struct {
        Gfill_int_style int_style /* file area interior style */
        Gint     style_ind       /* fill area style index */
```

```
Gint      colour  /*fill area colour */
} Gfill_rep;
```

In the following program segment three different interior styles are defined using three variables. The variable style1 has a style index 1 and colour 1 with HOLLOW interior style, style2 has a style index 2 and a colour 2 with interior style SOLID and style3 represents an interior style with a specified pattern.

```
/*variable declarations */
Gfill_rep style1, style2, style3;

style1.int_style = GHOLLOW;
style1.style_ind =1;
style1.colour =1;

style2.int_style= GSOLID;
style2.style_ind = 2;
style2.colour =3;

style3.int_style =GPAT;
style3.style_ind = 2;
style3.colour=3;
```

Now a GKS function set_fill_area_index can be called with any one of the variable style1, style2 or style3 as its parameter to set the required attribute to the primitive fill area. Similarly the following typedef statement, define a data type to declare polyline representation, when the aspect source flag is set to GBUNDLE.

```
typedef struct {
Gint type;          /* line type */
Gfloat width; /* line width scale factor */
Gint colour; /* polyline colour */
} Gline_rep;
```

It is a general programming practice in graphics programs to set different output primitive representations at the beginning of the program. So that later, only the corresponding indices for each polyline representation can be used to get lines with specified style, width and colour, associated with a workstation. To set a polyline representation the programmer can write the following code.

```
Gint ws-id ; /* workstation */
Gint line-ind ; /* polyline index */
Gline_rep *line_rep1,
*line_rep2 ; /* polyline representation */
```

```
line_rep1 = (Gline_rep *) malloc(sizeof(Gline_rep));
ws-id = 1;
line-ind = 1;
line_rep1->type = 2;
line_rep1->width = 1.0;
line_rep1->colr = 3;
gset-line_rep (ws-id, line-ind, line_rep1);
```

The function gset_line_rep associates the following attributes of polyline or workstation 1 to line index 1. The variable line_ind stands for line index.

```
line type = 2
line width scale factor = 1.0
and line colour = 3
```

Now if a set of poly lines are to be drawn with these attributes. The only thing the programmer has to do is to set the polyline index to 1 before calling the function for polyline. The function *gset-/ine-ind* sets poly line index and gpolyline draws the line.

```
gset-lind-ind (1);
gpolyline (*array_pt);
```

The polyline is drawn with the attributes assigned to line index 1. The argument *array-pt is a pointer of type Gpt which stores the set of vertices, which will be connected by lines with attributes set in line index 1. i.e., the type of line with a dashed pattern specified with an index 2, normal width and a colour specified with an index 3 on workstation 1. To draw a rectangle, array-pt can be set as shown below. array _pt is declared as

Gpt *array-pt;

To draw the rectangle given in Fig.5.35, five coordinate pairs has to be given. Because the line will start at 1 and end at 1. The following statements assign these values to the pointer variable array -pt. A pointer variable array-pt is declared with its type as Gpt. The malloc statement allocates memory for the array and the following statements assign values to the respective variables. The line index is set as I and then the function *gpolyline* is called to draw the rectangle.

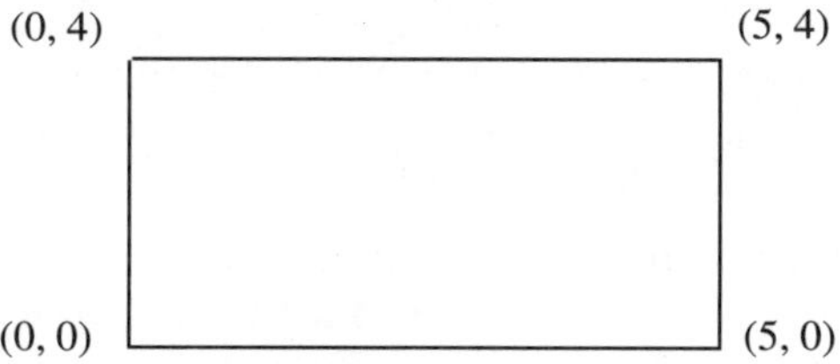

Fig. 5.35 A Rectangle

```
array-pt = (Gpt *) malloc (5* size of (Gpt)) ;
array_pt->x = 0.0 ;
array_pt->y = 0.0 ;
(array-pt+1)->x = 5.0 ;
(array-pt+1)->y = 0.0 ;
(array-pt+2)->x = 5.0 ;
(array-pt+2)->y = 4.0 ;
(array-pt+3)->x = 0.0 ;
(array-pt+3)->y = 4.0 ;
(array-pt+4)->x = 0.0 ;
(array-pt+4)->y = 0.0 ;
gset-line-ind (1) ;
gpolyline (array-pt) ;
```

In the above, the data values, are explicitly defined. Instead, a for loop can be used and point data can be read from a file as shown below.

```
for (i=0; i<5; i++) {
        fscanf (in_file, "%f %f", & (array-pt+i)->x,
            & (array-pt+i)->y) ; }
```

All the subsequent calls to function polyline will generate lines with the attributes associated with line index 1. The above method of setting attributes is by using the bundled concept. Individual attributes can be set using the functions shown below.

gset-linetype (line-type) set the line type attribute to that speci- fied by variable line-type. *gset-linewidth (line-width)* sets the line width attribute to that specified by variable 11ne-\fidth. Similarly the function *gset-line-colr -ind (line-colr -in d)* sets the line colour. When more workstations are attached, attributes can be set by bundling rather than individual setting. Attributes for other primitives are also set exactly the same as above. Typical functions for setting text attributes are discussed below.

Function *gset-tezt-rep* is called for setting text representation. It has the following form.

```
gset-text-rep (
Gint ws-id;        /* \forkstation identifier */
Gint text-ind, /* text index */
Gtext-rep *text-rep /* text representation */
    ) ;
```

Here the pointer variable text-rep is of data type Gtext.Iep, which is defined as:

```
typedef struct {
        Gfontprec fontprec;        /* font and precision */
        Gfloat expan; /* character expansion factor */
```

```
Gfloat space; /* character spacing */
Gint colr; /* text colour */
  } Gtext_rep;
```

Gfontprec is again a GKS defined data type and is described in gks.h as shown below.

```
typedef struct {
Gint font; /* text font */
Gtext_prec prec; /* text precision */
} Gfontprec;
```

Gtext-prec is a data type for setting the value of variable prec to either STRING, CHAR or STROKE. It is achieved by using an enum type definition as shown below.

```
typedef enum {
GSTRING..PREC,
GCHAR_PREC,
GSTROKE_PREC
} Gtext-prec;
```

The variable defined using datatype Gtext prec can take any one of the values GSTRING_PREC or GCHAR-PREC or GSTROKE-PREC. These corresponds to the string, char and stroke precision respectively. The fonts are identified by number 1..... n, where n is the number of text fonts available in the GKS implementation. The following code will set a text representation with text index Ion workstation 1.

```
/* variable declaration */
Gfontprec fpl ;
Gtext_rep *text_rep ;
 Gpt .*textpos ;
Gchar *char-string ;

/* attribute setting */
fpl.font 1 ; /* font type 1 */
fpl.prec = GCHAR-PREC ; /* char precision */
text_rep->fontprec = fpl ;
text_rep->expan = 2.0; /* char exp fac = 2.0 */
text_rep->space = 5; /* character spacing = 5 */
 text_rep->clr = 2; /* text colour */
gset_text_rep(1, 1, text_rep) ;
```

Similarly different combinations of text attributes can be set. Before calling *gtext* to ou~put character, a required combination can be selected by setting an appropriate text index as shown below.

```
        textpos = (Gpt *) malloc (size of (Gpt)) ;
        textpos->x = 100.0 ;
        textpos- >y = 50.0 ;
        char-string = "GKS testing" ;
        gset-text-ind (1) ;
        gtest(textpos, char-string) ;
```

A character string GKS testing will be displayed at coordinate (100.0, 50.0) with the string left justified. The function *gset-text-ind* sets only font, precision, character expansion factor, character spacing, and text colour. The other attributes character height, character up vector, text path, and text alignment can be set in individual mode. Because the previous set of attributes are workstation de- pendent they are generally set in bundle mode. They can be set in individual mode also. Individual settings of the second set of attributes are discussed below.

gset-char -ht (char -ht) sets the character height. The height of the subsequent character strings displayed through the text output primitive will be the value assigned to the float variable char_ht. *gset-char-up-tlec (*char-up-vec)* decides the orientation of characters displayed. The argument char-up-vec is of Gpt type. The follow- ing code rotates the characters by *45°* in anticlockwise direction. A vector defining this angle is (-1.0, 1.0). Original up vector is (0.0, 1.0) and up vector after rotation is (-1.0,1.0). The values defining up vector are only relative. For instance (1.0, 1.0) and (5.0, 5.0) specifies the same direction.

```
        j
Gpt *up-vector ; 1* declaration *1
up-vector = (Gpt *) malloc (size (Gpt)) ;
up-vector->x = -1.0 ;
up-vector- >y = 1.0 ;
gset-char-up-vec (up-vector) ;
```

Text path is set using *gset-text-path (text-path)* function. The argument text-path is of data type Gtext-path, which is defined in gks.h, and is as shown below.

```
        typedef enum {
GNORMAL-VERT,
GTOP-VERT,
GCAP-VERT,
GHALF -VERT ,
GBASE-VERT,
GBOTTOM-VERT
        } Gtext_vert ;
```

Fig.5.36 (a) illustrate different horizontal text alignments and (b) different vertical alignments.

Fig. 5.36   Text Alignment

The C language binding of GKS provide 212 different functions to write programs for graphics. These functions are divided into nine different groups. They are described below in brief. It is not the aim of the present book to give details of all the GKS functions. A few commonly used functions are discussed, so that using those functions, readers can write graphics programs.

5.7.10.5   *Control Functions*

These functions mainly set the operating states of GKS. Some workstation control functions are also included in this category. The first GKS functions to be called in any program using GKS is *Open GKS*. The function name and arguments are given below:

```
gopen-gks(Gchar err-f, size-t mem) ,
```

err-f is the error file name, to which all the error messages generated during running a GKS program is directed. Generally GKS programs do not stop execution even after generation of error messages. The second argument mem specifies the memory available for GKS. This function puts the GKS operating state to *GKS opened*.

The last G KS function called in any program which uses G KS in *Close GKS*. This does not have any arguments. This function sets the operating state to *GKS not opened*. The function name is:

```
gclose-gks() ; .
```

Another operating state of G KS is *at least* one *workstation opened*. The function name and parameters are:

```
gopen-ws (Gint wsid, /*workstation identifier *1
         Gconn-id conn-id, 1* connection identifier *1
         Gws-type ws-type) 1* workstation type *1
```

ws_id identifies the workstation opened. conn-id is the connec- tion identifier. This specifies the communication port of the computer system to which the workstation is connected. This parameter decides the output channel to be selected by GKS to route the graphics output. The gconn-id is a printer character string. The workstation type is an integer which is set by the GKS implementor. The function *gclose-ws(ws.-id)* closes the workstation.

Another set of functions which sets and rests the operating state of GKS is *activate workstation* and *deactivate workstation*. The function *gactivate-ws (ws.-id)* activates a workstation identified by ws-id and *gdeactivate-ws (ws-id)* dactivates it.

5.7.10.6 Output Functions

The six functions that come under this category are those which display output primitives. They are :

```
gpolyline (Gint num_pt, 1* no.of points *1
          Gpt *array_pt); 1* array of points *1
 gpolymarker (Gint num_pt, Gpt *array-pt);
gtext (Gpt *text-pos, 1* text position *1
          Gchar *char_string); 1* character string */
gfillarea (Gint num-pt,
          Gpt *array_pt);
gcell-array (Grect *rectangle, 1* cell rectangle *1
          Gdim *dim 1* colour index array dimm .*/
          Gint *colr); 1* colour index array *1
```

In the data types used in the above functions, all except Grect and Gdim have been defined. Grect is defined as

```
typedef struct {
Gpt p ; 1* lower left corner *1
Gpt q ; 1* upper right corner *1
 } Grect;
and Gdim is defined as
typedef struct {
          Gint xJiim; /* dimension along x *1
          Gint yJiim; 1* dimension along y *1
          } Gdim;
```

5.7.10.7 Output Attribute Functions

The output attributes control the appearance of output primitives on the display surface of workstations. Functions to set output attributes are divided into two categories. First category consists of functions to set workstation independent primitive attributes and second category consists of functions to set workstation dependent primitive attributes. The first category has twenty five (25) functions and the other has six (6). Many of these functions are already been described in an earlier section.

5.7.10.8 *Transformation Functions*

These functions set the viewing transformations of GKS. There are seven (7) functions
defined for this purpose. Every GKS pro- gram uses these functions quite often for setting and
selecting various transformations, both normalization as well as workstation. The syntax of
these functions are shown below.

```
Set Window
gset-win (Gint tranJlum, 1* transformation number */
         Glim *win-lim) 1* window limits */
 where Glim is defined as
          typedef start {
          Gfloat x_min; 1* x minimum limit *1
           Gfloat x_max; 1* x maximum limit *1
           Gfloat y_min; 1* y minimum limit *1
           Gfloat y_max; 1* y maximum limit *1
} Glim ;
Set viewport
          Gset_vp ( Gint transform, /* transformation number */
            Glim    *wp_lim); / viewport limits */
```

A normalization transformations can be set using these functions. Let the window size
[0,0] [1000,1000] and viewport size [0.0, 0.5] [0.0,0.5]. The following code sets a
normalization transformation number 1 with above window and viewport sizes.

```
        /* declarations */
        Glm *win_lim, *vp_lim ; Gint trans_num ;
        Gwin_lim = (Glim *) malloc ( sizeof (Glim));
        vp_lim = (Glim *) malloc ( sizeof (Glim));
        win_lim ->        x_min = 0.0 ;
        win_lim -.>       x_max = 1000.0;
        win_lim ->        y_min = 0.0;
        win_lim ->        y_max = 1000.0 ;
        vp_lim     ->     x_min = 0.0 ;
        vp_lim     -.>    x_max = 0.5;
        vp_lim     ->     y_min = 0.0;
        vp_lim -> y_max = 0.5 ;
        tran_num = 1;
        /* set normalisation transformation 1 */
        gset_win ( tran_num, win_lim);
        gset_vp (tran_num, vp_lim);
```

Like this many normalization transformations can be set and at any time one of them can be selected using function select normalization transformation, the syntax for which is shown below.

```
gset-norm-tran ( Gint norm-tran-num) ;
```

The function set workstation window and set workstation viewport set the workstation transformations.

Set workstation window

```
gset-ws-win (Gint ws-id, Glim *ws-win-lim);
```

Set workstation viewport

```
gset-ws-vp (Gint ws-id, Glim *ws-win-lim);
```

These functions are also used similar to set window and set viewport. The other two functions in this category are set clipping indicator, which turns on or off clipping and *set viewport input priority,* which sets the relative priorities of viewports for the purpose of input.

5.7.10.9 *Segment Functions*

These set of functions are used to create and manipulate seg- ments and also to set segment attributes. Segment functions are again divided into two categories. C language binding of G KS define eight (8) functions to create and manipulate segments. They are:

Create segment

```
gcreate-seg (Gint seg-name);
```

Close segment

```
gc/ose-seg ( ) ;
```

Rename segment

```
grename-seg (Gint o/d-seg-name, Gint new-seg-name);
```

Delete segment

```
gde/-seg (Gint seg-name);
```

Delete segment from workstation ,

```
gde/-seg-ws (Gint ws-id, Gint seg-name);
```

Associate segment with Workstation

```
gassoc-seg-ws (Gint ws-id, Gint seg-name);
```

Copy segment to workstation

```
gcopy-seg-ws (Gint ws-id, Gint seg-name);
```

Insert segment

```
ginsert-seg (Gint seg-name, Gftaot tran-matrix [2] [3] );
```

The transformation matrix tranJnatrix of size 2 x 3) transforms the segment segJ1ame) before putting it into the viewing pipeline. As the names of functions and arguments are obvious) they are not explained in detail. The second set of segment related functions set different segment attributes.

Set Segment Transformation

```
gset-seg-tran (Gint seg-name, Gftoat tran-matrix [2] [3] );
```

Set Visibility

```
gset-vis (Gint seg-name, Gseg-vis seg-vis);
```

Set Highlighting

```
gset-hight (Gint seg-name, Gseg-det seg-det);
```

Three data types Gseg-vis, Gseg-high and Gseg-det are used in the above segmentation functions. They specify the values that variables seg-vis, seg-.high and seg-det take respectively. They are defined in gks .h as shown below.

```
typedef enum {
        GVIS, 1* visible *1
        GINVIS 1* invisible *1
        } Gseg-vis;
typedef enum { GNORMAL, 1* normal *1
        GHIGHL    1* highlighted *1
        } Gseg-.highl;
typedef enum {
        GUNDET, 1* undetect *1
        GDET 1* detect *1
        } Gseg-det;
```

Set Segment Priority

```
gset-seg-pri (Gint seg-name, Gfloat seg-pri )
```

Segment priority variable seg-pri varies between 0.0 and 1.0. The relative numbers assigned as priorities to different segments de- cide the order in which segments are displayed, when they are re- generated, This attribute setting is extremely useful when segments overlap each other .

5.7.10.10 *Input Functions*

All the functions for graphics input are grouped under this sec- tion. When the graphics program expects an input, first it is necessary to initialize the input device. GKS provide six (6) functions to initialize logical inout devices, one each for locator ,stroke, valuator , choice, pick and string. The following function is a typical initialization function for locator device.

Initialize Locator

```
        ginit-loc (Gint ws-id, 1* workstation identifier *1
        Gint loc_num,, 1* locator device number *1
        Gint init_norm-tran_num,
        Gpt *init-loc-position, 1* init loc posn *1
        Gint pet. 1* prompt and echo type *1
        Glim *echo-area, 1* echo area *1
        Gloc-data *loc-data) 1* locator data array *1
```

In the above function, argument loc-data of type Gloc-data is an implementation dependent type and is defined in gks .h. The variable loc-data stores the data records, which are positions located using the input device. Initializing locator require many parameters to be specified. Out of them the parameter pet, i.e., prompt and echo type dependes on the specific GKS implementation. They are:

1. ws-id- workstation identification number
2. loc-num -device number allocated to locator in GKS implementation
3. init_norm-tran_num -This initial value, serve for starting display of prompts and echos and for setting initial measure values. This also facilitates the application program to adjust the input device to some pre- defined value.
4. pet -Prompt and echo type is again implementation dependent
5. echo-Area -Rectangular area specified as the coordinate pairs of lower left and upper right corner
6. ini t-loc-posi tion -Is the initial position, where the cursor should locate when it is initialized.
7. loc-data- This parameter may contain required values and some additional information. In the case of a stroke devices, the data record contains items defining input buffer- sizc in number of points.

Once the input device is initialised, the next step is to set the operating mode to either REQUEST, EVENT or SAMPLE. One function is defined for each logical input device, for setting its operating mode. As an example, function for *set locator mode* is shown below.

```
        gset-locJnode( Gint ws-id, 1* workstation id *1
            Gint loc_num, 1* locator device no.*1
            Gin-mode op-mode 1* operating mode *1
            Gecho-sw echo-sw); 1* echo switch *1
```

Where op-mode in a variable of Gin-mode type, which is defined as an enum in gks .h and are shown below.

```
typedef enum {
        GREQ, /* for REQUEST */
        GSAMPLE /* for SAMPLE */
        GEV /* for EVENT */
        } Gin-mode;
typedef enum {
        GECHO, /* to echo prompt */
        GN-ECHO /* to supress echo of prompt */
        } Gecho..sw
```

The variable echo-sw controls the echoing of prompt on the dis- play surface.

The next set of functions are input functions in three different operating modes for each of the logical input devices. One typical function *reque..t locator* is given below.

```
greq-loc (Gint ws-id, /* workstation identifier */
 Gint loc_num, /* locator device number */
 Gin-st *in-st,   /* OUT input status */
 Gint *norm-tran-num, /* OUT normalisation transform no */
 Gpt *loc-pos); /* OUT locator poBition */
```

greq-Ioc returns three values, the position located and the normalisation transformation is used to convert the position values to world coordinate system and a status. This status can take values OK, NONE or NO-IN and is defined in enum shown below.

```
typedef enum {
        GOK, 1* If position returned *1
        GNONE, 1* If break facility involved *1
        GNO-IN 1* If no Input *1
        } ;
```

5.7.10.11 *Metafile Functions*

Functions for metafile interface of GKS are provided under this category. There are four functions for metafile interface. These functions are used to create metafiles and read information from metafiles. The G KS metafiles contain information on every output primitive that is displayed after opening the MO (Metafile Output) workstation. The functions are :

```
Write Item to G KSM
gwrite-item (Gint ws-id, /* workBtation id */
```

```
Gint item-type, /* item type */
Gint item-data-length, /* item data rec 19th */
 Gitem-data *item-data); /*item data record*/

Get Item Type from G KSM
gget-item-type(Gint ws-id, /* workstation id */
        Gint item-type, /* item type */
        Gint item-data-length); /* item data rec lgth */
Read Item from GKSM
gread-item (Gint ws-id, /* workstation id */
        Gint max-item-data-length, /* max data rec lgth */
        Gitem-data *item-data) ;
Interpret Item
ginterpret-item(Gint item-type, /* item type */
        Gint item-length, /* item length */
        Gitem-data *item-data); /*item data record*/
```

Now International Standards Organisation is working on a separate metafile standard called Computer Graphics Metafile (CGM), which is expected to be accepted by both ISO and ANSI.

5.7.10.12 Inquiry Functions

GKS provides 103 functions for getting information's on various items like, transformations, state list variables, primitive attributes, segment status, state of input devices, various facilities available in the GKS implementations, predefined attribute representations, pixel information etc. The application program can any time get information from G KS using these inquiry functions.

5.7.10.13 Utility Functions

Two utility functions are provided in GKS to initialize and modify transformation matrices, to be operated on segments for manipulating them. The function Evaluate Transformation Matrix generates a transformation matrix with a given value, whereas, Accumulate Transformation Matrix modifies the already defined transformation
matrix.

```
Evaluate Transformation Matrix
      geval-tranJflatrix (
            Gpt *fixed-pt,
            Gvec *shift-vec,
            Gfloat angle,
            Gvec *scale-vec, ;
```

```
            Gcoord-sw coord-sw,
            Gint *err-ind,
            Gfloat tran_matrix [2][3]) ;
Accumulate Transformation Matrix
        gaccum-tran-matrix (
            Gfloat tran-matrix [2] [3] ,
            Gpt *fixed-pt,
            Gvec *shift-vec,
            Gfloat angle,
            Gvec *scale-vec,
            Gcoord-sw coord-sw,
            Gint *err-ind.
            Gfloat tran-matrix [2] [3]);
```

The utility function *evaluate transformation matrix* generates a matrix of size 2 x 3, from the single operation specified in the parameter list. The second function *accumulate transformation matrix,* accumulates any number of transformation operations translate, scale and , rotate in any order of multiplicity within one matrix. This function expects an input matrix which is initialized by the function *evaluate transformation* matrix.

5.7.11 GKS -Example Programs

The language independent G KS functions and language bindings that map the language independent functions to specific functions in C are discussed in earlier sections. The same program written in different programming languages will look very much different, as the way in which they use the different data types vary. Four ex- ample programs are given below to illustrate the way one might use the *GKS/C* binding to develop graphics programs. The first two programs are intended to do the same task. The first one is written conforming to the standard C binding discussed above and in the second one only basic data types are used similar to that of FOR- TRAN binding. They illustrate generation of graphics output using GKS. The third program demonstrates the programming for graph- ics input using locator device. Segmentation and use of modeling transformations on segments are illustrated in program 4. Necessary comments and annotations are given in the program itself so that, the program needs no additional explanations. At first instant the programs seem too long. That is because many lines are used exclusively for defining the coordinates of points. In practical situations, the data to be plotted or drawn will be available in the variables. Also the statements for opening and closing gks and workstations are more or less the same irrespective of the length of the program.

Program 1 -Graphics Output (Standard C Binding)
This program creates an image shown in Fig.5.37.

242

```c
#include <gks.h>

1* definition of constants *1

#define GKS-ERR "gks.err" 1* name of GKS error file *1
#def ine DEF_BUFFER GDEF_MEM_SIZE 1 * let GKS choose the buffer size *1
#define PC-WS      1                1* work,station identifier *1
#define CONN-1D   1                1* connection identifier *1
#define WS-TYPE   1                1* workstation type *1
#define TRAN-NUM 1                 1* normalization transformation number *1
#define WHITE     0                1* colour definition *1
#define BLUE      1
 #define RED               2
main ( )
{
static Glim window = {0.0, 150.0, 0.0, 150.0} ;
static Glim viewport = {0.0, 1.0, 0.0, 1.0} ;
static Gcolor-rep colr = {
{1.0, 1.0, 1.0},           /* 0 = white *1
 {0.0, 0.0, 1.0},          1* 1 = blue *1
{1.0, 0.0, 0.0},           1* 2 = red *1
 } ;
static Gpt         caption-pos = {55.0, 5.0};
static Gchar caption = "HOUSE",
static G-text-aign cen_half={GCENTRE._HOR, GHALF-VERT};
Gpt        *block-1,       *block._2 ;

1* define coordinates of blocks *1

block-1 = (Gpt *) malloc (5*sizeof (Gpt));
block_2 = (Gpt *) malloc (3*sizeof (Gpt)) ;

block-1 -> x = 10.0 ;
block-1 -> y = 10.0 ;
(block-1+1)->x = 100.0 ;
(block-1+1)->y = 10.0 ;
(block-1+2)->x = 100.0 ;
(block-1+2)->y = 80.0 ;
(block-1+3)->x = 10.0 ;
(block-1+3)->y = 80.0 ;
(block-1+4) = block-1 ;
(block_2+0) = (block-1+3) ;
```

```c
(block_2+1)->x = 50.0 ;
 (block_2+ 1) ->y = 120.0 ;
(block_2+2) = (block-1+2) ;

/* open GKS and activate a workstation */

gopen-gks (GKS-ERR, DEF_BUF) ;
gopen-ws (PC-WS, CONN-ID,WS-TYPE) ;
gactivate-ws (PC-WS) ;

/* set viewing pipeline transformation */

gset-win (TRAN_NUM, &window) ;
gset-vp (TRAN_NUM, &viewport) ;
gset_num-tran (TRAN_NUM) ;
gset-ws-win (PC-WS., &viewport) ;

/* in workstation transformation. it is assumed that the full display surface
is used
for displaying the image */

/* set colour representations */
for (i=0 ; i<3; i++)
 {
gset-colr_rep(PC-WS, i, &colr [i])
 }
/* The bottom rectangle is filled with full RED colour using fill area
primitive.
Fill area interior style and colour index in set first */

gset_fill-int-Btyle (GHATCH) ;
gset..fill-colr-ind (WHITE) ;
gfill-area (5, block-1) ;

gset-line-colr-ind (RED) ;
gpolyline(3, block_2) ;

/* put caption */
gset_char_ht (0.25) ;
gset_text_align( &cen_half);
gset_text_color_ind (BLUE) ;
gtext ( & caption_pos, caption) ;

/* close workstation and GKS */

gdeactivate_ws (pc_ws) ;
```

```c
        gclose_ws(pc_ws);
        gclose_gks();
    }
```

Program 2 – Graphics Output

Only basic data types are used in this program similar to that of FORTRAN binding.

```c
    #include <gks.h>
    #define GKS_ERR "gks.err"
    #define DEF_BUFFER GDEF_MEM_SIZE
    #define PC_WS           1
    #define CONN_ID         1
    #define WS_TYPE         1
    #define TRAN_NUM        1
    #define WHITE           0
    #define BLUE            1
    #define RED             2
    main()
    {
        float colr =  { { 1.0,       1.0,    1.0},
                    {0.0.  0.0,    1.0},
                    {1.0,  0.0,     0.0}    } ;
        char caption = "HOUSE" ;
        float *x1, *y1, *x2, *y2; int I;

        x1= (float * ) malloc ( 5 * sizeof(float) );
        y1 = (float * ) malloc ( 5 * sizeof(float) );

        *(x1+0) = 10.0 ;      *(y1+0) = 10.0 ;
        *(x1+1) = 100.0 ;     *(y1+1) = 10.0 ;
        *(x1+2) = 100.0 ;     *(y1+2) = 80.0 ;
        *(x1+3) = 10.0;       *(y1+3) = 80.0 ;
         *(x1+4) = 10.0 ;     *(y1+4) = 10.0 ;
        x2 = (float *) malloc (3 * sizeof(float)) ;
        y2 = (float *) malloc (3 * sizeof(float)) ;

        *(x2+0) = *(x1+3) ; *(y2+0) = *(y1+3) ;
         *(x2+1) = 50.0; *(y2+1) = 120.0 ;
        *(x2+2) = *(x1+2) ; *(y2+2) = *(y1+2) ;

    gopen-gks (GKS-ERR, DEF_BUF) ;
```

```
gopen-ws (PC-WS , CONN-ID, WS-TYPE) ;
gactivate-ws (PC-WS) ;
gset-win (TRAN_NUM, 0.0, 150.0, 0.0, 150.0) ;
gset-vp (TRAN_NUM, 0.0, 1.0, 0.0, 1.0) ;
gsel-num-tran (TRAN_NUM) ;
gset-ws-win (PC-WS, 0.0, 1.0, 0.0, 1.0) ;

for (i=0; i<3; i++)
gset-colr_rep (PC-WS, i, &colr[i]) ;

gset_fill_int_style (GHATCH) ;
gset_fill-colr-ind (WHITE) ;
gfill-area (5, xI) ;

gset-line-colr-ind (RED) ;
gpolyline (3, x2) ;
gset-chr-ht (0.25) ;
gset-text-lign (GCENTRE_HOR, GHALF -VERT) ; gset-text-colr-ind (BLUE) ;
gtext (55.0, 5.0, caption) j
gdeactivate-ws (PC-WS) ;
gclose-ws (PC-WS) ;
gclose-gks () ;
}
```

Both the programs given above are intended to do the same task. But the first program uses a number of GKS defined data types like Glim, Gpt, Gcolor_rep, G-text-align etc, whereas, the second program uses only the basic data types float, char and int. Beginners may find the second program easy to understand. But the use of G KS defined data types will make the program more organised, structured and standard.

Program 3 -Graphics Input

This program illustrates the use of graphics input using locator device. The program locates two points on the output device and draws a rectangle with the two located points as opposite vertices. Locator device is used in request mode.

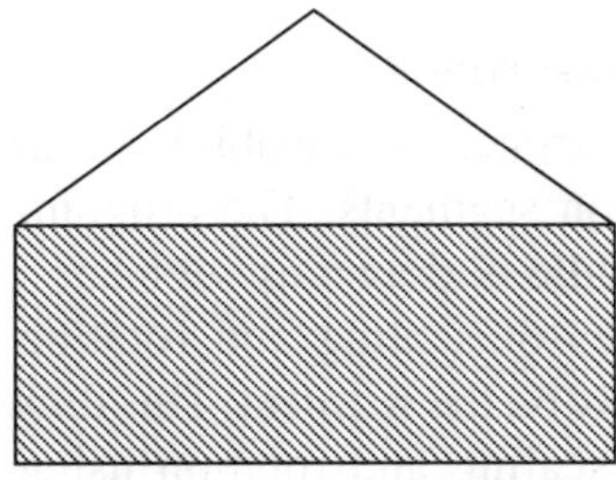

Fig. 5.37 Output of example program 1

```
#include <gks.h>
main() {
    Gpt points [5], fp, sp ;
    Gpt origin = { 0.0, 0.0} ;
    Glim echo-area = { 0.0, 1.0, 0.0, 1.0} ;
    Gin-st status ;
    int ntr ;
    gopen-.gks ("err.gks", GDEF-MEM-SIZE) ;
    gopen-ws (1, CONN-ID, 1) ;
    gactivate-ws (1) ;
    1* initialise locator with pet 2 *1
    ginit-loc (1, 1, 0, &origin, 2, &echo-area) ;
    greq-loc (1, 1, &status, &ntr, &fp) ;
    if (status == GOK) {
    1* initialiser locator with pet 5 *1
    ginit-loc (1, 1, 0, &fp, 5, &echo-area) ;
    greq-loc (1, 1, &status, &ntr, &sp) ;
     if (status == GOK)
     {
        points[0] .x=fp.x ; points[0] .y=fp.y ;
        points[1].x=sp.x ; points[1].y=fp.y ;
        points[2].x=sp.x ; points[2].y=sp.y ;
        points[3].x=fp.x ; points[3].y=sp.y ;
        points[4].x=fp.x ; points[4].y=fp.y ;
        gpolyline (5, points) ;
     }
    }
gdeactivate-ws (1) ;
gclose-ws(1);
gclose-gks ();
}
```

Program 4 – Segments and Transformation

The program given below demonstrates the capability of GKS to perform segmentation and apply modeling transformation on segments. The program draws the spiral shown in Fig. 5.19. First the square in the middle is drawn as segment 1. Then transformation matrix is evaluated for appropriate values of scaling and rotation using GKS function *evaluate transformation matrix* and is apply on the segment. This draws the second square. This matrix is then updated to accumulate scaling and rotation using the GKS function *accumulate transformation matrix* and the square is repeatedly drawn 36 times to get the final of the spiral.

```c
#define PI 3.14159
#include <gks.h>
#include <math.h>

main()
{
    Glim window = {-100.0, 100.0, -100.0, 100.0};
    Glim viewport = { 0.0, 1.0, 0.0, 1.0 } ;
    Glim device = {0.0, 639.0 , 0.0, 349.0 };
    Gppt fixed-pt = {0.0, 0.0 };
    Gvec shift-vec = { 0.0, 0.0} ;
    Gvec scale-vec = {1.0,0.0 };
    Gcoord_sw sw = Gwc;
    Gint error ; Gfloat marix[2][3], that = 5.0 * PI / 180.0 ;
    Gpt pt [5]; float side = 10.0, sf ; int i ;
    sf = sin ( (double) that ) + cos ((double) that) ;
    pt[0].x = -side/2.0 ;        pt[0].y = -side / 2.0 ;
    pt[1].x = side/2.0 ;         pt[1].y = -side / 2.0 ;
    pt[2].x = side/2.0 ;         pt[2].y = side / 2.0 ;
    pt[3].x = -side/2.0 ;        pt[3].y = side / 2.0 ;
    pt[4].x = -side/2.0 ;        pt[4].y = -side / 2.0 ;

    gopen-gks ( "err.gks", 5) ;
    gopen-ws ( 1, "" , 1) ;
    gactivate-ws (1);
    gset-win (1, &window ) ;
    gset-ws-win (1, *viewport) ;
    gset-ws-vp (1, &device);
    gsel-norm-tran (1) ;

    gcreate-seg (1) ;
        gpolyline (5, pt) ;
    gclose-seg () ;

    geval-tran-matrix ( &fixed-pt, &shift-vec, that , &scale-vec, sw,
    &error, \ matrix) ;
    scale-vec.x = sf ;
    scale-vec.y = sf ;
    for ( I=o; I< 36; I++)
    {
        gset-seg-tran ( 1, matrix) ;
```

```
        gcopy-seg-ws(1, 1);
        gaccum-tran-matrix ( matrix, &fixed-pt, &shift-vec, that, &scale-
        vec, sw, &error, matrix) ;
    }
    getch();
    gdeactivate-ws (1) ;
    gclose-ws (1) ;
    gclose-gks ();
}
```

5.8 COMPUTER AIDED DRAFTING

In engineering the process of drawing is linked with design. Any design is finally represented in the form of drawing so that construction or production can be carried out. Sixty percent of works hours in most engineering design offices are taken away by prepearation of drawings. Replacing the present manual drafting with computers and specialised peripherals requires large investments. This transformation from manual to computer aided drafting improves the quality of drawings produced and makes the production faster. Storage of drawings requires very less space and their revision on a date can be done much faster than the present manual techniques.

5.8.1 Principles and Concepts

Computer Aided Drafting uses sophisticated equipments in the place of pencil, pen, paper and drafter. The equipments include a computer, graphics screen, plotter, digitizer, mouse etc.Techniques and styles of preparation of drawing are modified, when computers are used instead of conventional drafting tools As already been dis- cussed in earlier sections, drawings can be visualised as collection of lines, curves, polygons, text etc. Hence combining these basic elements or objects by placing them in appropriate positions, dimen- sioning the objects and adding detailed notes on the drawing are the activities involved in preparation of drawings.

Computer aided drafting is a modelling process, hierarchical in nature. In the first level, a drawing is treated as a collection of points with colour attributes associated with it. Representing drawings as a collection of lines and curves can be thought of as the next level of modelling. End points of lines and a set of attributes like line colour, thickness of line and line type represent lines at this level of modelling. Similarly curves are repr~sented in many ways like, (i) centre, radius, beginning angle and ending angle; (ii) three points passing through the curve etc. with attributes similar to that of lines. Using the above information, the lines or curves can be drawn, positioned anywhere, erased, moved, copied etc. In the third level of modelling, the drawings are represented as objects, also called blocks or symbols. This enables one to define objects and create symbol libraries for different application areas. In the case of a building drawing, objects for door, window, step, sunshade etc. can be created and positioned at appropriate locations. The figures which are repeated several times are defined as blocks for easy and fast preparation of drawings. Points, lines or curves defining the object are combined and treated as single entities and are identified by separate names, so that they can be pointed by input devices like mouse, light pen or a keyboard entry for manipulation.

The drafting programs enable one to define objects at different levels of modelling and manipulate them to produce drawings. A drafting program is one, which when loaded into the computer sys- tem creates an environment to prepare drawings interactively. Most drafting packages are menu driven. Commands can either be entered directly or selected from a list displayed on the screen. The effect of every command entered is immediately displayed on the screen, so that modifications and corrections, if necessary, can be made faster. Components or blocks can be defined by pointing the set of primi- tives constituting the block by any input device and giving a specific name to it. Once a block has been defined, it can be reused any num- ber of times on the same drawing or on some other drawings. The blocks defined can be enlarged or reduced to any required size. They can be reflected any number of times or stretched to get different styles. Drawings can be logically divided into different layers and layers can be selectively displayed individually or combined. This feature of layers is a powerful one. For instance, in building drawing, the architectural plan can be placed on one layer, electrical fixtures on another, plumbing on another layer and so on. If one is interested only in plan and electrical fixtures, only those layers can be be made visible with the others invisible.

A computer aided drafting system can be regarded as a graphics equivalent of a word processor. It creates, edits, repeates, transforms and translates graphics elements instead of words in a wordprocessor . i.e., the drawings generated can be treated similar to the reports from a wordprocessor .

Computer aided drafting improves the consistency of the draw- ings, because drawings produced at different times will be exactly similar. Once a drawing is created and saved, it can be reproduced very fast. At every time of production, if any changes are to be car- ried out, it can be done very fast using the editing features provided by the drafting program.

One of the most important features of any drafting package to be used for preparing engineering drawing is the dimensioning fa- cility. Most drafting programs offer a semi-automatic dimensioning facility, requiring only the specification of the end points of the di-mension. Annotations and notes are to be added to any drawing for its completeness. The text facility with many attributes like size, font, orientation, justification etc. provide a very flexible control to include notes and annotations on drawings.

Any engineering product, let it be a building or a machine el- ement, is an object with three dimensions. To give all the details of the product, it is necessary to' give different views of the prod- uct projected onto a two'dimensional plane like plan, elevation, side view, isometric view, perspective view, section etc. In a two dimen- sional drafting system, the designer has to do a large amount of homework to create different views of the product separately with no logical relation between them. Many drafting programs support three dimensional modelling, where the product can be prepared in three dimensions and different views of the product can automati- tally be produced. One of the major advantages of this system is that any change made in the original model in three dimension will immediately reflect on all the views. Instead of separately produc- ing all the views in two dimensions, generating the object in three dimensions automatically creates the required v jew with all associ- ated attributes. As only 2D views can be displayed on a screen, the edges of the objects are transformed into lines on a plane, depending on the view point and view direction. All the attributes are then represented as in two dimensions.

The operation of a 3D drafting system uses the same equipment and is conceptually the same to that of a 2D drafting system. Only difference is that in 3D, the objects are made up of surfaces and solids, whereas in 2D they are made up of lines.

Before the designer or the draftsman starts preparing drawing using a computer aided drafting system, he should have a clear pic- ture or idea of what he is going to draw. The CAD system will be ready to accept commands and display the images on the screen, immediately after it is loaded into the memory of the computer. All the drafting systems are driven by a command language, where the commands -generally short -are either entered through the key-board or selected from a screen or tablet menu. As it is very difficult to remember all the commands, the menu control system to input the commands makes the job of the draftsman easier, since the com- mands are displayed in the menu. The user only has to pick it using input devices. Using a mouse to pick the commands is one of the efficient techniques since the coordination between the eye and hand is very effectively used.

Since it is impossible to fit all the commands in a menu and display it all at a time, menus are organised hierarchically with com- mands on one menu causing submenus to appear. The general con- trolling features like draw, edit, display etc. are kept at the topmost level in the hierarchy, so that when the drawing editor of the drafting package is loaded this top level menu appears on the screen. Screen menus are generally organised in two ways. In the first, a portion of screen is reserved for the screen menu as shown in Fig. 5.38.

First the top level menu appears and subsequently when a com- mand is given, the submenu for the command occupies the same space that the top level menu occupied. First the screen menu area is cleared and the submenu appears. The second type of menu or-ganisation uses pull- down menus, where the main menu and the sub-menu for the selected item appears simultaneously. The sub- menus are displayed in pull-down windows, which overlap the draw- ing area as shown in Fig. 5.39. Once an item is selected from the submenu, then the latest window disappears and the parameters for the command selected are accepted through the dialogue area in the screen and the effect of command is simultaneously displayed in the drawing area. This type of menu organisation as shown in Fig.5.39. This takes less space on the screen as only the topmost one line is occupied for displaying the main menu.

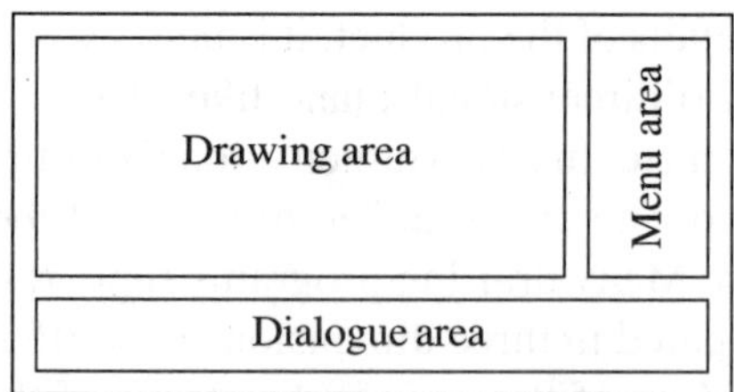

Fig. 5.38   Screen Menu Organisation -type 1

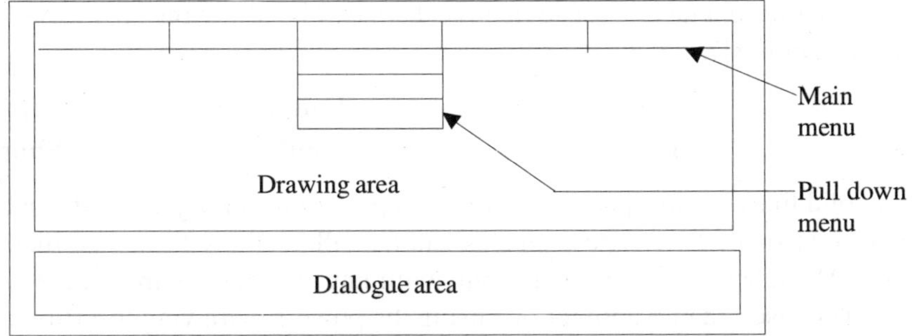

Fig. 5.39 Screen Menu Organisation -type 2

A drawing, then, is constructed by a sequence of individual commands, and the numeric data with which they operate. These commands can be put in a file and the drafting system can be asked to execute them in sequence. This facility can be indirectly utilised to graphically display the results of some computations. The program written in any high level programming language creates a file with the commands of the drafting program and the parameters are the results of computation. The file thus created can then be submitted to the drafting program to execute the commands in sequence, which simultaneously displays the action of the commands.

As a drafting medium, the computer is much more versatile compared to the traditional media. The problem has been in making this versatility available without getting into difficulties of this high technology medium. Many drafting packages are in use around the world, which demands only little knowledge about computers as far as the users are concerned.

5.8.2 Drafting Packages

Capabilities and versatilities of the drafting system vary depending on the type of computer on which they are implemented. AutoCAD, VersaCAD, DOGS etc. are few popular commercially available drafting systems presently in use across the world. These systems provide a variety of features required for producing engi- neering drawings. Out of these, AutoCAD has become more or less a defacto standard in drawing industry. The latest revisions of Au- toCAD are very powerful and provide separate language, by which computations and drawing activities can be carried out simultane- ously. A brief description of AutoCAD is given below:

AutoCAD is a computer aided drafting package, which provides a complete environment for preparation of engineering drawings. It has got almost all the capabilities described above. It supports both keyboard entry of commands and selection from either a screen menu or a tablet menu. The AutoCAD drawing editor helps one to cre- ate drawings or make changes - edit -on already prepared drawings. Entities created can be erased, moved or copied to form repeated patterns. AutoCAD also provides many drawing aids that helps one to prepare engineering drawings accurately. It has ability to build a complex object from simple ones and then manipulate it as a block. Rectangular or circular arrays of objects can be constructed, and even entire drawings can be inserted into the one, which is currently being drawn. Drawings can be generated in different layers, for se- lective display. The following are the built-in entity types provided in AutoCAD.

Lines	**Traces**	**Points**	**Circles**
Arcs	**Text**	**Solid**	**Shapes**

Traces are solid lines of any specified width. Shapes are small objects that can be created and stored in special shape files. These shapes can be called at any time, just like any other entities. Au- toCAD supports text in many fonts with any size and desired angle of rotation. One drawing can be inserted into another one using the powerful drawing insertion technique. Any number of layers can be defined and various portions of the drawing can be assigned to dif- ferent layers. Colour and line types of lines are associated with each layer. A few advanced features of AutoCAD are listed below.

- Smooth arcs can be drawn to connect two lines.
- Objects can be filled with specified pattern or cross hatched.
- Aspect ratios can be varied at any time.
- Objects can be dragged to vary their locations and sizes.
- Existing objects can be mirrored about a specified horizontal or vertical line. The original objects can either be retained or deleted.
- Semi automatic dimensioning facility is provided for linear, an- gular, diameter and radius dimensioning.
- A built-in programming language AutoLISP provides a pro- gramming environment, so that AutoCAD commands can be called along with programs written for computations.
- Drawing exchange files and script fi~es can be used to interface programs written in other high level languages with AutoCAD.
- AutoCAD provides techniques to define and extract attributes of entities. This feature is used in extracting information from a drawing for processing by other programs or to transfer it to a database.

The script file facility of AutoCAD is very useful in interfacing graphics to other programs through files. A script file is nothing but a sequence of commands which is executed sequentially when the command SCRIPT is invoked in AutoCAD. The following C program illustrates the generation of a script file through a program. The algorithm given in page 204 is used to draw the spiral. The program generates a script file to draw the spiral shown in Fig.4.19. This is drawn using only the LINE command of AutoCAD. As part of the spiral will lie outside the display, a ZOOM command is given finally with an *'e'* option to bring the complete spiral within the screen.

Program 5 -To Create AutoCAD Script File

```c
#include <math.h>
#include <stdio.h>
#define PI 3.1415927
```

```c
FILE *outp ;

struct pt {
      float x ; float y ;
      } ;
main ()
{
      float Bide, theta, sf ;
      float Bcale-lactor, thetar ;
      outp = fOpen("spiral.scr", "w") ;
      Bide = 10.0 ;
      theta = 0.0 ;
      scale-lactor = 1.0 ;
      sf = sin(5.0*PI/180.0) + cos(5.0*PI/180.0) ;
      thetar = 0.0 ;
      draw-square (side, thetar, scale-factor) ;

      while (theta < 180.0)
      {
            theta += 5.0 ;
            thetar = theta*PI/180.0 ;
            scale-factor *= sf ;
            draw-square (side, thetar, scale-factor) ;
      }
fprintf(outp, "ZOOM\n") ;
fprintf(outp, "e\n") ;
}
draw-square(side, thetar, sf)
 float side, thetar, sf ;
 {
      struCt pt *org-pt, *new-pt ;
      float sd2 ;
      org-pt = (struct pt *) malloc (sizeof(struct pt)) ;
      fprintf(outp, "LINE\n") ;
      sd2 = side/2.0 ;
      org-pt->x = -sd2 ;
      org-pt->y = -sd2 ;
      new-pt = rotate(org-pt, thetar) ;
      fprintf(outp, "%f, %f \n ",new-pt->x* sf, new-pt->y* sf);
      org-pt->x = sd2 ;
```

```c
        org-pt->y = -sd2 ;
        new-pt = rotate(org-pt, thetar) ;
        fprintf(outp, "%f, %f \n",new-pt->x* sf, new-pt->y* sf);
        org-pt->x = sd2 ;
        org-pt->y = sd2 ;
        new-pt = rotate(org-pt, thetar) ;
        fprintf(outp, "%f,%f\n" ,new-pt->x* sf, new-pt->y* sf) ;
        org-pt->x = -sd2 ;
        org-pt->y = -sd2 ;
        new-pt = rotate(org-pt, thetar) ;
        fprintf(outp, "%f,%f\n",new-pt->x* sf, new-pt->y* sf);
        org-pt->x = -sd2 ;
        org-pt->y = -sd2 ;
        new-pt = rotate(org-pt, thetar) ;
        fprintf(outp, "%f,%f\n" ,new-pt->x* sf, new-pt->y* sf) ;
        fprintf(outp, "\n") ;
        return;
}
rotate (opt, thetar)
struct pt *opt ;
float thetar ;
{
        struct pt *npt ;
        npt = (.truct pt *) malloc (sizeof (struct pt)) ;
        npt->x = opt->x*cos(thetar)-opt->y*sin(thetar) ;
        npt->y = opt->y*cos(thetar)+opt->x*sin(thetar) ;
        return (npt) ;
}
```

This program produces a script file by name SPIRAL.SCR, which can be run in AutoCAD environment by giving SCRIPT com- mand. A portion of the script file showing a few lines in the beginning and at the end is shown below.

```
LINE
-5.000000, -5.000000
5.000000, -5.000000
5 .000000 .5 .000000
-5.000000,5.000000
-5.000000, -5.000000
```

```
LINE
-4.924039,-5.868241
 5.868241,-4.924039
4.924039,5.868241
-5.868241,4.924039
-4.924039,-5.868241

.....

....
89.259082,89.259099
-89.259099,89.259082
 -89.259082,-89.259099
89.259099,-89.259082
89.259082,89.259099
ZOOM
e
```

The AutoCAD output of this script file is the spiral shown in Fig.5.18.

There are many drafting packages available with varying degrees ;) of capability on different computers and CAD workstations. One of ;" the most important feature a designer would expect from a drafting package is the ability to use the results of analysis and design program directly, so that the possible loss of information during transfer of data by indirect means could be avoided. One such example is the script file facility of AutoCAD. Here the data transfer is through files. It would be ideal from a designer's point of view to have a facility by which one can call the drafting functions through the programming language itself, so that the data structures of the program could be made use of to pass the parameters to the drafting functions.

5.9 COMPUTER GRAPHICS IN CAD/CAM/CAE

It has already been observed that Computer Graphics playa very important role in communicating design information between the designer and the computer system. It provides techniques for representing, presenting and storing pictures and also for interacting with them. The efficiency of the CAD process and the acceptance of the systems by the designer depends a lot on its graphics capabili- ties. Graphics support software systems are used to write programs for various graphics functionalities. To facilitate porting of graph- ics programs across different hardwares, standards are adopted both for graphics functionality as well as for language binding. Graphical Kernal System (GKS) is the standard accepted by ISO for graphics functionality for 2D graphics and its language binding in different programming languages. GKS-3D is an extension to the GKS, which defines viewing of three-dimensional objects. Both GKS and GKS- 3D meets the needs of about 80% of graphics applications. GKS-3D is limited to only viewing. 3D modelling is one of the very impor- tant requirement in CAD/CAM/CAE applications. A new standard PRIGS (Programmer's Hierarchical Interactive

Graphics System) is emerging as a standard for specifying an application programmers interface to a rich, device-independent graphics environment. PRIGS provide all the viewing capabilities of G KS-3D in a compatible man- ner, but in addition it supports creation, modification and viewing of a geometric model. In PRIGS elements are structured into hierarchies with structures calling other structures and inheriting at- tributes from present structures. One of the powerful features of PRIGS is the facility to allow selective editing of the contents, to allow the results of interactive sequences to be displayed without completely redefining the displayed structures.

Another important development in Computer Graphics is the emergence of more and more sophisticated hardware systems. The capabilities and the interface details of these devices vary from one another. This makes it difficult to implement device-independent functionalities in these devices. To help the implementors of graph- ics packages across these heterogeneous hardware systems, another standard called Computer Graphics Interface (CGI) h~ been de- fined, which specifies functional and syntactic specifications for the exchange of device independent data and associated control informa- tion between the devices and the graphical functions. CG I defines an idealized abstract graphics device capable of accepting input and generating, storing and manipulating pictures. It contains facilities for generating graphical primitives; controlling the appearance of graphical primitives; inquiring device capabilities, states and char- acteristics; controlling graphics devices; generating and controlling groups of primitives (segments); and obtaining graphical input. It serves as a standardised, device independent interface for graphics package implementors to write to. This greatly eases the burden of writing device drivers.

The Computer Graphics Metafile (CGM) is another important development in the area of Computer Graphics. It specifies standard for exchanging pictures among diverse applications and across sepa- rate programming environments. Graphics information is captured at an interface and placed in a graphics *metafile,* on a secondary stor- age device. These picture files can be stored, and reused as a library of predefined pictures.

The two phases in the use of metafiles are *generator phase* and *interpreter phase.* In generator phase, a metafile is created, whereas, in the interpreter phase a metafile is read and interpreted. A brief overview of G KS metafiles is discussed in section 4.7.7. G KS metafile is a sequence of GKS commands that are used to generate a picture at the level of GKS workstation. Whereas, Computer Graphics Metafile (CGM) represents a snapshot of the final image that a program has created. CGM provides a file format suitable for storage and re- trieval of picture description information. It describes pictures in a completely device-independent manner. The G KS metafile interface can write or read metafiles following CGM standards.

The four standards -GKS and GKS-3D, PRIGS, CGI and CGM- together provide standard techniques to both implementors and users of graphics software systems, so that the graphics programs become device-independent, operating-system independent and portable across wide range of hardware systems available. All these four standards are defined in a compatible manner.

In CAD/CAM/CAE, it is also often required to have digital exchange of database information among different CAD systems. IGES, the Initial Graphics Exchange Specification is a mature mechanism by which engineering drawings, 3D-wireframe and surface models, finite element mesh descriptions and other product information can be exchanged among various systems. The major difference between a metafile and IGES is that, metafile is only a description of a picture for the purpose of displaying it, whereas, IGES defines specifications for organising of product data in a complete manner , so that the data can be exchanged or shared by various CAD systems. In the field of manufacturing, it is required to associate various non-geometric data in addition to geometry. IGES does not address this problem. PDES, the Product Data Exchange Specification pro- vide mechanisms for not only completely representing the product as a database, but also for associating non- geometric data such as manufacturing features, tolerance specifications, material properties, surface finishes etc. IGES and PDES have different technological objectives and are in different stages of development. IGES is a us standard, while PDES represents the US contribution to the inter- national standard on product data exchange. Although, PDES does not contribute much to graphics, it provides facilities to develop a conceptual schema for representation of mechanical objects. The schema also will support some viewing functions, which are again drawn from other graphics standards.

The above discussion gives a brief overview of the developments that are going on in the field of computer graphics standards with special emphasis on CAD/CAM/CAE. The material provided in the present chapter on computer graphics is sufficient for beginners in the area of CAD. The fundamental principles described in the ear- lier sections will enable users and programmers to understand better the underlying theoretical aspects of various graphics mechanisms. Brief descriptions of GKS functionality and graphics programming using G KS will take the designers from the mathematical basics of computer graphics techniques to programming aspects for CAD applications.

References

1. Arnold,D.B. and Bono,P.R.;(1988),CGM *and CGI -Metafile and Interface Standards for Computer Graphics,* Springer -Verlag, Berlin, Germany.

2. Berger, M., (1986), *Computer Graphics with PMCal,* The Benjamin/ Cummings Publishing Company Inc., California, U.S.A. 3. Besant, C. B. and Lui, C. W. K., (1986), *Computer Aided Design and Manufacture* 3rd ed., Affiliated East- West Press Pvt. Ltd., New Delhi, India.

4. DeLucchi,C. J., (1989), *The AutoCAD Cook Book,* John Wiley & Sons Inc., New York, USA.

5. Encarnacao, J. and Schlechtendahl,E. G., (1983), *Computer Aided Design- Fundamentals and System* Architectures,Springer -Verlag, Berlin, Germany.

6. Enderle, G. Kansy, K. and Pfaff, G., (1988), *Computer Graphics Programming, GKS- The Graphics Standard,* Springer- Verlag, Berlin, Germany.

7. Fanx, I. D. and Pratt, M. J., (1979), *Computational Geometry for Design and Manufacture,* Ellis Horwood, Chichester .

8. Hagen,P.J. W .,(ed.),(1984), *Eurographics Tutorials-83,* Springer -Verlag, Berlin, Germany.

9. Harrington, S., (1983), *Computer Graphics -A Programming Approach,* McGraw-Hill, New York, U.S.A.

10. Hop good, F. R. A., Duce, D. A., Gallop, J. R. and Sutcliff, D. C., (1983), *Introduction to Graphical Kernal System (GKS),* Academic Press, London, U .K.

11. Kunii, T. L. (ed.), (1983), *Computer Graphics -Theory and Applications,* Springer-Verlag, Berlin, Germany.

12. Newman, W. M. and Sproull, R. F., (1979), *Principles of Inter- active Computer Graphics,* McGraw-Hill Book Company, New York, U.S.A.

13. Plastock, R. A. and Kalley, G., (1986), Theory and Problems of Computer Graphics - Shaum's outline series, McGraw-Hill Book Company, New York, U.S.A.

14. Rogers,D.F ., (1985), Procedural Elements for Computer Graph- ics, McGraw-Hill Book Company, New York, U.S.A.

15. Rooney, J. and Steadman, P., (1990), Principles of Computer Aided Design, Affiliated East- West Press Pvt Ltd., New Delhi, India.

16. Sproull,R.F ., Sutherland, W.R. and Ullner,M.K.,(1989), De- vice- Independent Graphics, McGraw-Hill Book Company.,New York,USA.

17. User's Manuals -AutoCAD -rel. 10, (1988), Autodesk Inc., U.S.A.

18. Voisinet, D. D., (1986), Introduction to Computer-Aided Draft- ing, McGraw-Hill Book Company, New York, U.S.A.

Exercises

1. Using the function line (xstart, xend, ystart, yend), write a function polyline for any given number of points n. A single point is to be plotted when n=l.

2. Modify the function line (xstart,xend,ystart,yend) by adding one more parameter line-type, to draw lines of different types.

3. Represent an ellipse in parametric form and write a function to scan convert it.

4. Similar to the modelling transformations described in section 4.4, represent reflection and shearing transformations in matrix form in homogeneous coordinates.

5. Write an algorithm to implement a segment table.

6. Use the line function and write a complete program to draw grids with desired spacing.

7. Develop an algorithm for generating solid objects as combina- tion of three dimensional primitive shapes, defined as a set of surfaces.

8. Develop and implement an algorithm for full viewing operations for a perspective projection.

9. Using standard GKS library write the following functions.

    move(x,y) -set current cursor position to (x,y)

draw(x,y) -draw a line from current cursor position to (x,y)

vecrel -all the subsequent moves and draws after a call to this functions will be relative to current cursor position.

vecabs -resets the relative vector environment to absolute

10. Using G KS library functions, write a mini-drafting package with line, arc and text facility.

11. Write a program using GKS, to simultaneously display on the screen, the movement of stylus on a digitizer surface.

12. Write a program to draw contours with specified contour inter- val for the given positions and reduced levels of a set of points.

13. Implement the 3D transformations to display 3D objects using GKS- 2D package.

14. Add a set of functions to display 3D objects in the available GKS-2D library.

15. Write a program to display a simply supported beam. Create a menu to select type of loading on the beam and its magnitude. Depending on the choice, the program should draw the shear force and bending moment diagram for the beam.

16. For a given pipe network, the discharge through the pipes are known. Write a program to display the pipe network, with the width of the line representing the pipe proportional to the discharge through the pipe.

17. A finite element mesh data consists of a set of nodes and a set of elements. The x,y,z coordinates of all the nodes and connectivity of all the elements are given. Write a program to display the mesh display node numbers display element numbers shrink and display the elements for a given shrink factor 18. Using GKS functions write a program to display a traffic in-tersection with various traffic turns to view different possible conflicts.

19. A truss is analysed with a set of loading. Write a program to display the truss with loading details in a viewport at the top left corner and a force vector diagram in a larger viewport on the remaining area on the display surface.

20. Using animation techniques, generate a display to show the sec- tional view of cylinder of an IC engine with the reciprocating piston and connecting rod.

CHAPTER 6

Data Base Management System

6.1 INTRODUCTION

Data base management is one of the most rapidly growing area of information science. Data Base Management System (DBMS) is widely used in data processing applications, because of its inherent nature of efficiently handling large amount of data. In early stages of computing DBMS did not find much application in engineering. This was because computers were used only for limited applications in engineering and for specific tasks like analysis, design, detailing etc. However, in commercial data processing large amount of data f have to be handled with relatively less numerical computing and DBMS is used for a wide range of applications. Recent advances in hardware and software technology have made it possible for design engineers to make use of computers in a much more effective manner for solving engineering problems. This improved scenario of computer applications resulted in integrating various phases of design and I manufacturing / construction leading to computer aided engineering of large systems. For efficiently solving engineering problems with large amount of data efficient mechanisms for data storage, retrieval and manipulation are required. Database management system pro- vides such mechanisms to application programmers to improve the effectiveness and efficiency of the programs.

Database management system consists of a collection of inter- , related data and a set of programs to manipulate the data. The data - f contained in the database is an integrated whole with no artificiality introduced by separate files. The primary goal of any database management system is to provide an environment for storing information into, retrieving information from and manipulating information in a database.

The conventional method of handling large amount of data is by using files. In a, traditional file processing system, each file exists independent of each other, where the application programs directly store as well as retrieve data from the files as shown in Fig. 6.1. On the other hand in a database processing system, data items are made i inter-related and are integrated. Data in a file are directly accessible by an application program, whereas, data in a database cannot be directly accessed by external programs. The external programs interact with the database through the database management system as shown in Fig. 6.2.

Database management system consists of a large number of complex programs. It merely acts as a data librarian; where data is stored along with the description of its format. It not only retrieves the data correctly, but also carries out integrated processing of data. A few advantages of processing data using a DBMS are I enumerated below:

- *DBMS eliminates data redundancy and inconsistency*
- *Accessing data is easier.*
- *Data accessing facility can be extended to multiple users by , database sharing.*
- *Data security constraints can be easily enforced addition*
- *Standards can be enforced*
- *Conflicting requirements by different application programs can be balanced.*

All these advantages of using a database management system in data manipulation is possible if the amount of data to be handled is reasonably large and there exists relationships between different data Items. In simple and trivial problems, traditional file processing may

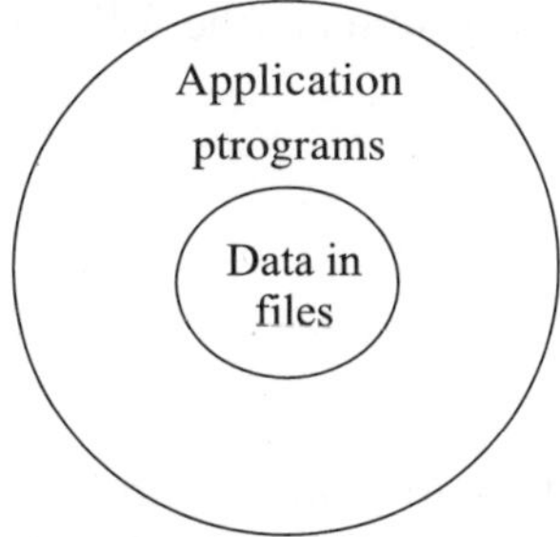

Fig. 6.1 Traditional File processing System

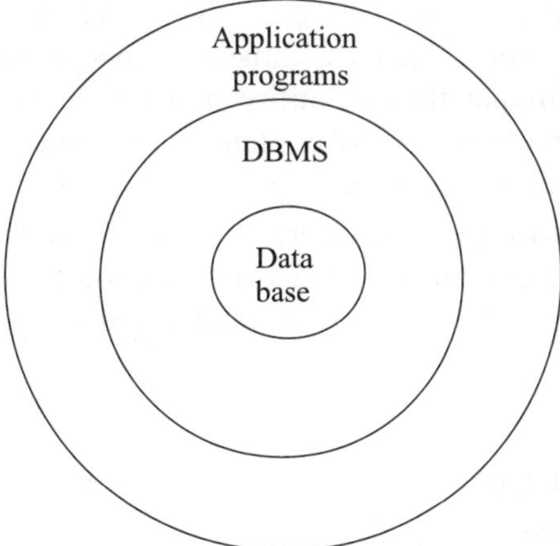

Fig. 6.2 Database Processing System

still be efficient. Large engineering problems are always decomposed into smaller tasks and many of these smaller tasks share data. In such cases storing data in a database and manipulating it through a database management system is ideal. Eventhough DBMS has many advantages, it has some disadvantages too compared to traditional file processing. They are enumerated below:

1. DBMS is expensive and require more system resources.
2. DBMS require more hardware resources and its operating cost is high.
3. Accessing and manipulating databases from application programs require additional skill.

Components of database management system and various data .models in use are described in this chapter. Concepts of relational database model are explained with the help of an example from engineering domain. The chapter also illustrates the use of query

language for manipulating data in relational databases. Nature and requirements of engineering databases are discussed towards the end of the chapter.

6.2 COMPONENTS OF A DATABASE SYSTEM

The main components of a database system are the following.

- Hardware
- Programs
- Data

6.2.1 Hardware

Though database management system does not require any special hardware features, it does involve special programs and overhead data. As database processing addresses the problems with large amount of data, it may not be possible to store the whole database in main' memory of the computer. Hence, even during processing large portion of the database reside on the secondary storage devices and as and when required the relevant portions are loaded into the main memory. In a database processing environment, in to a portion of the database, the main memory has to house a few frequently used utility programs of the DBMS and the application program which uses the data from database. Hence, the computer for database processing requires more primary as well as sccondary storage with a faster CPU.

In 1982 dedicated database machines were introduced into the market. They are special purpose computers that perform database functions in a much more efficient manner. They did not find wider applications and are yet to be established

6.2.2 Programs

Main programs involved in a typical database processing are:

- Application Programs
- Utility Programs
- Operating System

Fig. 6.3 shows how these programs interact for database processing. Application programs are written in any of the high level languages for a specific application, which uses database. The utility programs of the database management system provide facilities for creating, updating and deleting of databases along with a set functions to manipulate the data in the database.

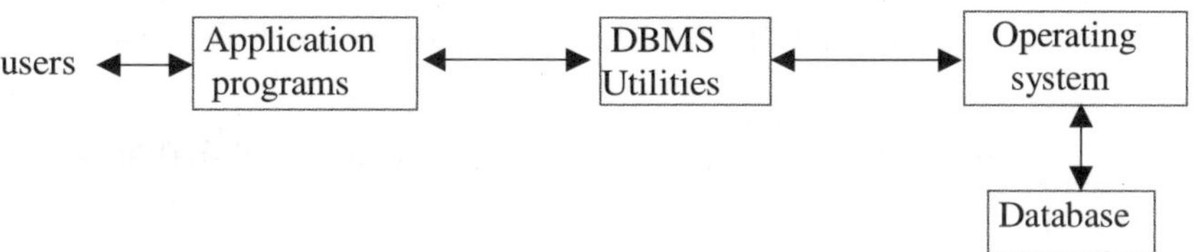

Fig. 6.3 Programs Involved in Database Processing

The functions of the utility programs of DBMS include:

- define and store database structure
- load database data
- provide different data access methods
- store and manipulate data
- provide multiple views of data
- provide mechanisms for data security
- provide facility to access data by multiple users

6.2.3   Data

A database is a self describing collection of integrated files. Files are collection of records. It may be noted that bits are grouped Into bytes or characters, characters are grouped Into fields and fields are grouped into records. Most high-level programming languages support a notion of record type. For example, m C programming language, a record is nothing but a structure.

```
struct room {
        char *room_name ;
        float length;
        float breadth;
        char f loor _type ;
};
```

This C statement defines a record called room with four fields Each field has a name and a type associated with it. In a typical application, several such record types may be necessary. To be a database two additional information are required in of addition to the above data. They are :

> - information on description of data
> - information on relationship among different sets of records

The term file has different meaning when used within and out side a DBMS environment. In a file processing environment, files are grouped together physically. Whereas, in DBMS logical collection of a set of records may not exist as. a physical collection. Thus the logical data representation scheme IS different from the physical level of data representation. The three levels of data abstraction in DBMS environment are shown in Fig. 6.4.

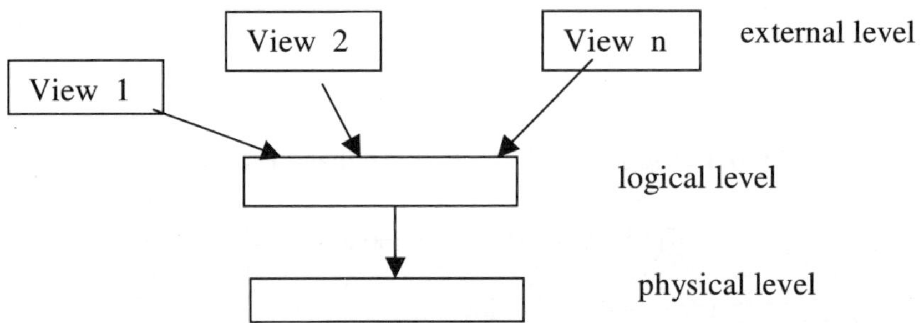

Fig. 6.4 Data Abstraction Levels in a DBMS

The lowest level, i.e., the physical level has the data stored on hardware devices. User programs cannot access them directly. They have to go through the logical level to access the data. The external level defines the different views of the database as required by the external or user programs. One user program may not require all the data in the database. Hence the user/application programs view only the required information from the database. That means different programs will have different views of the database depending on their requirement of data. Such views are external to the database and are specified at the external level. Also it is not necessary that different views should contain altogether different data. There can be common information in different views.

The conceptual level also called schema level describes the entire database, where data description, data relationships, data semantics and data constraints are defined. These definitions form data models. The data models are divided into three classes, viz., object-based logical models, record-based logical models and physical data models.

6.3 DATA MODELS

Object-based logical models are used for describing data at the conceptual and view levels. They are very close to human logic. Many different models are available to describe object-based logical models. The most important among them are semantic data model and entity-relationship model. Semantic data model provides a facility for expressing meaning about the data in the database. The Entity-Relationship model (E-R model) is based on a perception of a real world which consists of a collection of objects called entities and relationships among these objects. An entity is an object, which can be uniquely distinguished from other objects.

For instance, the designation, physical dimensions and weight per unit length uniquely describe a particular rolled steel section. The set of all entities of the same type and relationships of the same type are termed as *entity* set and *relationship set* respectively. Examples of entity set are:

all rooms in a building

all elements in a finite element mesh

all bearings in a machine

An E-R model may define certain constraints to which the con- tents of a database must confirm. Entities and relationships are to be distinguished and a database model should specify how this can be carried out. This is achieved using the concept of *primary key*. An entity-relationship model may define certain constraints to which the contents of a database must confirm. One important constraint is the number of entities to which another entity can be associated via a relationship. For relationships involving two entity sets, there can be relationships like one-to-one, one-to-many, many-to-one and many-to-many. Schematic representation of these relationships are shown in Fig. 6.5.

Record-based logical models define the overall logical structure of the database as well as higher level description of its implementation. Three different record-based logical models are widely used. They are:

1. Hierarchical Model

2. Network Model

3. Relational Model

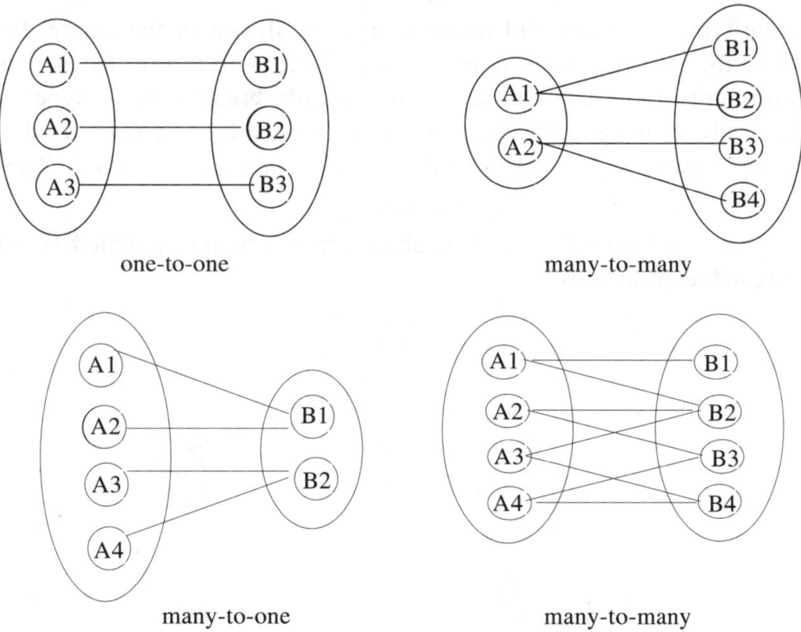

Fig. 6.5 Different Types of Entity Relationships

Physical data models are used to describe data at the lowest level. There are very few physical data models in use. Some of the widely known ones are :

1. Unifying model

2. Frame memory

For designing and using database for a particular application, a detailed knowledge of record-based logical models is required. The three widely used record-based models are described in detail in the following sections.

6.3.1 Hierarchical Model

In a hierarchical data model, which is based on a tree structure, nodes and links are used to represent respectively entities and relationships. Each node has a collection of attributes associated with it, which describe the entities represented by that node. The relationships formed in a hierarchical model are only one-to-many or one-to-one relationships between nodes. As a result of this there can not be any cycles. A general form of hierarchical data model is shown in figure 6.6.

Here the objects Bl, B2, B3, Cl, C2 and C3 are entities and the relationships are expressed in the form of a tree structure. This concept is illustrated below with the help of an example. Consider the building plan shown in Fig. 6.7.

A number of entities can be defined in a building. They are : building, room, wall, door and window, floor, roofetc. Relationships between the different entities can also be defined. The entities can be organised depending on their relationships. Such an organisation of entities based on hierarchical model is shown in Fig. 6.8.

Only a few typical entities and relationships are shown in the figure. Each entity is completely described using a set of attributes associated with it. For instance, the attributes associated with entity room can be room_name, length, breadth, floor -type, wall-on-East, ..etc. When a database using hierarchical model is designed, one has to decide a schema to construct the tree structure. The schema primarily depends on two factors. They are:

1. types of queries expected on the database

2. the degree to which the overall database schema being modelled fit into the given entities and relationships.

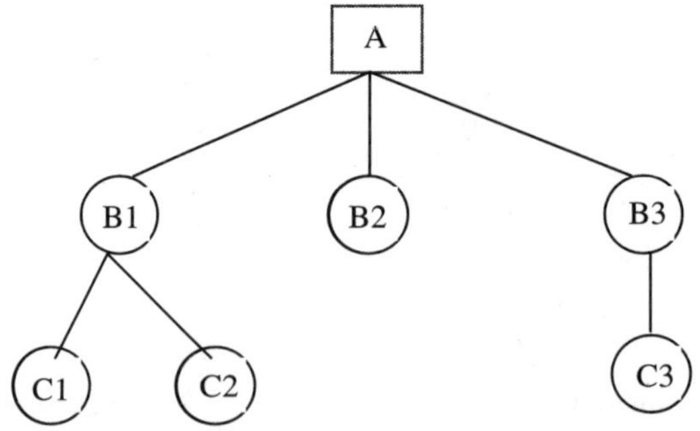

Fig. 6.6   General Form of Hierarchical Data Model

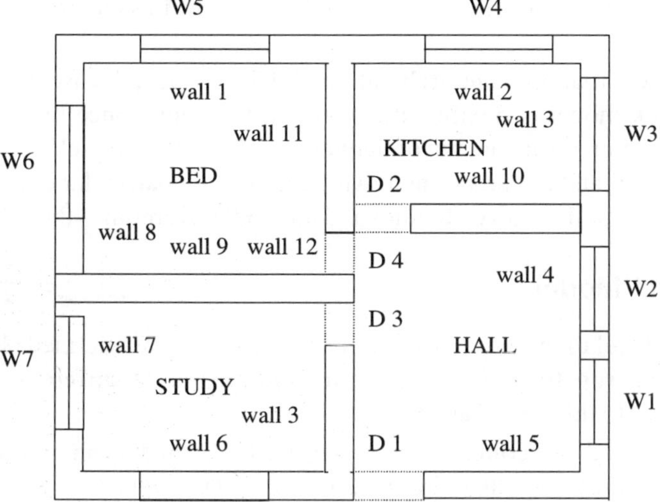

Fig. 6.7   Plan of a Building

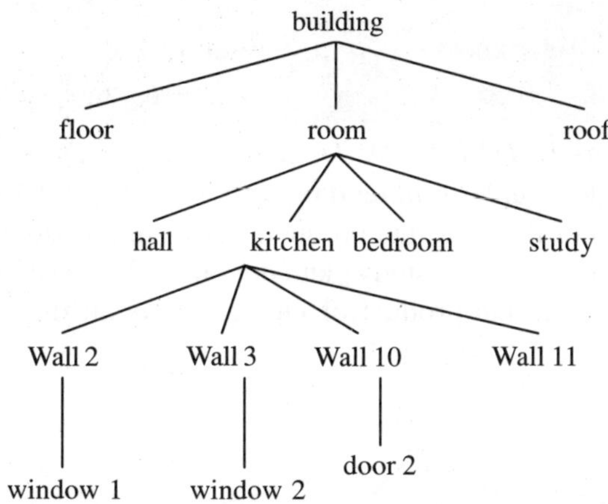

Fig. 6.8   Hierarchical Model of a Building Database

Accessing a particular data item in hierarchical model requires the complete knowledge of path to the entity from the root.

6.3.2 Network Model

Network model differs from hierarchical model in one aspect, i.e., network model can have many-to-many relationships. In network a given entity set can have any number of links or relationships. The many-to-many relationships in a network model allows direct path between entities rather than the hierarchical approach. The same building database can be represented in a network data model as shown in Fig. 6.9. Only a few entities and relationships are shown in the figure.

It may be noted that the hierarchical model is a special case of network model. Eventhough network model is flexible, it is difficult to change once the network schema is defined. One of the main disadvantage of network model is that the relationships are integral part of database model and are predefined. Also accessing a particular data item requires the knowledge of the path to the entity. Relational data model overcomes these limitations.

6.3.3 Relational Model

In relational model, relationships between entities are not pre- defined. Relationships are defined only during run time. Here the term *relation* has a different meaning. A few terminologies related to this model are explained below.

A *relation* is defined as a collection of tuples, each of which is an ordered set of attribute values $< dl, d2, d3, ...dn >$ such that dl $\hat{I}$ $Dl,d2$ $\hat{I}$ $D2,d3$ $\hat{I}$ $D3,...dn$ $\hat{I}$ $Dn,$ where $Dl,D2,D3,...Dn$ are n given domains, which are not necessarily distinct. Domain D is nothing but a set of possible values for some variables. A few examples of domains are :

Domain	room-name	-	characters
Domain	wall-thickness	-	numeric ^{3} 0.5
Domain	floor –type	-	character { mosaic, marble, tiles }

Given a set of domains $Dl,D2,D3,...Dn,Dl$ X $D2$ X $D3$ X Dn is the cartesian product, which is a set of all possible n-tuples $< dl,d2,d3,...dn >$ such that dl $\hat{I}$ $Dl,d2$ $\hat{I}$ $D2,d3$ $\hat{I}$ $D3,...dn$ $\hat{I}$ $Dn.$ A relation is a subset of the cartesian product. For example, domain Dl be a set of four room names { hall, kitchen, bed-room, study} and domain $D2$ be a set of six areas { 200, 160, 120, 100, 130, 80 }. The cartesian product of Dl and $D2$ is all the possible combinations,

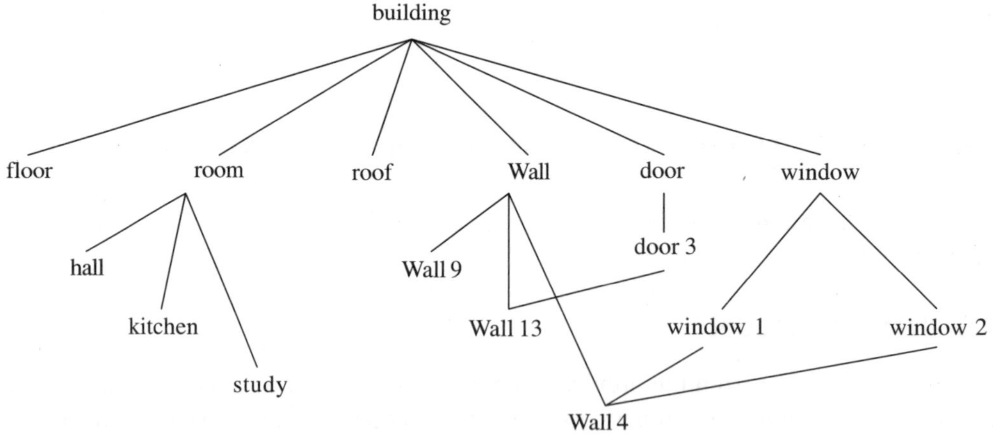

Fig. 6.9 Network Model of Building Database

which will be 24 tuples. A subset of the cartesian product with 4 tuples can be written as shown below which is a relation.

Dl	D2
hall	200
kitchen	160
bedroom	200
study	120

A relation can be visualised as a two dimensional table with columns as different attribute values and rows different tuples. A typical relation is shown in Fig. 6.10.

Computer Narne	CPU	CO-Processor	Make	Main Memory	Disk Space	Graphics Card
Ganesh	8088	8088	Turbo	640 Kb	20 Mb	MGA
Herman	80286	80287	Mark 2	2 Mb	40 Mb	EGA
CECL	80386	NULL	AT386	4 Mb	80 Mb	VGA
lndus	68030	88066	Nexus	8 Mb	350 Mb	Custom

Fig. 6.10 A Typical Relation

A relation is identified as a set of tuples with a value of each attribute in every tuple is drawn from meaningful domains. A rela- tional database model can be visualised as a collection of relations. A building database for the building plan shown in Fig. 6.7 is shown in figures 6.11 through 6.14. As the database is shown for the purpose of illustrating the features of relational model, only minimum required information is included.

Room_name	length	breadth	fioor-type	wall1-E	wall 2-E	wall 1-W	wall 2-W
hall	6.5	3.2	marble	wall 4	NULL	wall 12	wall 13
bedroom	5.5	4.0	mosaic	wall 11	wall 12	wall 8	NULL
kitchen	4.0	3.2	tiles	wall 3	NULL	wall 11	NULL
study	5.0	4.0	mosaic	wall 13	NULL	wall 7	NULL

Fig. 6.11 Relation ROOM

Wall_name	thickness	type	length	origin_x	origin_y
wall 1	one-brick	load-bearing	4.0	0.0	10.5
wall 2	one-brick	load-bearing	3.2	4.0	10.5
wall 3	one-brick	load-bearing	4.0	7.2	6.5
wall 4	one-brick l	load-bearing	6.5	7.2	0.0
wall 5	one-brick	load-bearing	3.2	4.0	0.0

(Fig. 6.12 Contd.)

(Fig. 6.12 Contd.)

Wall_name	thickness	type	length	origin_x	origin_y
wall 6	one-brick	load-bearing	4.0	0.0	0.0
wall 7	one-brick	load-bearing	5.0	0.0	5.0
wall 8	one-brick	load-bearing	5.5	0.0	10.5
wall 9	half-brick	partition	4.0	0.0	5.0
wall 10	half-brick	partition	3.2	4.0	6.5
wall 11	one-brick	load-bearing	4.0	4.0	10.5
wall 12	one-brick	load-bearing	1.5	4.0	6.5
wall 13	one-brick	load-bearing	5.0	4.0	5.0

Fig. 6.12 Relation WALL

The database has four different relations, viz., room, wall, door and window. In addition to the room name, dimensions and floor type information, details of the walls of the rooms are also included. The bedroom has got 2 walls on eastern side and hall has two walls on western side. All other rooms have got only one wall on each side. Because of this, provision is made for two walls on each side, when the relation room is designed. Thus the relation room has 12 attributes. Only eight are shown in Fig. 6.11. Relation wall has six attributes. They are: wall_name, thickness, type, length, origin-x and origin-y. Relation door has 6 attributes and relation window has 7 attributes. The attribute names and tuples are shown in Fig. 6.11 through 6.14.

Door_name	width	height	offset	type	wall_Name
door 1	1.2	2.1	0.0	flush	wall5
door 2	1.0	2.1	0.0	panelled	wall 10
door 3	1.0	2.1	0.0	panelled	wall 13
door 4	0.8	2.1	0.2	panelled	wall 12

Fig. 6.13 Relation DOOR

Window_name	width	height	h_offset	v -offset	type	wall_name
window 1	1.5	1.5	1.0	0.6	glazed	wall 4
window 2	1.5	1.5	4.0	0.6	glazed	wall 4
window 3	1.5	1.0	0.7	1.1	glazed	wall 3
window 4	1.5	1.0	0.8	1.1	glazed	wall 2
window 5	2.0	1.5	1.0	0.6	glazed	wall 1
window 6	2.0	1.5	2.0	0.6	glazed	wall 8
window 7	1.5	1.5	2.0	0.6	glazed	wall 7
window 8	2.0	1.5	1.0	0.6	glazed	wall 6

Fig. 6.14 Relation WINDOW

If a two dimensional table has to be called a relation, then it should satisfy a few conditions. First, there cannot be any duplicate tuples. An examination of the four relations shows that there are no duplicate tuples in the relations. There should be difference in at least one of the attributes. One or more of the attribute(s) in a relation can be defined as key(s). Key(s) uniquely identify a tuple in a relation. For instance, in the relation ROOM, room_name can be defined as a key. The value of key attribute is different for different tuples. But a key has to be always defined and it cannot be null. In the relation room, the value for attribute wal12-E is null. Hence, attribute wal12-E cannot be defined as key.

It has been stated that the basic architecture of database management system define three levels, viz., external level or views of user programs, conceptual level and physical level. At the conceptual level the schema is defined by a Data Definition Language (DDL). At the physical level the data organisation is defined using types of records, physical devices and access mechanisms. User has no or limited control over the physical level of data. DBMS itself controls the access mechanisms at the physical level.

A Data Manipulation Language (DML) provided by the DBMS provide operators for manipulating and processing the data in the database. Relational Data Base Management System (RDBMS) uses operators based on relational algebra for retrieving and manipulat- ing information from database. An application which uses database, would like to have a specific view of the database. The view has to be created by extracting the required information from the database. RDBMS defines a set of operations for this purpose. Out of them, the three basic operations project, select and join are used for manipulating data stored in database. The working of these operations are described below.

PROJECT

The PROJECT operator generates a new relation from an existing relation, containing only a subset of attributes. The effect of typical PROJECT operation is shown in Fig. 6.15.

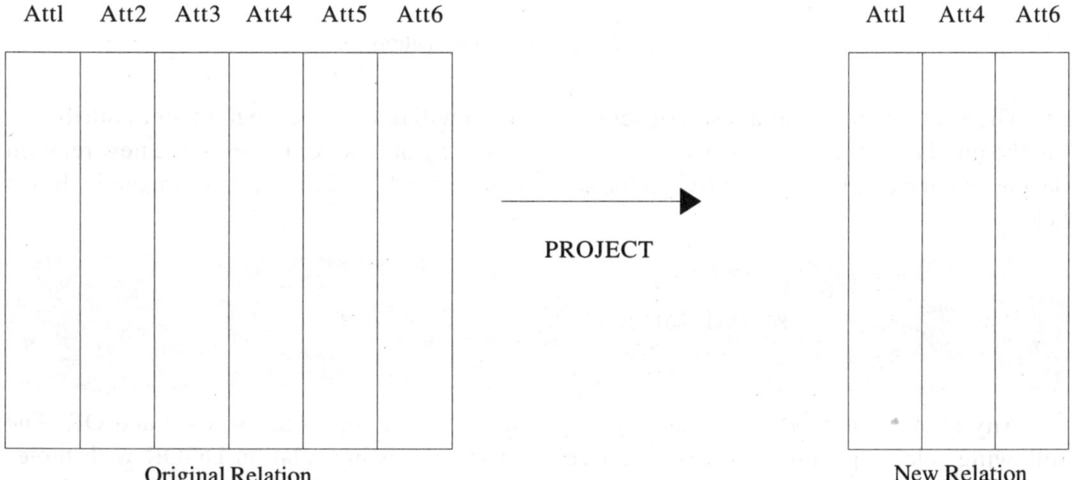

Fig. 6.15 PROJECT Operation

The number of tuples in the new relation will be the same as that in the original relation. The attribute(s) to be projected: are specified in the PROJECT operator as shown.

```
PROJECT <original-Ielation>
OVER <att1, att4, att6>
```

The tuples in the new relation can either be listed on a display device or it can be stored. The effect of the above project command is a new relation with three specified attributes att1, att4 and att6. Depending on the requirement of the application program the at- tributes to be projected can be decided. For creating the derived relation with the projected attributes a new relation name can be associated with the project operation.

SELECT

SELECT operation generates a new relation from an existing one such that the value(s) of some attribute(s) satisfy specified constraints. The effect of a typical SELECT operation is shown in Fig. 6.16.

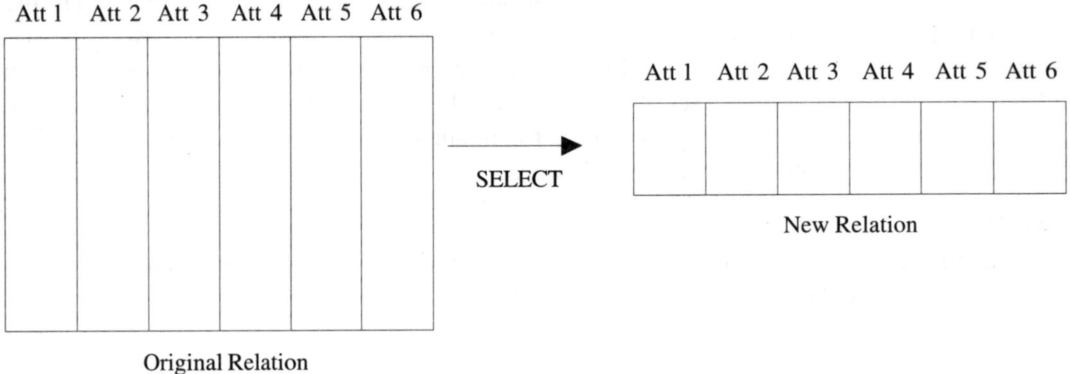

Fig. 6.16   SELECT Operation

The relation created as a result of select operation will have the same number of attributes, but the number of tuples will always be less or equal. The number of tuples in the new relation depends on the conditions specified in the select operation. A typical select command is shown below:

```
SELECT
FROM <original-Ielation>
WHERE <conditions>
```

Any number of conditions can be grouped using logical oper- ators AND and OR. The following select operation creates a new relation from existing relation DOOR with tuples where the value of attribute height is greater than 2.0 and value of attribute type is panalled.

```
SELECT
FROM        DOOR
WHERE       height >2.0 AND
            type = panalled
```

JOIN

The operators PROJECT and SELECT essentially deal with one relation at a time, which is not much different from traditional' file processing. As databases consist of a collection of relations, operators capable of extracting information from more than one relation are required to effectively extract and manipulate data from databases. JOIN operation is such an operation, which joins more than one relation based on specified conditions. JOIN operation generates a new relation from two existing relations containing a common domain by concatenating the attributes from both the relations, where values in common domain have specified relationships. For example, consider the relations DOOR and WINDOW.

```
JOIN      DOOR      AND      WINDOW
```

The above definition creates a new relation, which will have 13 attributes, i.e., 6 from door and 7 from window. The total number of tuples generated will be 32, which is obtained by multiplying the total number of tuples in both the relations. Such a JOIN operation may not be desirable always. One can define attributes with common domain so that only those tuples with required information are present in the newly created relation. The following JOIN operation creates a new relation, which will have tuples with wall names wallS, wall10, wall12 and wall13. That means it lists the tuples of walls which has doors, with all the 13 attributes.

```
JOIN          DOOR AND WALL
OVER          wall_name
```

In general, to get the required information from the database, one may have to use the the three basic operators PROJECT, SELECT and JOIN either individually or in combination. Any complex query into a database can be decomposed into a sequence of PROJECT, SELECT and JOIN operations. Query language associated with database management system allows one to manipulate in- formation stored in database. A brief description on database query languages is given in next section.

6.4 QUERY LANGUAGE

For users to request information from the database, some kind of language support is required in DHMS. A *query language* which is a DML class of language helps a user to obtain the required information from the database. Generally query languages are high level languages and are procedural in nature. Structured Query Language (SQL) is one of the most popular query language commercially used. International Standard Organisation (ISO) has recommended a standard specification for SQL. SQL provides two sets of commands, viz., Data Definition Commands and Data Manipulation Commands.

Data Definition Commands are primarily used to create and delete relations, create and delete index tables, define structure of databases and relations etc. The formal definition of a typical data definition command for creating the relation ROOM is shown below.

```
CREATE TABLE ROOM ( room_name char(8)
                    length      real
                    width       real
                    ........)
```

The exact syntax of the command may vary slightly in actual implementations. Few other examples of data definition commands are: CREATE DATABASE, CLOSE DATABASE, ALTER DATABASE, DROP TABLE, CREATE INDEX, DROP INDEX) CREATE VIEW, DROP VIEW etc.

Data Manipulation Commands of SQL provide facility for modifying the relations and querying information from the database. The four data manipulation commands supported by SQL are:

```
QUERY (SELECT)
UPDATE
DELETE     and
INSERT
```

The query command provided by SQL is SELECT. In SQL all the three basic operations are achieved through SELECT command itself. The syntax of SELECT command is :

```
SELECT <attribute-list>
FROM <relation-list>
WHERE <condition-list>
```

A PROJECT operation can be done using the above query command in the following manner.

```
SELECT wall_name, type
FROM WALL
```

This query command lists the values of attributes wall_name and type of all the tuples from relation wall. The command

```
SELECT *
FROM WALL
type = partition
```

lists those tuples from relation WALL, whose values for the attribute type is partition.

SQL query command is used for JOIN operation as shown below. The following query lists the value for attribute door_name of .ll the doors in hall. For that first the relations ROOM and DOOR ,re joined, then the attribute door-.name is projected and finally a se- ection of tuples is made satisfying the conditions given in WHERE clause. The conditions checks for any door on the walls of the room all. This query command not only does a natural join but subsequent PROJECT and SELECT operations are also carried out. To .void a project, i.e, to list all the attributes of relations ROOM and)OOR, a wildcard character * can be given.

```
SELECT DOOR.door-name
FROM ROOM, DOOR
WHERE ROOM.room-name = hall AND
          (DOOR.wall-name = ROOM.wall 1_E OR
           DOOR.wall-name = ROOM.wall2J1 OR
           DOOR.wall-name = ROOM.wall1_W OR
           DOOR.wall-name = ROOM.wall2_W OR
           DOOR.wall-name = ROOM.wall1_N OR
           DOOR.wall-name = ROOM.wall2_N OR
           DOOR.wall-name = ROOM.wall1_S OR
           DOOR.wall-name = ROOM.wall2_S)
```

UPDATE, DELETE and INSERT are the other data manipuation commands. These commands are used to modify the contents >f a relation. The command

```
INSERT
INTO              ROOM (bath, 2.0, 2.0, tiles. :.)
```

adds a tuple with specified attribute values into the relation ROOM. The command

```
DELETE
FROM      DOOR
WHERE     type = flush
```

deletes all the tuples from the relation DOOR, which has the value for the attribute type is flush. Attribute values can be updated llsing the UPDATE command. For example, the command

```
UPDATE WALL
SET thickness = half-brick
WHERE type = partition
```

modifies the value of the attribute thickness to half-brick, of all the tuples with value of attribute type is partition.

SQL query command either lists the tuples in the new relation or stores them. As different application programs are interested in different information from the database, the application program creates new relations from the existing ones in the database, using data manipulation commands of query language. These new relations, which are derived from the existing ones are derived relations, which are nothing but views at the external level. The SQL can be used in two different modes, viz., direct querying and querying through programs. The querying through programs is very helpful in using data in databases along with regular programs. It.is done using inter- faces provided between the programming language and the database. Here SQL query commands are embedded in the source code of the programs. Many commercial database management systems provide! such facilities, where SQL is supported within traditional programming languages like FORTRAN and C. INGRESS is one such DBMS developed at University of California, Berkeley. The following SE- LECT command get the values of attribute length and breadth for the room hall from the relation ROOM and stores it in variables hI and hb.

```
SELECT length, breadth
INTO $hl, $hb
FROM DOOR
WHERE room_name = hall
```

Such facilities in programming languages will relieve the programmers from designing complex data structures and developing large programs for accessing information for these data structures. As the data is organised and stored in the databases, the DBMS takes care of lower level programs for storing and accessing data. But for effective utilisation of capabilities of DBMS, the database has to be designed properly, by taking into account the type of data and the type of query that would be used to access the information from the database.

6.5 DESIGN OF DATABASES

Introduction to databases with various data models and mechanisms for defining and manipulating databases have been discussed so far. When CAD programs are designed which use databases, one should look into several aspects related to the design of databases. A brief description on design of relational databases is given in the following section.

Three different record-based logical models for databases are defined in previous sections, viz., hierarchical, network and relational models. Hierarchical and network models are the earlier ones and relational model is relatively new. Out of these, relational model is more popular compared to the other two. This is mainly due to the fact that the relationships among entity sets are not predefined in relational model. In addition, computer implementation of relational model is much easier. Depending on the type of applications, one may choose the model that suits the application. Sometimes the inherent properties of the problem itself may require a particular type of data model for effective data management. For instance, for a problem where all the relationships can be defined in the form a tree structure, a hierarchical model may be more suitable compared to other two. Hence, depending on the nature of the application to be solved, one has to select a proper data model for logical organisation of data in the database. A few aspects related to the design of relational databases are discussed below.

Design of databases has to be done very carefully, since improper design will result in some undesirable properties like: repetition of information, loss of information and inability to represent certain type of information.

Repetition of information not only wastes space, but also it makes the updating of information difficult. If the same information is repeated in several places in a database, and that information has to be updated, the database management system has to update the information at all the places, otherwise it will generate inconsistency in the database. Such inconsistencies may lead to generation of erroneous reports. Hence deciding on number of relations and attributes in each relation, has to be done after careful study on the information that has to be obtained from the database.

Consider the relation ROOM. Hall has only one wall on the eastern side, where as bedroom has two walls on eastern side. One way is to define an attribute wall OD east and provide two values to that for the tuple with room name bedroom. In such a case, some attributes will have one value, whereas some others two. Having more than one value to an attribute is not allowed in a relational data model. A state with all the attributes having single value is called 1st normal form. To make the relation room to first normal form, two separate attributes can be defined for wall on each side, viz., wall1-E, wall2-E, wall1_W, wall2_W etc. Now some attributes in some tuples will have null-value, which of course is allowed in RDBMS. Now the relation room is in 1st normal form. At the time of designing a database itself one has to see that all the relations should be in first normal form.

It is desirable to have all the non-key attributes in a relation dependent on the key. If this condition is satisfied in a relation, the relation is said to be in 2nd normal form. Another important point that. has to be borne in mind during the design of database is that no attribute should be functionally dependent on other attributes. For instance, consider the relation room. The user programs using the database uses the information area of rooms in addition to length and breadth. Just because of that if one adds an attribute area also to the relation, that becomes functionally dependent on the attributes length and breadth. Always one can compute the area given the length and breadth of a room. Hence adding an attribute area leads to storing dependent information in the database. Having functionally dependent attributes not only wastes space, but creates inconsistency when values of independent attributes are updated. A relation with no functional dependencies among non-key attributes is said to be in 3rd normal form. Two more normal forms are defined, which are not discusssed here. .Readers may refer to anyone of the books given in references at the end of the chapter to get more information on normalization. CAD programmers should see that the relations designed satisfy various normal forms, which not only makes the database consistent, but also makes it efficient.

6.6 REQUIREMENTS OF ENGINEERING DATABASES

In this chapter we have so far discussed the essential features of a database management system. Most of the commercial databases are developed for business applications, where the nature of requirement follows a specific pattern. Whereas, in engineering applications, computing in some domains may be very similar to business computing. But the nature of majority of applications differ from one another and most of them being unique. Hence in engineering databases or design databases designers expect much more facilities for organising and manipulating design data. Before going into the details of what designers expect from Engineering Data Base Management System (EDBMS), let us summarise the facilities provided by the traditional DBMS.

Primarily, traditional DBMS provide effective logical schemas for efficient storage, retrieval and manipulation of information. They provide the concept of transaction, which is a sequence of operations that together perform a unit of work. A transaction always maintains consistency in a database. Traditional DBMS provide mechanisms for data security, protection, concurrency control, crash recovery and automatic integrity management. High level query languages are integral part of any DBMS. In addition to the query language facility, they provide the users with friendly interfaces for interaction with databases.

Of course , all these facilities are required in design databases also. But the nature of engineering design problems demand much more capabilities. Most of the modern day systems are relational database systems. In many of the engineering design applications, designers prefer to organise data as complex objects in contrast to business applications, where the most prefered representation is tables. Such representations in the form of objects fall into hierarchical category. Most of the engineering systems, when decomposed also form a hierarchy tree. To model such problems using databases, in addition to relational structure one should be able to incorporate hierarchical model also into database. systems.

As design descriptions in different engineering domains are rep- resented differently, design database systems should provide provision for representing multiple and correlated design descriptions. In addition, there should be facility for capturing the dependencies across different representations. When designs are represented using multiple descriptions a change made. in one representation may not reflect in others. Hence mechanisms should be provided for automatically changing dependent information in all the representation, when changes are made in one of them.

Another important feature of any engineering design problem is that from the primary data entered by the user, the system generates large amount of secondary data. These secondary data has to be effectively managed to avoid any kind of inconsistency. Storing derived data along with primary data may cause problems of data dependency. Hence a typical design database should have the capability to handle generic data, which is not a common feature in business databases.

Interfaces with programming languages is one of the most important requirement of design database systems. As many existing programs are coded in languages like FORTRAN or C, capability to interface databases with the languages help in using the data in database in a much more effective manner. For instance, graphics programs can create a view with the geometry data of the artifact and display it on the monitor, whereas, the analysis programs can create a view with geometry, material properties and loading data to carry out analysis.

Design interactions require much stricter expression of consistency. The support for integrity constraints available in traditional databases are of very simple form, like salary *of* an *employee must* be greater than zero. Design databases should support complex con- straints. Constraints should check for all the dependencies between attributes, when any changes are made in the database.

Design databases or in general, engineering databases should support broader range of domains like booleans, vectors, arrays, knowledge represented as rules etc. It should also support graphic as j well as geometric primitives as domains. Both syntactic and semantic transnational facilities should be provided between databases and applications representation. Data models where relation names as attribute values can take advantage of both relational as well as hierarchical model. In an engineering design computing environment, the above model will provide facilities to represent complex objects.

There are many engineering applications which are predominantly data processing oriented. Such applications can directly be automated using database system concepts. Commercial database management systems like INGRESS, ORACLE, dBASE-III etc. can directly be used to implement those applications. INGRESS and ORACLE support SQL queries from host languages like FORTRAN and C. dBASE-III is a relational database management system avail- able on personal computers under MS-DOS environment. It provides facilities to export and import data from other- environments. But neither dBASE-III relations can be created nor relations created using dBASE-III can be directly accessed from host language programs. Hence such database systems can be used only in those applications where it is fully data processing oriented. It would be ideal to have a programming environment that allows use of all the necessary soft- ware tools like graph'ics, knowledge based processing and database management from a host language like C. A description of such an integrated programming environment is given in chapter 8.

References

1. Date, C. J., (1981), *An* Introduction to Database Systems. *vol.1,* 3rd ed., Narosa Publishing House, New Delhi, India.
2. Date, C. J., (1983), *An* Introduction to Database *Systems - vol.* 2, Addison -Wesley Publishing Company, Reading, Mas- sachusetts.,U .S.A.
3. Encarnacao,J. and Schlechtendahl,E.G.,(1983) ,*Computer Aided* Design - Fundamentals and System *Architecture,* Springer Verlag, Berlin, Germany.
4. Katz, R. H., (1985), Information Management *For Engineering Design,* Springer-Verlag, Berlin, Germany.
5. Korth, H. F. and Silberschatz,A., (1986), Database System Con- cepts, McGraw-Hill Book Company, New York, U.S.A.
6. Martin,J .,(1976), *Principles of* Database *Management,* Prentice -Hall, Englewood Cliffs, N.J., U.S.A.
7. Prakash,N.,(1984), *Understanding* Database Management, Tata McGraw -Hill Publishing Company, New Delhi, India.
8. Ullman, J. D., (1988), *Principles* of Database *System,* Galgotia Publications pvt. Ltd., New Delhi, India.

Exercises

1. State the essential features which distinguish database process- ing from traditional file processing.

2. Write a detailed report on the advantages of having database management system in engineering computing.

3. For a typical engineering design problem of your choice draw the schematic diagrams showing the organisation of data in three different data models, viz., hierarchical, network and relational models.

4. Compare the advantages and disadvantages of hierarchical, network and relational models.

5. What are the properties of a relation? Prepare a typical relation for any example problem of your choice and explain the the terms domain, *tuple* and *attribute* with reference to the relation prepared.

6. Explain the term normalization.. What is the importance of normalization in relational database model?

7. What are the requirements of an engineering database management system? Justify each of the requirement with suitable examples.

8. For the building database shown in section 5.3.3, formulate queries for the following items using SQL.

    (a) list the room names which has two walls on at least one side.

    (b) list the names of all external walls.

    (c) list the names of walls, where percentage opening> 30.

    (d) list the names of windows on eastern side of the building.

9. Describe the terms Data Definition Language and Data Manip*ulation* Language. Describe the constructs provided .by SQL for data definition and data manipulation.

10. Enumerate the important points to be taken into consideration when a relational database is designed for a given engineering application.

11. Illustrate the features of a relational database management system using anyone of the commercial database systems like INGRESS, ORACLE, UNIFY or dBASE-III. Use any problem of your choice for illustration.

CHAPTER 7

Knowledge Based Expert System

7.1   INTRODUCTION

Computer Aided Design/Engineering addresses a wide variety of problems in engineering, where the problem solving is done using computers. Many software tools assist the engineers in developing effective programs for various engineering activities, right from the conceptual stage to the construction/ manufacturing or sometimes the maintenance stage. The type of information to be processed during the different stages of engineering vary depending on the nature of the problem. It is always a common practice to sequentially describe the problem solving process; which decomposes the overall problem into a sequence of subproblems. Then these subproblems can be solved independently in a manner following the sequential order, ultimately to complete the solution process of the overall problem. Many subproblems which deal with the quantitative aspects of engineering may have algorithmic procedures for solving; whereas other subproblems dealing with heuristic and ill-structured aspects are difficult to implement. Recent developments in computer technology, especially in the field of Artificial Intelligence, make it possible to simulate. *human-like* reasoning in computer systems. Such systems popularly known as Knowledge Based Expert Systems (KBES) have generated much excitement in the engineering community. Artificial Intelligence techniques improve the efficiency of the engineering de- sign process by allowing one to move towards inferential computing from that of algorithmic computing, which indeed simulate problem solving method by humans. 'The variety of knowledge representation methods make it possible to segregate the engineering design knowledge based on the knowledge structure.

The term Expert Systems and Knowledge Based Systems are used in many contexts. At this stage, we think it is appropriate that the terminology is made more clear and specific. Generally the term Expert System is used where problem solving is done mainly using symbolic processing. The numeric processing component in this case is as less as possible or even nil. Only small portions of integrated problems can be solved using expert systems, where decision making based on expert knowledge is involved. Most of the problems in engineering, when decomposed into subproblems for the purpose of solving, show different behaviour. The problem solving strategies vary from one subproblem to another. Some may have more of symbolic processing with very less numeric processing, and others vice versa. Expert systems have a major role in those problems where symbolic processing is predominant. But when the subproblems are integrated to form the complete problem solving model, it is required to properly interface all the subproblems. Knowledge Based Models can be adopted in such cases to integrate the different modules representing different subproblems. Such integrated systems are called Knowledge Based Systems, where Expert System form a major component. This chapter initially focuses the attention on techniques offered by Expert Systems to deal with ill-structured aspects of engineering knowledge, majority of which are heuristic in nature. Then a brief discussion on Knowledge Based Problem Solving Models is presented.

7.2 ARTIFICIAL INTELLIGENCE

Artificial Intelligence (AI) has been one of the intensive areas of research in Computer Science for the last two decades. It is difficult to precisely define Artificial Intelligence and a few of the possible definitions by the leading researchers are given in references [1,2,3]. According to Rich [1], Artificial Intelligence is the study of how to make computers do things at which at the moment people are better.

It is observed that it is equally difficult to define human intelligence. Some of the essential activities associated with intelligence are listed in reference [3] and they are given below:

- *To respond to situations flexibility*
- *To make sense but of ambiguous or contradictory messages*
- *To recognize the relative importance of different elements of a situation.*
- *To find similarities between situations despite differences which may separate them*
- *To draw distinctions between situations despite similarities that may link them*

The above activities are difficult to simulate on a computer. The branch of science that deals with the mechanics of human intelligence is known as Cognitive Science. The research carried out on the working of human intelligence is very useful to AI scientists who work on computers to simulate the human intelligence.

The AI research works for nearly three decades (1960-1990) were concentrated on the general problem solving strategies and development of specialised programs. These approaches did not yield results for wider applications. Only in the late 1970s and early 1980s a breakthrough was made in AI research to make the program intelligent enough through the knowledge compiled in a specific domain of application. This has led to the development of Expert Systems which are special purpose programs with the knowledge for application to solve specific problems. This development has made tremendous impact and generated wide research activities in the use of AI technology for solving practical problems in various disciplines.

There are also other areas where AI technology is being increasingly used through considerable amount of research activities. They are:

- Natural Language Processing
- Speech Recognition
- Computer Vision
- Robotics
- Intelligent Computer Assisted Instruction
- Automatic Programming
- Planning and Decision Support

The various aspects of development of Expert Systems for engineering applications are described in the following sections.

In general, the problems where the techniques offered by expert systems will be useful, are classification, diagnosis, simulation, monitoring, analysis, planning and design. It can be seen that these problems lie in the derivation-formation spectrum, with the classification type of problems in the derivation end of the spectrum and design in the formation end. Their relative positions in the spectrum are shown in Fig.7.1. Nature of knowledge used and problem solving strategies vary from one class of problems to another.

The nature of knowledge very much influences the selection of representation schemes to be adopted. Control mechanism, also called inference mechanism to solve the problem, has to be identified depending on the nature of the problem and the domain knowledge. Research and development works are currently being carried out in many parts of the world on specific areas mentioned below.

- *Nature of engineering knowledge, its representation and impact on research and development in educational and professional practice.*
- *Inference mechanisms ideally suited for engineering design problem solving.*
- *Expert system development tools (shells) for developing prototype expert systems in various fields of engineering.*
- *Development of prototype expert systems in various domains of engineering.*

Expert systems differ from traditional program in many ways. Conventional programs handle data whereas expert systems handle knowledge. Conventional programs are based on

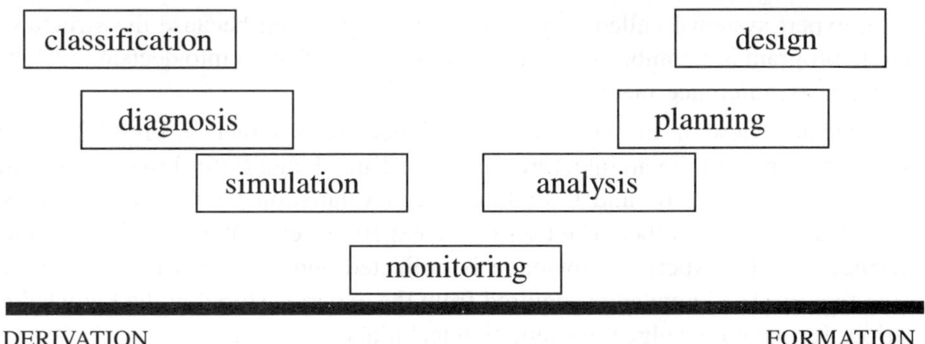

Fig. 7.1 Derivation-Formation Spectrum of Problem Classes

well defined algorithms, whereas expert systems are based on heuristics. When the conventional programs carry out algorithmic computing, expert systems do inferential computing. In addition to these, an expert system should exhibit expert performance with a high level of skill. Also it should have capability to explain to the user why a data is being asked and how the program arrived at a specific conclusion. In expert systems, the knowledge and. the control mechanism are logically separated, whereas in conventional programs, the data and the control mechanism are put together. The main advantage of separating the knowledge and the control mechanism is that, the knowledge part of the system alone needs to be replaced by the knowledge of other domains.

7.3 COMPONENTS OF AN EXPERT SYSTEM

An Expert System is a computer program designed to act as-an expert to solve a problem in a particular domain. The basic strength of the program is due to the knowledge that it contains about a particular domain of interest. Hence the emphasis is on compiling the human expertise into the program which forms the knowledge base.

Having stated that the human expert knowledge forms the base for the expert system, it is now necessary to define an expert. Ac- cording to Paul E. Johnson and as described in reference [7], an expert is a person who through his training and experience is able to do things the rest of us cannot; experts are not only proficient but also smooth and efficient in the actions they take. Experts also know great many things and have tricks and methods for solving problems; they are also good at scanning through information and identifying quickly the relevant information in order to get the basic issues concerning a problem. They are good at recognising problems as instances of types with which they are familiar.

Human experts in any problem solving domain are rare and ley are not easily available to a user. Building expert systems helps) bring the expert knowledge in the domain to the user and thus enhances the user's skills in problem solving.

The heart of the expert system is the knowledge-base. Having the knowledge base alone is not sufficient since there must be a mechanism that directs the use of the knowledge and helps to arrive at a solution and this is referred to as Inference Engine. There should be n interface to the user for the usage of the system. Thus there are three important components of an expert system. An expert system I called a system and not a program because the structure of an "pert system program is a combination-of various elements that go into decision making viz., goals, facts, rules, inference mechanisms etc. [3,4,5,7].

The schematic view of an expert system architecture is shown in Fig. 7.2. The figure shows six components in the architecture. They are Knowledge Base, Inference Engine and Working Memory n one side and User Interface, Explanation Facility and a Knowledge Acquisition Facility on the other. The user of the expert system, interacts with it through the user interface and the expert's knowledge is collected and compiled through knowledge acquisition facility. The knowledge acquired from the expert is stored in the knowledge base using various formal knowledge representation techniques.

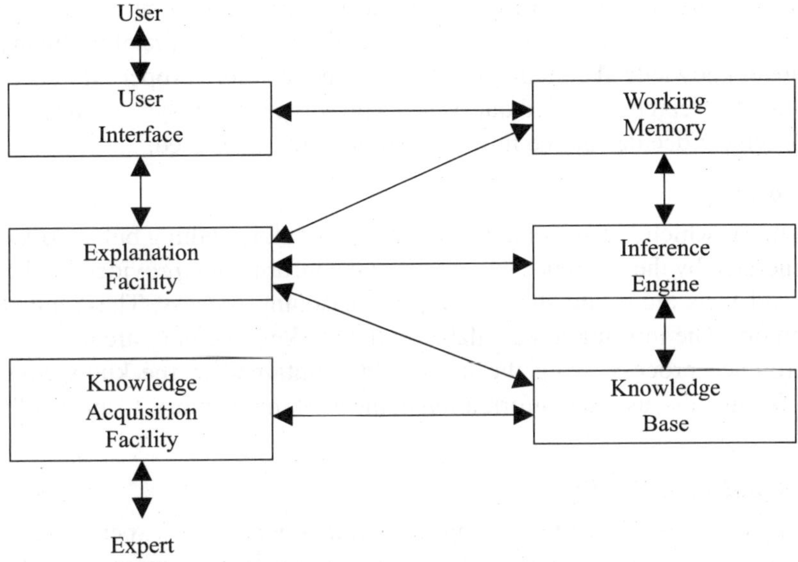

Fig. 7.2 Schematic View of Expert System Architecture

The process of developing and using an expert system involves' three individuals or groups of personnel. They are: the expert, the user and the knowledge engineer. The schematic view of the expert system shown in Fig. 7.2 shows only the user and the expert. The role of knowledge engineer is primarily to collect the knowledge from the expert, formalise the knowledge through various levels of abstraction, select a proper inference mechanism and implement the expert system. To achieve these things, the knowledge engineer should not only possess adequate knowledge of tools and techniques offered by Expert System Technology, but also should have familiarity with the domain knowledge. A reasonable amount of knowledge in the domain, helps the knowledge engineer to understand and represent the expert knowledge in a better way. The role and the functions of the different components of the expert systems are explained below.

Knowledge Base

The knowledge base is where the domain specific knowledge acquired from the expert is stored. The behaviour and action of the expert system entirely depend on the nature of the knowledge put in the knowledge base. Hence the knowledge engineer should take efforts to properly represent the knowledge in the knowledge base, without losing its, meaning and integrity. It is very much essential that the knowledge representation scheme adopted should be capable of handling complexities, inexactness, and uncertainties of engineering knowledge. The knowledge engineer may have to adopt different representation schemes at different stages of expert system development. These are described in detail in a subsequent section.

Inference Engine

It has already been mentioned that, expert systems do inferential computing and not algorithmic computing. The inference engine, which is nothing but the implementation of one or more inference mechanisms, carries out the search through the knowledge base either to prove hypotheses or to arrive at a conclusion. Depending on the nature of problem to be solved and the nature of knowledge I contained in the knowledge base, a proper inference mechanism is i selected and the search is carried out. When a prototype expert sys- ' tem is developed, the knowledge engineer decides on the inference strategy to be selected.

Working Memory

Working memory, which is also sometimes called context, is nothing but a workspace for the problem, generated by the inference engine, from the information provided by the user. Many hypotheses and facts are established during the reasoning process. These are stored in the working memory. The information available in the working memory are used for continuing with the inference process using the knowledge contained in the knowledge base. The explanation facility also uses the information in the working memory, to answer the queries of the user.

Knowledge Acquisition Facility

A knowledge acquisition facility is an optional component of an expert system. This very much depends on the expert system development tool used to implement the system. Any text editor can be viewed as a knowledge acquisition facility, since it provides an environment for the knowledge engineer or the expert to input the coded knowledge into the system. Many development shells allow the knowledge engineers to code the formal representation of the knowledge in a text file, following a specified syntax. Later, the knowledge in the text files are converted. into a form of data and stored in data structures for carrying out reasoning process. A good knowledge acquisition facility should have the capability to incrementally acquire the knowledge at various levels of knowledge abstraction and update the knowledge base.

Explanation Facility

Explanation facility is one of the most important components of an expert system. This provides a mechanism for the user of the expert system, to get more information on the inference process. Primarily a user will be looking for four different pieces of information during and after the. inference process. They are explained below:

When an expert system asks the user to enter a value for a variable, the user may not understand what the variable stands for. In such a case, the user would like to get a description of the variable, for which a value is sought. For instance, if the expert system prompts the user, to input a value for "plasticity index" and the user is not clear about what he/she has to enter, then the system should give either a brief or detailed description on plasticity index. The description should be capable of making the user understand what plasticity index is and the ranges of possible values it can take, etc. The knowledge base of the expert system should contain such information on variables for which explanations are likely to be asked for by the user.

When the expert system prompts for a value to be assigned to a variable, it is quite natural that the user is curious to know, Why the system needs a value for the variable displayed. The explanation facility should answer the user on this question of Why?

Once the inference is completed, the user would like to know, How the system arrived at a particular conclusion. The knowledge base of the expert system should be designed in such a way that the explanation mechanism can interact with it to provide the required answer to the user's query on How?

Displaying the complete line of reasoning would also be of interest to the user, i.e., the system should show the traces of complete reasoning process, explaining how each of the intermediate hypotheses or conclusions are drawn. These explanation capabilities are not only useful during the use of expert system, but also during the development stages for debugging.

User Interface

This component is an interface module for a user to interact with the expert system. A friendly user interface can provide nice interactive features, for easy and effective use of the system.

7.4 STAGES IN EXPERT SYSTEM DEVELOPMENT

Expert System development is a process, where the expert and knowledge engineer first interact to collect, compile and formalise the knowledge, then implement it using a development tool and finally test and validate with the help of the expert. The various stages in a developmental process are shown in Fig.7.3 and they are briefly described below:

Identification

As a first stage, it is required to identify the class of problems that the system will be expected to solve. That means one should identify where exactly the problem to be solved fits in the derivation-formation spectrum shown in Fig. 7.1. This identification of the problem class, enables the knowledge engineer to decide on knowledge representation schemes and inference mechanisms to be adopted. Also resources available for the developmental projects, in terms of availability of expert knowledge, constraints on time, hard- ware and software resources etc. are identified.

Conceptualisation

This stage primarily aims at compiling raw knowledge, deciding on possible decomposition of the problem solving process into subtasks, selecting proper inference mechanisms etc. The behaviour and nature of the domain knowledge is studied in detail to identify the concepts required to arrive at a solution of the problem. The control strategy for properly using the concepts is also identified at this stage.

Formalisation

During the formalisation stage, the knowledge engineer selects ~n appropriate representative formalism for the domain knowledge. Depending on the nature of the knowledge, one or more formal representation schemes may have to be adopted. Individual knowledge units and their relationships are identified and represented properly on paper, so that the domain expert can also browse through the same to check for any possible inconsistency or redundancy. Inference mechanisms are selected depending on the flow of information and underlying structure of the domain.

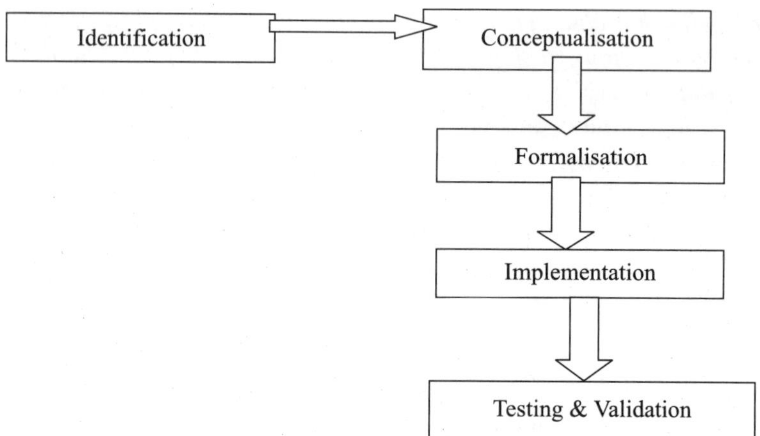

Fig. 7.3   Stages in Expert System Development

Implementation

An expert system development tool or shell is selected, which has the capabilities to represent the formalisms and inference mechanisms adopted in the previous stage. Knowledge base is coded into a form following the syntax of the knowledge interpreter of the shell. The coded knowledge is then entered into the computer using the editor program provided by the shell.

Testing and Validation

Once the coded knowledge is completely entered, the expert sys- tem is tested for its performance. The expert system is made to run on a large number of representative samples of test cases. The 8)'stem is debugged for any possible mistakes, during implementation. The validation of the expert system is usually carried out with the help of the expert who gave the knowledge contained in the knowledge base.

Out of the five stages, the conceptualisation stage is the most difficult, because experts generally do not structure their decision making in any formal manner. They also have difficulties in isolating and describing the steps of reasoning they take. According to Fenves et al [10], the shortage of good, practical Engineering Knowledge Based Expert Systems is due not so much to the limitations of present KBES frameworks (shells) as to the difficulty of compiling, organising and formalising that vast body of heuristic expertise which characterises the profession.

7.5   KNOWLEDGE REPRESENTATION

It can be seen from the previous section that the domain knowledge takes various forms, before it is coded into one or more representative formalisms. Proper representation schemes are to be used in different stages of developmental process. Once the knowledge is organised and represented in a formal manner, then it is the turn of the expert system development shell to convert and store it in proper data structures, so that the inference process can be started. In the present section, more emphasis is given on formal knowledge representation schemes.

As already seen, the domain knowledge of an expert system is organised and stored in the knowledge base. The computer program which simulates intelligent problem solving behaviour frequently interacts with the knowledge base. It is very important to note at this point that the problem solving procedure very much depends on the knowledge in the knowledge base. There are many ways to represent knowledge and it depends' on the type of knowledge to be represented in the knowledge base of the system.

Primarily the knowledge that is used for solving engineering problems can be classified into compiled, qualitative and quantitative knowledge. Compiled knowledge consists of experience of the experts in the domain, knowledge gathered from sources like hand- books, old records etc. The qualitative knowledge include common- sense, thumb rules, approximate theories, causal model of processes etc. The quantitative knowledge deals with numerical techniques, closed form solutions, domain concepts etc. A design engineer would generally use all these forms of knowledge in his design process. The amount of these different types of knowledge used will vary from problem to problem. It depends on the nature of the problem and its task complexity. In general, a problem of derivation nature will have more compiled knowledge, whereas a problem of formation nature will have more of quantitative and qualitative knowledge compared to the compiled one. This statement cannot be viewed as a generalised one, since the nature of the knowledge varies from domain to domain. The present section deals only with the representation of expert knowledge, i.e., compiled as well as qualitative knowledge.

The compiled as well as qualitative knowledge can be further classified into two broad categories, viz., declarative knowledge and procedural knowledge. Declarative knowledge, which is also called static knowledge primarily deals with the knowledge on the physical propreties of the problem domain. Whereas, procedural knowledge which is also called active knowledge deals with the problem solving techniques. For instance, consider a problem of traffic signal design. In this the knowledge about the traffic intersection, various approaches, flows, design goals or requirements etc. are represented as declarative/static knowledge, while the procedure of design, which contains the expertise of the experienced designers and the method of using the knowledge is represented as procedural or active knowledge.

The most common ways of representing knowledge are the following:

1. *Production Rules*
2. *Decision Tables*
3. *Frames*
4. *Semantic Networks*
5. *Predicate Logic*
6. *Conventional.Programs*

Knowledge Representation in the form of production rules is a very powerful and commonly used method for representing heuristic as well as control knowledge. Many of the prototype expert systems which are being used at present in industries, have major chunk of their knowledge in the form of production rules. Decision tables pro- vide easy means o(representing heuristic knowledge, which can be easily understood by an expert as well as a knowledge engineer. This feature of the decision tables make them a powerful means of representation for incremental acquisition of knowledge and adaptation of knowledge base to suit different requirements. Frame representation of knowledge is very useful where stereotyped situations are to be de- fined. Here a frame is visualised a knowledge unit, described by a set of slots. The frames can be networked using arcs, which semantically define the relationships between frames. Predicate logic provides an elegant, simple and mathematically strong model for representing knowledge and manipulating descriptions. The programs written in conventional procedural languages also contain good amount of knowledge. In knowledge based expert systems for engineering, one cannot avoid using functions and procedures written in procedural languages. Depending on the type of the problem and the specific requirements, one or more of these knowledge representation techniques can be used. In general, rules and procedures are used to represent control, active as well as procedural knowledge, whereas frames, semantic networks and predicate logic are used for storing static knowledge and description of objects. Decision tables can be manipulated to represent both the types of knowledge.

7.5.1 Production Rules

A rule base representation of knowledge consists of a set of rules, which may consist of both procedural or control' knowledge and heuristic knowledge. Each rule in the knowledge base has a left hand side (antecedent), consisting of either one or more conditions, and a right hand side (consequent), consisting of one or more actions. The actions specified in the right hand side are taken only if all the conditions in the left hand side are satisfied. A few typical rules in a knowledge base are given below:

1. IF environment is highly corrosive
   THEN steel beams are not preferred

2. IF flow is open channel flow
   AND Froude number is equal to 1
   THEN flow is critical

3. IF numerical computations are predominant
   THEN floating point co-processor is required

In all the above cases, when the IF portion of a rule is satisfied by the facts, the actions specified by the THEN portion are performed, and the rule is then said to be executed or fired. An inference mechanism of a rule interpreter acts on the rules in the knowledge base to arrive at a specified goal.

The knowledge to be stored in a rule base can be schematically represented in a net form as shown in Fig.7.4. Such a representation is called a knowledge net. A knowledge net is a computer model for implementing a knowledge base. Various facts, their inter- relationships and conditions for arriving at different hypotheses are represented in a knowledge net. Every node in the knowledge net represents a state. A state can be defined with a variable, an operator and a value. For instance, *Plasticity Index> 7* is a state, where the variable is *Plasticity Index,* operator is > and value 7. The nodes at the lowermost level represent initial states and

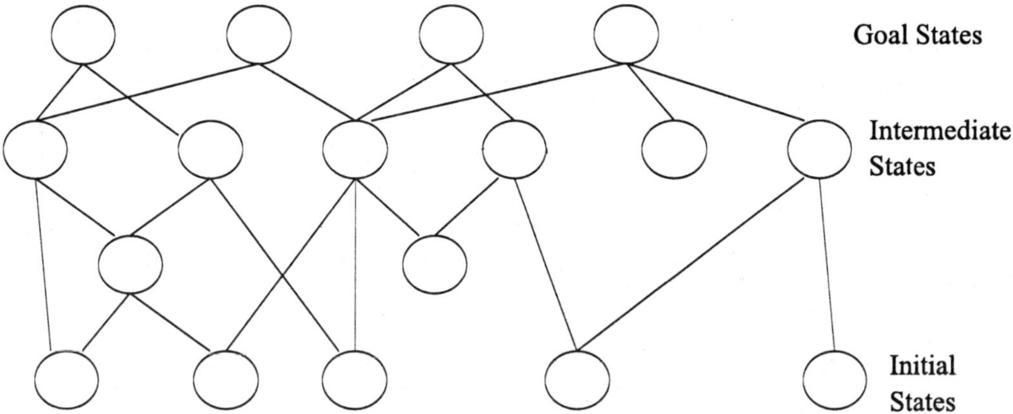

Fig. 7.4 A Knowledge Net

those at uppermost level represent goal states. The other nodes represent intermediate hypotheses. Depending on the nature of the knowledge, the relative number of goal states a node initial states vary. This is one of the governing criteria for selection of a proper inference mechanism to carry It reasoning.

A knowledge net can have four different types of nodes. They are leaf node, AND node, OR node and NOT node. The leaf node presents the initial states. Fig. 7.5 shows an AND node, wherein establish the state represented by the node, the states represented r all the three lower level nodes have to be satisfied. The rule that represented by the node is :

```
IF type of crack IS dormant
AND crack IS isolated
AND water conditions none
THEN repair method IS bonding with epoxy
```

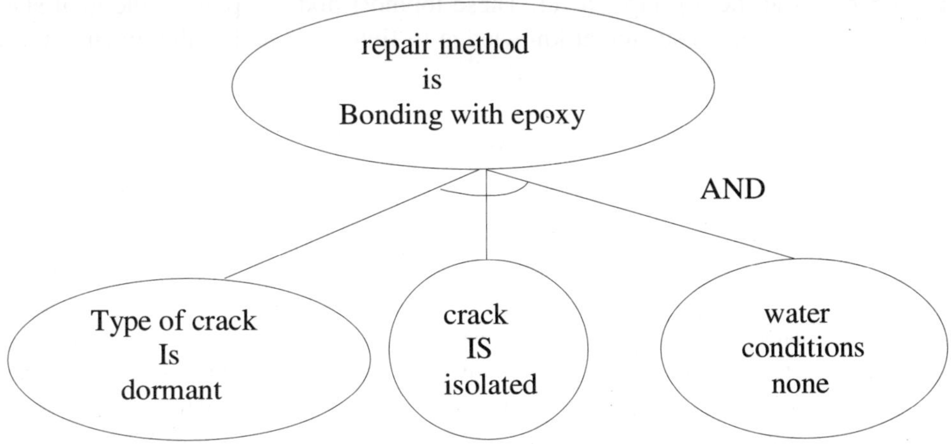

Fig. 7.5 An AND node

Here the first two states have a variable, an operator and a value, whereas the third state takes a value TRUE or FALSE. The variable in the first state is type of crack, operator is IS and value is dormant. Similarly in the second state, the variable is crack, operator is IS and value is isolated. These variables take character strings as their value. In the third state, only a variable is given, which means that it can take only two values, TRUE or FALSE and hence the variable is of boolean type.

An OR node is showed in Fig.7.6. Here it is sufficient that the states represented by anyone of the lower level node need be satisfied. The rule represented by the OR node is given below.

```
IF length of crack is increased substantially
OR glass strip IS cracked
OR crack width >= 0.05
THEN type of crack.IS active
```

In this case, the first state is described using a boolean variable, the second with a string variable and third with a numeric. In the third state, the variable is crack width, operator is '>=' and value 0.05.

Fig. 7.7 shows a NOT node in a knowledge net. The rule represented by the a NOT node is:

```
IF NOT the polymer is to be flame resistant
AND NOT the polymer is to be used as a thin film
THEN the flammability is appropriate
```

Here the hypothesis the flammability is appropriate is TRUE is set if both the supporting states are false.

A knowledge net can be visualised as a hierarchical organisation of one or more AND, OR or NOT nodes. A complete knowledge net for a soil classification problem is shown in Fig. 7.8. It has 8 nodes at the top most level. These topmost nodes represent the goal states. It means that the net contains sufficient knowledge to find out whether the given soil sample

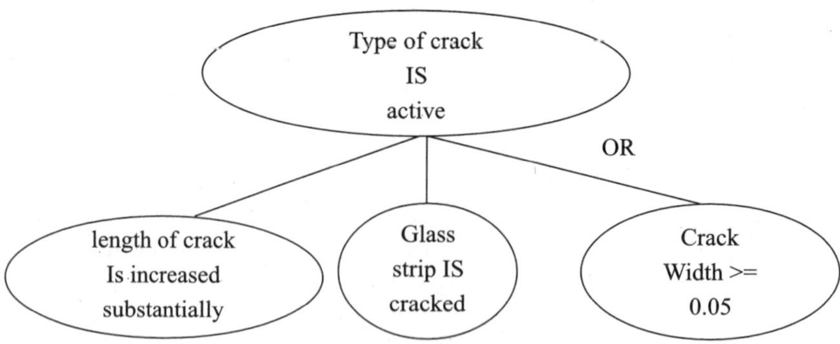

Fig. 7.6   An OR node

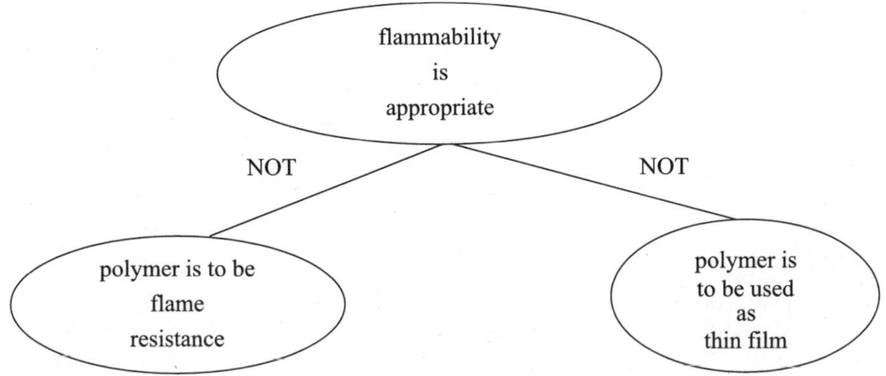

Fig. 7.7   NOT node

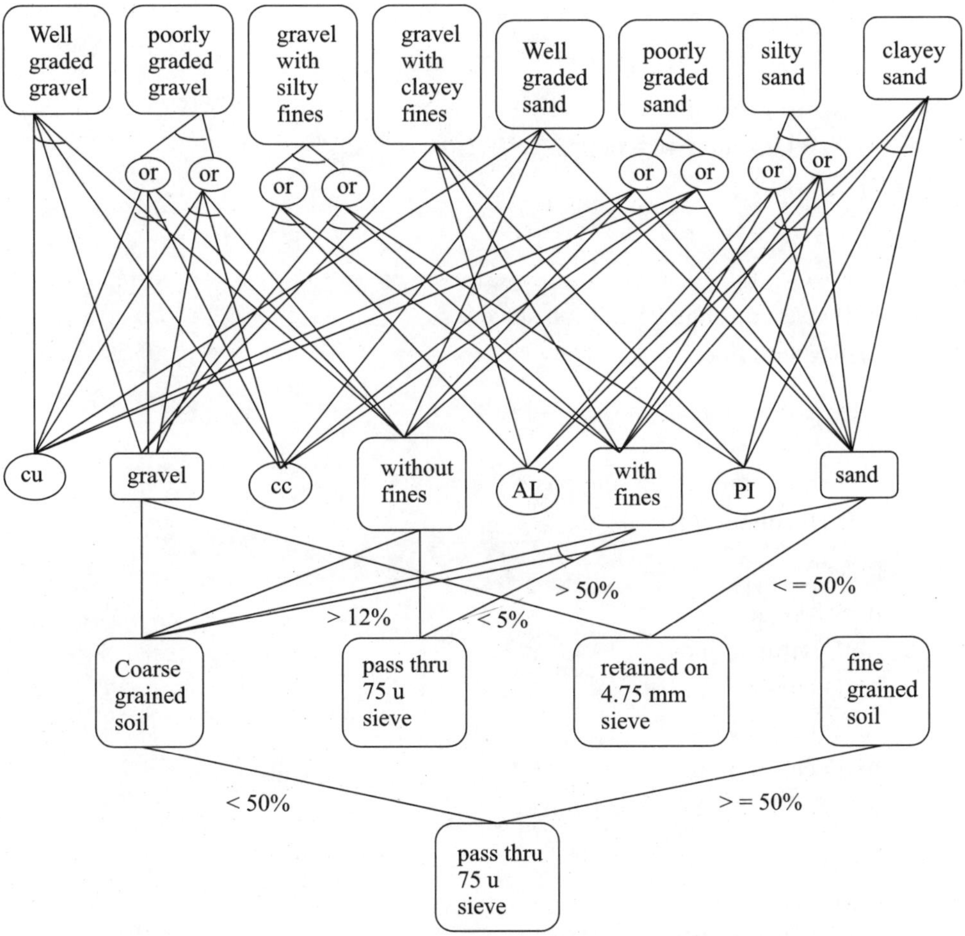

Fig. 7.8   Knowledge Net for Soil Classification

(ofcourse, coarse grained) is one of the eight types. Different search strategies are available to traverse through the net to classify the soil sample. The knowledge net shown in Fig. 7.8 is transformed into a set of production rules and are listed below.

Rule 1
IF pass through 75 micron sieve < 50 %
THEN coarse grained soil

Rule 2
IF pass through 75 micron sieve >= 50 %
THEN fine grained soil

Rule 3
IF coarse grained soil
AND retained on 4.75 mm sieve > 50%
THEN gravel

Rule 4
IF coarse grained soil
AND retained on 4.75 mm sieve <= 50
THEN sand

Rule 5
IF coarse grained soil ,
AND pass through 75 micron sieve < 5 %
THEN with fines

Rule 6
IF coarse grained soil
AND pass through 75 microns sieve > 12%
THEN without fines

Rule 7
IF gravel
AND without fines
AND cu > 4
AND cc >= 1
AND cc <= 3
THEN soil IS well graded gravel

Rule 8
IF gravel
AND without fines
AND cu <= 4

AND cc < 1
THEN soil IS poorly graded gravel

Rule 9
IF gravel
AND without fines AND cu <= 4 AND cc > 3
THEN soil is poorly graded gravel

Rule 10
IF gravel AND with fines
AND atterberg's limit IS below A-Iine
THEN soil IS gravel with silty fines

Rule 11
IF gravel AND with fines
AND plasticity index < 4
THEN soil is gravel with silty fines ,

Rule 12
IF gravel AND with fines
AND atterberg's limit IS above A-Iine
AND plasticity index > 7
THEN soil IS gravel with clayey fines

Rule 13
IF sand AND without fines '
AND cu > 6
AND cc > 1 AND cc < 3
THEN soil IS well graded sand

Rule 14
IF sand AND without fines
AND cu <= 6 AND cc <= 1
THEN soil IS poorly graded sand

Rule 15
IF sand AND without fines
AND cu <= 6 AND cc >= 3
THEN soil IS poorly graded sand

Rule16
IF sand AND with fines
AND atterberg's limit IS below A-Line
THEN soil IS silty sand

Rule 17

IF sand

AND with fines

AND plasticity index <= 4

THEN soil IS silty sand

Rule 18

IF sand

AND wi th fines

AND atterberg's limit IS above A-Line

AND plasticity index > 7

THEN soil IS clayey sand

These eighteen *rules* form the *rule* base for classification of coarse grained soils. Representation of knowledge in the form of *rules* is very widely used to describe the ill-structured knowledge. Rule based systems are relatively inefficient with respect to the execution time, because the reasoning mechanism has to carry out extensive searches through the *rules*. It has been reported in the literature that the slow down varies exponentially with the number of rules in the rule base.

The *problems* become *complex* when more and more variables are involved. In such cases, it is conceivable that all the facts avail- able may not completely pinpoint the causes. This gives rise to some uncertainty in the premise for structuring the knowledge base. This concept is *built* into the knowledge base by specifying 'confidence levels. As more facts that support a particular hypothesis are established, the expert becomes more confident. Conversely, if all the facts are not established to support a particular hypothesis, it can be said to be established with a lesser confidence level (provided some basic facts are established). Confidence is expressed in percentage. A confidence factor of 100 indicates that the fact or decision has been fully confirmed. A fact or decision that is not confirmed has a confidence factor of 0. The confidence factors associated with decisions in the system are obtained heuristically and their significance is only relative. That is, for example, a confidence factor of 75 signifies that the expert is 25% *less* confident in making that decision than the decision involving a confidence factor of 100. No other significance is to be attached to these values.

7.5.2 Decision Tables

We have seen rules offer a *powerful* technique for representing *complex* thoughts of experts. *Also* We have seen the *role* of knowledge nets in the process of knowledge elicitation, where it helps in removing inconsistencies and redundancies in the knowledge base. One cannot expect an expert of a specialised domain to understand these knowledge representation schemes. Depending on the capabilities of the expert system development shell, the knowledge engineer has to form the *rules* from the knowledge that has been acquired from the expert. In the process of transforming the knowledge into the form of *rules,* the knowledge engineer has to suitably modify the knowledge structure to some extent. Because of this transformation it would be difficult for an expert to go through the rules written according to the syntax of the development shell, and suggest corrections and modifications. Hence at the stage of knowledge acquisition, an appropriate knowledge representation scheme has to be adopted, which not *only* is capable of representing the knowledge without loosing its meaning, but also as simple as possible, so that both the knowledge engineer and expert can carefully go through it to have a better inter- action between them. Decision tables are simple form of knowledge representation technique, which is capable of representing heuristic as well as intuitive knowledge in a simple but efficient manner. Fig. 7.9 shows the structure of a decision table.

A decision table consists of four parts as shown in Fig.7.9. The top left portion contains a list of factors or conditions and the bottom left portion contains a list of actions. The right portion is divided into a number of columns. The top portion of the columns corre- sponding to list of conditions has entries representing the state of conditions in the antecedent part of a rule. The bottom portion corresponding to the actions has entries representing the actions to be taken if the antecedent is true. There can be three different entries in the top portion; they are T, F and nothing. An entry T means that the corresponding condition should evaluate to true. Similarly the conditions with entries F should evaluate to false. The conditions with no entry in the columns can take either true or *Base,* hence they are immaterial. The only meaningful entry in the bottom portion of the the columns corresponding to actions is X. The entry X indicates the actions to be taken if the corresponding conditions evaluate to the respective values specified. Fig.7.10 through Fig.7.13 shows four decision tables, which represents the knowledge contained in the 18 rules for the soil classification problem discussed in the previous section.

	Rule 1	Rule 2		Rule n
Factor 1	T		T	
Factor 2		F		
Factor 3				T
				T
	T			
Factor n		T		F
Action 1	X			
		X	X	
Action m				X

Fig. 7.9 Structure of a Decision Table

Pass through 75 micron sieve < 50%	T	F
Coarse grained soil	X	
Fine grained soil		X

Fig. 7.10 Decision Table-I for Soil Classification

Rule	13	14	15	16
coarse graine soil	T	T	T	T
retained on 4.75 mm sieve > 50%	T			
retained on 4.75 mm sieve <= 50%		T		
pass through 75 micron sieve < 5%			T	
pass through 75 micron sieve > 12%				T
gravel	X			
sand		X		
with fines			X	
without fines				X

Fig. 7.11 Decision Table-II for Soil Classification

	7	8	9	10	11	12
gravel	T	T	T	T	T	T
without fines	T	T	T			
with fines				T	T	T
cu > 4	T	T	F			
cc < 1	F	T				
cc > 3	F		T			
atterberg's limit is below A-line				T		
atterberg's limit is above A-line						T
plasticity index < 4					T	
plasticity index < 7						T
soil is well graded gravel	X					
soil is poorly graded gravel		X	X			
soil is gravel with silty fines				X	X	
soil is gravel with clayey fines						X

Fig. 7.12 Decision Table-III for Soil Classification

	Rules					
	13	14	15	16	17	18
gravel	T	T	T	T	T	T
without fines	T	T	T			
with fines				T	T	T
cu > 6	T	F	F			
cc > 1	T	F				
cc > 3	T		F			
atterberg's limit is below A-line				T		
atterberg's limit is above A-line						T
plasticity index < 4					T	
plasticity index < 7						T
soil is well graded sand	X					
soil is poorly graded sand		X	X			
soil is silty sand				X	X	
soil is clayey sand						X

Fig. 7.13 Decision Table-III for Soil Classification

The decision table approach for knowledge representation can be used either only at the knowledge acquisition stage, or both at the knowledge acquisition stage as well as as a formal technique for, knowledge representation. In the first case, the knowledge contained i in the decision table is transformed into rules before actual inference starts. Whereas in the second case, the inference engine directly uses the decision tables to carry out reasoning. In the direct approach, appropriate methods have to be adopted for implementing inference mechanisms, which uses the knowledge sources in the form of decision tables. As in the case of rules, uncertainty factors can be attached to various conditions and hypotheses in decision tables. At the stage of structuring knowledge, decision tables offer a simple and efficient method which improves the effectiveness of interaction between the expert and the knowledge engineer.

7.5.3 Frames and Semantic Networks

Minsky has introduced the concept of frame representation to define stereotyped situations. A frame is a unit of knowledge source described by a set of slots. Primarily there can be two types of slots in a frame, viz., abstract or concrete, depending on the information associated with the slots. A concrete slot would contain a specific value, whereas an abstract slot would contain descriptions that characterize any possible value for the slot. Depending on the situations, some slots are made relational in nature, where the slots contain information on the relationship of the frame with other frames.

The three slots of the frame for traffic intersection is shown in the Fig. 7.14. The two slots are concrete slots, which has values defined. The slot part- of is a relational one, which describes that traffic-intersection is a part of national highway.

Frame representing a beam is shown in Fig. 7.15. Here the slot bending_moment has a value compute_bm, which is a function, That means if the value for the slot is needed, then a function compute_bm can be called to compute the value. Semantic network representation of knowledge is very useful in representing static or declarative type of knowledge. Fig. 7.16 shows a typical semantic network representating the knowledge about a structure.

Here nodes such as building, beam, column, reinforced concrete etc. are related by means of links by semantics such as part- of, made-of, size etc. As the descriptive power of semantic networks are extremely good, they are well suited for representing declarative type of knowledge than procedural type of knowledge.

Traffic_intersection

no_of_legs	4
Part_of	National highway
traffic control	By signal

Fig. 7.14   A Frame represnting a Traffic Intersection

beam

name	beam_5
Part_of	building_A
material	reinforced concrete
size	300 x 600
b_moment	Compute_bm

Fig.7.15   A Frame represnting a Beam

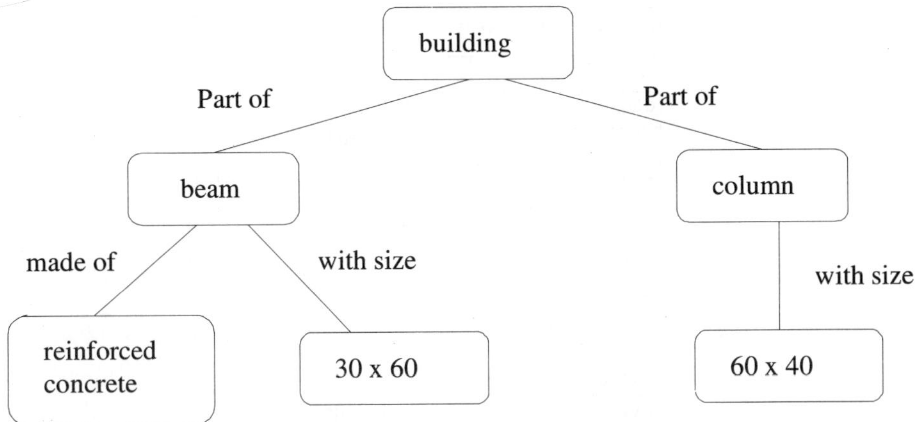

Fig. 7.16 A Semantic Network

The nodes of the semantic net in Fig.7.16 are just objects with- out any attributes attached to it. Even the descriptions of the objects are specified using links. The power of the semantic networks can further be improved to a great extent by representing the nodes as frames. This allows one to use the arcs or links of the network to specify only the relationships between frames. All the properties and attributes of the objects are described using slots. Fig.7.17 shows the modified semantic network shown in Fig. 7.16 using frames. The advantages of using frames as nodes of the network are obvious from the two figures.

A knowledge unit frame is described by a set of slots and a slot may either be an attribute to the object, that is described using a frame or a relation. As already illustrated, a relation slot is used to link two frames together. A hierarchy of frames can thus describe a set of concepts or objects which are related. Such hierarchical description of concepts or objects is generally called taxonomy. In a taxonomic description all the abstract information is kept at the top. Frames at the lower level inherit properties and attributes from their parent frames. This very effective technique of knowledge representation, helps in saving time in the definition of new knowledge. Fig. 7.18 shows a typical taxonomic description of structural steel frames as a hierarchy of frames.

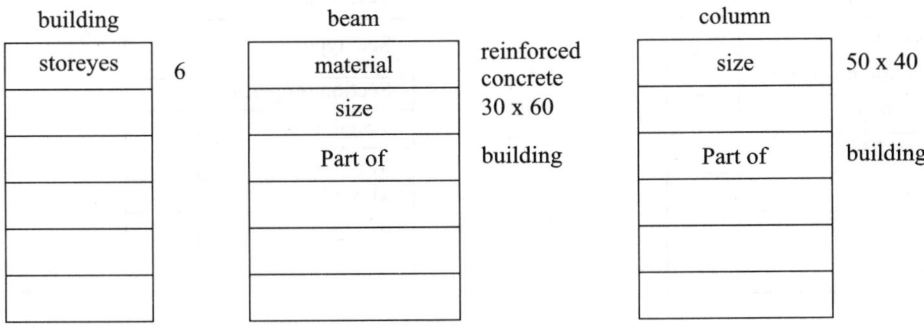

Fig. 7.17 Semantic Network with Frame

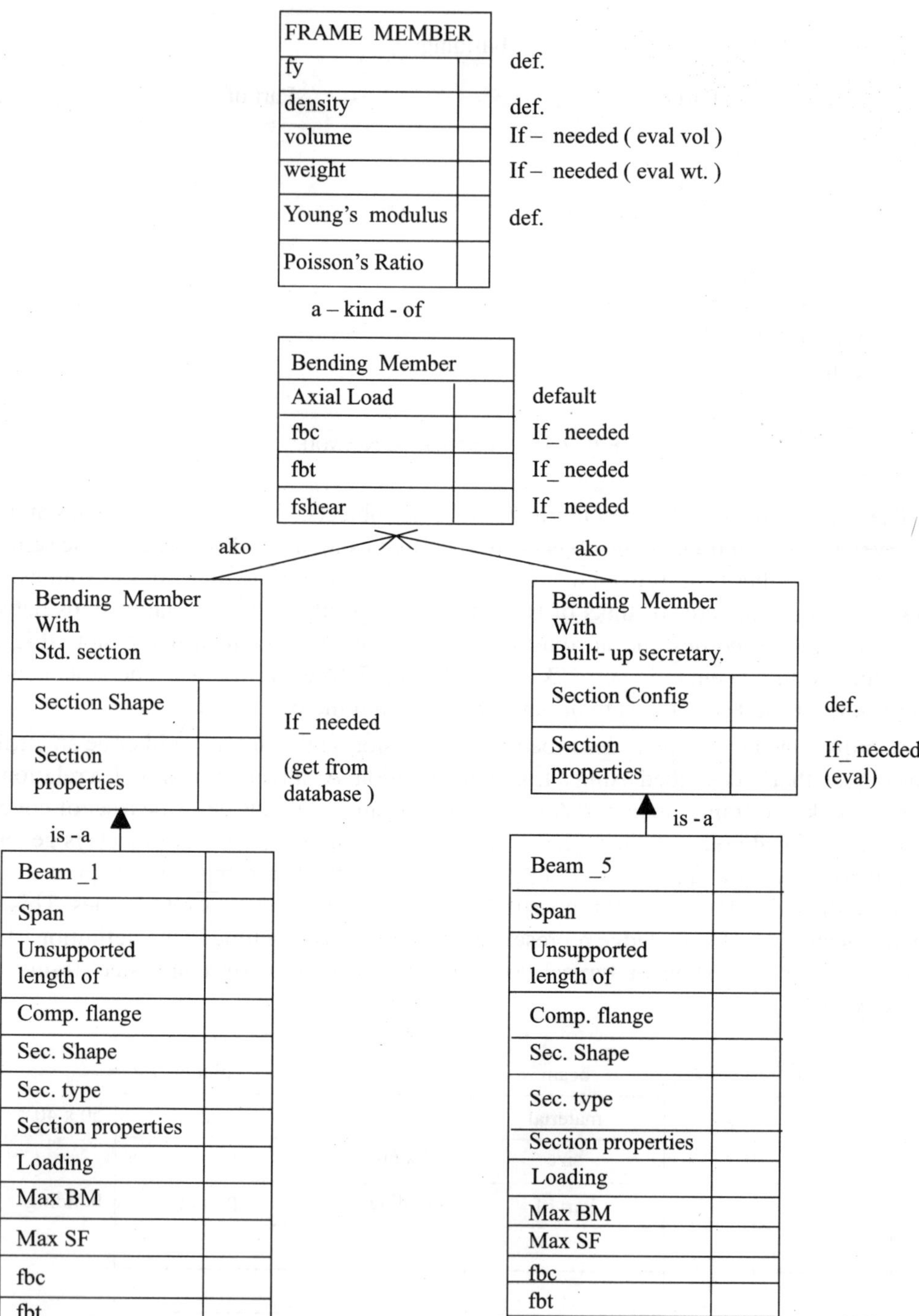

Fig. 7.18 Taxonomic Description of Structural Steeel Members

The attributes or relations can be of many types. For instance, an attribute can be specified to be of either, default, value or a demon. These default, value or demon facets are required to properly represent the assumptions based on common sense knowledge in the specific domain, and to attach procedures which compute and return results to the attributes. If an information related to an attribute is specific, then it is considered to be of *value* type, and has got highest priority. In the absence of specific information, *default* values are assumed. For instance, consider the node for *bending member* in Fig. 7.18. The attribute *axial load* of the frame *bending member* is specified as a default type and is given a value 0. This means that by default, the axial load acting on any bending member can be treated as 0, unless it is explicitly given. This is a common assumption that any structural design engineer makes during the design process.

Also during the design process, it is required to compute the section properties of the member selected for design evaluation. In the case of a *bending member with standard section,* the attribute *section properties* is given an *if-needed* facet with a demon attached to it. When the design process requires this data, a procedure is automatically invoked, to obtain the data from a database. Such procedures which are automatically invoked without an explicit call is called a demon. It is nothing but a sleeping program which acts when some specified modifications are done in the network. In this case, when- ever a value for the slot section properties is needed, the demon is invoked and the value is fetched. One of the most important use of demons is to simulate common sense type of knowledge. For example, consider a case, where there are a number of frames and many attributes of different frames are dependent on a specific attribute of a specific frame. If a value is added to that specific attribute, all the related values in other frames have to be modified. This can be achieved by attaching an if-added demon to the attribute slot. This invokes the demon, whenever a value is added to the slot. The demon function will carry out the actions specified, without the user explicitly calling it.

Another interesting feature of the taxonomic representation of knowledge is that, it provides a mechanism to inherit attribute values from parent nodes and other nodes at higher level. For example, consider the taxonomic representation of *frame member* given in Fig. 7.18. During evaluation of the design, it is required to check the stresses with the allowable stress for the material. The allowable stress fy is given at the topmost node as a default attribute. Whenever the design process requires this value, the inheritance mechanism, traverses up the net and inherits the value for fy from the topmost node, as the value holds good for all the nodes below.

In a particular problem, it may be required to identify and separate the static as well as the procedural knowledge and represent them as semantic net in a taxonomic form and rules respectively. When the rules are to be executed after a proper match and select operation, it may be required to obtain facts about objects from the semantic network of frames. In such cases, the inference mechanism interacts with the static/declarative knowledge represented in the form of semantic net to proceed with the problem solving. In some cases, especially in design type of problems, data bases may be required to hold large amount of design data. In such cases, the database also contains knowledge, which is required by the inference mechanism for problem solving. This demands the inference engine to be capable of extracting knowledge not only from the rule base, but also from data bases, frames and semantic networks.

7.5.4 Meta-knowledge

The term meta-knowledge refers to knowledge about knowledge. As the size of the knowledge base grow larger and larger, and control strategy become more complex, it becomes increasingly difficult for the knowledge engineers to properly organise the knowledge and control mechanism. An ideal way out in such situations is to logically divide the knowledge into smaller ones, and have a higher level knowledge base, which contains the knowledge about the lower level knowledge bases and problem solving strategy. Fig. 7.19 shows a schematic organisation of meta-knowledge base and other problem solving knowledge bases. The knowledge base at the higher level is called meta-knowledge base. Depending on the control information, the meta-knowledge selects the current knowledge base to be used with appropriate reasoning mechanism. Meta-knowledge also helps in providing information about domain knowledge and adding new knowledge to the knowledge base.

7.6 INFERENCE MECHANISMS

It is not sufficient that expert knowledge be compiled in the knowledge base. There must be another component that directs the implementation of the knowledge. This component of the system is known as the control structure or the inference engine. The infer- ence engine primarily uses a search technique to arrive at conclusions based on the knowledge in the knowledge base.

The search methods used in the area of Artificial Intelligence are broadly classified into five types. They are :

1. *simple search*
2. *evaluation based search*

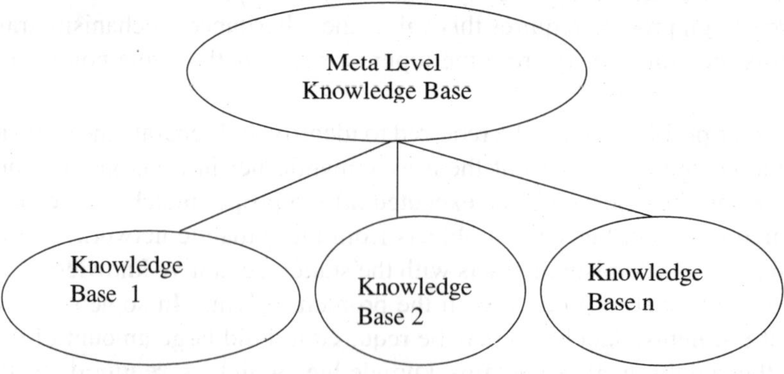

Fig. 7.19 Meta-knowledge and Problem Solving Knowledge

> 3. *games search*
> 4. *constraint search*
> 5. *controlled search*

Controlled search techniques are generally used for searching a solution path through a knowledge net. Forward chaining and back- ward chaining are the most Popular controlled search techniques commonly adopted. As these searches carry out deductions at various stages of search, they are also called inference mechanisms. Working of these mechanisms are explained in detail below.

We have seen the various knowledge representation schemes adopted for building Knowledge Based Expert Systems. The purpose of the various inferencing strategies is to arrive at a solution for the given problem, by conducting exhaustive searches through the knowledge base, which may be either only a rule base or a combination of rule base and semantic network.

Any intelligent problem solving system must have the ability to think and act. This capability is the one which differentiates the expert system from conventional programs. The conventional programs Carry out just blind actions, whereas expert systems has a reasoning mechanism, which is generally implemented by combining pattern matching and pattern recognition capabilities.

Inference mechanism is a kind of search technique, where a given pattern is matched against a set of stored patterns. Simple search techniques can be used for problem solving using knowledge stored in *rules*. A rule, as discussed earlier has an antecedent and a consequent. The antecedent consists of a pattern, whereas, the consequent contains a set of actions. These actions are performed, when the pattern in the antecedent matches with the one being tested. As the action of one rule changes, the state of the stored patterns, it leads to other rules being matched. This process of pattern matching and carrying out a set of actions can be visualised as a reasoning process and can be modelled as a chaining of rules in a particular manner to arrive at conclusion.

The most commonly used inferencing models are *forward chaining* and *backward chaining*. In both these strategies, the current state of patterns are stored in a *working* memory, which is also sometimes called *context*. A detailed description of these inference mechanisms with examples is given in the following section.

7.6.1 Backward Chaining

In backward chaining process, the reasoning starts with a given goal. Here the rules are scanned in a manner that those whose con- sequent action can lead to the goal are found. The patterns in the antecedent of these rules are checked with those in the working memory. If the pattern matches, then the rule is fired. If not, a new subgoal is defined, which is the pattern of the antecedent of the previous rule, and search is continued. The details of *backward chaining* is explained using the knowledge net shown in Fig. 7.6 and the rule representation of the knowledge net.

Assume that the goal is to diagnose given soil sample. The goal variable is defined as soil. The topmost nodes of the knowledge net represents the goal states and the leaf nodes, initial states. Once the goal variable is defined, the backward chaining inferencing mechanism starts as follows.

There is no information available now in the working memory. The mechanism creates a goal stack and a rule stack, and the goal variable is pushed into the goal stack. The inference mechanism scans through the rulebase, for a rule with the goal variable in its consequent. In the example considered, rule- 7 has the goal variable soil in its consequent. The rule no.7 is pushed into the rule stack as shown below schematically in Fig.7.20. As the working memory does not contain any facts, the pattern in the antecedent part of the rule could not be matched. There are four variables in the antecedent of rule-7.

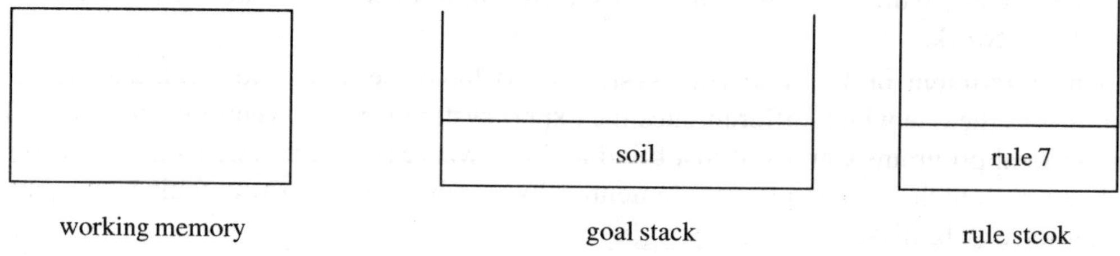

Fig. 7.20   Working Memory, Goal Stack and Rule Stack -I

```
Rule selected: Rule 7
IF gravel
AND without fines
AND cu > 4 AND cc >= 1
AND cu <= 3
THEN soil IS well graded gravel
```

Now it is necessary to know the state of the variables in the antecedent of rule- 7 to prove or disprove that the consequent of rule- 7. The first variable gravel is pushed into the goal stack, and the current goal is set to gravel. The mechanism searches for a rule in the rulebase, whose consequent has the variable gravel. Rule-3 satisfies this condition and is selected, and the rule number is pushed into rule stack. The state of the stacks and the rule selected is shown in Fig.7.21.

```
Rule selected: Rule 3
IF coarse grained soil
AND retained on 4.75 mm sieve > 50 %
THEN gravel
```

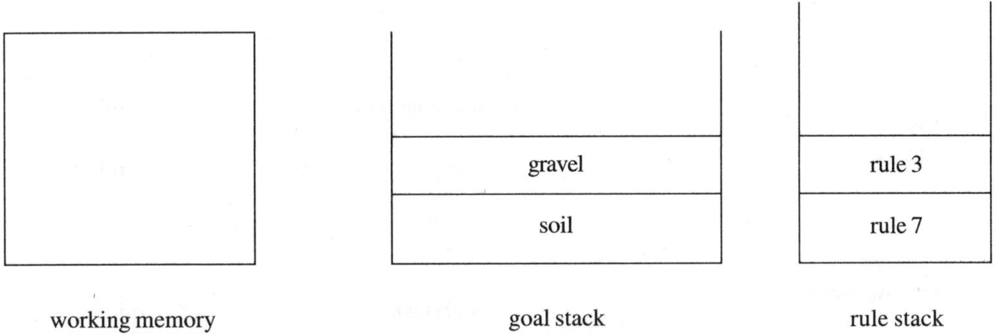

working memory   goal stack   rule stack

Fig. 7.21   Working Memory, Goal Stack and Rule Stack -II

Even now, working memory is empty. The antecedent of rule-3 has two variables, and more facts are required to prove wheiJ1er the soil is of gravel type or not. The first variable in the antecedent of rule-3 coarse grained soil is pushed into the goal stack and is shown in Fig. 7.22. The search is again continued for a rule with coarse grained soil in its consequent. Rule-1 satisfies this.

```
Rule selected: Rule 1
IF pass through 75 micron sieve < 50 %
THEN coarse grained soil
```

There is only one variable in the antecedent part of rule-1 and it is required to know the state of pass through 75 micron sieve, to deduce whether the soil is coarse grained soil or not. The variable pass through 75 micron sieve is pushed to the goal stack and the rule base is searched for a rule with this variable (current goal) as its consequent. As no such rule exists, it means that this variable lies in a leaf node of the knowledge net and the data has to be obtained by querying the user. The user response is put into the working memory and the goal stack is popped. The present state of the working memory and the stacks are shown below in Fig. 7.23.

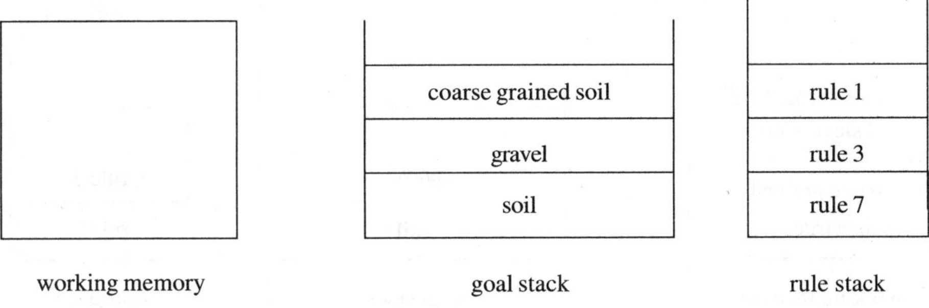

working memory   goal stack   rule stack

Fig. 7.22   Working Memory, Goal Stack and Rule Stack -III

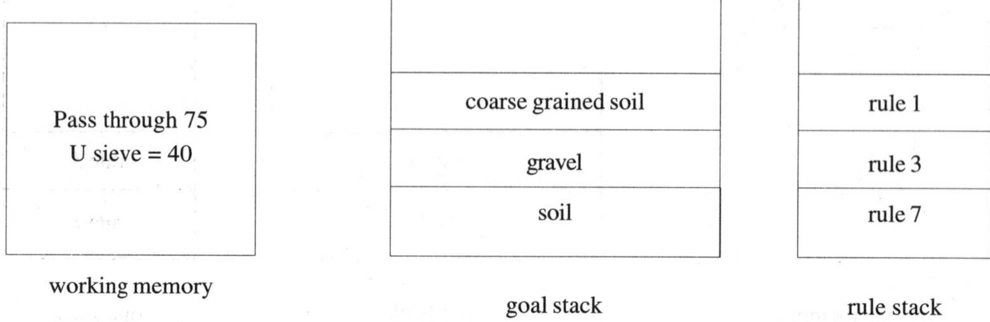

Fig. 7.23   Working Memory, Goal Stack and Rule Stack -IV

Let the user response to the query for pass through 75 micron sieve be 40. That means the antecedent part is satisfied and hence the rule can be fired. As a result of the rule being fired, one more fact is added to the working memory. Then the goal stack and the rule stack are popped. The modified working memory and the stacks are shown in Fig.7.24.

Now the variable at the top of the goal stack is gravel and it is on the consequent part of rule-3. This information is available to the inference mechanism from the rule stack. Out of the two variables in the antecedent part of rule-3, one is satisfied and is available in the working memory. Now the second variable retained on 4.75 mm sieve is pushed to the goal stack. The rule base is searched for a rule with the above variable at consequent. As there is no rule to satisfy this condition, the user is queried to get the data as before. Let the user response to the query be 38. This information is added to the working memory as a fact. As the condition of rule-3 is not satisfied, the" rule could not be fired, and it is proved that the soil sample is not gravel. The goal stack and the rule stack is popped. Now as the first condition itself of rule- 7 is not satisfied {i.e. gravel is not true), it is proved that the soil is not well graded gravel. Hence rule-7 is popped out of rule stack, making the variable soil at the top of the stack.

The rule base is scanned for the next rule with soil as its variable in the consequent. Rule-8 satisfies this condition, and hence this rule number is pushed to the rule stack, and the antecedent part of this rule is examined. The first condition is that gravel should be true. The present facts in the working memory proves that gravel is not true or gravel is false. As the

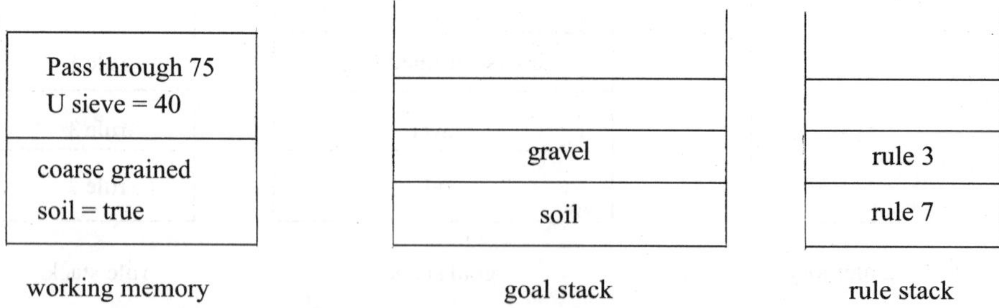

Fig. 7.24   Working Memory, Goal Stack and Rule Stack -V

match fails, the rule also fails, and the rule number is popped out of the stack. Similarly rules 9, 10, 11 and 12 fails, as one of the conditions in their antecedent is that gravel must be true. Then rule-13 is selected, and the antecedent is examined. The first variable is sand and is not available in the working memory. Hence it is pushed into the goal stack (Fig.7.25).

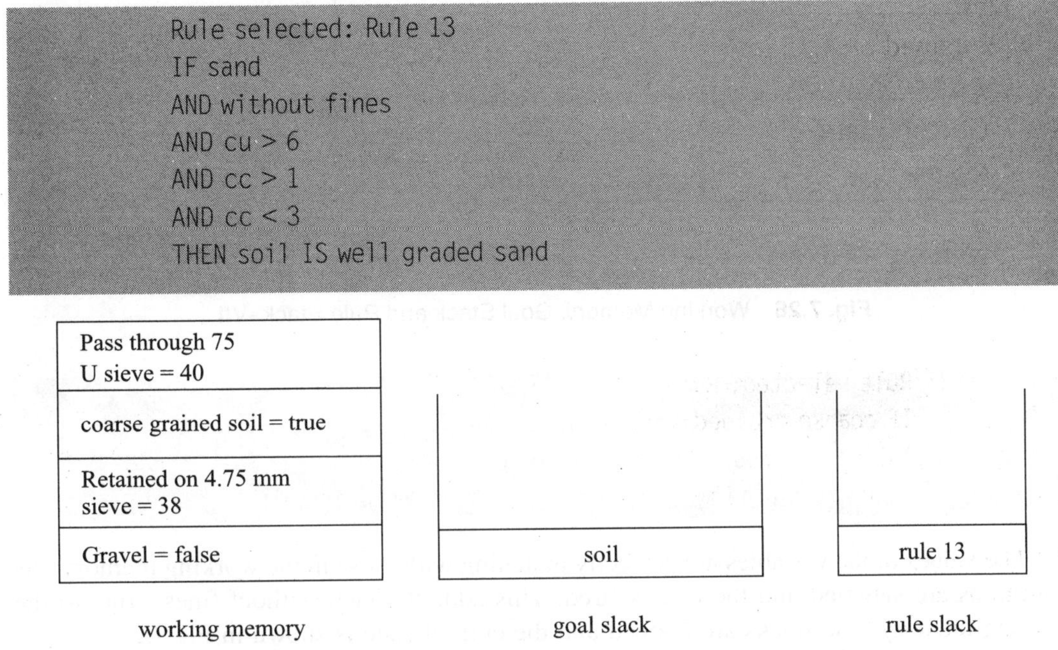

Fig. 7.25 Working Memory, Goal Stack and Rule Stack -VI

A search through the rule base for a rule with sand in consequent shows that rule-4 satisfies this, and it is selected.

Now the pattern in the antecedent part of rule-4 matches that with the values in the working memory, and the rule is fired. This firing of rule-4 adds the variable sand to the working memory with its value to be true. Both the stacks are popped, which makes the present state as shown in Fig. 7.26.

As the first variable in the rule-13 is proved to be true, the second one is examined. To satisfy it, the variable without fines should be true. This variable is now pushed on to the goal stack, and as a result of search it is found that rule-6 has the variable without fines in its consequent. Rule-6 and variable without fines is pushed into the respective stacks.

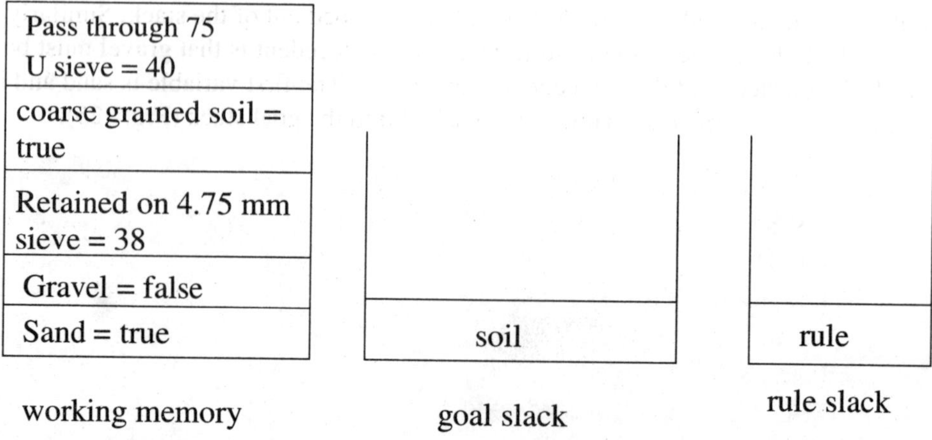

Fig. 7.26 Working Memory, Goal Stack and Rule Stack -VII

```
Rule selected: Rule 6
IF coarse grained soil
AND pass through 75 micron sieve > 12
THEN without fines
```

The values of the variables are perfectly matching with those in the working memory, the conditions are satisfied and the rule is fired. This adds the fact, without fines -true, to the working memory. The stacks are popped and the current state is shown in Fig.7.27.

Now as the two conditions in the antecedent of rule-13 is satisfied, the third variable is examined. The variable cu is pushed to the goal stack and searched for the rule to prove the

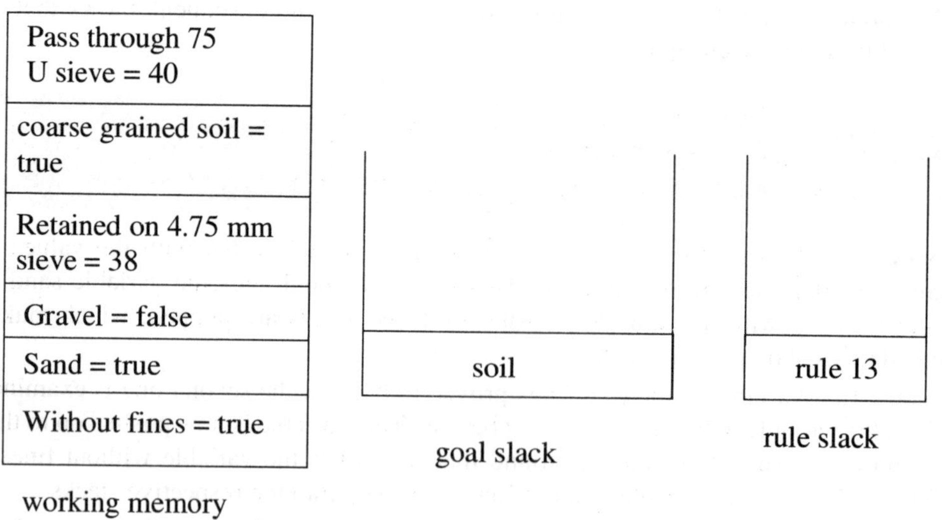

Fig. 7.27 Working Memory, Goal Stack and Rule Stack -VIII

value of cu. As there is no rule with cu in the consequent, it is queried and the data is obtained, and which is added to the working memory. Let the value of cu be equal to 6. This violates the third condition of rule-13 and hence the rule is discarded and the rule stack is popped. The next rule with goal variable soil is rule-14 is added to the rule stack.

```
Rule selected: Rule 14
IF sand
AND without fines AND cu <= 6 AND cc <= 1
THEN soil IS poorly graded sand
```

The first three conditions of the rules are satisfied with the values in the working memory. Now the fourth condition is examined. A search through the rule base shows that the variable cc cannot be deduced, because it does not appear in the consequent part of any rule. Hence, it is queried and the data is obtained. Let the user response to the query for cc be 5. This is added to the working memory. This violates the fourth condition of rule-14, and hence it is discarded and popped from the rule stack. The next rule selected is rule-15. The rule with the states of working memory and the stacks are shown in Fig.7.28.

```
Rule selected: Rule 15
IF sand
AND without fines
AND cu <= 6
AND cc >= 3
THEN soil IS poorly graded sand
```

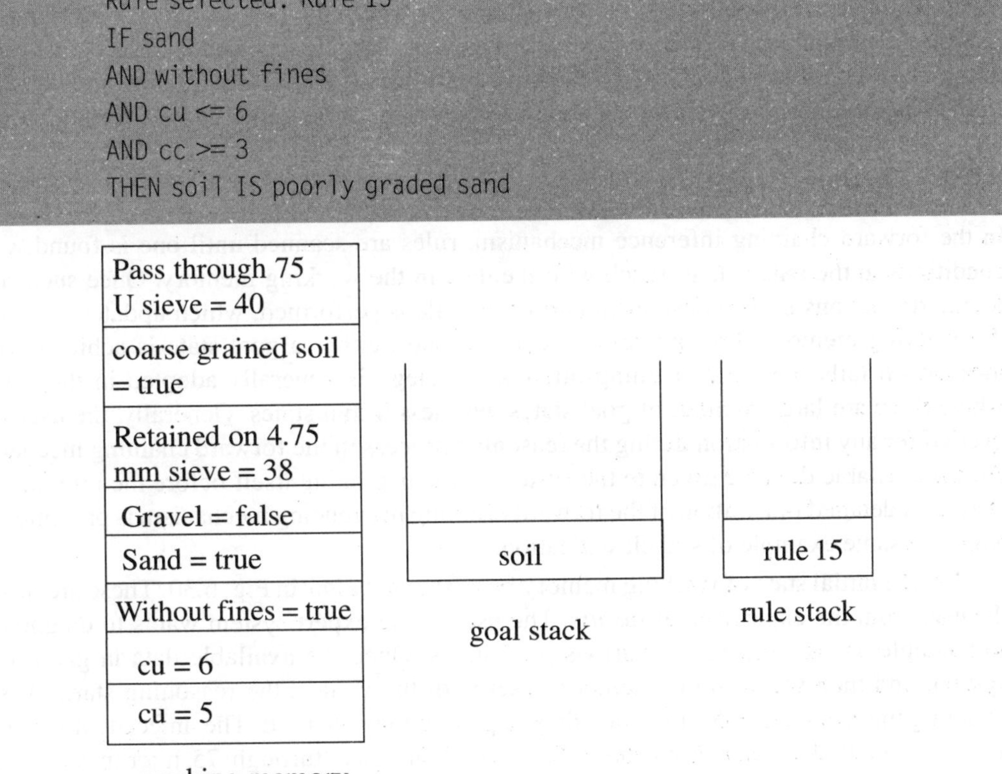

Fig. 7.28 Working Memory, Goal Stack and Rule Stack -IX

The pattern in the antecedent of the rule-15 is matching with that in the working memory, and rule-15 is fired. This proves that the soil sample is poorly graded sand. Now a value is obtained for the goal variable soil, the stacks are popped and they are empty. This indicates that there are no more goals to be proved.

In backward chaining inference process, the search is carried out based on the goal. Hence this inference mechanism is also known as *goal driven.* Here the questions required to prove the current goal are asked. The order in which the questions are asked depends on the order of rules appear in the rule base. Only those questions associated with the variables appearing in the rules selected are asked. For instance, atterberg. s limit and plasticity index are two variables used in the rulebase. The questions associated with these variables were not asked as these has relevance only when the variable with fines is true. A close examination of the rules deducing the above two variables shows that, there was no necessity to use two different variables with fines and without fines, because when with fines is true, without fines must be false and vice versa. Similarly the variables gravel and sand could also could be combined as, both of them cannot be true at the same time. Only for the purpose of illustration and clear understanding, such explicit variables are used in the present example.

Most expert systems are implemented in such a way that, during the process of reasoning, the user can ask questions like *how* a variable was deduced and *why* it needs a specific data input. Another interesting information one would like to know is the line of reasoning. This lists all the facts in the working memory, and the rules fired to arrive at the goal, and is shown in the knowledge net (Fig. 7.29} by drawing solid lines (Other lines are drawn using dashed lines. Line of reasoning connects all the states which are true in the knowledge net.

7.6.2 Forward Chaining

In the forward chaining inference mechanism, rules are scanned until one is found, whose conditions in the antecedent match with the data in the working memory. Once such rule is found, the actions in the consequent part of the rule is performed, which updates the facts in the working memory. This process is repeated until, either a goal state is achieved or the mechanism fails. Forward chaining inference strategy is generally adopted in those cases, where there are large number of goal states with less initial states. Generally, the user is not queried for any information during the reasoning process in the forward chaining mechanism. All the available data are given to the system in the beginning itself before the inferencing is started. A detailed illustration of the forward chaining inferencing mechanism is presented here using the same example of soil classification.

Let the initial state of working memory be as shown *below* in Fig. 6.30. These are input by the user from the experimental *results.* The user of the expert system wants to diagnose the soil sample as one among the various goal states. Once the available data ia given to the system, and then the working memory is set with the values, the reasoning starts. It starts scanning the *rules* the order in which they appear in the *rule* base. The antecedent part of the *rule-l* is satisfied by matching the value of variable pass through 75 micron sieve in the working memory. As it is *less* than 50, the *rule (rule-l)* is fired and the action in the consequent

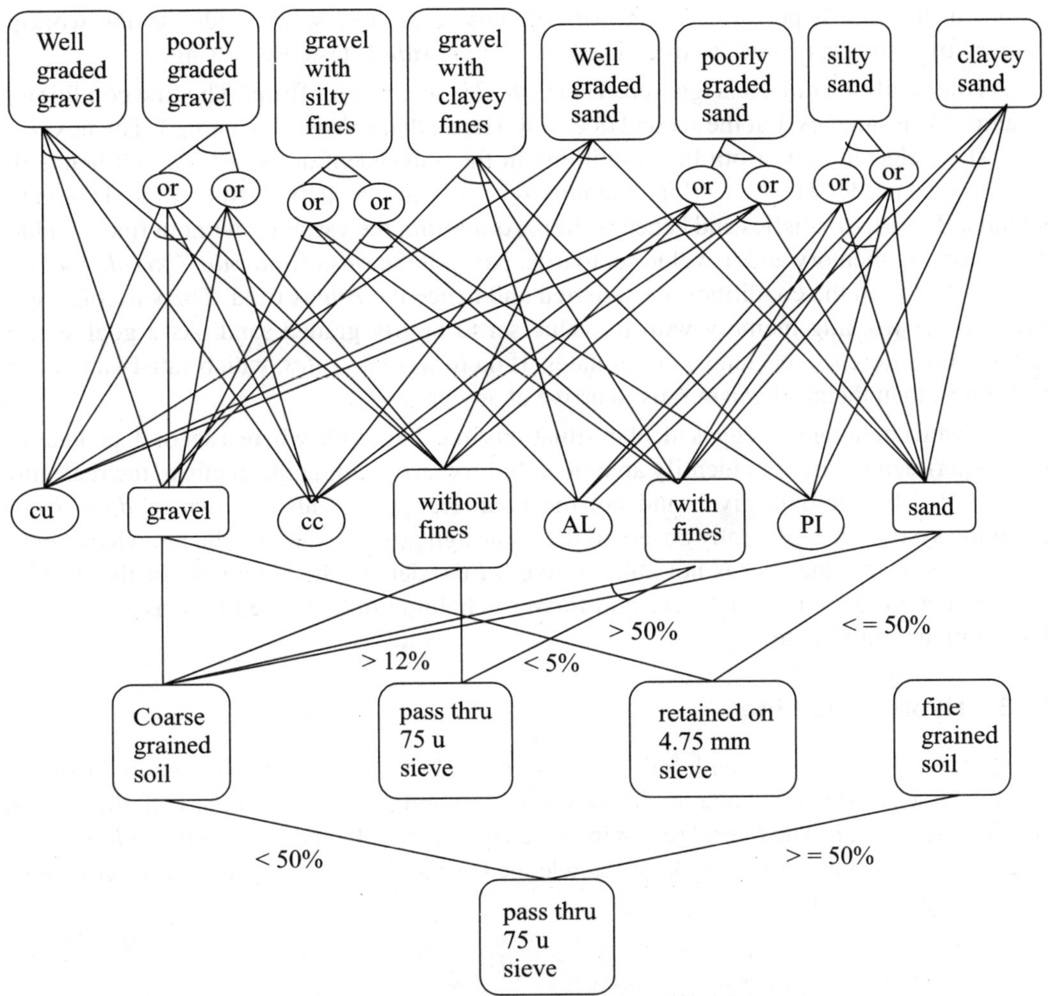

Fig. 7.29 Line of Reasoning

Initial Stale of Working Memory

Pass through 75 u   sieve = 40
Retained on 4.75 mm sieve = 38
cu = 6
cu = 5

Fig. 7.30 State of Initial Working Memory

portion of the *rule* is performed. The variable coarse grained soil is added to the working memory by setting its values to true. Then the second *rule* is tested for firing.

As the condition rails, it is ignored. Then *rule-3* is selected for firing. The first condition in the antecedent satisfies, but the second does not. Hence that *rule* is also ignored. The next *rule* (*rule-4*) is selected now. Both the conditions in the antecedent are satisfied, and hence the variable sand is added to the working memory with its value set to true. Now *rule-5* is selected but fails. But *rule-6* satisfies and hence is fired. As a *result,* the variables without fines is added to the working memory and its value set to true. Now all the *rules* from *rule-7* to *rule-14* fails. But in *rule-15,* all the conditions are satisfied and hence the *rule* is fired. The variable soil is added to the working memory with its value set to poorly graded sand. As a goal state is reached, the inference mechanism terminates. If there were no *rules,* which satisfy any of the goal states, then the mechanism fails to arrive at any goal.

Forward chaining strategy is ideal in situations like diagnosis, where a set of data obtained from experiments is used to identify an object. In forward chaining mechanism, the reasoning is controlled by the data given and not the goal. Hence it is also known as *data driven* reasoning system. It is generally observed that in design prob*lems,* where the knowledge net is quite *complex,* and the user is not able to give *all* the data in the beginning of the *problem* solving, a combination of backward and forward chaining may be used to arrive at the goal state from the initial state.

7.6.3 Hybrid Chaining

Hybrid reasoning first starts with forward chaining and when- ever a data is required from the user, backtracks to the leaf node of the knowledge net and gets it to continue with the forward chaining mechanism. The hybrid reasoning mechanism is explained *below with an illustrative example.* The following is a portion of knowledge base for selection of a floor/roof system for multistoryed buildings.

Rule 1
IF length to breadth ratio > 2.0
THEN one-way floor system

Rule 2
IF one-way floor system
AND breadth of room < 6.0 m
THEN span IS small

Rule 3
IF one-way floor system
AND breadth of the room >= 6.0 m
AND breadth of the, room < 9.15 m
THEN span IS medium

Rule 4
IF one-way floor system
AND breadth of the room >= 9.15 m
AND breadth of the room < 13.75 m
THEN span IS large

Rule 5
IF span IS small
THEN suggest RCC one-way slab

Rule 6
IF span IS medium
AND PSC is available for use in slabs
THEN suggest PSC ~ne-way slab

Rule 7
IF span IS medium
AND Aesthetics are not important
THEN suggest RCC one-way slab with deep beams

Rule 8
IF span IS medium
AND Aesthetics are important
AND formwork for waffle slab is available
THEN sugest RCC one-way slab with shallow beams

Rule 9
IF span IS medium
AND Aesthetics are important
AND formwork for waffle slab is not available
THEN suggest RCC one-way slab with deep beams

Rule 10
IF span IS large
AND PSC is available for use in slabs
AND formwork for waffle slab is available
THEN suggest PSC one-way slabn with small beams

Rule 11
IF span IS large
AND Aesthetics are not important
THEN suggest RCC one-way slab with deep beams

> *Rule 12*
> *IF span IS large*
> *AND Aesthetics are important*
> *AND PSC is not available for use in slabs*
> *THEN suggest RC one-way slab with deep beams with false ceiling*

From the nature of the knowledge contained in the rules, it is evident that, the system finally has to suggest a structural system based on the data provided by the user. The selection process very much depends on the data provided by the user. This shows that a forward chaining inferencing strategy is ideal in such situations. In forward chaining, the user has to supply the basic data and the sys- tem either arrives or fails to arrive at a goal state, depending on the data available. In the above example, the size of the rooms, availability of prestressed concrete for use in slabs, aesthetics requirements, and availability of formwork for waffle slab system are the necessary data. One can give these data and finally the system will arrive at a goal state. In such case, a conventional forward chaining strategy can be applied to carry out reasoning.

But in many situations, the designer may not know what are the data items necessary to begin the reasoning process, but he can give a starting variable, which need not always lie in a leaf node of a knowledge net. He can answer the queries, depending on the expert questions asked by the system. In such a situation, conventional for- ward chaining strategy fails. Otherwise, the system has to inform the user in the beginning itself, what are the data required to select a roof/floor system. In many cases, some of those data items sought in the beginning may not be relevant at all, based on the values sup- plied for other data. In such circumstances, the designer will not be in a position to supply all the necessary data in the beginning itself, for conventional forward chaining. This demands a better reasoning strategy for design type of problems. A hybrid strategy is basically data driven, but carries out backtracking during the reasoning process, to get necessary data from the user.

The hybrid chaining strategy starts reasoning from any node in the knowledge net depending on the initial variable specified by the user. Only a starting point is given to the reasoning system, and it asks for the necessary data as and when required. For example, the designer knows that variable span is the most important one, based on which only the selection process progresses in the case of the roof/floor selection system. But span is not in a leaf node in the knowledge net, as it is a deduced variable. And it is deduced based on the data length and breadth. In a hybrid reasoning strategy, the system sets span as the current goal and tries to prove it by getting data for length and breadth from the user, following the backward chaining principle. Then it proceeds forward depending on the order in which the rules appear in the rule base. Every stage when data is required to deduce a variable, the system backtracks and gets the data from the user. This combination of keeping the overall direction of reasoning forward and backtracking as when required, makes it a hybrid reasoning mechanism. It is seen that, the number of searches through the solution space to obtain the solution, are much less com- pared to that of backward chaining, and it also gets the necessary data from the user as and when required. These advantages makes the hybrid mechanism an ideal one for design kind of problems. An illustration of the hybrid inference mechanism is given below, with the knowledge base for roof/floor selection system as an example.

The initial variable given by the user be span. As it is not a variable at a leaf node, it has to be deduced. The system first proceeds in a backward chaining manner and gets data from the user for length and breadth of the room and finally deduces the span to be either small, medium or large. Let the values of length and breadth of the room are such that it is a one-way system and the span is medium. This is obtained by firing rule-! and rule-3. Now the rule- 6 is selected for firing. The conditions in the antecedent of rule-6 are examined. It s seen that the first condition is matching that with that available in the working memory. But the second one is not available. The current goal is set as availability of prestressed concrete for use in slabs. This data is obtained by querying the user following a backward chaining procedure. If the user responses with a no, rule-6 is discarded and rule- 7 is selected for firing. In a similar manner, the mechanism proceeds in forward direction and finally arrives at a goal state.

This hybrid strategy is found to be very suitable in such cases, where the knowledge net is very large, and the user of the expert system does not know about what are the data to be supplied in the beginning.

7.6.4 Common Sense Reasoning

The inference mechanisms described above are the ones which are generally used to search through the knowledge bases represented in the form of rule lists. Knowledge about the physical properties of problems are generally represented by means of semantic networks, where the nodes of the network are described using frames. In many cases, only a few basic information are given to the system, and the system is expected to infer many related information using the basic ones, which should simulate reasoning based on common sense. Incorporation of such common sense based reasoning or assumption based reasoning in the expert systems make them more and more intelligent. Various inference, reasoning or deduction mechanisms can be used to simulate common sense in an expert system. This is illustrated with the help of a simple example. Assume that we have stored an information regarding relationship between A and B, such that B is son of A and A is male. Then the common sense tells that A is father of B. If an expert system should show an intelligent behaviour, whenever father of B is referred, it should refer to A, without our explicitly mentioning it. This can be achieved either by using predicate logic or by using frames to represent the piece of knowledge. In the case frame representation, an *if-added* demon is attached to the slot representing son-of frame B. That means, whenever a value is added to the slot son-of of the frame B, the mechanism automatically creates a slot father-of to the frame A, and adds a value B there. That means the if-added demon has acted and related information has been created during run time. This action which is done automatically when some value is added to some specified slot of a frame, is called demon actions. Many other kind of demon actions can be defined, depending on the nature of problem under consideration. These facilities provide interesting mechanisms for simulating common sense in expert systems, which are very essential in engineering design applications.

7.6.5 Inexact Reasoning

Inexact reasoning deals with inference mechanisms where confidence levels also called certainty factors or degrees of belief are associated with facts. If every fact required to establish a hypothesis has a confidence level associated with it, then depending on the values of confidences, the confidence level of the hypothesis varies. Many theories have been tried to simulate confidence of expert decisions, still a rational and acceptable one is not available. Implementations based on empirical and probabilistic theories work for some cases, and they give absurd result in other. Fuzzy set theory has also been tried for implementing inexactness in decision making during reasoning. Implementations based on belief functions seem to be most appropriate, but the mathematical basis of belief functions are not yet fully developed.

7.7 KNOWLEDGE BASED APPROACHES FOR ENGINEERING DESIGN

The various knowledge representation schemes along with different inference mechanisms have been described in the previous sections. Expert systems can be developed for narrow domains using the principles described above. But many engineering problems cannot be strictly identified to resemble one of the class of problems that lie in a derivation-formation spectrum. Also expertise from many different specialisations are. required to solve the problem completely. The nature of the knowledge of these specialisations also may be different from one another. Conflicting ideas may come from different specialised fields, which are to be resolved to make the solution to the problem acceptable from all points of view. Deep knowledge on each of the specialised area is necessary to effectively improve the performance of the design. In such cases, expert systems alone may not provide a solution. Hence knowledge based models are to be formulated which control the overall problem solving, of which expert systems and other programs form a component. To understand this in greater detail, consider the following example of a building design.

Right from the conceptual stage of building planning to the stage of construction and maintenance, different expert knowledge is put in. Based on the functional requirements of the building, the architect does the planning and prepares architectural drawings. During the planning process itself, the architect has to get information (expert advice) from the experts in the fields of circulation, ventilation, lighting etc. Once the planning is complete, the struc- tural engineer comes into picture and evaluates the planning from the structural strength and safety point of view. Sometimes he approves the plan as it is and suggests a structural system to carry various loads that come on the system and does the analysis and de- sign of the structural system and prepares drawings. If the plan given by the architect is not structurally acceptable, the structural engineer suggests modifications based on his expertise and the architect modifies the plan and corresponding drawings. Here the interaction between the two experts is essential to obtain an acceptable design. Once the structural drawings are made, the quantity surveyor computes the quantities of materials required for construction at various stages, and finally the construction engineer starts his work. The construction engineer may face many difficulties during the construction process, for which again he would require advice from the architect, structural engineer and environmental expert. This clearly illustrates that the engineering design of building system is a process which can be carried out only by the cooperation and interaction between the experts in different domains of building engineering. Similarly any engineering design process also requires expertise from various disciplines, and these experts have to cooperate and interact with each other to arrive at an optimum acceptable solution for the design problem. When knowledge based systems are to be developed for integrated design systems, like the one for the building system explained above, there may exist many experts, and one has to generate knowledge base by collecting knowledge from many knowledge sources. The nature of the knowledge may be such that, there may be contradictions and conflicts in the knowledge, which have to be resolved only by interacting with respective knowledge sources.

Various strategies and models have been proposed to implement such a design procedure, where more than one domain of expert is involved. One such popular model is Blackboard Model.

The black board model simulates arising of contradictions and arriving of compromises to resolve the contradictions, when experts representing different domain interact with each other to arrive at an acceptable design. Critique based model is an alternative model being experimented by many researchers. This model critically evaluates a design generated by the expert representing the first specialised knowledge domain in the logical sequence, and generates a report. The report is then passed on to the experts of other related domains to suggest modifications in the design if necessary to suit the requirements of respective domains. This process of criticism and evaluation is repeated until an acceptable design is obtained. In both the models the experts are represented as knowledge sources created using one or more of the knowledge representation techniques. The black board model is described in the following section.

7.7.1 Blackboard Architecture

Blackboard architecture provides a framework for integrating different knowledge sources and representing multiple levels of problem decomposition. The design problem is reduced to subtasks, and separate knowledge bases are developed to represent knowledge for solving each of these subtasks. The knowledge bases may be com- posed of combination of rules, frames and procedures. The black- board model provides an inferencing mechanism, which controls the problem solving process. Fig. 7.31 shows the schematic representation of blackboard architecture.

A blackboard model basically has three components. First, the knowledge base, consists of many knowledge sources, that communicate with each other through a blackboard, and controlled by an inference mechanism. These knowledge sources are independent and contain knowledge in specific narrow domains. They do not directly communicate with each other. They participate in the problem solving process, through the blackboard, which can be considered as a global database. Generally the knowledge in the knowledge base is divided into three clauses, viz., strategy level, specialist level and resource level. The strategy level contain knowledge on task control, which determines the next course of action to be carried out based on the current solution state in the blackboard. Specialist level contains the expert knowledge required to solve subtasks. The resource level basically contain the analytical knowledge required for problem solving. Depending on the type and nature of problem any number of levels may be defined in the blackboard as shown in Fig. 7.31.

As mentioned earlier, the blackboard can be considered as a global database, where information generated by different knowledge sources, during problem solving is stored. Depending on the nature of problem, the blackboard can be decomposed into hierarchy of levels both vertically and horizontally. This decomposition is generally made based on the number of subtasks present in the solution process and the nature of interactions required between them. The various knowledge sources available in the knowledge base are associated with the corresponding levels in the blackboard. The various hypotheses in the blackboard which are distributed in different levels are related through the semantic relationships.

As shown in Fig.7.31, agenda (scheduler) and monitor are the two main components of the inference mechanism. Agenda keeps watch on the activities that are going on in the blackboard and generates an agenda of priorities of execution of various knowledge bases, based on the knowledge available at the strategy level. The monitor takes the knowledge source with the highest priority from the agenda and executes it. Depending on the nature of knowledge and the cur- rent state of problem solution, the monitor selects the proper control strategy to proceed with problem solution. The other features that can be included in a blackboard architecture are: explanation facility and a knowledge acquisition facility.

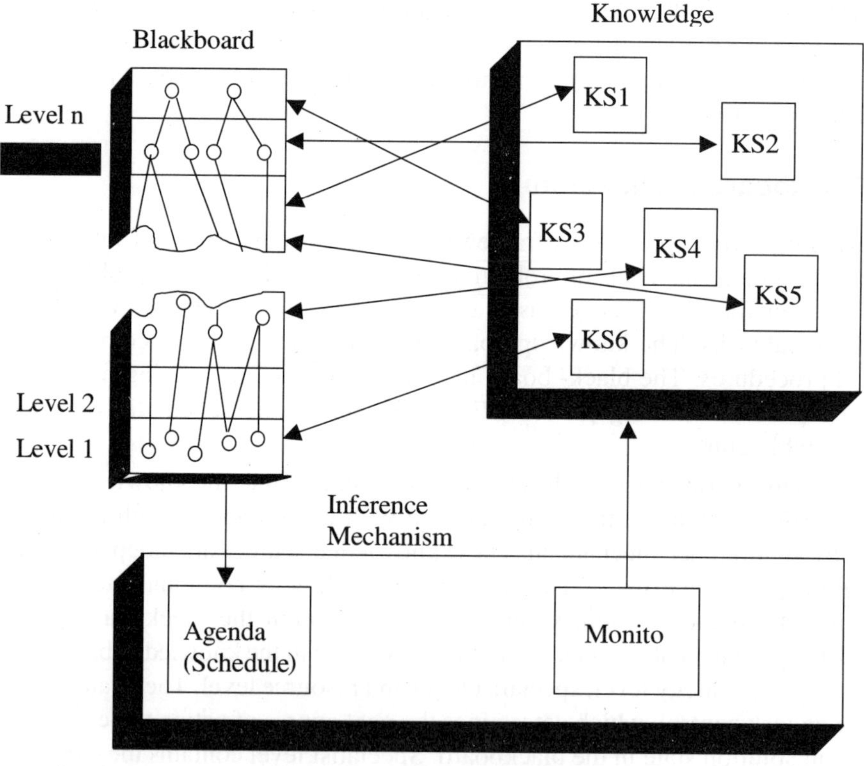

Fig. 7.31 Blackboard Model

Any engineering design problem can be treated as an expert co- operative process, with different knowledge sources. The blackboard data structure allows the knowledge sources to communicate with each other for proceeding with the problem solving. In most cases, knowledge sources are created in the form of rule lists. The rule lists in turn call procedures and get data from databases or other semantic structures. The blackboard system should have interfaces to external software systems, such as analysis, database graphics and mathematical packages. Another important requirement for any blackboard system from Computer Aided Design point of view is that, it should have the ability to simulate criticism and compromise among various experts.

Many expert systems are either developed or under development, using blackboard models. An integrated engineering design problem can be effectively implemented using a blackboard architecture, where exact simulation of expert problem solving can very well be achieved.

7.7.2 Other Knowledge Based Approaches

Researchers across the world have been trying to solve many engineering design problems using knowledge based approaches. As a result many innovative ideas are developed such as design synthesis, case based reasoning, database-knowledge base interactions and learning techniques.

Design synthesis is a process where feasible alternatives for engineering systems are generated by decomposing the system into a hierarchy of subsystems and elements, and then using expert knowledge on subsystems and elements. EDESYN is an engineering design synthesis environment developed at Carnegie Mellon University, and is used in many applications [18]. EDESYN knowledge base consists of a decomposition description of the system, constraints describing incompatibilities among subsystems and elements and a set of functions to carry out computations during synthesis process.

Case based reasoning primarily deals with extracting knowledge from existing designs for carrying out new designs. Many existing cases are stored in the knowledge base of the system. Whenever a new design is generated, the control mechanism of the model checks the validity and effectiveness of the new design with the ones stored in the knowledge base as cases.

In many engineering applications, large amount of data is required at the time of design process. As the data does not form the expert knowledge, it is not advisable to put it in the form of rules or semantic network of frames. A database will be an ideal form of storage in such cases. As a database management system takes care of manipulating the data stored in the databases, the control mechanism of the knowledge based problem solving model has only to interact with it to get data items from the data base. Hence access to data bases is a primary requirement of any knowledge based problem solving models.

Adaptive learning is another interesting technique which will improve the efficiency and effectiveness of knowledge based systems. The adaptive learning process stores the information related to al- ready carried out searches and uses it in subsequent searches. This narrows down the search space for the later sessions as a result of which the solution becomes faster .

7.8 BUILDING EXPERT SYSTEMS

Development of Expert Systems require software tools for rep- resenting knowledge in different representative formalisms, an inference engine with different inference mechanisms and explanation facilities. The personnel involved in an expert system can be classified into three categories, viz., domain experts, knowledge engineers and users. Domain experts and knowledge engineers contribute to the development of the expert systems, whereas users come into picture, once the development is completed. The knowledge engineer is the person, who has sufficient knowledge regarding the knowledge representation schemes, use of computer resources and development tools and programming languages to implement the expert systems on machines. It is also better that the knowledge engineer has some idea about the domain knowledge. The domain expert is an acknowledged expert in the specific domain and has enough knowledge to solve problems in his domain. The domain expert need not know, the intricacies of knowledge representation schemes, inference mechanisms and other related hardware and software tools. The knowledge engineer with a good knowledge of hardware and software tools, interacts with and extracts knowledge from the domain expert and properly represent it in a form, which the expert can go through and correct, if necessary. Once the representation schemes are finalised based on the nature of the knowledge, the knowledge base is created in the computer. Once the knowledge base is created, the knowledge engineer decides on the control strategy to be adopted for solving the problem. And finally when the implementation of the expert system is complete, the knowledge engineer along with the domain expert solves many problems using the expert system for the purpose of validating the knowledge contained in the knowledge base of the expert system.

Various knowledge representation schemes and control strategies have already been discussed in greater detail in earlier sections. The present interest is to know how these are implemented in a computer system to form a knowledge based expert system.

Conventional programs which follow an algorithm are developed using programming languages like Fortran, Pascal, C, Basic etc. Ex- pert systems are not conventional programs, but still one can use these languages to develop them. Expert systems mainly do symbolic processing compared to numeric processing done by conventional programs. Hence use of conventional programming languages to carry out symbolic processing may not be ideal. Hence separate languages were developed to handle symbolic processing in a much more efficient manner. Two such languages are LISP and Prolog. The following section provides a brief overview of these languages and their role in developing expert systems.

Building expert systems involve extensive programming. Here the programming is used for all the activities right from structuring, formalising and coding the knowledge, till completing the testing and validation. A knowledge engineer does these tasks for developing and implementing expert systems. Basically a knowledge engineer has two choices. First choice is to use a programming language, and the second one to use an appropriate expert system development shell. Use of programming languages for developing prototype ex- pert systems are not recommended, because the knowledge engineer has to first implement at least an inference mechanism and an explanation facility in the language chosen, and then implement the knowledge net using appropriate data structures. This is very inefficient from the point of view that, the knowledge and the inference engine are not separated. But there are some programming languages, specifically designed for Artificial Intelligence applications. These languages have built-in inference mechanisms and provide easy methods for representing knowledge. In these languages separating the inference engine from the knowledge can be achieved, but one has to write large codes to incorporate an explanation facility, which is an important component of expert systems.

The second choice is more suitable as far as the development of expert systems for engineering applications design are concerned. This is because the expert system development shells provide an environment for the knowledge engineer to implement prototype expert systems in a domain of his her choice. An expert system development shell essentially provides a knowledge editing facility, an inference engine with one or more control strategies and explanation facilities. These are domain independent frameworks. It is to be noted that all these shells are developed using either conventional programming languages or using special purpose AI languages like LISP or Prolog. The following section provides a brief description review on the general purpose AI languages LISP and Prolog, rule based language OPS5. Hybrid languages like Art, Knowledge Craft and Knowledge Engineering Environment (KEE) provide a number of facilities for the developers of the expert systems. Many expert system development shells like EMYCIN, GEPSE, Personal Consultant plus, INSIGHT 2 etc. are commercially available, which provide interactive environments for developing and using expert systems.

7.8.1 Artificial Intelligence Languages

The most popular and common AI language LISP, an acronym for *LISt Processing,* was invented by John McCarthy, about two decades ago. It is a symbolic processing language. One of its main features that made it an extremely attractive programming language for AI, is its use of list as a data structure. A list in LISP is a sequence of elements, in which each element may either be an atom or another list. The term atom, means a single object. LISP allows recursive techniques in programming. The design of LISP is such that it allows one I..ISP program to be used as data for another LISP program. The advantage of this feature being, (1) the declarative and procedural knowledge can be easily integrated. LISP programs keep track of the instructions that have been executed, how often each has been executed and in what order they have been executed. This feature is very useful for designing explanation facilities in expert systems. LISP is an interpreted language. A LISP program interacts with the programmer in every phase of development, which facilitates in obtaining additional information needed to solve problems. The basic structure of LISP is fairly straight forward. LISP also allows defining procedures for carrying out numeric manipulations and evaluation of expressions.

Prolog was developed in France in 1973, and uses predicate calculus to solve problems. Prolog is basically a *theorem proving system* using the formal logic techniques. Like LISP it is also a declarative language. Prolog uses only data about objects and their relation- ships. A Prolog program is a collection of facts and the relation- ships among these facts. It means that in Prolog, the program is a database. Characteristics of Prolog database makes it an ideal

324

language for problems, which are solved by reasoning rather than algorithmic computing. To write programs for numerical and string computing, Prolog is very inefficient, eventhough there are many versions of Prolog which provide facilities to call functions written in other conventional programming languages. For developing expert systems, the backtracking capability of the language can be made use of. It is also possible to simulate forward chaining in Prolog. It is much simpler compared to LISP, and has the backtracking feature built-in, which helps very much in developing expert systems.

Official Production System (OPS5) is a rule based programming language, developed at Carnegie Mellon University, USA. OPS5 essentially has a working memory, a production memory and an inference engine. Working memory stores the data or facts about the problem. Production memory contains productions or rules. The inference mechanism of OPSS is based on a find-select-execute cycle. In the select state, all the rules where conditions are satisfied are searched and found. There may be more than one rule, whose conditions are satisfied. These rules form a conflict set, from which a rule is selected for firing. The select state selects the rule for firing from the conflict set based on a criteria called specificity ordering. Specific ordering means that the most specific rule is selected for firing. A rule with more number of conditions in the antecedent is more specific. Execution state fires a rule, and which modifies the contents of working memory. OPS5 uses a concept of regency for selecting working memory elements. For selecting a working memory element it is assumed that more recent items are more relevant. The find-select-execute cycle is repeated, until the goal is satisfied. The inference mechanism of OPS5 is essentially forward chaining. It is a very easy to use rule based language.

7.8.2 Expert System Development Tools

Even though languages like LISP and Prolog offer a number of facilities for developing Expert Systems, expert system development shells remove the burden of developing the basic framework for knowledge representation and inference mechanisms from the knowledge engineer. A number of expert system development shells are commercially available with many more additional features. These development shells provide an environment, which makes Expert sys- tem implementation an interactive session with the computer system. These shells generally provide the following facilities.

1. *A knowledge editor, which helps one to create and edit knowledge bases. The editors are menu-driven and interactive, so that the knowledge engineers can enter the rules or details or frames in a very easy manner.*

2. *Many of these shells provide alternate control strategies, like backward chaining, forward chaining and other reasoning strategies.*

3. *The explanation facilities provided by these shells, helps the knowledge engineers, to improve the effectiveness of the expert systems implemented, by adding more relevant information on many objects and variables to avoid ambiguity while using the expert system.*

4. *A few of these shells provide interface with external programs, like databases, invoking procedures written in other high level languages, interface to graphics programs etc.*

These shells are developed using high level languages like, LISP, Prolog, C, Pascal etc. Eventhough the languages like C or Pascal are not tailored to handle symbols, the programs are written to carry out symbolic processing as well as numeric processing effectively, as any Computer Aided Engineering problem would require both these capabilities. As far as the knowledge engineers are concerned, they need not go into the programming details of these shells. The shells provide them an interactive environment for developing Expert Systems. The requirements of an expert system development shell for engineering problems should have the following capabilities.

1. Facilities to represent knowledge in the form of rules, semantic networks and frames.
2. Interaction between various knowledge representation schemes. 3. Capability to interact with external programs and databases.
4. Organisation of rule bases in a hierarchical manner with meta levels.
5. Capability to describe taxonomies and inherit properties from higher level nodes.
6. Facilities to associate certainty factors or belief factors with facts.
7. Knowledge acquisition facility, which helps experts as well as knowledge engineers to effectively interact with each other .
8. Knowledge adaptation facility where modification of existing knowledge in the knowledge base is possible.
9. Explanation facility which helps the users of the expert system to interact with it during run time.
10. The inference engine should have a number of inference mechanisms so that the knowledge engineer can select the appropriate ones depending on the requirements.
11. A friendly user interface, which makes users interaction with the expert system an effective one.
12. An interactive environment where all the components of the shell are integrated.

Besides these basic requirements, the development tool should have capability to address problems specific to engineering design. Design can be conceived of, as a series of tasks and subtasks. Some of the tasks can be grouped together on the basis of the methodology adopted to solve them. In another words, solution of these tasks comprises of using generic nature of these methodologies. It is evident that if these generalised methodologies are incorporated as components in the development shell, they can be repeatedly used by the expert system for solving tasks that are addressed by them. Two such generic components are:

1. A design synthesiser that can generate all feasible solutions for a given task that satisfy certain predefined constraints. This tool will be required to use domain specific knowledge and synthesise solutions for problems in that domain.
2. A facility for design criticism that will be able to examine al- ternate solutions and generate critical reports based on certain predetermined criteria. This tool is required to use domain specific knowledge to critically evaluate possible solutions of a design problem.

In addition, a knowledge acquisition facility that will provide the framework for acquisition of knowledge from experts is also a vital ingredient of the framework. Fig. 6.32 shows the architecture of a typical knowledge based expert system development tool for engineerig design, which has the capabilities discussed above. Such a development environment for knowledge based expert system (DEK- BASE) is reported in reference 19 of knowledge bases not only helps at the stage of running the system, but it also makes the design of the knowledge bases much more this easier.

The performance of an expert system very much I the design of the knowledge base. Improper ordering of rules and conditions in the antecedent part of rules may some times make the expert system ask questions which are irrelevant. As an expert system is considered to be an intelligent program, the order in which questions are asked is very important. This can be achieved by proper design of the knowledge base. It may be not inconsistencies and other undesirable effects of a knowledge base can be tested using the knowledge net representation of the knowledge. Hence, a proper design always follows a systematic style of development, where first the knowledge net is drawn and it is verified before it is transformed in to rules. An extensive validation and testing of the expert system has to be carried out by checking the result for all the possible paths in the knowledge net. It is always better that the expert himself carries out the testing by giving different possible values for different data items.

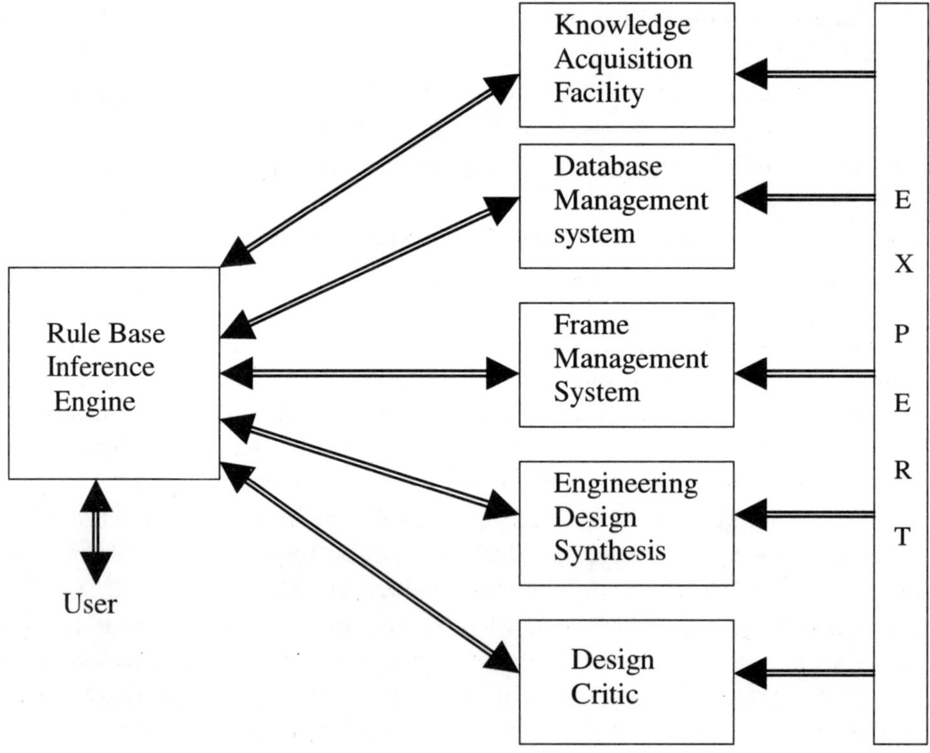

Fig. 7.32 Architecture of a KBES Development Tool

References

1. Rich,E., (1983), *Artificial Intelligence,* McGraw-Hill, New York, USA.

2. Winston, P. H., (1984), *Artificial Intelligence,* Addison- Wesley Publishing Co., Reading, MA, USA.

3. Mishkoff, H. C., (1986), *Understanding Artificial Intelligence,* B.P.B. Publications, New Delhi, India,

4. Hayes-Roth, F ., Waterman, D. A. and Lenat, D. A., (1983), *Building Expert Systems,* Addison -*Wesley* Publishing Co., Reading, MA, USA.

5. Buchanan, B.G. and Shortliffe, E. H., (1984), *Rule-Based Ex- pert Systems,* Addison- *Wesley* Publishing Co., Reading, MA, USA.

6. Winston, P. H. and Horn, B. K., (1984), *LISP,* Addison-Wesley Publishing Co., Reading, MA, USA.

7. Waterman,D.A., (1985), *A Guide to Expert Systems,* Addison- *Wesley* Publishing Co., Reading, MA, USA.

8. Clocksin, W. F. and Melllish, C. S., (1986), *Programming in PROLOG,* Narosa Publishing House, New Delhi, India.

9. Marcus, C., (1986), *PROLOG Programming,* Addison- *Wesley* Publishing Co., Reading, MA, USA.

10. Sriram, D., Maher, M. L. and Fenves, S. J., (1985), *Knowledge Based Expert Systems £or Engineering Design,* Int. *Jl.* Computers and Structures, *Vol.20,* No.1-3.

11. Bennet, J., Creary, L., Englemore, R and Melosh, R., (1978), *SACON: A Knowledge Based Consultant £or Structural Analy- sis,* Tech. Rep. STAN-CS-78-699, Stanford University.

12. Camacho, G. T., (1985), *LOW-RISE: An Expert System £or Structural Planning and Preliminary Design 0£ Industrial Type Buildings,* M.S. Thesis, Dept. of Civil Engg., Carnegie-Mellon University, USA.

13. Maher, M. L. *and* Fenves, S. J., (1984), *HI-RISE: A Knowledge Based Expert System £or Preliminary Structural Design of High Buildings,* Tech. Rep. R-85-146, Dept. of Civil Engg., Carnegie-Mellon University, USA.

14. Sriram, D. (1986), *Knowledge Based Approaches £or Structural Design,* Ph.D. Dissertation, Dept. of Civil Engg., Carnegie*Mellon* University, USA.

15. Kostem, C. N. and Maher, M. L., (1986), *Expert Systems in Civil Engineering,* ASCE Publication, USA.

16. Sriram, D. and Aday, R. A., (1987), *Knowedge Based Expert Systems in Civil Engineering,* Proc. 2nd Int. Conf. on AI Applications in Engineering Design, Boston, USA.

17. Sriram, D. and Aday, R. A., (1986), *Proc. Ist Int. Coni on AI in Engineering Problems,* Southampton, UK.

18. Maher, M.L., (1989), *EDESyN: An Engineering Design Synthesis Environment,* Tech. Rep., EDRC 12-31-89, Carnegie *Mellon* University, Pittsburgh, USA.

19. Shivakumar,H., Suresh,s., Krishnamoorthy,C.S. and Rajeev,S (1991), *Development Environment £or Knowledge Based Expert Systems in Engineering Design,* Tech. Rep. CE- 91-05, Civil Engineering Department, Indian INstitute of Technology, Madras, India.

Exercises

1. Discuss the *role* of Knowledge Based Expert System computer Aided Design.
2. What are the type of problems that can be solved better using techniques offered by KBES?
3. What are the essential components of an Expert cuss the role of each of the components in the overall work*ing* of Expert Systems?
4. What are the different stages in Expert System Development? Discuss the activities involved in each stage.
5. Explain different knowledge representation schemes that are *Commonly* adopted in Expert Systems.
6. Modify the structure of the decision table presented to incorporate OR clauses and ELSE clauses.
7. What is a knowledge net? Explain the terms Goal State and Intermediate State.
8. Take a classification problem of your choice and represent the knowledge required for the classification in a knowledge net, rules and decision table form.
9. What are the circumstances in which Frames and Semantic net works are *useful* ?
10. Name the different inference mechanisms used in expert systems. Discuss the features of the mechanisms.
11. Under what conditions hybrid inference mechanism is desirable compared to forward and backward chaining?
12. Describe how inexactness is incorporated in knowledge bases. Explain how confidence *levels* can be incorporated in an inference mechanism.
13. What is a blackboard model? When a blackboard model? When a blackboard model is ideally suited for problem solving?
14. Explain in brief the concept of" Engineering Design Synthesis", with an example of your choice.
15. What are the requirements of an expert system development shell for developing expert systems for engineering design applications.
16. Compare the programming languages C, Prolog and Lisp from the knowledge-based systems development point of view
17. Compare and discuss the capabilities and features of various commercially available expert system development tools.

CHAPTER 8

Analytical Tools

8.1 INTRODUCTION

The earlier chapters provided a deep insight into the different software tools used for Computer Aided Design of Engineering Systems. One of the most important steps in design of any engineering system is the analysis. The behaviour of the system is studied during this stage using suitable mathematical/analytical model of the system. Depending on the type, nature and behaviour of the problem the analytical modeling process varies. Large number of analytical tools are being used by design engineers to simulate the behaviour of the engineering systems in the real world conditions. An overview of a few such computer based analytical tools, which form essential components of many CAD systems are presented in this chapter.

The important processes involved in Computer Aided Design of engineering systems are conceptual design (preliminary design), engineering analysis, design optimization (review/ evaluation) and drafting as shown in Fig. 8.1. In the design of complicated or complex components, the first phase of conceptual design is aided by he geometric modeling graphics packages which have been briefly described in chapter 5. Extensive graphics support is required for geometric modeling of an engineering system. After the conceptual design, the preliminary dimensions and other details are to be arrived at, which constitute the preliminary design phase. It is at this stage that engineers are aided by the expertise and experience gained by other designers who are experts in their respective domains of application. The knowledge Based Expert Systems techniques, discussed in chapter 6 will enable into CAD programs.

After the preliminary design of the components design or the system itself, it is subjected to engineering analysis and then the adequacy of the components to meet the required performance specifications is checked. The introduction of computers and the rapid advance in hardware in the last two decades have significantly contributed to the development of powerful numerical tools for rigorous analysis and design. In the case of engineering analysis, the Finite Element Method has been developed and it provides a powerful numerical analysis procedure for solving complex and complicated problems of engineering design. The method

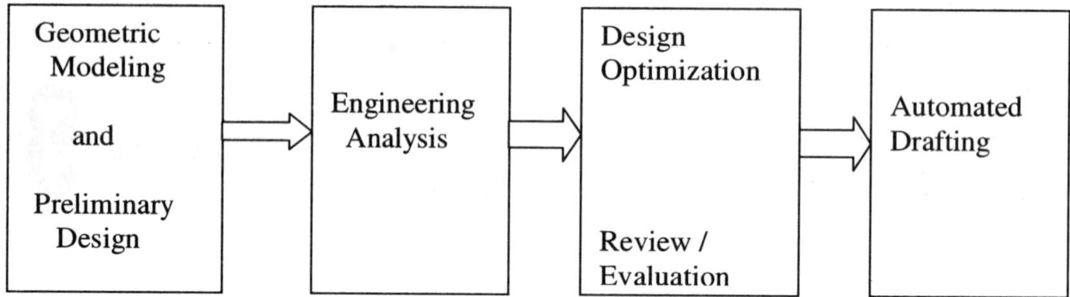

Fig. 8.1   Computer Aided Design Process

is very much computer-based and large number of software packages have been developed and are widely used in industries.

The other significant development is the development is the advances made in the numerical methods for mathematical programming techniques o arrive at optimal design. It is now possible to integrate analysis and design and formulate it as an optimization problem. The problems of engineering design are quite complex and non-linear in general, and a number of algorithms have been developed that can be used to arrive at an optimum solution.

In the development of a CAD package for any domain of application, the Finite Element Analysis and Optimization Techniques provide the analytical tools that are necessary to rationally analyse and design the system. These two subjects are taught as separate courses, and a number of text books are available and are listed under the References. In view of the importance of these two analytical methods, a brief introduction is given in this chapter. However, it is to be emphasized here that a CAD program developer should study the Finite Element Analysis and Optimization Techniques in greater detail for using them in the CAD system.

It may be added here that these two numerically based analytical methods require ue of commercially available software packages or development of software for a particular application. The software tools discussed in chapters 2,3,4 and 5 will be extremely useful for one to develop any special purpose software for solving a specific design problem.

8.2   FINITE ELEMENT ANALYSIS

In the realm of engineering design, the finite element method provides a powerful numerical technique for analysis. The method in the last two decades evolved from applications to structural engineering to several other areas of science and engineering such as solid mechanics, fluid mechanics, geo-mechanics, aeromechanics, bio mechanics, chemical reaction, nuclear reactors, acoustics, electromagnetic etc. In the description to follow, attention is focussed on the application of the finite element method to **stress analysis** in the area of solid mechanics as it forms an integral part of a CAD/CAM package.

The basic concept of the finite element method is that a body or a structure may be divided into smaller elements of finite dimension called finite elements. The original body or the structure is then considered as an assemblage of these elements connected at finite number of joints called Nodes. The properties of the elements are formulated and combined to obtain the solution for the entire body or structure. Figures 8.2 to 8.5 illustrate the finite element discretization of a few structures and solids.

For a given practical design problem, the engineer has to idealize the physical system into a finite element model with proper boundary conditions and loads that are acting on the system. The five basic steps involved in the finite element analysis are summarized in the following : [1,2,3,4,5].

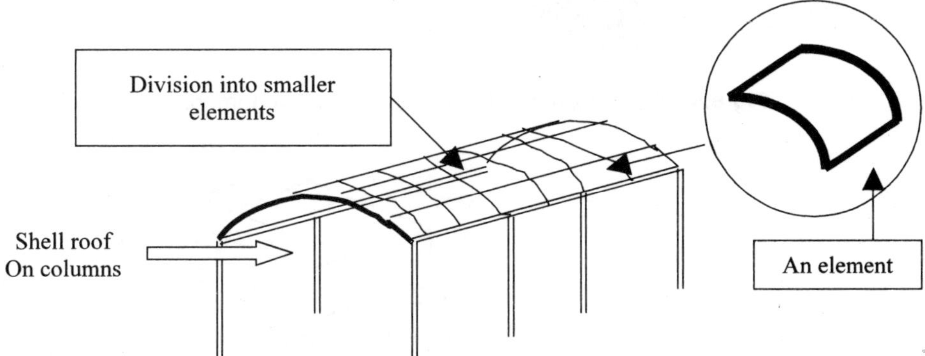

Fig. 8.2 Finite Element Discretization of a Cylindical Shell

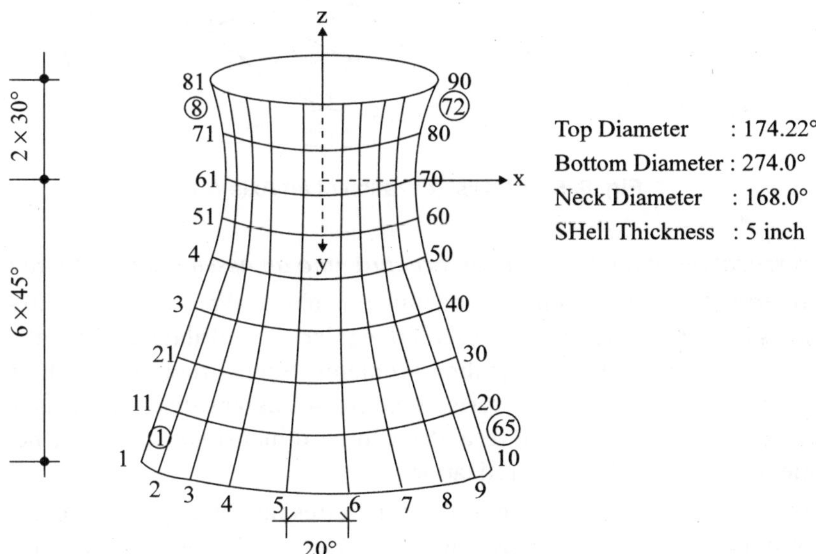

Fig. 8. 3 Finite Element Discretization of a Cooling Tower

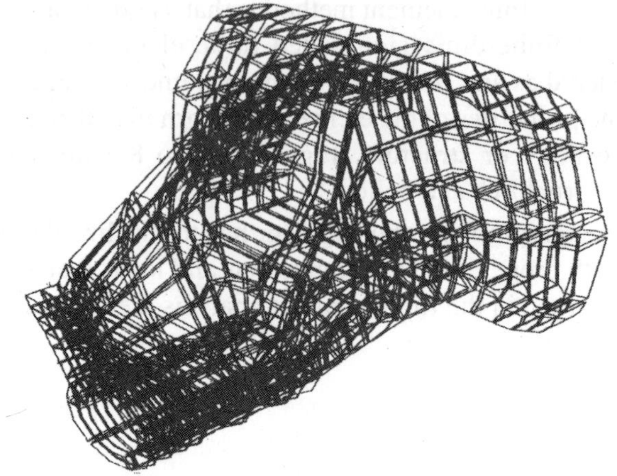

Fig.8.4 Discretization of rear spring of an automobile

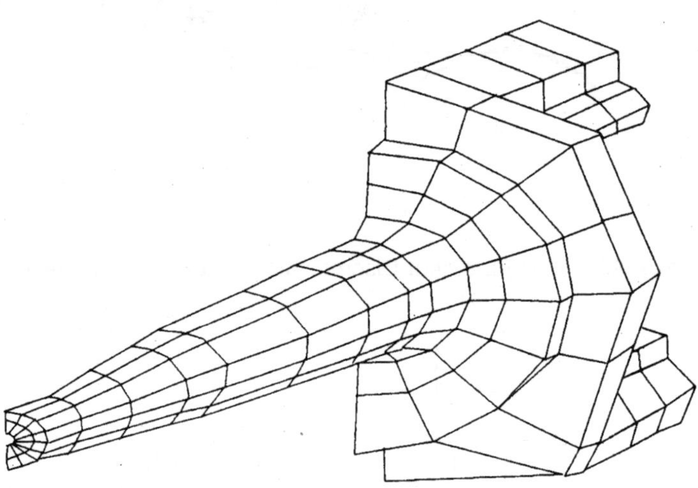

Fig. 8. 5 FE Discretization of an Axle Arm

Step 1 *Discretization of a given body or structure into an assemblage of finite elements.*

This step is referred to as finite element modeling of a physical problem. Fig. 7.6 shows some typical elements for various types of analysis. Triangular or quadrilateral elements are used for plane stress or plane strain or plate bending problems. Shell structures are discretized with either flat or curved shell elements. Axisymmetric solids are discretized using ring type elements. For problems which require a strict three dimensional analysis, hexahedral or tetrahedral elements are used for discretization.

The finite element modeling of a given problem requires human expertise and knowledge on the behaviour of the physical system and on various elements. Hence, it still remains as an art [6]. Since the finite element method is an approximate numerical method and the solution

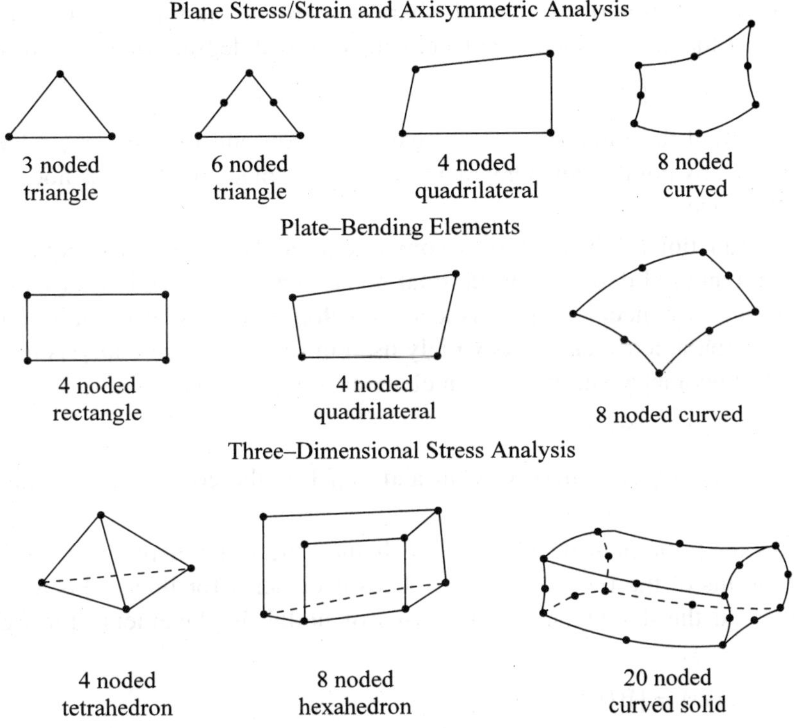

Fig. 8.6 Some Finite Elements used for Modeling Structures

obtained is not *exact*. The main types of errors are: (a) :mathematical modeling error, (b) discretization error and (c) roundoff errors. The first type of error is due to the approximation of the physical system and asumptions made in idealisation, and the third type of error is due to the accuracy level possible in a computer due to fixed number of digits used for calculations and with improved hardware this is being taken care of. The main error is therefore due to discretization, after finite element modelling of a physical system. In the last one decade considerable amount of research work has been carried out on error analysis/estimates and are described in reference [7]. After the errors are estimated the analyst would like to get improved solution to the problem. Research is also in progress to develop algorithms and software 80 that the initial mesh can be improved depending on the amount of error and it is referred to as *adaptive meshing* [7] .However, in the context of current usage of finite element analysis, the user takes decisions on the size and type of elements and try a few alternatives until the results are *satisfactory*. For the process of creating a finite element mesh, the pre-processor is very much helpful, especially the interactive graphics helps the user to create a finite element mesh and also to generate the necessary input to the analysis packages. The requirements and functions of a pre-processor are described in the next section.

Step 2 *Derivation of element equations for various types of analysis*

In the area of stress analysis one of the widely used formulations is based on *Displacement Model*. In this displacement model the variation of displacement inside an element is assumed

334

through polynomial functions, called shape functions, and is expressed in terms of displacements at the nodes (nodal displacements or nodal degrees of freedom) as,

$$\{u\} = [N]\{d\} \tag{8.1}$$

where [N] is called the interpolation or shape function and the vector $\{u\}$ expresses the displacements at any point in an element and $\{d\}$ the displacements at the nodes or degrees of freedom at the nodes.

The shape function [N] has to satisfy convergence and compatibility requirements and the order of the polynomial depends on the total nodal degrees of freedom of an element [1-5]. The shape function concept is also used to develop elements of complex curved shapes referred to as isoparametric elements widely used in finite element analysis to model curved geometries. The geometry variation of an element is expressed as,

$$\{x\} = [N]\{x_n\} \tag{8.2}$$

where $\{x\}$ is the coordinates of any point and $\{x_n\}$ h is the coordinates of the nodes of the element.

Following the principles of structural mechanics, the strain displacement relations can be expressed in terms of the first derivatives of displacements for linear elastic analysis. Thus having expressed the displacements in terms of nodal displacements through EQ. 7.1 it follows that,

$$\{\epsilon\} = [B]\{d\} \tag{8.3}$$

where $\{\epsilon\}$ is the vector of strains at any point and [B] is the strain displacement matrix, which can be obtained from Eq. 8.1 by taking the derivatives of [N] to satisfy the strain- displace helps the user Then, the stresses at any point $\{\sigma\}$ can be e the necessary the stress-strain relation, called constitutive reality functions of a behaviour of the material of the solid. Thus,

$$\{\sigma\} = [C]\{\epsilon\} \tag{8.4}$$

where [C] is called the constitutive matrix.

Using the Eq. 8.3, the above equation can be expressed in terms of nodal displacements as,

$$\{\sigma\} = [C]\,[B]\,\{d\} \tag{8.5}$$

Having obtained the above relations it is possible to use one of the two principles of structural mechanics, i.e., Principle of Virtual Displacement or Principle of Stationary Potential Energy to derive the condition of nodal equilibrium of an element subjected to static loads as

$$[k]\{d\} = \{Q\} \tag{8.6}$$

where [k] = stiffness mareix of an element and is given by the following equation.

$$[k] = \int\int\int [B]^T\,[C]\,[B]\,dv \tag{8.7}$$

It may be noted here that k_{ij} is the force in the displacement direction i due to unit value of displacement at j, with all other displacements neing held zero. The element nodal load vector $\{Q\}$ is obtained as shown below.

$$\{Q\} = \int\int\int [N]^T\{X\}dV + \int\int_{s1} [N]^T \{p\}dS \tag{8.8}$$

where $\{X\}T = [Xb \; Yb \; Zb]$, components of body force per unit volume, and $\{p\}^T = [Xs \; Ys \; Zs]$, components of external forces per unit area acting on the surface. The stiffness matrix [k] and the nodal load vector $\{Q\}$ are evaluated using numerical integration scheme and Gauss Quadrature is widely used in practice [1-5].

Thus, it may be observed that the fundamental assumption in a finite element is the variation of displacement through a chosen or assumed function and is expressed in terms of nodal displacements through Eq.8 .1. Then, the other relations, Eqs. 8.3 to 8.8 can be derived following the principles of structural mechanics and no further assumptions are involved. Also it may be noted that all the relations are expressed in terms of nodal displacements. Thus, if the nodal displacements of an element are solved for, the strains and stresses can be evaluated through Eqs. 8.3 and 8.5.

Step 3 *Assemblage of elements to obtain the governing equation for the whole problem*

The equations of equilibrium for the entire structure or body are obtained by combining the equations 8.6 for each element such that the continuity of displacement is ensured at each node where the elements are connected. The actual process thus involves assembling the stiffness matrices [k] and nodal load vectors $\{q\}$ of the elements using the connectivity information, i.e., relation between the degrees of freedom of the element and the corresponding global degrees of freedom. Consider the following example to illustrate the assembly process.

A cantilever beam is idealised as a plane stress problem and the finite element model consisting of five four nodded plane stress elements is shown in Fig. 8.7. The connectivity relation for a typical element 4 is shown in Fig. 8. 7b.

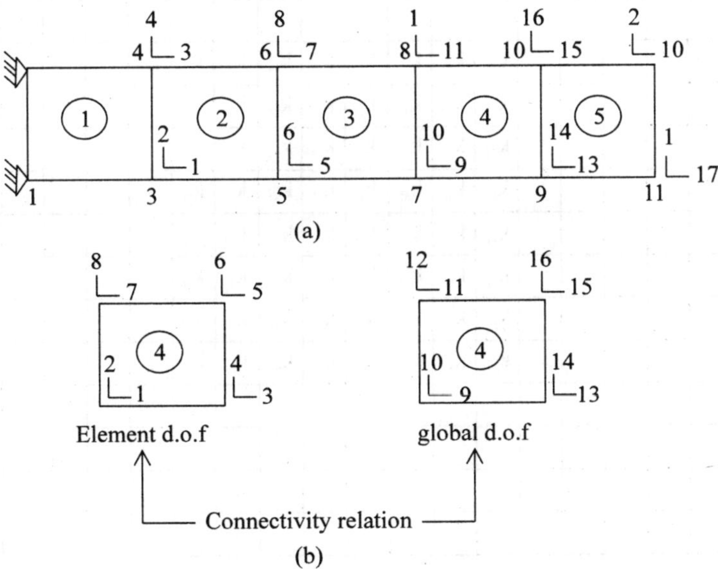

Fig. 8.7 Cantilever Beam as a Plane Stress Problem

336

As it has been observed that the stiffness coefficients refer to forces developed at the degrees of freedom, the coefficients of element stiffness matrix and load vector can be added directly to get global stiffness coefficients to correspond to the global degrees of freedom. This process of assemblage is referred to as *direct stiffness method* and is well explained in reference [5] . From the programming point of view the contribution from every element to the overall (global) stiffness matrix [K] involves transferring the element stiffness coefficients to the appropriate position, Ith row and Jth column (corresponding to global degrees of freedom) of [K] by making use of the connectivity relation. The contribution of element 4 to the overall global or structure stiffness matrix [K] and the nodal load vector { P} is shown in the following Fig.8 .8.

Thus the overall equation of equilibrium of the solid or structure can be obtained as,

$$E[k_n]\{d\} = \sum_{n=1}^{N} \{Qn\} \tag{8.9}$$

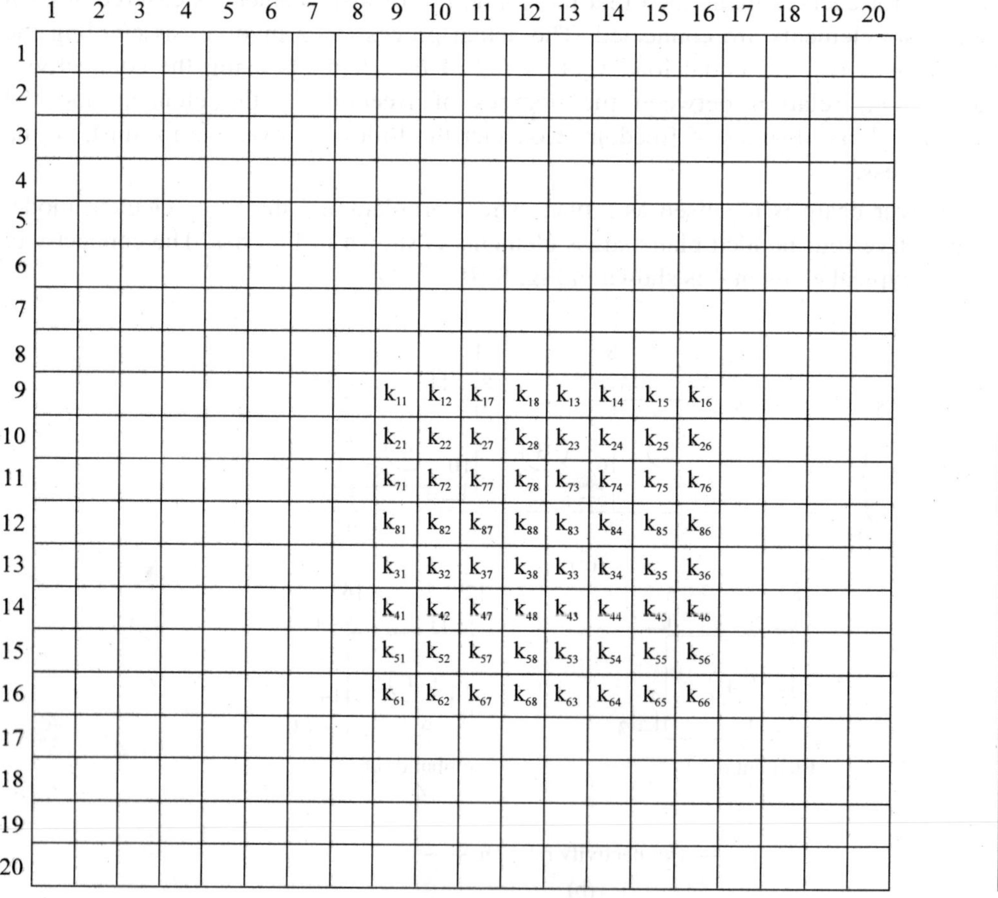

Fig. 8.8 Contribution of Element 4 to [K] and [P]

where N is the total number of elements in the assemblage. After imposing the boundary conditions, the equilibrium equation of the structure can be expressed as,

$$[K]\{r\} = \{P\} \tag{8.10}$$

where $\{r\}$ is the vector of unknown displacements at the nodes, i.e. vector of nodal degrees of freedom and $\{P\}$ is the vector of nodal loads.

Step 4 *Solution of the Assembled Equations*

The solution of linear simultaneous equations of Eq. 8.10 is computationally important since the number of equations in a realistic and *practical* application of finite element analysis is quite large. It may be observed here that in the case of *structural* analysis the equations are symmetric and banded in nature, i.e. the non-zero coefficients in the structure stiffness matrix [K] are within a bandwidth and the remaining coefficients are zero. The solution schemes adopted should *exploit* this symmetric and banded nature of the stiffness matrix [K]. *All* the solution schemes adopted in finite element analysis basically employ the Gauss elimination procedure or the variations of it depending on the storage scheme and technique adopted in storing the coefficients of [KJ. The reader may refer to the books [1-5] listed under references for further details on the solution techniques.

Step 5 *Post-processing of Results*

After solving the equilibrium equation (Eq. 8.10) by anyone of the techniques briefly described above, and obtaining the displacements $\{ r \}$ at the nodes, the displacements $\{ d \}$ at the nodes of each element can be obtained through the connectivity relations similar to the procedure adopted for assemblage of elements explained under step 3. Then using Eqs. 7.3 and 7.5, the strains and stresses at any point in an element can be computed. With the availability of computer graphics the results of analysis, i.e. displacements, strains and stresses can be further processed and presented in the form of contours or variation along a given 'section. This is the purpose of the post-processor and it very much helps the analyst in the design process.

8.2.1 Finite Element Programming

From the computational point of view, the five basic steps involved in finite element analysis can be well organised in a modular form for the development of a software package. There are three basic components in a finite element analysis program as shown in Fig.8.9 below:

The functions of the above three components of a finite element analysis package are highlighted in the flow chart given in Fig.8.10.

The requirements of pre and post processors and the capabilities of some of the available software packages are discussed in the next two sections. It may be observed here that the pre and post processors are *mostly* graphics oriented whereas the processor mod*ule* involves mathematical computations that require large arithmetic operations, i.e., *number crunching operations* in a computer.

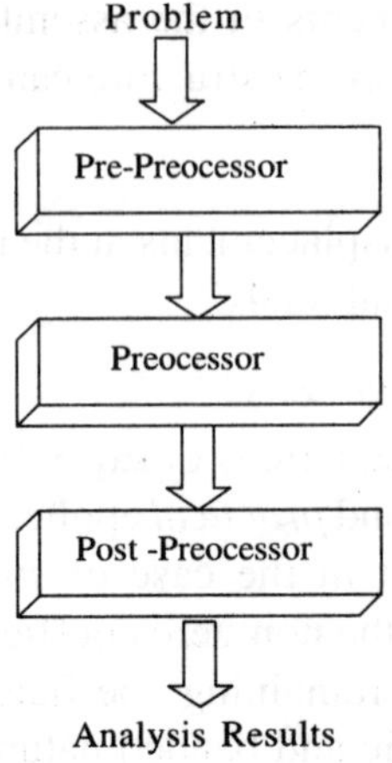

Fig. 8.9 Main Components of a FEA Package

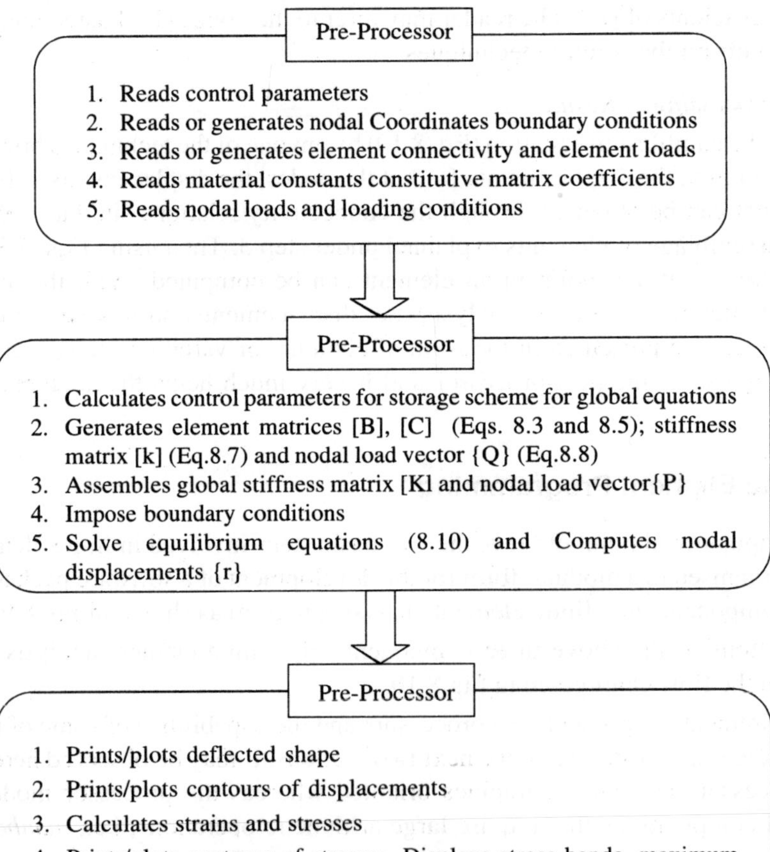

Fig. 8.10 Functions of the three modules of a FEA Program

8.2.2   Pre and Post Processors

Finite *Element* Analysis of practical problems require handling of large amount of input data. Manual preparation of input data is a tedious, time consuming and error-prone task particularly for three dimensional stress analysis of solids and shells. In a computer aided design environment a good and acceptable design is arrived at only after a few cycles of analysis and design procedure. Hence, it will be advantageous to have software which will aid in the preparation of input data and also in the interpretation of analysis results. Such programs are called pre and post processors to finite element analysis package. A pre processor creates the finite element model and the input necessary for a finite element analysis program. A post-processor program accepts the results of the analysis and generates tables, diagrams/pictures etc. for proper interpretation of results. The studies conducted by Clerk and Muller [8] show that the cost of a typical analytical solution can be divided as 80% of engineering cost and 20% of computing cost. The engineering cost consists of 65% of input data preparation and the rest for interpretation of results. Due to pre and post processing software development and use, the cost of input data preparation comes down by approximately 20%, that of results interpretation by 10% with a rise in computing cost by 30%, but results in 40% overall savings.

General Requirements of Pre and Post Processing

The preprocessor takes minimum input from the user, creates the finite element mesh and other data required for analysis, and displays the model for data-check and correction, if any, to be made by the user in an interactive mode. Graphical post- processing of finite element results helps to perceive the physical consequences of the analysis. Both the types of programs should be user oriented, graphics-based and hence easy to use with minimum instructions [9, 10, 11].

A large portion of the input data to finite element analysis is concerned with geometric idealization of the structure and mesh generation. Automatic generation of finite element meshes for two and three dimensional structures not only reduces a good percentage of man power expenditure of the total analysis time but also minimizes the errors. Graphics oriented edit facility should be available to edit and display the finite element model and also enable the user to input/generate additional data like loads, boundary conditions etc. The user should have on-line assistance by way of help screens, windowing/zooming, model rotation, change of view direction, element shrinking, removing hidden lines/surfaces etc.

The nodal values of the field variables are the immediate results of the finite element analysis. In such cases, the post- processor has to work out the higher order derivatives of field variables with reliable accuracy which are of interest in applications. For example, in structural/solid mechanics problems, the field variables are usually displacements, and stress/ stress-resultants are of interest in many design problems. The post-processor helps the user to judge the accuracy of the results by means of various graphical outputs, to identify the critical values and regions for design, and to decide upon the adequacy of modeling/design and the need for remodeling/ redesigning the component/structure/solid.

Methods of Finite Element Model Generation

The construction of a single complex planar or 3-D finite element model usually requires a variety of mesh generation techniques. A single pre-processor must offer many generation options in order to be sufficiently versatile in mesh generation. Several mesh gener- ation techniques which are available in commercial programs are as follows.

1. Single node and element generation: This technique is a tedious ,procedure. However, it can be very effective on models with a few higher order elements.

2. Digitizing input: Many users may have scaled drawings of a model. Outlines of the model or nodes and elements can be transferred directly into the program using an electronic digitizing tablet.

3. Pattern generation: Often an entire model can be generated by simply repeating a portion of the model.

4. Duplication: Portions of an existing model or the entire model can be translated, rotated, mirrored or scaled to generate another portion of the model.

5. Region generation: This model generation technique generates nodes and elements within a region bounded by previously defined lines.

6. Dragging generation: This mesh generation technique is used to extrude a fixed section of elements. Dragging a line creates 2-D or shell elements. Dragging 2-D elements creates 3-D elements of constant cross section.

Some of these methods of generation are illustrated in Fig. 8.11. Recent developments in automatic mesh generation algorithms include blending functions, coordinate transformations, automatic triangulation and encoding techniques in the form of quadtree and octree. Each of these techniques are designed for more automatic generation of finite element meshes using just the geometric description of the model.

When there is a need to analyze many geometrically similar finite element models, interactive mesh generation commands can be combined in a user written program based on a generic model which contains all the necessary model features. Dimensions in the generic model are interactively specified by the user and the program automatically generates an entire finite element model. Using this method a user can generate finite element models in minutes rather than hours.

Methods for Specifying Loads and Boundary Conditions

Manual generation of loads and boundary conditions for finite element analysis can be very tedious and time-consuming task. The user normally specifies the nod~1 point index and the value of each force component for each nodal load. Element loads are specified by element name, face name and load type. The following two techniques are used by interactive pre-processors to reduce the amount of effort required to specify load and boundary conditions:

1. *Menuing:* Nodal couples, nodal loads, element loads and node constraints can be generated by specifying the load or constraint type, the value and the appropriate node or element from the plotted model.

2. *Location* and *association:* Nodal points and elements have co- ordinates associated with them. This location can be used as a qualifier to determine if the node or element

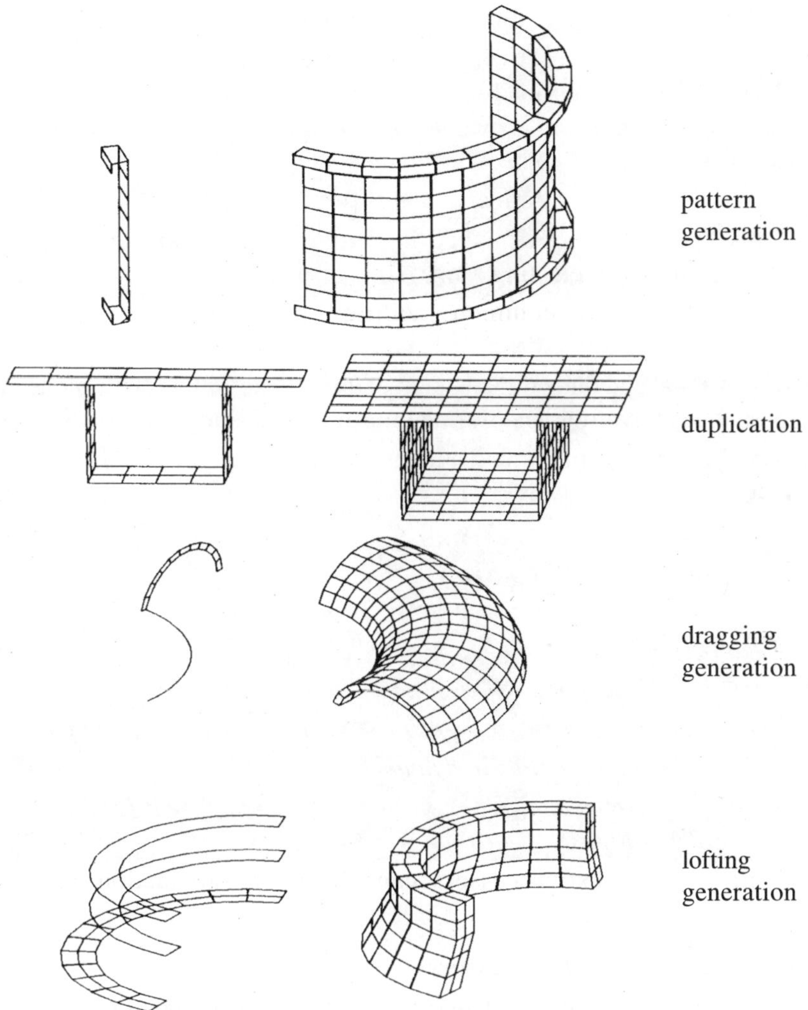

Fig. 8.11   Finite Element Model Generation - Methods

lies i) on an arbitrary plane ii) within the specified range of the global Cartesian or local coordinate system, or iii) on a specified surface. The node or element can be loaded accordingly. The nodal point and element can also be associated with the specific region which generated the node or the elements.

Of these two techniques, the latter is by far the most powerful. With locations and association, the user can apply loads and constraints to many nodes or elements with a single interactive command.

Graphical Output Facilities

The common graphical display and output facilities that are generally available in most of the pre and post processors are given below: [9,10,11].

1. Two dimensional and three dimensional mesh plots:

   The discretized model is shown with options to display element and node numbers, boundary conditions, and loads; to select a portion of a structure either by selecting range of element number or by selecting a window on the screen. Shrunk element plots are also available for checking element connectivity.

2. Two dimensional and three dimensional node plots:

   Here only the nodes are displayed in their respective positions, with options for numbering nodes and selecting range, similar to earlier case.

In addition to the above common facilities, post-processors have the following capabilities.

1. Two dimensional and three dimensional deformed meshplots: This plot can be separate or superimposed over the undeformed mesh plot to study the structural behaviour .

2. Search and display the maximum and minimum values of user defined variables based on the results of the analysis.

3. Plotting of results such as,

   - *Force and Moment Diagrams,*
   - *Contours and bands (eg. for stress, strain, tempera- ture, etc.),*
   - *Vectors (for stress, strain etc.),*
   - *Variation of stress or stress resultant along a user de- fined line/section of model,*
   - *Animation of structural movements, .Mode shapes in dynamic analysis,*
   - *Load -time -history plots in dynamic analysis,*
   - *Combine the effects of different analyses like different load cases or different load combinations.*

Some of the special post-processors can check on satisfaction of specific codal provisions.

Features of Typical Pre and Post Processors

The pre and post processors can be of two types: general and specific purpose types. The general purpose type processors can be coupled to many finite element packages and many even offer facility to process problems in different fields of engineering. On the other hand the special purpose processors work in connection with specific finite element analysis package and is usually available in an integrated form with that package.

The capabilities of the pre and post processors that form an integral part of a finite element analysis package are described in reference [9] .These are briefly mentioned in the next section along with description of some of the finite element analysis packages.

A good review of the general purpose, stand alone type pre and post processors is available in reference [10]. These packages handle a wide variety of geometries and element types. In order to give the readers an overview of the capabilities that are available in a general purpose processor, a brief description of PATRAN-G is given below.

PDA/PATRAN- G

This package has been developed by PDA Engineering Company, California, USA. It is a program system for finite element modeling and interpretation of analysis results. Its random access data base has unlimited capacity and automatic restart facility. All data transfers are performed automatically.

The preprocessor part consists of a geometric modeling phase, which precedes development of a finite element (analysis) model. This approach allows the user to optimize any number of analysis models for the particular type of analysis, i.e., static, dynamic, heat transfer, while assuring that the same geometry is being analysed.

Hardware Requirements:

Computers- VAX family, PRIME family, DEC, HARRIS, APPOLO, CDC Cyber. Graphics devices -Tektronix, Lexidat, Ramtek, Evans and Sutherland MPS & PS, DEC VS-11, Color Graphics Communication, Magatek, Advanced Electronic Design.

Interfaces available:

MSC/NASTRAN, COSMIC/ NASTRAN, ANSYS, ASAS, SAP, MARC, ADINA, ASKA, EASE2, SPAR(EAL).

Input format:

Free format command language. Interactive mode of operation. Digitizer, keyboard and cursor

Possibility of incorporating user's specific requirements:

Not directly, can be ordered from PDA.

Model generation:

Any 2D or 3D model can be created. The mathematical base for geometry modeling is the parametric cubic technique. Three different entities are available for the user during the geometry creation: parametric cubic lines, bi-cubic parametric patches and tri-cubic parametric hyperpatches. With these entities the solid geometry is created by using multi-level synthesis. Automatic mesh generation for uniform and non-uniform grid distribution, local mesh refinement and automated mesh transitioning and extensive element library for 1D, 2D and 3D element types are available.

Post-processing:

Any parameter of analysis can be visualised and interactively examined. Post processing capabilities include: de- formed geometry plots, element results display, mode shape, nodal variable, superposition results display, simultaneous load case display, color contour plots, solid color contours, etc.

Special Features:

Section property calculation, material property synthesis for orthotropic anisotropic materials, and for laminated and solid composites, model optimization (band width, RMS wavefront, max wavefront, profile), light source shading are available. Full color graphics which the user may selectively control and HELP commands are included in the system. CAD /CAM interface support is available for ANVIL 4000 and AD 2000, Applicon, Auto-trol, Computervision, Matra Datavision Euclid, Medusa, IGES Standards suppprt

Documentation:
Two-volume User Manual, study guides, News letter.

8.2.3   Finite Element Analysis Software packages

The rapid advances made in computer hardware and software led to significant developments in finite element analysis software. Finite element programming has emerged as a specialised discipline which requires knowledge and experience in the diverse areas such as finite element technology including foundations of mechanics, and numerical analysis on the one hand and the computational skills in areas of software technology including programming techniques, data structures, data-base management and computer graphics on the other hand. It requires several man years to develop a general purpose finite element analysis software with a processing capability and facility for the user to have a wide choice of several types of elements, analysis for different types of problems -static, dynamic, material and geometric nonlinear, coupled situations, heat transfer, interaction problems etc. and pre and post processing features.

A team of persons specialised in the areas mentioned above is required to develop a large and general purpose finite element analysis software package. Over the years finite element analysis software has become a big business due to the wide range of applications in diverse areas of engineering industries. It was estimated that by late 1980s there were about 500 user-oriented and several thousand research-oriented finite element program systems. A number of soft- ware reviews and bibliographies have been published and the details are given in references [iiI.

As it is not possible here to review the capabilities and compare different commercially available finite element analysis packages only the names of some of the popular packages are given below:

ABAQUS, ADINA, ANSYS, ASKA, COSMOS, GT-STRUDL, NISA, PAFEC, SAP, SESAM-80

The above list is not exhaustive and the reader may refer to publication [12] for more details including the addresses of developers etc. In order to give the readers an overview of the capabilities that are offered in a commercial software package, the major features are listed below:

- Element Library: The element library is a very important com- ponent in a package and allows the user to idealise the sys- tem and arrive at the finite element model as realistically as possible. The element library may include structural elements such as 3D rods (truss), beams, plane stress/strain and membranes in space, axisymmetric solids, shear panels, plates, thin and thick shells, shells of revolution, 3D solids, discrete stiff- eners for plates and shells and pipe elements. The user should have options to use lower or higher order elements in all the above types. Other elements may include matrix elements, substructures, and boundary elements. Other effects which can be modeled include gaps, friction, viscous dampers, cables, plastic hinges, and crack tip.

- Analysis Capabilities and Range of Applications
  - Linear static analysis
  - Nonlinear static analysis -nonlinear material, geometry, large deformations, stress stiffening, plasticity, creep, hyper-elasticity and rubber like material behaviour, temperature dependent inelastic properties, nonlinear contact problems.
  - Dynamic analysis -Eigen-value free vibrations, linear transient dynamics, spectrum analysis due to seismic loading.
  - Nonlinear dynamic analysis -material and geometric nonlinear effects, direct integration and different incremental approaches.
  - Harmonic response -steady state response of a linear structure subjected to harmonically time-varying loads.
  - Stability analysis -calculation of critical loads, bifurcation points, buckled shapes, large deflection analysis to determine the limit load for failure by bifurcation or snap through buckling.
  - Heat transfer -temperature distribution and heat flow within a body, linear and nonlinear analysis for temperature dependent material properties and temperature dependent convection boundary conditions, transient heat transfer analysis for time dependent temperature distribution.
  - Coupled field analysis -simultaneous solution of interaction of multiple field effect such as structural displacements, temperature and heat flows, solid and fluid flow interactions.
- Types of Loading -Option for analysis of the system due to several types of loading such as concentrated loads, line loads, axisymmetric loads, gravity loads, surface and volume loads, initial stresses, strains or velocities, thermal loading, centrifugal loading, deformation dependent loading, random loading, contact loading.
- Boundary conditions and constraints -Sliding interfaces, pre- scribed displacements, support at contact points, elastic foundation, multipoint constraints.
- Material Properties and Models -Material properties may be temperature-dependent, isotropic, or tho tropic or anistropic and multilayered composites. Nonlinear material behaviour such as plasticity, creep, elastic-strain hardening, visco-elastic or plastic.
- Pre and post-processing -Commercially available packages offer extensive pre and post-processing facilities as described in the earlier section.
- Interfaces with CAD /CAM systems -Interfaces to solid modelers and CAD programs are available to form an integrated CAD system.
- Design optimization -Until recently, finite element analysis has been used almost exclusively for the analysis of a user designed model. Some of the packages now offer sophisticated family of computer programs for optimum structural design -the capabilities include minimization of material volume, mass and weight for fixed

geometry by changing thickness and cross-sectional dimensions, optimization of structural shapes and optimization of parameters such as area, moment of inertia, thickness etc.

It is a difficult task to select a software system and the problems that are faced by the potential users of finite element analysis packages are [12]:

1. Getting information about, and sorting out, existing and avail- able finite element programs.

2. Identifying the program that is best suited for a particular purpose or range of applications.

In the selection of computer program for finite element analysis, the following points must be examined by the user:

1. Analysis capabilities to suit the given situation and also to projected range of applications.

2. Adequacy ofuser-oriented features and possibility of integration with other CAD programs.

3. Maintainability by the vendor in the supply of updates and new releases of additional capabilities.

4. Adequacy of user-support facilites which are necessary to get help in case of buge and problems faced in application areas.

5. Portability to different computer hardware platforms in view of rapid changes in hardware.

8.2.4 Current Trends in Finite Element Analysis Software

Current trends involve running interactive finite element codes on both larger and smaller computers. There is a strong trend towards implementing total finite element packages, which include interactive pre-processors, equation solvers and post-processors, on stand-alone workstations and personal computers. The application is ideally suited for small and moderate problems because it eliminates the queue time associated with batch computing and opens the door for interactive design and analysis.

At the other end of the computing spectrum, interactive finite element computing is performed on super-mainframe computers also. PATRAN-G is already operational on CRAY computer. The major advantage of using interactive super-computing is reduced response time for processing data and obtaining solutions for large models. On the super-computers, models with as many as 5000 degrees of freedom are small and may be solved in seconds. Such computing capabilities of super computers are needed in solving problems such as contact stress, crack propagation, penetration, material and geometric nonlinear systems under dynamic loading etc., where the problems are highly nonlinear and very large number of equations have to be solved for a number of iterations.

Developments are also directed towards merging it with the CAD and CAE technologies. Computer interfaces which allow the geometry from CAD data bases to be transferred directly to CAE data bases are being established [11] .

The finite element analysis requires experience and judgement in modeling the solid/structural system, choice of elements, decision on the type of analysis and in the interpretation of results. Users of the finite element packages require assistance in the above aspects and also needs expertise to use a particular package. The currently available software systems for finite element analysis are based on the traditional programming languages and do not have facility to incorporate the expert knowledge required to advise the engineer while solving the practical complex problems of engineering design. The recent developments in Knowledge-Based Systems seem to pro- vide a powerful software tool to address the above problems of finite element analysis [13].

A brief description of the expert systems developed for addressing specific problems of finite element analysis is given in reference [14]. Fenves [13] has proposed a KBES framework based on black- board architecture. Essentially three knowledge modules are required : finite element modeling, analysis and post-processing. They are referred to as Modeling, Analysis and Post-processor Consultants and their main functions are described in reference [14].

When the finite element analyst designs a mesh, the process involves a mixture of experience, intuition and guess work. Then after the analysis there is no reliable way of judging the acceptability of the solution and also methods to improve the solution. All these problema are subjects of intensive research under *Error Estimates* and *Adaptive Meshing* for finite element analysis currently being carried out at several universities [15]. While the work involved in *error esti*mates is mathematical including numerical analysis techniques, the *adaptive meshing* is heavily graphics oriented and the programming is quite complex [16, 17]. These advances would help to build the post-processor consultant with a facility to the user to define first a mesh sufficient to describe the geometry of the problem and state an acceptable level of error and the system will then automatically create a mesh that will achieve that level efficiently.

The reader may appreciate from the above discussion that the software tools discussed in Chapters 2 to 6 are needed to develop a Knowledge-Based Finite Element System that will widen the scope and use of this powerful technology.

8.3 OPTIMIZATION TECHNIQUES FOR ENGINEERING DESIGN

In a traditional design environment, the engineer would try different trial designs with a quest of arriving at a design that is optimum. With the development of mathematical programming techniques for optimization and rapid advances made in computer hardware and software technologies, it is now possible to formulate the engineering design problem as an optimization problem with the objective of minimising the cost or weight subject to satisfaction of all the conditions of design. In this section the subject of optimization will be introduced along with the description of a few algorithms and with this background the reader may be able to refer to books and publications listed under references [18-26] for additional information on this subject.

The term mathematical programming has been originally coined by Robert Dorfman in 1950 [18] and refers to the computational methods that are used to determine the *best* or *optimum* solution to a problem (design, planning or allocation of resources) that exhibits a structure which is represented by a mathematical equivalent, called a mathematical model. The generic term now encompasses linear programming, integer programming, nonlinear programming, dynamic programming and programming under uncertainty.

8.3.1 Mathematical Programming Concepts

In general, a mathematical programming (optimization) problem can be stated as follows.

Find the values of $x1$, $x2$, ..., xn that minimize (or maximize) the objective function $y(x)$ subject to a set of constraints as,

$$\text{Min } y = y\,(x1, x2..., xn) \tag{8.11}$$

subject to

$$f_j\,(x1, x2, ... xn) < = 0 \; j = 1, 2, ..., m \tag{8.12}$$

$$g_j\,(x1, x2, ..., xn) = 0 \; j=1, 2, ..., p \tag{8.13}$$

The function y (Eq. 8.11) is called the objective function and the function f_j and g_j are called the constraints of the problem. The first set of constraints (Eq.8.12) is referred to as inequality constraints and the second set (Eq.8 .13) as equality constraints.

If the objective function and the constraints are linear, the optimization problem is called a linear programming problem. If the objective function and/or the constraints are nonlinear the optimization problem is called a nonlinear programming problem. The above definitions are explained, below in the context of engineering design.

Objective function:

A function for which an extremum (minimum/ maximum) is sought, in the optimal design process. It is also referred to as merit function. Usually weight, cost or volume of the structure/solid/component is chosen as the objective function.

Design variables:

Design variables are those quantities defining a system and these are varied to achieve an extremum of the objective function. Generally the cross-sectional dimensions, thickness etc. are taken as design variables,

Constraints:

Constraints are mathematical functions which define the interaction between the design variables. Any acceptable set of design variables should satisfy these constraints and they are mainly of three types:

1. Inequality constraints
2. Equality constraints and
3. Side constraints

Inequality Constraints:

These constraints usually ensure safety gainst a failure mode or satisfactory behaviour under the given loading conditions. The limits imposed on stress at a section/point not to exceed the allowable value and the displacement at a node not to exceed the permissible limits are typical examples for inequality constraints. They are expressed as shown below.

$$\sigma/\sigma \text{ all} - 1 <= 0$$

$$\delta/\delta \text{ all} - 1 <= 0$$

Equality Constraints:

These are conditions that must be strictly satisfied for the design to be acceptable. In the case of solid/ structural mechanics problems, the conditions of equilibrium (Eq. 8.10)

$$[K]\{ r \} = \{ P \}$$

are to be imposed as equality constraints, but they are implicit as part of analysis procedure and are not stated explicitly. So it may be noted that the inequality constraints such as limits on press cannot be expressed explicitly since it requires a finite element analysis. This is largely the difficulty in formulating the optimization problem for engineering design as the analysis procedure needed to be embedded into the formulation.

Side Constraints:

The upper and lower bounds on the design variables are usually referred to as side constraints. Generally the idle constraints impose geometric restrictions on the design variables $10 < t < 20$ where t may be the thickness) due to coal provisions, fabrication or practical considerations, and availability of the sizes.

8.3.2 Classification of Optimization Problems

Optimization problems can be classified in several ways [20] .They are briefly discussed below.

- Classification based on existence of constraints: Based on the existence of constraints in the problem, the problem may be classified as
- Constrained optimization problem
- Unconstrained optimization problem
  - Classification based on nature of loading and constraints: Based on the nature of the loading and constraints encountered; the problem may be classified as
  - Optimization for static response; to include stress, displacement and buckling constraints and also single, or multiple load cases.
  - Optimization for dynamic response; to include response and frequency constraints.
- Classification based on the nature of equations involved:

  It is an important classification from computational point of view. The classification, is based on the nature of the equations for the objective function and the constraints. According to this classification, the problem can be defined as under:

- Linear optimization problem: If both the objective function and set of constraints are linear .
- Non-linear optimization problem: If either the objective function, or the set of constraints are non- linear; or both are of non-linear type.
- Classification based on design variables:
  - Depending on the permissible values of the design variables the problem may be defined as either integer programming problem or real-valued programming problem.
  - Depending on the types of variables required specifically for shape optimization, the problem may have either geometric, topological, or sizing variables.
- Classification based on deterministic nature of variables
  - Stochastic programming problem.
  - Deterministic programming problem.

8.3.3 Unconstrained Optimization Techniques

An unconstrained optimization problem aims at minimization (or maximization) of the objective function in the absence of constraints. Study of the techniques for unconstrained optimization is essential since many methods of solving a constrained optimization problem are converted into unconstrained optimization problem and solved using unconstrained solution techniques.

The unconstrained optimization techniques can be broadly classified into two categories i) single variable/unidirectional search techniques and ii) multi-variable optimization techniques. For optimizing a nonlinear function in single variable, a number of methods are available and they include golden section search, Fibonacci numbers, polynomial approximation methods to include quadratic and/or cubic interpolation techniques etc. [20] .

All the algorithms for optimizing functions of several variables are iterative and proceed from the current step to the next giving a better value of the objective function. Hence, basically the iterative steps can be stated as,

$$\{X\}_{k+1} = \{X\}_k + a_k \{S\}_k \qquad (8.14)$$

where $\{X\}_k$ is the vector giving "the values of the design variables $x1, x2, ..., xn$ at the iteration k, $\{S\}_k$ is the direction of search to locate the next better point, a_k is the step length along the direction $\{S\}_k$ i.e., it is a scalar along $\{S\}_k$ to locate the point $\{X\}_{k+1}$ at which the function $f(\{X\}_{k+1}) < f(X)_k$.

We would notice from Eq.8 .14 that once the direction of search $\{S_k\}$ is known, the step length Qk can be found out using any of the single-variable optimization techniques for the extremum value of the objective function with substitution of $f(\{X\}a_k + {}_k\{S\}_k)$ wherein only a_k is an unknown variable. One could use any of the techniques mentioned above for single variable optimization and guide-lines are given in many texts for proper choice of a method [20, 22, 24] .

Thus, it may be noted that various optimization techniques for multi-variable functions essentially involve in the development of algorithms/procedures to define the *best* search direction $\{S\}_k$ at a given point $\{X\}_k$. The iteration is continued until a specified convergence criterion is satisfied.

The techniques for multi-variable optimization can be broadly classified as i) Direct Search Methods and ii) Gradient Methods.

Direct Search Methods

Direct search methods have proved to be quite versatile for large scale complex problems, because they involve only function evaluations. They involve less complex computations and can effectively handle discontinuous functions. These methods are advanta- geous when the function evaluation is not computation ally expensive as these methods require a large number of function evaluation to achieve optimum. A number of direct search methods are avail- able and the *Pattern* Search *Method* of *Hooke* and Jeeves [20, 23] has been found to be computationally efficient in engineering design optimization. To illustrate the detailed steps involved in a typical optimization process, the direct search method of Hooke and Jeeves is explained in the following part of this subsection.

Gradient Methods:

The techniques which utilize the information of the first, second or possibly higher order derivatives of the problem functions come under this category. In general, the methods of optimization which require gradient information (usually the first derivatives of the function) are considered more efficient than the ones which do not-essentially because the gradient of the function has the property of steepest ascent/descent. The gradient of the function may be evaluated by either of the following techniques:

1. Writing explicit expression for the evaluations of the partial derivatives of the function; or

2. Evaluating the partial derivatives numerically by the use of finite differences [23] i.e., by the use of forward, backward or central difference formulae. In most of the problems of engineering design the constraint functions are not explicit and hence the gradients are evaluated by this numerical procedure which in- directly involves function evaluation.

The different gradient based methods used are given below:

* *Methods of Steepest Descent/ Ascent*
* *Newton Search Method*
* *Conjugate Gradient Method*
* *Method of Fletcher and Reevs*
* *Quasi-Newton/Variable Metric Methods and under this category, Davidon-Fletcher-Powell (DFP) method is reported to be stable and reliable for use.*

Direct Search Method of Hooke and Jeeves The direct search method of Hooke and Jeeves is a sequential search technique wherein each step of the method consists of two kinds of searches viz. the exploratory search and the pattern search.

1. In exploratory search, the objective function around a temporary base point in the direction of a particular design variable is explored. If the search improves the objective function, then a new temporary base point and new reference values are oh. trained for the exploratory search, in the direction of the next variable. This search is thus carried out for all design variables to obtain a new base point.

2. Once a new base point is obtained a pattern move in the direction joining the new base point with the previous base point, is made to obtain a new temporary base point for the exploratory search as discussed in (1) above, The idea of the pattern search is to gain useful information about the shape of the design space which can be used to accelerate convergence,

3. The process is continued likewise as discussed in steps (1) and (2) above, If any exploratory search or a pattern search in a particular direction fails to improve the objective function, that search is cancelled, As the search nears the optimum, the exploratory search in the directions of all the design variables will fail, in which case the step length is reduced and the procedure continued, The optimum value is obtained when the step length reaches some predetermined minimum. The method is illustrated for a function of two variables, in Fig, 8.10, The steps of Hooke and Jeeves method can be mathematically explained as below:

Step 1

Let $\{X\}_1{}^T = \{x1, x2, \ldots xn\}$ be the starting point. Let Δxi be the step length for exploratory search in the direction $\{e\}_i$ of the design variable with $i = 1, 2, \ldots, n$. Set $k = 1$.

Step 2

Evaluate the objective function, set $i = 1$ and start the exploratory search as given in Step 3,

Step 3

Now perturb the variable xi about the current temporary base point $\{X\}_{k,i-1}$ to obtain a new temporary base point $\{X\}_{k,i}$ as

$$\{X\}_{k, i} = \{X\}_{k,i-1} + \Delta x_i \{e\}_i \text{ if } y+ < y$$
$$\{X\}k, i = \{X\}k,i-1 - \Delta xi\{e\}_i \text{ if } y- < y$$
$$\{X\}_{k, i} = \{X\}_{k,i-1} \text{ if } y < min (y+, y-)$$

where
$$y+ = y(\{X\}_{k, i-1} + \Delta xi\{e\}_i)$$
$$y- = y(\{X\}_{k, i-1} - \Delta xi\{e\}_i)$$
$$y = y(\{X\}_{k, i-1})$$

This procedure is to be continued for all the temporary base points i.e.

for $i = 1, 2, \ldots, n.$

Step 4

If $\{X\}_{k, n} = \{X\}_k$ i.e., the search does not yield a better point; reduce Δx. by a factor. Set $i = 1$ and go to Step 3.

If the search of Step 3 above yields a better point, Set $\{X\}_{k+1} = \{X\}_{k,n}$ and go to Step 5 below.

Step 5

Establish the pattern direction

$$\{s\}_k = \{X\}_{k+1} - \{X\}_k$$

and make a pattern move to get $\{X\}_{k+1,0}) = \{X\}_k + \propto_k \{s\}_k$, where $\propto_k$ is the step length parameter which may be taken as 1 for simplicity, or can be found out by using any tech- nique for minimizing a function of one variable.

Step 6

Evaluate $y_{k+1} = y(\{X\}_{k+1,0})$, if $Y_{k+1} < Y_k$; set $k = k+1$ and go to Step 3; clsc, cancel the pattern move by setting $\{X\}_{k+1,0} = \{X\}_{k+1}$

Set $k = k+1$ and go to Step 3.

Step 7

The procedure is assumed to have converged if step lengths fall below a specified small quantity $\in$ and the process is terminated if all $\Delta x_i < \in_i$, which is user specified.

A flow chart is given in Fig.8.12 which explains all the steps needed for computer programming.

8.3.4 Constrained Optimization Techniques

A constrained optimization is concerned with obtaining a minimum (or maximum) of the objective function subject to constraints as given by Eqs.7.11 to 7.13. The methods of optimization can be classified into two broad categories: (i) Direct Methods and (ii) Transformation or Indirect Methods.

Direct Methods

In the direct methods, the constraints are handled in an explicit manner. These methods include the following:

- *Linear Approximation Methods -Where objective function and constraints are linearised (Sequential Linear Programming)*
- *Cutting plane method*
- *Move Limit Method*
- *Method of Feasible Directions*
- *Zontendijk's Method*
- *Gradient Projection Method*
- *Generalised Gradient Projection Method*
- *Pshenichnny's Linearization Method*
- *Quadratic Objective function and Linearized Constraints*
- *Sequential Quadratic Programming*
- *Recursive Quadratic Programming*

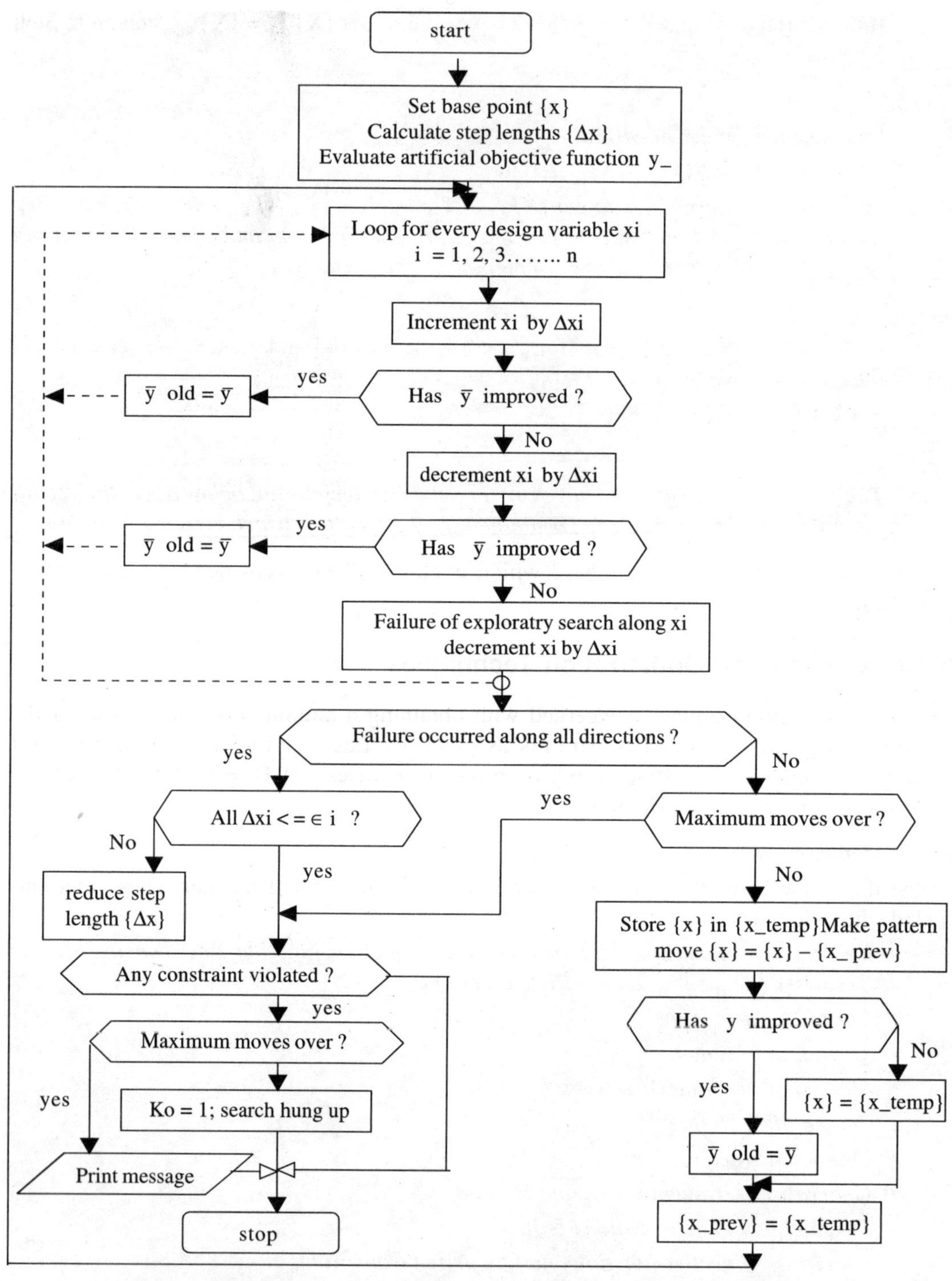

Fig. 8.12   Flowchart – Direct Search Method of Hooke and Jeeves

Transformation/Indirect Methods

These methods transform the constrained optimization problem into a sequence of unconstained optimization problems with the motivation to use well established unconstrined optimization techniques discussed in the earlier section. The general approach of the indirect methods will be to minimize (or maximise) the objective function as an unconstrained function but provide penalty to limit the constraint violations [19,20]. The transformation methods include:

- *Penalty Function Method*
- *Barrier Function Method*
- *Multiplier/Augmented Lagrangian Methods*

The two methods viz., Penalty Function and Barrier Function Methods, are simple to use in engineering design optimization. The formulation for the two methods and the solution technique are briefly described below:

Penalty Function Method

A very simple but powerful technique has been described by Siddal [23]. The basic concept is to add function often constraints to the original objective function y in such a way that artificial walls of rising slopes are thrown up as the search nears or reaches a violation.

The search is thus forced away from the violation. A simple strategy has the form,

$$ya = y(\{X\}) + 10^{20} \sum_{j=1,\,p} |gj\,(\{X\})| + 10^{20} \sum_{i=1,\,m} |fi\,(\{X\})| \qquad (8.15)$$

where ya is the artificial objective function and the second summation applies to the inequality constraints that are not satisfied or violated. Here the penalty is put on violations. As this penalty tends to infinity, the approximation becomes increasingly accurate. But the choice of penalty should be judiciously made so as not to cause over- flow problems in computer. A value of 10^{20} has been proved to be satisfactory in many computers. It has been reported by Siddal [23] that the technique is better suited to search methods than gradient methods. Only difficulty is that this technique does not handle well the equality constraints.

Barrier Function Method

This method is also known as *interior penalty function method* and it provides a sequence of improving feasible designs. This method is also referred to as Sequential Unconstrained Minimization Technique (SUMT) and the basic concepts are due to Fiacco and McCormic [25] .The artificial objective function is defined as,

$$ya = y(\{X\}) + (1/\sqrt{rk}) \sum_{j=1,\,p} [gj\,(\{X\})]^{2} - rk \sum_{i=1,\,m} (1/fi(\{X\})) \qquad (8.16)$$

here the penalty parameter *rk* are a decreasing sequence of positive values, ie., r1 > r2 > r3... > 0. It can be shown that if ya is minimized for a decreasing sequence of values of *rk* the unconstrained minima ya will converge to the solution y of the original problem as *rk* –> O [19,25].

During the optimization process, satisfaction of inequality constraints may be maintained by abandoning any infeasible step in the search for optimum by adding penalty values to $\bar{y}$. This term drives the solution to feasibility rapidly and the artificial objective function becomes,

$$\bar{y} = y(\{x\}) + \frac{1}{\sqrt{^r k}} \sum_{j=1}^{p} \bar{f}_j^2(\{x\}) - {}^r k \sum_{q_1} \frac{1}{f_j(\{X\})} + 10^{20} \sum_{q_2} |f_j(\{X\})| \qquad (8.17)$$

where q_1 = number of satisfied inequality constraints and q_2 = number of violated inequality constraints. This formulation handles well the equality constraints.

8.3.5 Genetic Algorithms for Optimization

Recent developments in artificial genetics have provided robust and powerful mechanisms for search and optimization. They are Genetic Algorithms (popularly called as GAs) based on natural selection and natural genetics. They combine the Darwinian theory of survival of the fittest with a structured but randomized information exchange to form a search algorithm. They are very much different from the traditional search or optimization algorithms. Genetic algorithms work with a coding of the parameter set, not the parameters themselves. They search parallely from a population of points and not a single point at a time as in the traditional methods. Genetic algorithms do not use any auxiliary information like derivatives for carrying out search through design space. Instead of deterministic transition rules they are guided by probabilistic information. A number of researchers are carrying out research activities both for developing better genetic algorithms and using the algorithms for search, optimization and machine learning. Reference [39] provides a self-study guide on Genetic Algorithms and their use for search, optimization and machine learning. In addition, genetic algorithms show potential for application to engineering optimization problems where the variables take discrete values. Almost all the variables in most of the engineering design problems are discrete in nature. The mechanism provided by genetic algorithms to handle discrete variables provide the algorithm the capability to produce more rational design solutions compared to other traditional optimization algorithms [40].

8.3.6 Software for Optimal Design

In the previous section it has been observed that several methods are available for solving nonlinear optimization problems of engineering design. The formulation of a design problem as an optimization problem including all the constraints and adopt a solution technique for solving the resultant nonlinear programming problem is a difficult task. This is essentially due to the differences in analysis and design formulation/models [27] .

The structural analysis model used is usually based on finite element method which requires discretization of the continuum. Once the discretization has been chosen, the number of basic analysis variables gets fixed (usually the degrees of freedom at the nodes) .Then the solution procedure starts as per the steps indicated in section 8.2.3 and the algorithm to be followed at each step is well defined. This well defined nature of formulation and computational steps make it possible to develop general purpose software packages and indeed, several of them are commercially available and are discussed in section 7.1. These packages are quite general and are applicable to solution of several problems in various disciplines.

The formulation of a design problem as an optimization problem is not as straight forward as analysis model. The problems that are faced are as follows:

1. Selection of objective function which may be cost, weight or volume of the structure and depending on the situation and type of the system it has to be chosen. Sometimes it becomes difficult to include all the fabrication costs in the formulation.

2. The choice and number of design variables depend on the type of the structural system.

3. The behavioral constraints are implicit functions and in general the formulation of constraints require a finite element analysis. For example, stress constraints can be evaluated only through analysis. In the case of large systems it is not possible to write these constraints explicitly.

4. The codal provisions and practical considerations should be stated in the form of constraints. These provisions make the formulation dependent on the code and make it more specific rather than of general application.

5. The optimal design formulation is usually nonlinear and complex in having large number of design variables and implicit constraints. There are a number of techniques for solving non- linear optimization problem as discussed in the earlier section. The choice of a technique depends on the type of problem on hand and it is difficult to categorically specify a particular solution technique for all cases.

From the above discussion it may be evident that unlike the case of finite element analysis, general purpose optimal design packages are not available. However, there is an increasing trend to include limited optimization capability in general purpose finite element analysis packages. In view of the growing importance of optimization techniques in engineering design environment, the algorithm based on penalty function methods is described below.

Program for Constrained Optimization using Penalty/Barrier Function Methods

One advantage of the penalty function methods is that complex constraints to satisfy codal provisions can be treated, their number can be large and is not a significant factor in computer time as is the number of design variables. These methods are also most suitable for solving explicit design problems where the evaluation of the objective function and constraints are simple and do not involve implicit structural analysis. However, if structural analysis is required for evaluation of the constraints, an iterative or sub optimization procedure can be adopted without much of difficulty [28, 29]. Another advantage, from practical point of view, is that available computer programs can be used for different problems with little programming effort by separating problem dependent module and the optimization solution technique module.

In view of the above mentioned advantages of the penalty function methods, the computational steps for developing a program are given below:

1. Start with an initial point $\{X\}_1$. In the case of interior penalty function the starting point must be a feasible one satisfying all the constraints. In the case of engineering design problems, the starting point $\{X\}_1$, i.e., initial values of the design variables, can be chosen from the knowledge of existing design practice, empirical relations etc. It does not seriously pose a problem at this step. Set k= 1.

2. Construct the artificial objective function y, using anyone of the equations 7.15 or 7.17 depending on the choice of penalty function or barrier function method .

3. Minimize y using anyone of the unconstrained optimization techniques. For example, the pattern search method of Hooke and Jeevs can be used for this unconstrained minimization. (Refer Flow chart presented in the previous section). Let the optimal solution be $[X]^*_k$.

4. Test whether $[X]^*_k$ is the optimum solution of the original problem satisfying the specified covergence criteria. If $[X]^*_k$ is found to be optimum, terminate the process, otherwise go to the next step.

5. In the case of interior penalty function method, assign the value of the next penalty parameter, r_{k+l} as, $r_{k+l} = c\, r_k$ where $C < 1$, and the value of c can be taken as 0.1, 0.2 or 0.5 etc. Suggestions are given in references [20,26] for the initial choice of r_l.

6. Set the new value of k = k+ 1, take the new starting point as $[X]_{k+l} == [X]^*_k$ and go to step 2.

The above steps and the flow chart given in the previous section for unconstrained optimization using Hooke and Jeevs method will enable one to develop an optimization program. In a particular design optimization problem the User has to develop program segments to construct the objective function and constraints and call this optimization program to get an optimal solution.

8.3.7   Interactive Design in CAD Environment

With the developments in CAD environment, there is an increasing trend to interactively involve the designer during the Optimization process [3O-33]. The interactive aspect provides the design engineer a capability to monitor the program execution, thereby en- abling him to instantaneously Use his engineering judgement, experience and intuition to interrupt execution, and pull back the design variables to a feasible and realistic region. The execution of the program can then be resumed by making sure that good part of the search is spent in a mathematically feasible and practically realistic manner -since the optimization algorithm would generally scan a very large design space, otherwise. The aspect of interaction is thus said to enhance the computational efficiency of an algorithm - a feature that is highly desirable in any optimization process.

8.3.8   Recent Advances in Design Optimization

The recent developments in the computer software and hardware, and AI technologies have made significant impact in the field of engineering optimization. The recent publications [33-37] indicate the growing interest and research activities currently pursued, and these are briefly discussed in the following.

1. Integration of graphics as a means of communication to prepare large input data and in engineering design optimization, finite element analysis becomes an integral part of *it*. The role of pre- processors for interactively creating the finite element mesh and other input data has been described in the earlier section. Similarly there is a need for a post-processor to display the desired results, after the analysis and optimal design is complete.

2. The developments in Knowledge Based Expert Systems as a part of AI technology make it possible to incorporate human judgement to a great extent. This feature is highly desirable in engineering design where the experience of an *expert* engineer is needed at several stages of design process. In addition, ex- pert knowledge is required for optimum design modeling and for selecting the most suitable algorithm for optimizing a specific problem at hand out of a number of optimization techniques. The increasing availability of software tools show potential for future research and development work on Knowledge Based Systems for Optimal Design [36-38].

3. The use of Data Base Management System has immense potential especially in view of the fact that a central data base can handle/process a large amount of data. Using DBMS facility it is envisaged, that development and integration of analysis, design, optimization and drafting programs will be simpler and the designer may find it more easy to use the integrated Computer Aided Optimal Design program [41].

4. Alongside the Data Base Management System, emerges an era of parallel computing i.e. Engineering Design Optimization on a network of computer workstations or by making use of parallel computers. The need for this aspect has been necessitated in computer aided design process, especially to cater for enormous computational time required for large scale problems requiring a general purpose finite element analysis program for different type of analysis for static and dynamic loading, design functions and optimization process. It has been indicated in recent publication [42] that parallel computing shows promise for applications. Application of genetic algorithms in engineering optimization also show good promise for implementing on parallel computers.

5. With the rapid advances in computer technology, endeavor now is to develop powerful and efficient mathematical programming methods, which seek to optimize the computational time and effort. Thus in the present day CAD environment there is vast potential to use various optimization techniques in the engineering design process.

8.4 PROGRAMMING ENVIRONMENT FOR CAD

We have seen that Computer Aided Design encompasses a wide variety of computer-based methodologies and tools for a spectrum of engineering activities like planning, design, analysis, detailing, drafting, construction, manufacturing, monitoring, management, process control and maintenance [43]. That is, CAD is more concerned with the use of computer based tools to support the entire life cycle of engineering systems. The earlier chapters of this book dealt in detail the different software tools which support development of CAD pro- grams. A brief review of two analytical tools, viz., Finite Element Method and Optimization Techniques, is given in the earlier sections of this chapter. Depending on the nature of problems to be solved, the software as well as analytical tools to be used vary. If different software tools work in different environment, the programming becomes difficult because of incompatibilities of different tools. A perfect coordination amon6 the software tools are essential, otherwise the programmer has to spend more time in designing the communication between different program modules and many times this may be a very difficult task. Hence a CAD programming environment en- compassing all the necessary software tools and with facility to call any required analytical tools will relieve the programmer from the redundant work of interfacing various program modules. In addition it also eliminates many other undesirable effects of such interface. Such a CAD programming environment provides the programmers a facility to use software tools like graphics, database management system and knowledge based systems from a program written in high level programming language like C. As such the standard C does not provide these facilities, additional efforts are required to implement necessary preprocessors and library functions following standard C features. This will enable the program to be portable on a wide variety of hardware and software platforms. Fig. 8.13 shows a typical CAD programming environment.

The various components of a CAD programming environment and interaction of a typical CAD program with these components are shown in Fig. 8.13. Essentially a CAD programming environment consists of a database management system, graphics support library, drafting module and an inference engine and a facility to call required analytical tools. Additional generic software components may be required, depending on the type of problem to be programmed. For instance, the problem of design of machine elements would require a geometric modeler and a problem of structural design would require a standards processor. A brief description on implementation aspects of a CAD programming environment by embedding the software tools into C programming language is given below.

A CAD program is a collection of different program modules and each module may contain a number of functions. An effective data communication between different modules can be achieved through a database management system. All or a portion of the data pertaining to the problem can be stored in the database, so that different modules can interact with it through a database management sys- tem (DBMS). This not only reduces the burden of writing separate routines for data management, but also improves the efficiency of the CAD programs. Most of the commercial database system packages provide only limited facilities for interfacing with external programs. This may not be adequate in a typical CAD programming environment. It may be convenient to use SQL for querying the database. But creating databases and manipulating the information stored in it using function calls though a program written in language like C will be more convenient and easier to use. A set of functions which allow data definition and data manipulation form a DBMS. If these functions are callable from a C program then it provides a complete interface with databases. A brief description of how a relational database management system can be embedded in C programming language is described below.

A relational database managememt system (RDBMS) consists of a set of programs which can create relations and manipulate the data stored in the relations. In a stand alone mode, the structured query language (SQL) is used to query the database to get required information. In

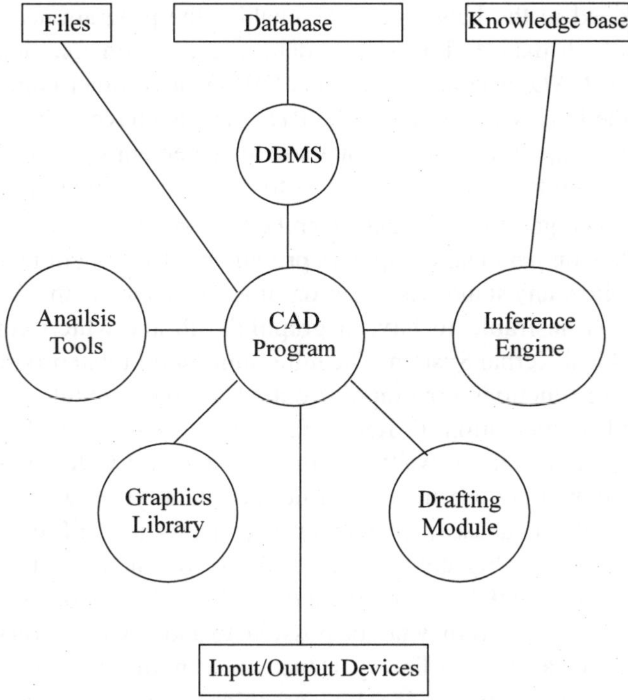

Fig. 8.13 CAD Programming Environment

language interface mode, generally SQL queries are embedded in language. The basic architecture of database systems shown in Fig.6.4 of chapter 6 shows three different levels. Implementation of RDBMS consists of designing a set of low level functions, which deal with the physical storage of data as well as different access mechanisms. It is necessary to have good design of data structures and search algorithms at this stage. The functions required to be developed at this stage are grouped into two different categories, viz., high level functions and low level functions. The low level functions are not accessible to application programmers. They get parameters from the higher level functions and carry out search to store/retireve data from the database. They define abstract data types for relations and conditions. These definitions along with the function type declarations are provided in a header file. Including this header file in any program using the DBMS provides the necessary datatypes to be used for accessing the database. The low as well as high level functions written in C are compiled and are made available at the time of linking the application programs. This organisation makes it possible to create and manipulate databases from C programs. The RDBMS library should contain all the necessary functions that can be called from CAD programs.

For instance, a datatype called RELATION can be defined to refer the relations in the database. Since functions in the RDBMS library are also written using the standard language features, there will not be any difficulty in porting the programming environment from one computer to the other. By this process of adding additional header file and functions, the

DBMS gets embedded in the language. This enables the programmers to carry out all the database functions both data definition and data manipulation functions -anywhere in the program. To port the CAD programs using this DBMS on to other computer systems, along with the program the library functions of the RDBMS also have to be compiled on the new machine. This type of implementation of database management system completely eliminates the problem of explicit interfacing of databases to programs written in C.

In a similar manner, graphics also can be embedded into C programming language. Many C language compilers on personal computers provide built-in functions for graphics actions. Since they do not follow any standards, the programs written using these functions will not be portable. Hence it is desirable to have a graphic's library which conforms to graphics standards like Graphical Kernal System. The minimum support that programmers expect from a graphics library are functions for graphics output, graphics input, viewing and modeling transformations and segmentation. G KS provides functions for all the actions enumerated above. A set of functions can be written using the standard C features for these graphics actions. These functions may use many user defined data types, which can be defined in a header file. Similar to the database management system, this header file with the GKS function library adds graphics capability conforming to the G KS standard to the C programming language. In contrast to the DBMS implementation, the difficulty one may face here is using different input/output devices. It may not be possible to add device drivers for all the available graphics devices in such a graphics library. Hence one can limit the number of drivers only to the minimum required interactive devices like, graphics screen, keyboard, mouse and digitizer. It is not strictly necessary to have device drivers for hard copy devices like printers and plotters. Standard drafting packages like AutoCAD can be used to generate hardcopies of graphics output. Since these drafting packages have device drivers for a wide range of input/ output devices, the output can be routed to these using interface files. For instance, script files can be used as interface files for AutoCAD.

Another software tool that will be frequently used by CAD programmers is Knowledge Based Expert System. Of course it may not be possible to incorporate all the facilities of a KBES into a programming environment. The two main components of any KBES are the knowledge base and inference engine. The inference engine acts on the knowledge stored in the knowledge base to carry out reasoning. As the nature of database processing and knowledge processing is different, the strategy adopted for embedding DBMS in programming language cannot be adopted here. Databases are created either in stand alone mode or through programs. Many relations may be created or deleted during the solution process. But it is not the case with knowledge. The knowledge itself is of different type. Some type of knowledge describing the physical objects can be created during the solution process. But the knowledge used for carrying out the problem solution, i.e, the active or the procedural knowledge does not change depending on the context. This knowledge base contains knowledge about the path to be adopted for problem solution depending on the context. The former type of knowledge is normally stored in frames. Whereas, the active or procedural knowledge is stored in the form of rules with IF and THEN clauses. The manipulation of knowledge stored in the form of frames can be embedded in languages. But it is not advisable to create or update rulebases from a program. Hence it may be appropriate to have an inference engine with facilities to create and edit knowledge bases separately. The inference engine may be defined in such a way that it can get data from the user interactively or from frames or from a database. The inference engine should also be capable of running external pro- grams with good data communications facility between them. The number of inference mechanisms provided in the engine may be limited to two or three like backward chaining, forward chaining and hybrid chaining. Since the inference engine and the CAD program can interact with the database and rules can call external programs, any kind of interaction between the knowledge base, database and the data stored in the working memory can be achieved by suitably designing the CAD programs.

A programming environment described above supports different software tools graphics, database management and knowledge based processing from the same environment. It may be noted that almost all CAD programs use these software tools. In addition to the software tools described: above, many programs may require additional software support for carrying out mathematical analysis. The term analysis is used here for any kind of numerical processing like finite element analysis, standard equations solution, statistical analysis and optimization techniques. Depending on the requirement, the programming environment should provide facility to call any of these analytical tools from the CAD programs. Data communication I to and from these programs can be achieved either through database or through files. Many analysis programs may be old and may not use the database techniques for data handling. In such cases interface can be achieved using traditional file processing. Any activities specific to a problem can be separately programmed and stored as analytical tool, and can be called from the CAD program as and when required. But there are some generic software tools which are frequently used in some applications. Two typical examples are ge- ometric modeler and standards processor. In the case of computer aided design of machine elements, geometric modeling helps one to transform the conceptual idea of the designer to a computer model. Details of geometric modeling is described in chapter 5.

Standards processing refers to the activity where specifications provided in the design codes are organised and effectively used in carrying out designs. Design standards are evolved over a period of time based on material properties, construction practices, and the experience gained by the designers. Depending on the advancement of research and expertise gained from professional practice the design standard specifications may change from time to time. Embedding these standards into CAD programs by hard coding it, makes it very difficult to modify it at a later date to reflect such changes. Hence it is advisable to separate the standard provisions from the programs, ;which makes the CAD programs standard-independent and hence robust. This also makes the programs more flexibile. Standard processors store the standards in databases as well as in knowledge bases, depending on its nature. In most of the cases, some part of the standard specifications goes into database and other part into knowledge base. The knowledge base - database interaction facility provided by the programming environment offers excellent capability for standards processing in CAD programs.

One of the primary requirement of any CAD program is good user-interfaces. The user interface influence a great extent on the acceptability of the program by the professional designers. The user interface should be made as natural and as simple as possible. For instance, asking a designer to enter a large amount of numerical data following specific formats has to be totally avoided. These type of data input was designed for computers of 6Os, 70s and early 808, where interactive processing was not possible. But the introduction of terminal-based computer systems has totally changed the input scenario. Interactive query gave way to formatted input to some extent. Still old programs expected data input similar to that of batch processing. Introduction of computer graphics and graphics devices have revolutionized the interactive computing. Graphics based user- interfuse were designed which made the data input simple and natural. Digitizers are being extensively used for easy and simple data input. Instead of converting geometric information into numerical data and then entering it, digitizers can be used to directly enter the geometric information using the drawings of the object. In addition- to geometric information other data items can also be entered using good user-interfaces. For designing good user-interfaces, data can be classified into different groups and input Screens can be designed for each group separately. Window-based input Screens are convenient and easier to enter data. Display of online help information for the data that is currently being entered improves the effectiveness of the user-interface and minimizes the erroneous data entry. User-interfaces should be designed in such a way that it is possible to correct wrongly entered data items before going onto the next screen or window. It is also advisable to incorporate data validation wherever possible during the data entry.

It is evident from the above discussion that a Programming Environment with all the modules will greatly simplify the task of developing an integrated CAD software. The software tools that are presented in this book would form a first step in this direction and the prospective CAD programmer will benefit by the use of these tools for efficient design and development of CAD software in a particular field of application in engineering. The analytical tools provide the necessary mathematical background for formulating the analysis and design problems of computer aided engineering.

References

1. Zienkiewicz,O.C., and Taylor,R.L.,(1989), *The Finite Element Method,* Vol.1, Basic Formulation and Linear Problems, Mc Graw- Hill (U.K) Limited.
2. Cook,R.D., (1981), *Concepts and Applications 0£ Finite Element Analysis,* Second Edition, John Wiley, New York.
3. Bathe, K.J. and Wilson,E.L., (1976), *Numerical Methods in Finite Element Analysis,* Prentice-Hall Inc., Englewood Cliffs, New Jersy.
4. Reddy, J.N., (1984), *An Introduction to the Finite Element Method,* McGraw-Hill, New York.
5. Krishnamoorthy, C.S. (1987), *Finite Element Analysis -Theory* and *Programming,* Tata McGraw Hill Publishing House, New Delhi.
6. Cook, R.D., (1988), *Remarks about Modeling,* Lecture Notes in Engineering, Vol.37, Finite Element Analysis for Engineering Design, J.N.Reddy, C.S.Krishnamoorthy and K.N.Seetharamu, (Eds), Springer- Verlag, Berlin, Heidelburg, pp.177-189.

7. Babuska, I., Zienkiewicz,O.C., Cago,J. and De A Olivera,E.R., (Eds), (1986), *Accuracy Estimates* and *Adaptive Refinements in Finite Element Computations,* John Wiley, New York.

8. Clerk, C.V. and Muller,R.,(1981), *GIFTS-1100: Graphics Oriented Interactive Finite Element Time Sharing System,* In a Handbook of Finite Element Systems, (Ed) C.A.Brebbia, CML Publications, England.

9. Mackerle,J., (1983), *Review of Pre* and *Post Processor Programs in the Major Commercial General Purpose Finite Element Packages,* Advances in Engineering Software, Vol.5, No.1, pp.43-53.

10. Mackerle,J., (1983), *Review of General Purpose Pre* and *Post Processor Programs for the Finite Element Applications,* Advances in Engineering Software, Vol.5, No.1, pp.148-159.

11. Kardestuncer, H. (Ed), (1987), *Finite Element Hand Book,* Mc- Graw Hill Book Co., New York.

12. Kardestuncer,H., (Ed.), (1987), *Survey of some Finite Element Software Systems,* Chapter 5 in Part 4 Finite Element Method Computations in the Finite Element Handbook, McGraw Hill Book Co., New York.

13. Fenves,S.J.,(1986), *A Framework for Co-operative Development of a Finite Element Modeling Assistant,* Realibility Method for Engineering Analysis, K.J.Bathe and D.R.J.Owen, (Ed), John Wiley, U.K.

14. Krishnamoorthy,C.S., Krishnakumar,R. and Rajeev,S., (1989), *Expert System Framework for Finite Element Analysis,* Proc. Int. Conf. on Engineering Software, Ramakrishnan,C. V ., Varadarajan,A. and C.S.Desai, (Ed), Narosa Publishing House,New Delhi.

15. Ainsworth, M., Zhu, J .Z., Craig, A. W. and Zienkiewicz, O.C., (1989), *Analysis of the Zinenkiewicz-Zhu A- Posterior: Error Estimator in the Finite Element Method,* Intl JI. Num. Methods in Engineering, Vol. 28, pp.2161-2174.

16. Noboru,K., (1986), *Adaptive Grid Design Methods for Finite Element Analysis,* Computational Methods in Applied Mechanics and Engineering, Vol.55, pp.129-160.

17. Baehmann, P.L., Shepherd,M.S. et al, (1987), *Robust Geometrically Based Automatic Two Dimensional Mesh Generation,* IntI. Jl. for Num. Methods in Engineering, Vol.24, pp.1043- 1078.

18. Himmelblau, D.M., (1972), *Applied Nonlinear Programming,* McGraw Hill Book Co., New York.

19. Luenberger, D.G., (1973), *Introduction to Linear and Non- linear Programming,* Addison- Wesley, Mass.

20. Rao, *S.S.,* (1979), *Optimization Theory and Applications,* Wiley Eastern Limited, New Delhi. I 21. Haug and Arora,J.S., (1979), *Applied Optimal Design,* Wiley Interscicnce, New York.

22. Vanderplatts,G.N.,(1984), *Numerical Optimization Techniques for Engineering Design with Applications,* McGraw-Hill, New York.

23. Siddal, J.N., (1972), *Analytical Decision Making in Engineering Design,* Prentice Hall, Englewood Cliff.

24. Arora, J.S., (1989), *Introduction to Optimum Design,* McGraw Hill Book Company, New York.

25. Fiacco, A.G. and Mccormick, G.P.,(1008), *Nonlinear Programming Sequential Unconstrained Minimization Techniques,* John Wiley & Sons, New York.

26. Lavary, R.K. (Ed), (1988), *Engineering Design -Better Results through Operations Research Methods,* Elsevier Science Publishing Co., New York.

27. Schmit, L.A., (1981), *Structural Synthesis -Its Genesis and Developments,* AIAA Journal, Vol.19, 124g..1263.

28. Schittkowski, K. (Ed), (1984), *Computational Mathematical Programming, NATO* ASI Series, Springer- Verlag, Berlin. 29. Kavlie, D. and Moe,J., (1971), *Automated Design of Frame Structures,* JI. Struct. Div., ASCE, Vol.97, No.ST-1, Pp.33-62. 30. Krishnamoorthy, C.S., (1988), *Optimal Design of Reinforced Concrete Frames Using Mathematical Programming,* Engineer- ing Design: Better Results through Operations Research Methods, (Ed) R.R.Lavary, Elsevier Science Publishing Co., New York.

31. Krishnamoorthy, C.S. and Rajeev, *S.,* (1989), *Computer-Aided Optimal Design of Reinforced Concrete Frames,* Proc. Int. Conf. on Engineering Software, C. V.Ramakrishnan, A. Varada- rajan and C.S.Desai, (Ed), Narosa Publishing House,New Delhi. 32. Mota Soares, C.A (Ed)., (1986), *Computer Aided Optimal Design: Structural and Mechanical Systems, NATO* ASI Series, Springer- Verlag, Berlin. ,

33. Arora, J.S. and Tsong, C.H., (1988), *Interactive Design Optimization,* Engineering Optimization, Vol.13, Pp.173-188.

34. Mota Soares, C.A (Ed)., (1986), *Integrated CAD/FEM/ Optimization Techniques and Applications,* Computer Aided Optimal Design; Structural and Mechanical Systems, Springer-Verlag, Berlin.

35. Cheng, F .F .(Ed)., (1986), Recent *Developments in Structural Optimization,* ASCE Publication, Structures Congress.

36. Arora, J.S. and Baenziger,G., (1986), *Uses of Artificial Intelli- gence in Design Optimization,* Computer Methods in Applied Mechanics and Engineering, Vol.54, pp.303-323.

37. *Knowledge-Based Structural Design* and *Optimization,* (1987) Computer Applications in Structural Engineering, D.R.Jenkins, (Ed), ASCE Publication, pp.54-113.

38. Rajeev, S. and Krishnamoorthy,C.S., (1987), *Expert System for Optimal Design* of *Structural Members,* Proc. of Second IntI. Conf. on AI in Engineering held at Boston, USA, pp.405-419.

39. Goldberg, D.E., (1989), *Genetic Algorithms in Search, Opti- mization* and *Machine Learning,* Addison- Wesley Publishing Co., Massachusetts, USA.

40. Rajeev, S. and Krishnamoorthy, C.S., (1991), *Computer Aided Optimal Design of Structural Systems using Genetic Algorithm,* Tech. Rep. CE-06-91, Dept. of Civil Engineering, Indian Insti- tute of Technology, Madras, India.

41. Park, G.J. and Arora,J.S., (1987), *Role of Database Manage- ment in Design Optimization Systems,* JI. of Aircraft, Vol.24, No.11, pp.745-750.

42. Schnabel, R. B., (1985), *Parallel Computing in Optimization,* Proc. of the NATO Adv. Study Institute on Computational Mathematical Programming, K.Schittkowski (Ed), Springer - Verlag, Berlin, Germany.

43. Besant, C.B. and Lui,C. W .K., (1986), *Computer Aides Design* and *Manufacture,* Affiliated East-West Press Pvt. Ltd., New Delhi, India.

Review Questions

1. What are the five basic steps involved in finite element analysis of a structure/ solid ? Briefly explain these steps.

2. Describe the philosophy of finite element analysis for solids and structures.

3. What is meant by pre and post processing? Explain the role of pre and post processing in finite element analysis of engineering systems?

4. Explain different methods used for generating finite element meshes.

5. What is the role of geometric modelling in finite element analysis?

6. What are the different errors encountered in the results of finite *element* analysis? Describe the developments that are taking place in the area of error analysis leading to refinement of meshes?

7. Compare the pre and post processing capabilities of three different finite *element* analysis software packages.

8. What are the graphical output facilities that are generally available in pre and post processors.

9. What is the role of knowledge based expert systems in finite *element* analysis of engineering systems?

10. Briefly describe the nature and type of problems, .where Supercomputing power is required for carrying out analysis.

11. Give a note on the role of optimization techniques in engineering design problems.

12. Take a design problem of your choice and formulate the objective function and constraints. Examine to which category the optimization problem belong to and state which mathematical programming technique is most suitable to *solve* the problem.

13. What is meant by implicit form of constraints? Give an example where the constraints cannot be expressed explicitly in terms of design variables.

14. What are the basic differences between gradient methods and direct search methods?

15. Develop a computer program based on the direct search method of Hooke and Jeevs and test it with standard mathematical programming problems.

16. What is the essential difference between exterior penalty function method and interor penalty function method? For a given engineering design problem, how will you select the appropriate penalty function method?

17. What are the basic issues that are to be looked into when analysis and optimization programs are to be integrated?

18. Why interactive design is more relevant in CAD environment?

19. What is the role of artificial intelligence in design optimization ?

20. What is parallel computing? How parallel computing will help in expediting the optimization process?

21. How a programming environment with database management system, graphics system and knowledge base processing system interacting with each other, will help a CAD programmer?

22. Elaborate on the role of RDBMS in a CAD programming environment.

Index